The Private Sector in Soviet Agriculture

This volume is sponsored by
THE CENTER FOR SLAVIC AND EAST EUROPEAN STUDIES,
UNIVERSITY OF CALIFORNIA, BERKELEY

The Private Sector in Soviet Agriculture

By Karl-Eugen Wädekin

Edited by George Karcz

Second, enlarged, revised edition of
Privatproduzenten in der sowjetischen Landwirtschaft
Translated by Keith Bush

UNIVERSITY OF CALIFORNIA PRESS
BERKELEY, LOS ANGELES, LONDON

University of California Press
Berkeley and Los Angeles, California

University of California Press, Ltd.
London, England

ISBN: 0-520-01558-4
Library of Congress Catalog Card Number: 76-95322

Printed in the United States of America
Designed by Steve Reoutt

RUSSIAN AND EAST EUROPEAN STUDIES

Alan A. Brown and Egon Neuberger, eds., *International Trade and Central Planning.*

Gregory Grossman, ed., *Money and Plan. Financial Aspects of East European Economic Reforms.*

Charles Jelavich, *Tsarist Russia and Balkan Nationalism. Russian Influence in the Internal Affairs of Bulgaria and Serbia, 1879–1886.*

Jerzy F. Karcz, ed., *Soviet and East European Agriculture.*

Nicholas V. Riasanovsky, *Nicholas I and Official Nationality in Russia, 1825–1855.*

To the memory of

GEORGE F. KARCZ

Scholar, Friend, and Colleague

Contents

Tables

Foreword

by Gregory Grossman
University of California, Berkeley

The scholarly study between the covers of this book bears eloquent testimony on two scores. On one hand, it brings out in forceful fashion the complexities and contradictions, the paradoxes and problems, the achievements and agonies of Soviet agriculture as reflected in its — still surprisingly large, after four decades of "complete collectivization" — private sector. On the other hand, it demonstrates vividly how difficult it continues to be, nearly two decades after Stalin's death, to get at the essential facts of this sector, and therefore also of Soviet agriculture as a whole.

This is Dr. Wädekin's second monographic study of the private sector in Soviet agriculture. But while it builds on his *Privatproduzenten in der sowjetischen Landwirtschaft* (Cologne, 1967), it is much more than a mere translation and updating of the German book; rather, the thorough revision and rewriting that went into the English-language book have turned it into an essentially new work. Even those familiar with the German book — and perhaps especially they — will want to examine the present work; and, incidentally, they will surely appreciate Keith Bush's most competent translation in the face of many terminological difficulties.

This book is dedicated to the memory of the late George F. Karcz, Professor of Economics at the University of California at Santa Barbara until his untimely and suddenly death in December 1970 at the age of forty-nine. Professor Karcz was one of the leading specialists on Soviet and East European agriculture in the West, that is, one of an all-too-small band of dedicated scholars laboring in a vast and difficult field. When Dr. Wädekin's aforementioned German book was about to appear, Professor Karcz perceived its great importance and from that point on gave generously of his burdened time and his boundless energy to the cause of helping bring out this English-language version. He was not to see the fruit of his efforts, and the author's dedication of the present book to his memory is a fitting tribute to a devoted and productive scholar whose work was so tragically cut short in mid-career.

In undertaking his research Dr. Wädekin was confronted with a formidable problem of evidence. The official Soviet data on the private sector in Soviet agriculture continue to be sparse and often misleading — for reasons that the reader will be able to deduce as he proceeds through the book. The statistical compendia that began appearing again in 1956 after a hiatus of twenty years may have eased the task for many students of Soviet economic problems, but they are of only limited assistance in an investigation of private agriculture. The author was thus forced to resort to the slow and painful "archaeological" method of digging up innumerable bits and pieces of information, sifting them to discard the unrepresentative and the deliberately deceptive, and fitting the pieces together into a rich and broad picture. It is a method that is well known to all students of the Soviet economy who had to confront Stalin's statistical blackout. It was of course also the method employed, say, by the late Naum Jasny in his monumental study, *The Socialized Agriculture of the USSR* (Stanford, 1949), to break through official secrecy and prevarication in order to arrive at a fair picture of reality in the Soviet countryside since collectivization. Nearly a quarter century has passed since then, much has changed in the USSR and even in Soviet agriculture, but the same tedious "archaeological" digging is still necessary to discover the facts in an area that the Soviet authorities are determined to keep from view. We are all grateful to Dr. Wädekin for his persistence and patience.

The first thing that will probably strike the uninitiated reader of this book is how much private production there is four decades after mass collectivization. As late as the second half of the 1960s, 30 percent of the gross value of Soviet agricultural output was produced on private account. For some products this share was considerably higher — about 40 percent for vegetables, meat, and milk, and more than 60 percent for potatoes and eggs. This private production provides a major source of income, both in kind and in money, for the members of collective farms, for the workers at state farms, and for millions of families whose chief source of livelihood is outside agriculture. By some estimates, in the early 1960s the private sector absorbed about 40 percent of the total labor input in agriculture. It supplies the relatively small but important open (kolkhoz) market, which functions alongside the gigantic official retail-sales network, and in this way benefits the general consumer.

One of the most instructive aspects of Dr. Wädekin's study is the light that it sheds on the intimate and organic links between the private sector and the larger, socialist sector in Soviet agriculture, as well as between the private sector and the economy at large. Not only has private production been so far indispensable in meeting the food requirements of the country — which of course explains why it has been tolerated by the authorities — but at the same time the *opportunity* to engage in private agriculture has been an important form of remuneration for involvement in *socialist* production. Moreover, private and socialist agriculture are intricately interrelated in resource use, in mutual commodity flows, and the daily life patterns of tens of millions of people. The picture that emerges is one of great complexity and delicate adjustment.

This delicate adjustment occurs paradoxically in a setting that is marked by gross and clumsy management of agriculture by the authorities. However, the shortages and disequilibria that result from this state of affairs only serve to create new opportunities for the millions of private producers. These tiny undertakings are woefully short on resources of all kinds, but they are long on adaptability and resilience in the quest for material advantage when given a chance (which does not always happen). Indeed, one of the most interesting passages in this study is the vivid account of the remarkably swift adjustment of some private producers to changing opportunities for profit making. One cannot help being reminded of the enterprising and energetic peasant Khor' immortalized in Turgenev's *Sportsman's Notebook;* his ghost must be very much alive in the minds of the Soviet authorities as they perennially battle to contain the peasant's private plot within its miniscule prescribed limits. But lest one obtain from this account the false image of "penny capitalism" at work over the length and breadth of Soviet Union, one should also bear in mind that other powerful fictional portrait: the miserably poor, single and forsaken, doggedly laboring and suffering kolkhoz woman who is the saintly hero of Solzhenitsyn's story *Matrena's Home*. She, too, is a significant statistic in Dr. Wädekin's book.

The private sector is of course an anomaly in the socialized, centralized, planned economy of the USSR. Economically it is backward, ideologically it is alien, politically it is suspect, and morally it stands in the way of the creation of the new socialist and communist man. But it utilizes labor, land, energies, and drives that would otherwise be largely lost; it produces an important part of the food supply; and it provides income where the socialist economy fails to do so. The dilemmas of this "uneasy coexistence," in the author's phrase, and the ebb and tide of official restriction and relaxation, are fully and judiciously presented in the chapters that follow, especially in the concluding one. The cold war between the Party and the peasant goes on, even if the latest phase has been one of greater toleration. The reader will also ask the question that has been constantly asked about the private sector in Soviet agriculture ever since it emerged from the collectivization of the countryside: What is its future? There is no prediction in this book, for that would inevitably have to rest on a much broader vision of the future of the Soviet economy and society, which obviously falls outside the scope of this study. Nor will the writer of this foreword be so bold as to look into the crystal ball. But to understand the Soviet economy as it has been and as it is, one can hardly do without this definitive study.

Preface

to the Enlarged, English-Language Edition

The present book was originally intended to be no more than a translation of its German predecessor *Privatproduzenten in der sowjetischen Landwirtschaft* (Cologne, 1967). Later it was decided to enlarge the original by the present Chapters VIII, IX, and X dealing with Soviet policy toward the private sector since Stalin's death. Most of Chapters VIII and IX is based on my articles in *Osteuropa* (Stuttgart) and *Sowjetstudien* (Munich), and the first section of Chapter X on one in *Problems of Communism* (Washington). I am grateful to the editors of these three periodicals for consenting to use the articles here. Although the appendices of the German version were dropped to save space for the new chapters, the American edition became more voluminous; the bulk was further increased because, during the translating and editing process, material was added that deals with recent developments and incorporates new information, which became available to me only after 1967. (These emendations are documented in the footnotes and bibliographic references; to make room for them, some footnotes of the German version were dropped; the reader searching for full documentation is referred to these.)

In the end, virtually a new book emerged. If it is also a better book, most of the credit should go to the translator and the editor.

During the process of rewriting and editing, I was at times ready to give up the Sisyphian task. If I did not, thanks are due primarily to the unrelenting energy and intellectual strength of the late Professor George F. Karcz, who from the beginning believed in the book. Besides, I am greatly indebted to Professor Gregory Grossman, for his helpful interest, to Mr. Keith Bush, the translator (except for Chapter VI, translated by Karcz), and to the University of California Press. The Bundesinstitut für Ostwissenschaftliche und Internationale Studien, Cologne, has to be gratefully mentioned; the Institut had sponsored the German version, held the rights to it, and took a benevolent attitude toward translation and emendations of the work.

In one of the many letters we exchanged, Karcz encouraged me by citing the motto of the prewar Polish cavalry: *Tuum fac, nec respice finem*. I can think of no better motto for a book owing so much to this sincere friend, whose early tragic death casts a shadow on this publication.

K.-E. W.

1

Private Plot and Livestock Holding—A Basic Right of the Soviet Citizen

In the Soviet Union, private farming still accounts for more than a quarter of total agricultural output. It is more than just an adjunct of the kolkhoz system, which permits kolkhozniks to tend their own small plots of land and keep a little livestock within the limits of the kolkhoz statute. Sovkhoz and nonfarm workers and employees situated in rural areas, in small towns, or on the fringes of cities also tend private plots and raise livestock for supplemental income. The nonfarm population living in the countryside increased from twenty-nine million in 1955 to about thirty-four million in 1967,[1] and moreover millions of kolkhozniks have become sovkhoz workers and employees. Thus, the private sector outside the kolkhozes has become much more significant, and kolkhoz private plots have decreased in number and—up to 1964—in size. More than two-fifths of private farming, accounting at present for about 13 percent of the Soviet gross agricultural output, is carried out by nonfarm workers and employees. This leaves at most three-fifths of the private output—or 15 to 17 percent of total farm output—for kolkhozniks and sovkhoz workers and employees (cf. below, p. 56).

Frequently the significance of the private sector in agriculture is measured by the amount of land involved, but this is misleading. Crops are less important than livestock and animal products, which account for about two-thirds of total private agricultural production. Fodder is therefore the main problem of private farming. Except for potatoes, only a small amount of fodder is grown on private plots; grain, hay, straw, green fodder, and silage come from the socialized sector, partly as wages-

[1] These figures are discussed further in Karl-Eugen Wädekin, "The Nonagricultural Rural Sector," J. A. Millar, ed., *The Soviet Rural Community* (Urbana, Chicago, London: 1971), p. 163 ff.

I

in-kind. In addition, private producers have the right to graze their live-stock on unused or little-used state and kolkhoz land.

The policy of the Soviet authorities toward the private agricultural sector clearly shows to what extent they are prepared at any given time to let economic necessity take precedence over ideological misgivings. Private agricultural production is in many ways alien to the Soviet sys-tem. Economically it is alien because it is not amenable to direct planning and involves unsocialized labor. Socioeconomically private agricultural production is alien, because for a large part of the population, it consti-tutes a basic livelihood that the state or collective system does not ade-quately provide and because such unregulated earning power reduces the effect of state policy on incomes. Politically and ideologically it is alien because it involves private ownership of cattle as well as of small agricultural implements and buildings, thus contradicting the Marxist–Leninist position on socialization of the means of production. To be sure, the land is not privately owned and remains state property, its use sub-ject to sundry regulations. Nevertheless, from the standpoint of practical economics, the institution of individual plots and private animal holdings resembles private ownership of the means of production.

Ideologically, the position of Soviet authorities and authors is clear and has never varied much. Private production is considered a transitional phenomenon that will gradually die out as progress is made towards a perfect communist social order and as the kolkhozes and sovkhozes be-come able to supply the entire population with food. This position was reaffirmed by the Party program of 1961. Until the demise of Khrushchev, the opinion was widely held in the Soviet Union that the private sector of agriculture was a "relic of capitalism, contradicting the economic con-ditions of the life of society and negatively influencing the building of communism" [*173, 60*]. Today this position is officially rejected, but it probably has not disappeared completely in so short a time.

However, socialized agriculture in the Soviet Union has at no time been able to feed the whole population adequately. Private production, therefore, has been and still is indispensable. Moreover, when harsh meas-ures are taken against the private sector, the socialized sector also suffers, so that not only private agricultural production but all agricultural pro-duction declines or stagnates. Even if total output expands, the private sector cannot be abolished in the foreseeable future. Population growth, combined with rapid industrialization and urbanization, makes greater demands on agriculture every year, in terms of both quantity and quality.

Thus, although the basic Soviet ideological position on private farming has remained essentially the same ever since collectivization, practical economic and social policies have shifted to cope with the problem of food supply. Soviet leaders have had to utilize the contributions of small private producers to solve the food problem. But they would like to be able to discourage private production so that its significance will decline in accordance with their ideological prediction.

If only the output of the kolkhozes and sovkhozes could be increased sufficiently—and, more important, rapidly—then most of the problem would be resolved.[2] But this has proved impossible, and so the private sector has been summoned to the rescue and appropriate concessions have been made. This is precisely what happened during the second half of the 1930s, during the Second World War and the early postwar years, after Stalin's death, and again after Khrushchev was deposed. Whenever Soviet authorities believed that they had mastered the food problem and could dispense with, or at least reduce, the private sector, it again proved indispensable and again demanded concessions. (For the development of the private sector in kolkhozes during Stalin's reign, a period not dealt with here, see the unusually informative outline given recently by V. B. Ostrovskii [275, 68–82].)

All land in the Soviet Union is "state property, that is the common property of the people" (Article 6 of the Constitution of the USSR); however, land may be made available for the use of organizations and private persons. It may be farmed either by the state through the medium of state enterprises, among which the sovkhozes play the principal role, by collective farms—the so-called agricultural artels or kolkhozes[3]—or by individual persons or families. However, this use of the land is strictly limited and allows little freedom for exploitation beyond actual farming operations [58, 29]. The Soviet jurist M. I. Kozyr' is very outspoken on this issue [197, 50, 53, 51]:

---

[2] But G. I. Shmelev [339a, 135–136] rightly makes it a point that even then, with general living standards and expectations rising, the need for additional money income to satisfy other than food requirements would provide some inducement to produce and sell private agricultural output where labor is not fully employed in the public sector.

[3] Artel is a traditional Russian word for a collective amalgamation. It is frequently used as a synonym for kolkhoz, the prevailing term at present. This is an abbreviation for kollektivnoe khoziaistvo or collective enterprise. There are also fishing and hunting kolkhozes, but these play a quantitatively minor role.

In the Soviet Union, land is withdrawn from civil use, it is not a good, it has no value and may not be considered as a possession in the normal, civil law sense of the word. . . . The land remains the property of the Soviet government as the sole owner. . . . Land is made available for use in the form of private plots . . . on the basis of special legislative acts on the allocation of land, passed by the corresponding state organs.

The private plots of land granted to the kolkhoz households, with the kolkhoz as the intermediate owner, play an important part in furnishing subsistence. Indeed, in economically weak kolkhozes this plot and the privately owned livestock are the main source of subsistence, and until a decade or so ago, practically all kolkhozes were economically weak. The plots of workers and employees in sovkhozes and throughout the nonfarm economy are relatively less significant and generally smaller than those of the kolkhozniks. The amount of livestock kept—both *de jure* and *de facto*—on the private plots is quite considerable in relation to the size of these plots.

The socioeconomic and legal position of the kolkhoznik cannot be likened to those of the traditional farmer. Therefore the Russian term *kolkhoznik*, not the English equivalent *collective farmer*, is used throughout this book. The private sector of production, which consists primarily of animal husbandry but is based on the use of small plots of land by families and individuals, is described in the Soviet Union as "personal subsidiary farm" (*lichnoe podsobnoe khoziaistvo*). The term *private farm* is sometimes used in this study with the understanding that it describes the peculiar Soviet minifarm rather than a complete farm in the Western sense of the word. In most cases we employ the term *private plot*, a synonym already used extensively in Western writings. To emphasize the most important part of the phenomenon, we occasionally speak of the *private plot and livestock holding*. In aggregate terms we refer to the *private sector* and to *private subsidiary farming*. Conversely, the Russian term *obshchestvennoe khoziaistvo*, which describes farming activities of the kolkhoz or the sovkhoz, refers to the *public sector* or (as in most direct translations from the Russian) the *socialized sector*.

The terminology applies equally to plots of the sovkhoz workers and employees. A distinction is drawn between plots and livestock holdings of the kolkhozniks and those of other individuals only when this is considered necessary, because the discrepancy has lost much of its earlier significance except in discussions of individual or collective urban gardens. These will be called gardens in specific cases. The size of the private plot depends largely on whether it is located in a rural or an urban area, but there are currently many workers and employees living in the countryside whose plots and livestock holdings differ only marginally from those of the kolkhozniks. And although for many kolkhozniks—in contrast to workers and employees—the income from private agricultural production used to be the main source of income and means of subsistence, the rise in kolkhozniks' money income from the public sector has made this a secondary income, albeit still indispensable for many.

In Soviet literature, a distinction is made between the property of the state enterprise and that of the cooperative kolkhoz. This allegedly reflects the basic character of the private plots and livestock holdings on the two kinds of farm. However, for our purpose this does not have much practical significance any more. Soviet authors refer only seldom to the altered situation.[4] One of the few exceptions is Iu. V. Arutiunian, who clearly states: "As owners of personal subsidiary farms, kolkhozniks do not differ in principle from workers and employees."[5] Especially with the growing number of sovkhozes, private plots have assumed great significance and differ only marginally from the plots of kolkhozniks. This is especially true where the sovkhoz is a converted kolkhoz, as is often the case. Occasionally the agricultural activities of urban workers and employees are considered to be "a third form of private agriculture" [*173*, 60], but they are generally—although undeservedly—neglected by most Soviet writers and are not shown separately in recent Soviet statistics. Nevertheless, some differences remain. G. V. D'iachkov enumerates them under four aspects [*87,* 40–42].

There is a sociopolitical difference, insofar as the private plot is "not the rule" for sovkhoz workers, but it is an intrinsic part of kolkhoz life. This is usually true only for urban areas, and does not alter the character of the private plot.

"The private plots of workers and employees are not connected with their work in state enterprises." This is not true for sovkhozes and many other enterprises and organizations, where the plots of workers and employees are made dependent, in size at least, upon work in these very

[4] For example [*303,* 117]

[5] [*51,* 55.] Cf. *ibid.,* 51–54, 95. See also [*56a,* 26]. Kornienko states in a similar vein [*193,* 40]: "Private subsidiary farming is not related to one of the forms of public socialist property but is rather inherent in both of these forms under the conditions of agricultural production. Not only kolkhozniks, but also sovkhoz workers, teachers, doctors, and others have subsidiary plots."

enterprises and organizations (cf. Chapter III). Generally the right to a plot is associated with employment relationships [*330*, 10]. D'iachkov contends further that sovkhoz workers and employees work on their plots only during their spare time. But this also applies to most, although not to all, of the kolkhozniks' work on their private plots; only a minor proportion is performed by kolkhozniks who should be working on the kolkhoz, but who absent themselves from the public sector or are permitted to do so.

The private subsidiary plot is of less importance to workers and employees than to the kolkhozniks, and many workers and employees have no plots or livestock at all. This is true in general, although there are exceptions; moreover, D'iachkov understates the numerical importance of the nonkolkhoz private plots and gardens.

A greater part of the kolkhozniks' private produce goes to the market, and they sell part of their wages-in-kind on the market; workers and employees, on the other hand, consume almost all of their private production themselves. This is a difference of degree, not of principle, and in sovkhozes even the degree differs less than is generally believed.

Thus the differences are there but they are no longer decisive and are not important enough to justify the use of different terms. In this writer's opinion, L. Kalinin is right when he says [*153*, 58]:

The private plots and livestock holdings of kolkhozniks in the future, when cooperative-kolkhoz and all-people's property merge, will hardly vanish but will rather be transformed into the private subsidiary plots of workers and employees. There is little to distinguish between them even now, despite their differing backgrounds. Therefore, in our opinion, the distinction drawn in economic and statistical literature between the plots of the workers and employees and the private plots of the kolkhozniks is already obsolete and should be replaced by a single designation such as "personal subsidiary plots of the toilers" or "private family plots."

The private ownership of agricultural means of production[6]—"livestock, poultry, and minor agricultural implements" (Article 7, Paragraph 2 of the Constitution of the USSR)—and the private use of land are not only quantitatively but also qualitatively limited. This is evident from the stress laid upon the term *personal property* as opposed to *private property*. Personal property may serve only for personal consumption. In fact it represents a distinct and isolated sphere of production [*193*, 40],

---

[6] Also in Soviet terminology these are referred to as "the means of production," although the point is seldom made as clearly as, for example, in [*223*, 23, 26].

a private sphere of production in an economy in which almost all productive activities have been socialized. The close interdependence with the public sphere (see Chapter VII) does not essentially change this situation. It is thus appropriate to call it the private sector of agriculture (cf. Chapter II).

Article 1 of the old Soviet Civil Code stipulated: "Civil rights [which include the right of possession] shall be protected by law except in those instances when they are exercised contrary to their socioeconomic purpose." The new Principles of Civil Law of 1961 have a corresponding Article 5 which precludes any exercise of civil rights which contradicts the purpose of "the socialist society during the period of building of communism." This provision can be broadly interpreted, and its application to private plots has varied during different periods and in different parts of the Soviet Union. The regulations for the kolkhozniks' private plots and livestock holdings are laid down in the kolkhoz statutes, but these too are not unchangeable and are not everywhere uniform. Any encroachment of private farming beyond the established norms—however these may be established—is regarded as a "serious offence against Soviet law."

The principal reason given by Soviet authors for the continued existence of the private sector is economic necessity resulting from the still inadequate level of collective agricultural production. The second reason is the political consideration of the "centuries old attachment of the peasant to his piece of land" which "has not yet completely died out and which it would be erroneous to ignore." [7] However, this psychological factor is at present attributed only secondary significance and will decline further with time. A. G. Koriagin goes so far as to maintain that this consideration "no longer has any appreciable significance." [8]

The private agriculture of the individual farmers and small artisans, whose right to exist and whose limitations are also established in the Constitution of the USSR (Article 9), is not dealt with in this work. Their significance has been diminishing since about 1950. In 1959 and 1960, only about ten thousand hectares were cultivated by individual peasants and others in their statistical category, mainly in the western

---

[7] [404, 6]. See also [184, 148] and [354, II, 330]. Only recently have some Soviet authors rejected the reference, current under Stalin and Khrushchev, to a "petty-bourgeois" mentality of the kolkhozniks; see, for example [230, 57]. Venzher, an exception, had criticized this term as early as 1962 [397, 65].

[8] [192, 361]. For a more cautious formulation, see [180, 94].

Ukraine, Belorussia, and the Baltic republics [87, 42]. Since then no data on land area in this category have been published, and it is presumed that these holdings have diminished even further. The number of households in this sector declined from sixty thousand in 1960 to less than twenty thousand in 1964 [204, 73; 223, 26]. The size of land and livestock holdings owned by what in Soviet terminology is called an individual farmer (*edinolichnik*) is, on the average, not greater than that of the plots and livestock holdings of kolkhozniks [339a, 37–39]. Officially this represents the only really private sector of Soviet agriculture; in reality, however, the problem of the private sector centers upon the personal plots of the kolkhozniks and of the workers and employees.

This study will not deal with nonagricultural private production such as construction, forestry, fishing, hunting, and the picking of mushrooms and berries. N. S. Lagutin estimates that 84 percent of the net output of the Soviet private sector was derived from agricultural production in 1962 (the proportion in the kolkhoz sector being 89 percent, and among workers and employees 76 percent). Most of the remainder was accounted for by private construction.[9]

In Western writings, great attention has always been paid to the private sector of Soviet agriculture. To be sure, judgment was often influenced by incorrect evaluations of the actual state of affairs. Sometimes exaggerated estimates were advanced, and on other occasions the propagandistic claims of the Soviet authorities concerning the minor significance of the private sector were more or less uncritically accepted.[10] This can largely be attributed to the fact that Soviet media had released only meager and sharply distorted data and information about this sphere of the economy. The first, albeit faltering, progress in this regard became evident with the overall improvement of Soviet statistics after 1958. Another more marked step forward was taken after the removal of Khrushchev. The better statistical information as well as the more propitious political—and thence psychological in the news media—atmosphere made itself felt in Soviet writings on the subject. The most recent examples—before the final manuscript for this book was revised—of this more sophisticated approach were the books by Belianov [56a] and Shmelev

---

[9] [204, 77]. Cf. *ibid.*, 72, n. 1, and 84–86.

[10] Among the notable exceptions are the following studies: Wronski [422], Newth [261], and Sakoff [315]. The last two are particularly recommended because they consider regional differences within the enormous area of the Soviet Union.

[*393a*]. But there have been quite a number of similar treatments since 1965, as the documentation of the following narrative will show.

Only on this greatly improved basis was it possible to start writing this book, which deals with only one of many symptoms—yet a particularly characteristic one—of the present internal and economic situation in the Soviet Union.

2

"Personal" or "Private"?

The existence of the private sector in Soviet agriculture can be regarded as a concession linked to collectivization, but one which may someday be withdrawn. Communist authorities tend to use the adjective *personal* rather than the term *private,* thus avoiding the implication that a capitalist element has been retained in the socialist system. It is debatable whether the Soviet practice is hypocritical or whether the use of the Western concept of private (or the term *private sector*) would indeed be misleading in this context, as Soviet writers contend.[1]

Nancy Nimitz was undoubtedly correct when she said: "Private agriculture is still indispensable. Far from being an anachronism, it has been a necessary condition for the survival of socialized agriculture" [262, 23]. Nowadays this is also conceded by Soviet authors.[2] T. I. Zaslavskaia writes: "The existence [of the private plots] has so far been the condition for the successful development of the kolkhozes."[3] It remains to be seen whether this function may be attributed to a private sector in the normal sense of the term or to a specific, organic constituent of the socialist agricultural system. Some Soviet authors who write in the latter sense may be doing so to protect the private sector from the attacks of dogmatists. Thus we may read: "The obscuration of the distinction between the personal plots and the private farms, the unjustified analogy between them, was conducive to the establishment of those distortions [of the Party line] with regard to the personal plots, against which the Party has repeatedly spoken out [after the fall of Khrushchev]."[4] An officially authorized textbook, published in the mid-fifties, equated the private farming of the

---

[1] For a typical polemic on this subject against "present-day bourgeois economists, historians, and sociologists" see [291, 79]; see also the polemic against the author of this book by M. Postolowski in *Sowjetunion heute,* no. 23/24 (1968), p. 14.

[2] See, for instance [104, 215].

[3] [427, 63]; see also [87, 39].

[4] [339, 28]. A good example of the defensive argument is found in [307, 65].

kolkhoznik with that of a small peasant and considered it the "birth-mark" of the old "capitalistic" social order. Such analogies were drawn by several Soviet writers during the Khrushchev period, and a Russian translation of a Polish study of the USSR appeared in 1965 using the term "private farming on plots" [87, 35–36, 58, 81]. Recent Soviet writings have tended to eschew this analogy. But G. I. Shmelev [339a, 36] recently complained that there still are authors in the Soviet Union who speak of the "private [*chastnyi*] sector" and of "*chastniki*" (people selling privately what they have grown).

Much of the conflict between Soviet and Western interpretations is a matter of semantics. The Russian word for private—*chastnyi*—has a stronger implicit sense of separation than the Western meaning. In Marxist-Leninist Russian usage, *chastnyi* has acquired a much more limited sense than private in the Roman and Germanic languages, and this accounts for much of the Soviet hairsplitting with this term. Soviet theorizing in this area further suffers from the fact that there are no clearly defined concepts of property, possession, use, disposition, and so on. Very few Soviet authors are aware of this deficiency,[5] although Iu. V. Arutiunian observes perceptively that "under the conditions of Soviet society" the functions of possession, disposition, and use "may not and usually do not coincide" [51, 37].

Writing in the summer of 1968 in a Soviet journal, N. Kornienko demanded "that personal property should occupy a significantly greater place in scientific research and in the course of political economy than has been the case until recently" [194, 31]. Ever since the removal of Khrushchev, Soviet authors have repeatedly emphasized that the private sector is not "private" in the political–economic sense of the word, but that it is an organic component of the kolkhoz and of the socialist system.[6] I. A. Vishnevskii termed it "the personal property of the citizens . . . a new category, born of socialism," and he prophesied that such property would not wither away under full communism but would instead attain "its full development."[7] The question of whether there will be "personal" property under full communism is still a matter of dispute among Soviet authors [see 223, 25].

[5] An exception was the allusion by I. A. Vishnevskii at a conference in Kiev; see [280, 93].

[6] For example: [292, 36]; [272, 69]; [180, 94]; [345, 6]; [91, 48]; [373, 183]; [87, 38].

[7] According to the conference report in [280, 93].

According to V. G. Venzher, "in a social–economic sense, the Central Statistical Administration is absolutely correct to include the private plots of the kolkhozniks, workers, and employees as part of socialist agriculture in the statistical yearbooks" [396, 49]. He does not mention that this is true only in the summary section of the cited yearbook, while a clear statistical distinction is made between state (sovkhozes and other state agricultural enterprises), collective (kolkhozes) and "personal" agriculture in the purely agricultural section of the compendium. Moreover, the "personal" agricultural sector—which, as we shall see, is by no means inconsiderable—is very perfunctorily treated in the yearbook, which would hardly make sense if it were viewed as a bona fide component of the socialist sector.

Three pages later, Venzher[8] limits his argument to work performed in this sector, declaring:

Would it not be more correct, from the social point of view, to regard the personal farms of the kolkhozniks, workers, and employees as their personal property, as the property of the workers of the socialist society, as one of the aspects of the appearance of personal property relations in socialism, while [considering] the labor applied on the personal plots as labor representing social labor in its concrete form, which at the given stage of our development is still called upon to fulfill a certain social function—namely, to help meet the still inadequately satisfied requirements of society for agricultural produce?

This argument is clearly tenuous. If labor is qualified as socialist merely on the grounds that it helps to satisfy social requirements, then the same qualification could apply to the labor of really independent individual peasants. Venzher's sequel is no more convincing when, after reviewing the "exploitative" relations of a really peasant agriculture, he continues:

For this reason, the concepts of "individual peasant holdings" or "individual sector" or "private sector" [here Venzher uses the Russian word chastnyi] may in no way be applied to the characteristics of the personal plots of the kolkhozniks, let alone those of the workers and employees.

V. B. Ostrovskii offers the following definition [275, 20]:

As distinct from private property resulting from the exploitation of alien labor, personal property under socialism primarily concerns the sphere of consumption . . . the personal subsidiary economy of the kolkhozniks represents a special form of personal property which generates income. . . . The personal

[8] [396, 52]; similarly [87, 39].

farm liquidates, as it were, the [quantitative] gap between [their] earnings and the labor income of the workers and employees.

The argument concerning the socialistic function does not hold water, but a case could be made for an exploiting nature of the Soviet agricultural system as a whole consisting merely of small family farmers—"state bondsmen," who exploit neither one another nor the urban workers and employees but are all exploited by—to use Djilas's term—another "New Class" in the kolkhozes. Of course, no one will concede the existence of the New Class or of state bondage in works published in the Soviet Union. Nevertheless, the existence of exploitation is not a valid criterion for differentiating "private" from "personal" agricultural production. When D'iachkov cites the absence of hired labor as one of the features distinguishing the private plot from the small private capitalist farm [87, 38–39], he overlooks the fact that not only the traditional small farmers but also quite sizable farms manage to operate without hired labor in any modern, mechanized agricultural system.

However, for Venzher too, "the functioning of the personal plots contains some contradictions." Lagutin calls them "a special form of personal property," and I. Laptev refers to them as a "special historical category" to be considered neither as "related to private property" nor as a "socialized" enterprise or economy.[9]

The inherent contradictions are evident, and the only problem is how much importance should be ascribed to them. Kornienko has devoted two essays specifically to "personal property under socialism"; in them he does not limit himself to agricultural private property (which he calls personal).[10] He speaks of "the socialist nature of personal property," but advocates that quantitative limits be set also on the personal ownership of consumer goods, lest "unduly excessive personal property forms a brake on social progress, [and] turns into a breeding ground for tendencies [fostering] private ownership." For instance, the size of a family house in private ownership should be limited, and a Soviet citizen should not own more than one car. Yet he grants that "under certain circumstances" —for instance, in a kolkhoz—the means of production could be private property. In such a case it would be essential that "they lead only to individual production, sufficient for providing for the existence of the producer. Beyond these limits private property begins. For this reason, the

---

[9] [396, 53], [204, 71]; [210, 27–28].
[10] For the following quotations, see [193, 38] and [194, 24–25, 28].

individual ownership of the basic means of production is not personal but private ownership." With such a definition, the private plots of the kolkhozniks during the past three decades must definitely be classified as "private," because they undoubtedly provided most of the personal consumption requirements as well as cash from sales of surplus produce for nearly all kolkhozniks and still do today for a part of the kolkhoz population (see pp. 56, 89, below). Kornienko criticized those overzealous authors who maintain that personal property can exist only under socialism, while under capitalism all property is by definition private. Such hairsplitting would in fact present too facile a resolution of the problem since, by definition, the following formulation would emerge: Private property under socialism is *eo ipso* personal and not private. The logical extension of this argument—which V. K. Logvinenko [*223*, 26] emphatically denies—is that the property of the few remaining individual peasants and artisans in the Soviet Union is also not private but personal, because this property is derived from their own personal labor and not from the exploitation of alien workers. But Logvinenko also feels that such "private" property in the "socialistic" Soviet Union differs fundamentally from "private property under conditions of capitalism."

V. E. Grigorovskiy and M. A. Alekseev [*128*, 6, 21–22, 24, 26, 30], who take issue with the "bourgeois ideology" of the private character of the "personal" plots, also know that the socioeconomic nature of those plots cannot be defined merely as an "organic element of the socialist system." They therefore term personal plots as "a special, specific form of socialist agricultural production" and as "a special variety of personal property under socialism." [11] The problem remains, of course, of where these peculiarities are to be located between "socialist" and "private"; this depends largely upon what is meant by "private." For Grigorovskiy and Alekseev, as for most Soviet authors, "private" can only refer to the economic system of the small Russian peasants before collectivization. At least they concede that the labor applied to private plots appears to be "in private form" and therefore "the splitting of the sphere of application of the kolkhoznik's labor inevitably means the splitting of his material incentive."

Kornienko also does not really resolve the problem. He introduces the neutral concept of "individual" property and declares [*194*, 23]:

[11] Similarly [*87*, 39].

When an individual does not participate in social production but organizes his own private production, then his property is individual and yet not personal but private property. It is the individual ownership of the means of production. . . . Private and personal property under socialism are united by the fact that they are both based upon the personal labor of the producer. The source of personal property under socialism is labor applied in production based upon the public ownership of the means of production. For this reason, the very essence of personal property originates from the fact that it may consist, in the main, of consumer goods.

In his second article, Kornienko ascribes to the private plots the distinction of representing "separate, detached production" which "presupposes a certain setting aside of the means of production," thus once more putting it into a special category among other personal property. But he qualifies this by saying that these means of production are "not decisive" [*193*, 40-41].

Yet this definition leaves two problems unresolved. First, how can such personal ownership of consumer goods—according to Kornienko's own admission—turn into private ownership when held in excess (although this depends on earnings) so that it preserves "private property tendencies" [cf. *303*, 161]? And second, why does the peculiarity of kolkhoz conditions automatically turn the private plots into private property when the kolkhoz wages are too low (so that the private income becomes the main source of income) and/or the kolkhozniks cannot be fully employed in the socialized sector of the kolkhoz? In the past, the latter has been the case in many parts of the country, and it still is true in some regions.

Other authors, who deal with kolkhoz conditions in a more extensive manner, contrast the mutuality and inner relationship of the social and personal (private) sectors of Soviet agriculture with the inner contradictions of property in the private plots and their means of production. V. A. Morozov, for instance, writes [*250*, 176]:

The kolkhoz household is based on, and its distinctive feature is, the relationship between the kolkhoznik's subsidiary farm and the social economy of the kolkhoz, the dependence of the former upon the latter. The private plot is no longer private [*chastnoe*], isolated, it is becoming auxiliary, supplementary. . . . The existence of the personal plot is in every instance subject to the participation of its owner in social production. The members of the kolkhoz household (apart from invalids, old-age pensioners, and some other groups) are obligated to work in the kolkhoz. If this condition is not fulfilled, the statutes of the agricultural artel provide for the diminution of the plot. The dependence upon the social economy turns the personal plot into a form of material incentive. Even more: during that period when the Leninist principle of material interestedness was grossly ignored, the private plot was in fact the only stimulus to participation in social production.

The same thoughts were advocated more precisely by Zaslavskaia. She dismissed the critiques, aired during Khrushchev's administration, of the personal sector. Another Soviet author, M. Makeenko, wrote: "The notion of the personal plot as an alien body in the socialist economy is unfortunately still very frequently propagated" [230, 62–63]. Zaslavskaia stated [427, 57]:

In connection with the administrative curtailment of the personal plots, which was carried out here and there, opinions were also aired on the subject: According to these views, the plot did not belong to the forms of the socialist production but represented a private [chastnyi] sector in the socialist economy. As an argument against this false thesis, many economists point out that the kolkhoz peasantry cannot at the same time belong to socialist and to private production, that there is no paid labor on the personal plots,[12] and so on.

We would like to support this contention and would point out, in addition, the role of the personal plots in the formation of the gross income and of the consumption fund of the kolkhozniks as shown in the above-cited data. These reveal the essential nature of the personal plot as a form of production which guarantees, on the one hand, the extended reproduction of the work force and the satisfaction of the necessities of life of the kolkhozniks and, on the other, the active participation of the social economy of the kolkhoz in accumulation. The operation of the social economy of the kolkhoz cannot take place in current conditions without the personal plot. In the same way, the personal plot of the kolkhozniks cannot exist without the social economy, which is distinguished [from the plot] by its higher labor productivity and which yields a large part of the agricultural output.

The socialist character of the personal plot does not, however, exclude the possibility of these laborers acquiring a speculative income not derived from work.

The arguments of Morozov and Zaslavskaia, which are also found in more recent Soviet publications and which are repeated in essence by Grigorovskiy and Alekseev [128, 23–24], boil down to the following:

---

[12] Of course there is in practice. See, for example, the reference in [212, 152]; also the private haymaking for another in return for money in [251, 48–51] (on p. 53 he shows how this practice may be disguised as a "social commission"). However, a private deal like this involving paid labor can certainly not be openly sanctioned. On urban plots, too, the use of hired labor is forbidden [55a, 99].

1. One class (the kolkhoz peasantry) cannot at the same time belong to both the socialist and the private spheres of production.

2. On the basis of the kolkhoz statutes and general Soviet law, the operation of the private plot is rendered impossible if its owner does not also cooperate in kolkhoz work.

3. The private plot presents problems (that is, becomes "private" rather than "personal") only when it yields more than the subsistence minimum for its owner and thus may lead to the emergence of "speculative" profits (as a result of the distorted price structure of the Soviet economy).

4. The kolkhozniks were unable to exist without the private plot, because their incomes from kolkhoz work—at least until recently—did not guarantee their material needs and reproduction (extended reproduction of the work force).

5. Similarly, the kolkhozniks were unable to exist solely on the output of the private plot; the social sector produces a large part of the produce necessary for their sustenance, as well as most of the fodder for their livestock, and accumulates the capital needed for the maintenance and raising of this production.

The first theoretical–declamatory point need not be treated here. The second and third points are not very convincing either, setting as they do only normative and quantitative limits on productive activities but not qualitatively changing these activities. Using an extension of the same argument, it might be pleaded that the terms "money lending" and "interest" are used in a special sense in a country where money lenders who do not pay taxes and do not serve in the armed forces are expropriated (the second point). Moreover, a money lender still lends money, even if there are restrictions on the maximum amount of loan or a maximum rate of interest to be charged.

On the other hand, the last two points are significant. Because of their diminutive size, the private farms cannot indeed exist on their own, in much the same way that the dependent day laborers on the former north German estates could not live from their allotments and had to rely on payments in cash and kind for their work on the estates. Conversely, the kolkhoz is dependent upon the labor of the kolkhoz families just as the estates were upon the day workers and their families. A kolkhoz (or an estate) cannot exist as an economic unit without its dependent labor force; the two parts, although distinct in certain respects, cannot be treated as two completely distinct phenomena. This is the point of departure for the Soviet authors.

Does this, however, mean that the private plot cannot be considered private in the Western sense of the word because the farm of which it is a part—the kolkhoz—is not private? Modern economics has long since refuted the Marxist–Leninist dogma whereby there can be no private capitalist undertaking unless the entrepreneur is in the legal sense the owner of the means of production; this also applies to agricultural undertakings. In the economic sense, a private undertaking can also exist if the entrepreneur is autonomous in what he produces and how he disposes of it but is subject to certain rules about the land use rights to a private plot, the ownership of livestock, farm buildings, and agricultural implements, and the provision of a certain amount of labor in the public sector.

Whether this private output exceeds the minimum needed for subsistence is immaterial. Let us take the case of a kolkhoz family who can grow only enough potatoes so that, with the potatoes received from the public sector, it has just enough for the family and its pigs. It would still be up to the family to decide whether they should slaughter the pigs in the fall and sell potatoes to purchase—for example—more hay for their cow. Or they could grow a large quantity of onions instead of potatoes in the hope that, with the proceeds of the sale of onions, they could buy enough potatoes in the fall to satisfy their needs and also buy a calf in the spring. An essential condition to all this, of course, is a relatively free market which enables such sales and purchases. For this reason the kolkhoz market (see Chapter VI) is a necessary extension of and indeed a necessary component of the private agricultural sector.

I. Pavlov is quite correct in stating [286, 22]: "The real essence of the kolkhozniks' rights and duties concerning their private plots consists of freedom to work these plots within the limits set by law and, above all, to dispose of the output produced there."

There clearly exist many different ways of disposing of the produce of the plot, and it would obviously be misleading to deny that such dealings have a small-scale business character. It is a business decision when one decides whether to limit consumption for the time being in order to invest (in extra feedstuffs, young animals, better seed) to secure a future higher income or to consume to the maximum extent at the present time.

Under these circumstances, the thoughts of I. Stadniuk's kolkhoz chairman are far closer to reality and more honest than all the theorizing [364, no. 8, 54]:

How can one get out of this contradictory situation when the state's interest in a surplus of produce coincides with the interests of the peasants in their plots and personal livestock, even though the state despises the private property strivings of people. . . . Yet there's nothing terrible about that because the consciousness of the villagers is anyhow determined in the last analysis by the life of the kolkhoz.

Yet Stadniuk's last phrase, comforting though it may be to a Communist's ear, misses the heart of the matter—just how does the life of the kolkhoz, in its entirety (including the private plots), determine the consciousness of people? Soviet writers also are well aware that "many specific traits of peasant everyday life, especially in the life of the family, are closely bound with the existence of the kolkhozniks' private plots" [369, 317].

Yet kolkhoz life does in fact contain one feature which limits the private character of the plot and considerably limits the number of different petty entrepreneurial decisions mentioned above (cf. Chapter VII). This is the fact that the kolkhoznik is crucially dependent upon the kolkhoz not only for his own personal subsistence but also for farming his plot. The kolkhoz is in a position to influence the scope of plot farming to a significant extent by refusing or limiting its allocations of fodder, grazing rights, and payments-in-kind. This is also true, to a lesser degree, for workers and employees and especially for those employed in sovkhozes. Conversely, however, the kolkhoz or sovkhoz is also dependent on the labor of the kolkhozniks (and sovkhoz workers and employees) and on their work performance as small entrepreneurs.

The plots cannot be considered to be fully private, nor can the kolkhoz or sovkhoz economy be regarded as purely social. However, although the social character is predominant in the kolkhoz or sovkhoz economy, the plot is to be regarded primarily as private in view of its special position and role within the socialist state and economic system. The specific peculiarities of this system must never be overlooked if we are to understand why the existence and functioning of "personal" small-scale producers repeatedly cause the agricultural authorities so much trouble.

3

The Rules of the Game

The only members of the Soviet population who still have land in their own right for agricultural use are the independent peasants (*edinolichniki*); these people are not members of collectives and are engaged in farming as their principal occupation using their own labor. The land of the *edinolichnik* consists of the plot adjacent to the dwelling (*priusadebnyi uchastok*) and a piece of land usually situated outside the settlement. The former may amount to 0.2 hectare including the land under buildings (0.1 hectare in irrigated regions), and the latter may total up to 1.0 hectare (0.5 hectare in fruit and root crop areas and 0.1 hectare in irrigated regions).

This division of the agricultural land is no longer of great intrinsic importance, because the number of *edinolichniki* is constantly diminishing and the total area of their land holdings is minimal (see pp. 7–8). But the division does serve to illustrate the position of the kolkhoz population in relation to the kolkhoz and of their use of land. The plots of land situated outside the settlements—plots which belonged to the once independent peasants—were incorporated into the land cultivated by the kolkhozes when collectivization took place. Although the state is the sole owner of all land, it allows the kolkhoz to use it. The kolkhoz in its turn grants the household (*kolkhoznyi dvor*) the individual use of the plot adjacent to the house.

The kolkhoz household retains many of the characteristics of the old peasant household, not in the economic sense but in its complicated juridical functions which intersect several legal spheres: It is defined as a "family and labor community."[1] In order to comprehend the nature and

---

[1] [*165*, 471–472]; [*241*, 97]; for a detailed discussion see [*404*, 22–23]. Kinship is not an essential prerequisite of this association and may be replaced by membership in the joint household: see [*404*, 32]; [*219*, 12 ff.]. The household may consist of two or more families; see I. Pavlov [*286*, 23].

the peculiarities of the private subsidiary farm, which belongs to the entire household and not to the individual, it is necessary to understand the special legal nature of the kolkhoz household and of the kolkhoz family; we discuss them here for this reason. The concept of kolkhoz household was sanctioned by Stalin in 1935 through its inclusion in the model statute of the agricultural artel, but a precise legal definition is still lacking.

The household list of the village soviet determines which households in a community are considered kolkhoz households and thus have a claim to a private plot. However, the kolkhoznik is given no documentary title to the use of this land. By its legal derivation, the kolkhoznik's private plot is clearly distinguished from the plot of the worker and employee, although the difference is no longer always recognizable by looking at the size of the plot—especially after the recent conversions to state farms. At least initially, former kolkhozniks who continue to reside in sovkhozes are allowed to retain their private plots in the old dimensions (see p. 297). A difference lies also in the fact that the juridical character as a legal person, which was enjoyed by the former peasant household under Russian and also Soviet law, is still not indisputably accorded to the kolkhoz household even in the latest Soviet writings. In contrast, no Soviet author appears to doubt that in workers' and employees' households, only the individual members are legal subjects, especially with regard to their land use rights.

For the above reason, the rights of ownership for each group are established in two separate articles (Nos. 7 and 10) in the Constitution of the USSR. One is regulated through civil law and the other through kolkhoz law, while explicit reference is made to "two kinds of personal property in the USSR." This difference stands out particularly when a kolkhoz household is converted into a worker's or employee's household. Only recently has there been a movement toward approximating the rights of the kolkhoz population to those legal norms valid for the rest of the population; this also corresponds with the actual development of the subsidiary farms.[2]

Similarly, there are certain peculiarities in the position of the individual members within a kolkhoznik's family (see below). The personal property of the individual member and the common property of the household exist side by side.

[2] [241, 98]; [303; 117]. At a conference of Soviet jurists in November 1965, V. A. Kikot' termed "a legal category such as the kolkhoz household" an "anachronism"; see [185, 95].

B. A. Liskovets differentiates the kolkhoznik household from other households according to its place in the economic process [*219, 6-7*]:

A household [*khoziaistvo*] whose members (or at least one of them) belong to an agricultural or fishing artel, [who] take part in kolkhoz production by means of personal labor, [who] have personal use of a private plot which is allocated to them within the framework of the norms prescribed by the statute of the agricultural artel. . . . The kolkhoz household receives its principal [or basic] income from the participation of its members in the social economy of the artel.

The right of the kolkhoznik to the use of a private plot is stipulated also in the Model Charters of 1935 and of 1969, as well as in the Constitution. The new Land Law (Art. 24-25), passed in December 1968, did not alter the existing regulations. (For details of the 1969 Model Charter not dealt with here, see below, Chapter X, Addendum.)

The permitted area of the private plot of a kolkhoz household comprises up to 0.5 hectare and—until the new statute (Model Charter) of 1969—up to 1.0 hectare in regions with unexploited land and very extensive agriculture.[3] Up to 1969, the area under buildings and—since the mid-1950s, the front gardens—were excluded [*64, 4-5; 68, 159*], although the latter was not precisely defined and was subject to dispute [*452, 21 September 1968*]. The private plot is counted as part of the kolkhoz's "land fund" set aside for private farming and is furnished by the state for the use of the kolkhoz and not of the individual kolkhozniks. The land fund may be increased—either in its entirety or only that portion reserved for private plots—only with the permission of the superior state authority; this may occur, for example, if the number of members or households in the given kolkhoz has risen sharply [*64, 3; 140, 19-20*]. Such extension is also provided for in the new Land Law (Art. 24). Occasionally, though seldom, this occurs illegally; in fact, in 1962 N. D. Kazantsev deemed *any* expansion of the portion of the land fund set aside for private plots as illegal and indicated that kolkhozes should try to reduce these portions [*165, 480*]. At the beginning of the 1960s, an area of 1.7 million hectares of the kolkhozes' land fund set aside for private plots was not allocated out to individuals and half of this land lay

---

[3] This is the model regulation which permits rare local deviations. In the legislation of 1935, the size of private plots was "defined and stipulated in the republics and provinces by means of joint decrees of the soviet and party organs of the republics and provinces and laid down in the statutes of the individual kolkhozes" [*286, 23*].

fallow.[4] The individual has no legal appeal against directives concerning the size and allocation of private plots. These directives are decided upon by the highest organs of the kolkhoz (the general assembly or council of plenipotentiaries), and the individual may not go to court.

Preconditions for the right to use a private plot are membership in the kolkhoz and active participation in its work. This also holds true for the so-called mechanizers, who joined or rejoined kolkhozes as members when the Machine Tractor Stations (MTS) were abolished in 1958.

Kolkhoz members are allowed to exchange plot usage rights among themselves within the limits laid down by the statute for each household, provided that the kolkhoz assembly or council approves. Disputes between kolkhoz families over private land use are resolved by the kolkhoz leadership or, in the final instance, by the kolkhoz assembly or council.

After the decree of 6 March 1956, the kolkhozes themselves were permitted and, indeed, were urged to determine the size of plot through amendment of their statutes. The criterion for deciding the size was the degree of active participation in work in the public sector and not the numerical size of the household. The new Model Charter of 1969 (Art. 42) again takes into consideration the household size in addition to labor participation. When, at the instigation of Khrushchev in 1950, the creation of the giant kolkhozes of today was begun through amalgamation, the first indications of such alterations in the size of private plots were mooted. At the time, it is true, it was said that "as a rule" the norms for private plots and livestock holdings should remain at their previous levels, but it was also added that these norms could be altered by a two-thirds majority of the kolkhoz assembly.[5]

The official trend in the decrees of 1950 and 1956 was toward a reduction in the size of the private plots. This was indeed the prime cause for the decline in the privately used area in kolkhozes [340, 137, n.]. Later a minimum size of 0.15 hectare was recommended, and reductions to 0.03 or 0.05 hectare—which had actually occurred—were denounced as an excessive implementation of the official policy, except when several able-bodied members of one household participated not at all or to an

[4] S. A. Udachin, "Ratsional'noe ispol'zovanie zemli," [391, 27]. By 1968, about one and one-half million hectares had not been allocated, of which some two-thirds lay fallow; see [387, 23].

[5] Decree of the USSR Council of Ministers of 17 July 1950, "On Measures in Connection with the Enlargement of Small Kolkhozes," in [321, 47]; cf. [206, 136].

insufficient degree in the public sector without valid reason.[6] Moreover, it appears that the norms for private plots and for livestock holdings were often independently determined by the kolkhoz chairmen without the decision being referred to the assembly or council, although this ran counter to the statutes.[7] However, the many instances of reduction were at the time termed "absolutely appropriate and opportune."[8] Then, shortly after Khrushchev's removal, the Central Committee of the Communist Party of the Soviet Union (CPSU) issued a decree (of 27 October 1964) on the lifting of all kinds of restrictions on private plots and livestock holdings. On the basis of this decree, the individual union-republics issued their own—not quite uniform—decrees (see p. 319 ff). In general, recent trends have been against a reduction of the plots, although opinions have differed on this issue.

After 1964, many spoke out against the size of the private plot being made dependent on the degree of "active participation" in the public sector. On this fundamental aspect of the whole issue, a Soviet jurist declared, at the beginning of 1966: "It cannot be acknowledged as correct that at the present time the resolution of all these problems is left to the judgment of the kolkhoz itself."[9] A few kolkhozes did annul the connection between the size of the plot and the amount of work put in to the public sector, but these represented a minority [440, 9 July 1965; 140, 7], and the Model Charter of 1969 did not support them.

The private plot may not be reduced because the household consists entirely of aged or infirm members who are able to contribute little or no labor to the public sector. There was, however, a tendency in the amendment of statutes after 1956 for many kolkhoz leaderships to deprive aged and infirm kolkhozniks, who were no longer of any use to

---

[8] [64, 8–9]. A decree of the RSFSR Council of Ministers of 18 May 1957 sought to check excessive measures against private land use by the nonkolkhoz population who resided in kolkhozes (mostly ex-kolkhozniks) and elderly kolkhozniks whose younger family members worked outside the kolkhoz. This decree, titled "On Cases of Abuse Against Private Plots of Workers, Employees, Pensioners, and Other Citizens Residing on the Territory of Kolkhozes," was summarized in [60, III, 457–458] and in [346, VIII, 79].

[7] This may be deduced indirectly from an observation in 1967 that in this respect renewed adherence to the statutes will "create a firm guarantee of the preservation of the legal interests of the kolkhozniks" [313, 100, n. 10].

[8] [269, 33]. For examples of reductions accomplished by altering the statutes, see [140, 5–6].

[9] [287, 93]; see also V. S. Karpik and N. V. Storozhev, "Razvitie kolkhoznoi demokratii na sovremennom etape," [147, 29]; [381, 22].

the kolkhoz, of their membership and therefore of their right to a private plot.[10] This was sometimes also applied to members who were performing their military service,[11] presumably on the grounds that they would not return to the kolkhoz afterwards. The Land Law of 1968 (Art. 25) and the new model statute (Art. 42) explicitly affirm the kolkhozniks' rights to the private plots in such instances.

On the other hand, a legitimate ground for reducing the size of the plot arises when individual able-bodied members of a household voluntarily (*samovol'no*) leave the kolkhoz. However, such absence does not affect the membership in the kolkhoz and the right to a private plot if it is officially approved and is of a temporary nature, and if the individuals concerned return to the kolkhoz or come back for regular periods in order to work their private plots and to take part in the kolkhoz work. However, the kolkhoz authorities do not always appear to have observed this rule.

The private plot may be withdrawn completely only if all able-bodied members do not participate in the public sector and work outside the kolkhoz, or when aged members move away (for example, to live with their children in the town), returning for only a few months each year to work the plot. It is then considered that "the household ceases in essence to be a kolkhoz household."[12] If, however, there are several household members who are engaged in other enterprises as workers or employees, but who "nevertheless live in the household and work the private plot and livestock holding together with other members of the household who are kolkhozniks," then the character of the private plot is retained. Such "mixed households," as they are called, are often to be found nowadays.[13] Even if only one member of the household has remained a kolkhoznik, the right to a private plot is preserved, since this right devolves on the family or household. However, as soon as the actual kolkhoznik members of the household leave or die and the only remaining members

[10] [404, 29]; [334, 34]. There were many such instances as late as 1965; see [452, 4 November 1965].

[11] An actual instance is cited in [229, 81]; see also [171, 23].

[12] [64, 11–12]. In the same connection, [404, 30] declares: "A household may under no circumstances be considered as a kolkhoz household if it contains no single kolkhoz member." Similar viewpoints now appear to be generally accepted among Soviet authors, in contrast to the wide differences of opinion in the 1950s: see, among others, [337, 616, especially n. 72]. There are Soviet citizens who live in Leningrad and still use private plots in the country; see [452, 21 September 1968].

[13] [404, 27]; see also [219, 7, 67]; [311, 163 f.]; [238, 84].

are those who legally work outside the kolkhoz, then the plot should be reduced to the dimensions customary for rural workers and employees.

For both the reduction and the confiscation of the private plot, a formal decision of the kolkhoz assembly or council is necessary, and certain procedures are to be observed. This is not always done in practice.

A new kolkhoz household is usually formed when a member of a kolkhoz family marries and sets up house; this is called a *vydel* (apportionment). In such instances, either a private plot of a size in accordance with the statute "may be" allocated from the land fund of the kolkhoz set aside for this purpose or, when this "appears to be impossible," the old plot may be subdivided and a share given to the new household.[14] This claim to an additional plot in connection with a family division has contributed substantially to a breakup of the enlarged kolkhoz families; occasionally fictitious family divisions were undertaken.[15]

Apart from the dwelling house—which up to 1969 was not included in the area of the private plot (see above)—the right to the plot may be inherited only by descendants and relations who are members of the kolkhoz in question. The right to the plot lapses "(a) when the household consists of fictitious kolkhozniks, who are detached from the life of the artel and are actually cut off from it; (b) if the kolkhoznik leases his private plot or transfers it to another person [this is forbidden, see below]; (c) if the kolkhoz household moves to another district; (d) if all members of the household are deceased, and (e) if all household members voluntarily give up their private plot." [64, 17]

The boundaries or locations of the private plots may be altered if this is in the interests of the kolkhoz, as long as the dimensions remain unchanged. If the land upon which a kolkhoz is situated is incorporated into an urban municipality, this does not basically alter the land use rights of the kolkhoz or of its individual members, but the size of private plots may be reduced within the framework of urban development schemes. Other plots of land may be allocated in compensation from the fund set aside for private plots, but only insofar as such land is available.

All adult members of a kolkhoz household enjoy equal material rights, but the head of the household—who need not necessarily be a man or the oldest member—is their representative and may act in their name

---

[14] [64, 15–16]. The second possibility is regarded as exceptional; see [219, 27].
[15] [172, 216]; [140, 18]; [103, 75]; see also the decree of the CC VKP (b) and Sovnarkhom SSSR of 27 May 1939, "O merakh okhrany obshchestvennykh zemel' kolkhozov ot razbazarivaniia," [90, II, 589].

in dealings with the outside world. The subsidiary farm with its means of production such as outbuildings, tools, livestock, seed and plants, together with the dwelling house (not regarded as a means of production), is considered to be "personal," that is, as private property of the entire household. The dwelling house may not be withdrawn once its occupants cease to be members, but the kolkhoz should, wherever possible, purchase it. As far as buildings are concerned—unless they are purchased to be razed [16]—the kolkhoz has the first option to purchase and must first expressly renounce this right. Similarly, before the right to a private plot may be transferred to a purchaser or to an heir[17]—who must normally be a kolkhoz member—the agreement of the kolkhoz is necessary for the sale to be considered legitimate. Such sales and purchases of houses occur "very frequently," and recently it was demanded—unsuccessfully—that the related problems of land use be regulated in the new Land Law [452, 14 September 1968].

As increasing numbers of specialists and other leading personnel move into the kolkhoz villages and have rights to private plots and dwellings as employees or as members of the kolkhoz, the regulations concerning the sale and purchase of this right acquire increased practical significance. These regulations can lead to difficulties, because the decision of a kolkhoz "to refuse the purchaser of a building the use of the plot of land upon which it stands, in fact limits the ability of the kolkhoz household in disposing of the dwelling house" which is the property of the household. This refers not to the private plot but to the legally authorized building plot, and "an answer to this question is to be found neither in the legislation nor in other authoritative documents" [404, 100]. Such a situation gives plenty of scope both for arbitrariness on the part of the kolkhoz direction and for circumvention of the regulations by the kolkhozniks.

Neither the ownership of nor the right to use the plot may serve for the "exploitation of others' labor" or the "systematic attainment of an unearned income." For this reason, any leasing or hiring of equipment, machinery, livestock, vehicles, or right of land use is forbidden.

---

[16] With log houses, which are still very common, it is not unusual for the entire house to be taken down and put up again on a new site or to be moved without being dismantled. For a description of these practices, see [200, 85–89, 115–117, 130–133, 242–244].

[17] The right to use land is fairly often the object of a purchase, de facto if not de jure; see, for instance, [101, 75–76] and [336, 89].

The private plot and livestock holding with all the appurtenances—
as distinct from items of personal use which belong to the individuals—
are the collective property of all members of the household; these count
as "personal property" although they do not belong to any one person
[*58*, 30, 34–35, 41]. Until the last household member dies or the household
is dissolved with the agreement of all its members—the *razdel* (partition)
—only the right to the relevant share (undivided) may be inherited and
only by those who have qualified for membership through active participation in the work of the household and its plot. Thus whenever a household member dies or leaves, there ensues a hypothetical redistribution
among the remaining household members. Only after the dying out or
dissolution of this "family and labor community" can the claims to an
inheritance be entertained in the general sense of Soviet civil law; these
claims do not, however, apply to the right to the private plot, because
that right ceases to exist once the legal subject is no more.

This retention of archaic familial legal rights of ownership, observing
the principle of equal rights for each member of the family, recalls the
thinking of the Slavophiles and narodniks (populists) of the nineteenth
century and forms a strange blend with the spiritual heritage of the Stalin
era.[18] It serves to "consolidate the kolkhoz system," and the following
formulation is characteristic [*404*, 74]:

The recognition of the general property of the kolkhoz household as the
common possession of its participants corresponds with the task of consolidat-
ing the kolkhoz system, in that it offers a number of advantages to those
members of the household who continue to work in the public sector of the
kolkhoz.

This could also be phrased rather more bluntly: Those who leave
the kolkhoz are subject to several disadvantages regarding property rights
which are not applicable to other Soviet citizens. Worthy of note is a
recent development which provides for a diminution in the size of the
plots belonging to sovkhoz workers and employees if they leave the farm
(see p. 36).

The state of property rights described above has led "in the actual

---

[18] From this it would appear that the institution of the kolkhoz household was
initially accepted by the Bolsheviks only as a necessary evil and as a concession to a
still too strong tradition. However, it seems that the advantages for the kolkhoz
system were soon recognized: see [*337*, 616–617, 620].

life of the kolkhoz village" to cash incomes—both from kolkhoz work
and from work outside the kolkhoz—being considered part of the common income of the household [19] and merged with the private income
from the private plot. Yet this is understandable, because the reason family members are able to earn a living from so many sources lies in the
way in which the work of the kolkhoz household is distributed, especially
between the male and female members. Work on the private plot is essential for the family income. It is performed mainly by women—as well
as children, the aged and invalids—and this frees the men for the main
tasks in the kolkhoz or outside the farm (and also some of the able-
bodied women for work in the kolkhoz livestock sector), without affecting adversely the housework or the plot.

Certain maxima are laid down for the livestock holdings in the
same way as for the size of the private plots. These were determined by
the Model Charter of 1935 and in most regions consisted of "one cow,
two calves, one sow with young or two sows with young where this is
considered necessary by the kolkhoz authorities, ten sheep and/or goats,
an unlimited amount of poultry and rabbits and up to twenty beehives."
These add up to the equivalent of 2.5 to 3 livestock units. In some areas
the private poultry holdings—for which no limits are specified—reach
a considerable size. Most kolkhoz families in the Kursk oblast in 1966,
for example, owned between twenty and thirty geese [449, 20 March
1967]. In crop regions with a developed livestock sector, these norms were
about two-and-a-half times as great, apart from the bee holdings. The
norms were even larger in regions where "crop growing is of minor significance and where livestock raising plays a decisive role." Finally, in
"nomadic regions where crop growing is virtually insignificant and where
livestock raising is the chief form of agriculture," the norms went up to
"eight or ten cows with young, one hundred to one hundred and fifty
sheep and/or goats, an unlimited amount of poultry, up to ten horses and
five to eight camels for personal use." The statute did not specify the age
covered by the expression "young animals" and this has been exploited
by "certain kolkhozniks" [404, 77].

In 1956, kolkhozes were also given the right to alter the maximum
holdings of livestock; until the removal of Khrushchev this usually meant

[19] [219, 30]; [404, 80–82]; Kazantsev [165, 486–487] even deduces from this the
prescriptive duty of all household members to put their earnings in the "family
chest.'

a reduction.[20] This tendency was also observed as early as the decree of 17 July 1950 (see p. 23, n. 5) and the "success" of the measure was evidenced by the rapid decline in private livestock inventories.

Since 1956, alterations to the statutes have been carried out in differing ways and with differing emphases so that, at least up to 1969, neighboring kolkhozes may have dissimilar provisions concerning the number of animals which each household is allowed to keep.

The new Model Charter, published in 1969, was more specific in this respect. In its Article 43 it allowed as an upper limit: "One cow with calves of up to one year, one calf of up to two years, one sow with piglets of up to three months or two hogs for fattening, [and] up to ten sheep or goats" as well as an unspecified number of beehives, poultry, and rabbits. Regional variations are left to the discretion of the union-republican councils of ministers.

It is generally and officially recommended to the kolkhozes and local authorities that they allow the grazing of privately owned livestock on certain kolkhoz lands and issue feed to kolkhozniks, as part of their payments-in-kind or otherwise.[21] However, a charge may be made for private grazing if not all members of the household put in the obligatory minimum amount of work in the public sector. The plots should be used for growing plants and, basically speaking, should not be left to grass. (For details, see Chapter VII, p. 220.)

A further limitation on the economic effectiveness of the private plot and livestock holding is the stipulation that the income derived from

[20] This was officially approved; see [362, 30]. Cf. [165, 45–46]. For an example from a later period, which is explicitly described as not an isolated case, see [334, 34]. This tendency was also positively appraised in [269, 33]. From 1960 on, in new statutes in those union-republics where livestock raising is the principal kind of farming, the top limits were lowered to twenty-five small livestock, and the limits in mountainous regions—where only livestock raising was possible—were set at fifty small livestock. See [457, 20 October 1960] and [463, 28 January 1961].

[21] [189, III, 521]. The model statute of 1935 recommended that feed be issued to those "working conscientiously in social production . . . as far as this is possible." However, as Shmelev [339, 36] correctly observes, this formulation was to be understood as "something desirable, rather than obligatory, for the [kolkhoz] leadership." Kazachkin [164, 13] speaks very decidedly of a "right," without it being at all clear where this right is formally based. But perhaps he is referring to a provision of the kolkhoz's inner regulations when he cites: "The kolkhoz members also enjoy the right to utilize the meadows and pastures of the kolkhoz for the livestock in their personal possession." The Model Charter of 1969 (Art. 43) more generally demanded help by the kolkhoz "in providing livestock with feed and grazing areas."

them may not represent the "basic income" of the household (Constitution of the USSR, Article 7). This is mirrored by the demand, common in Soviet writing, that the private plot serve only as a source of ancillary income, "only an additional expedient for the family budget." [22] Income from the private plot should not exceed the basic income from the "social economy of the kolkhoz." Other earnings, even quite legal wages from outside the farm, may not theoretically constitute the chief source of livelihood if the household is to be counted as kolkhoz household.

Such stipulations conveniently overlook the fact that, until the early sixties, the income from the private plot and related sources usually constituted the main source of livelihood for the kolkhoz population, because earnings from the kolkhoz public sector were very inadequate. Arutiunian says quite openly [51, 40–41]: "If this quantitatively miserable plot is turning, under some conditions, into the main source of income, this is, of course, to be explained not by its development but by the weakness of the social sector, the inadequate resources allocated to the payment of the kolkhozniks' labor." Nevertheless, this regulation represents a means of limiting the private plot and livestock holding, although until now it has been brought up more in theoretical pronouncements and rulings on principle than in actual practice. I am not aware of any instance where this regulation has been applied in practice; this does not rule out the possibility of exceptional cases but confirms its overall lack of significance.

WORKERS AND EMPLOYEES

The term "private plot" (*priusadebnyi uchastok*) is also employed to describe those plots of land which are placed at the disposition of workers and employees. It denotes a piece of ground situated next to and around the dwelling house (*pri usad'be*) even though formerly the word *usad'ba* usually meant a farmstead or an isolated peasant house. Nowadays it generally refers to a group of farm buildings or dwelling houses in a sovkhoz or kolkhoz (or in an MTS when these existed). As a result, in addition to covering the kolkhoznik's private plot, the term *priusadebnyi uchastok* applies in general to a plot of land in the country upon which a privately owned one- or two-family house is standing or is to be constructed. In urban areas, it is mostly called an *usadebyni uchastok* and is granted by decision of the local authorities (municipal soviets)

[22] [458, 11 November 1965]. The Russian word "podspor'e" meaning "auxiliary, ancillary" is often encountered in this context.

[55a, 21–22]. As with the kolkhoz households, only the house itself may be sold—not the use rights to the adjoining plot, although in practice it does happen that the ground itself is really the object of the sale [168, 341] if it is situated on urban territory. In urban areas the right to use the plot is transferred to the new owner of the house on the plot, but this does not apply in rural areas.[23] The right of urban plot use is "inseparably connected with the personal ownership right of the living houses situated on these plots" [55a, 96]. In the event of a dispute between Soviet citizens over the right to use land, the case is settled either by the kolkhoz or by a "comradely court"; as a rule, however, it may not be brought before a normal court [452, 14 September 1968].

The individual urban worker or employee is granted such a plot of land for himself and for his heirs for perpetual use when an entry is made in the land register. Thus his tenure is more firmly assured than that of the kolkhoznik, because it may not be removed by any members' or plenipotentiaries' assembly without any further legal recourse. Of course, only a certain proportion of workers and employees possess such a plot of land. For urban plots the agricultural tax does not have to be paid. But from residential sites a small so-called land rent is levied, which does not have to be paid for other urban gardens, pastures, and so on [55a, 18]. When the land lies outside urban territory, the workers and employees are generally obliged to pay agricultural taxes at the same rates as kolkhozniks. This also shows that the plot of the rural worker or employee does not differ greatly from the kolkhoznik's plot in the economic sense and is distinguished only by the size permitted and by the social status of its owner.

A Soviet jurist gives the following definition for the worker's or employee's plot and livestock holding, based solely on the social status of the owner [219, 6]: "The subsidiary economy of a worker or employee is one whose owner does not belong to a kolkhoz or fishery artel but who works in other cooperative, state or social enterprises, institutions, or organizations."

The normal area of a worker's or employee's plot in rural communities is a maximum of 0.15 hectare, including the front garden (see [452, 21 September 1968]), and the space occupied by the dwelling house and outbuildings. In irrigated regions, the dimensions are one-half of the above. However, quite a few exceptions are valid for various professions.

[23] [452, 9 September 1968]; see also Art. 33 of the 1968 Land Law.

The regulations for rural communities have some effect on the actual state of affairs in towns and in "urban-type settlements."[24] Many towns have grown out of, or have incorporated, villages and in such instances the previous tenure rights are retained. Nevertheless, once a community has become a town, usually no further really agricultural plots are distributed. Instead, since 1948, either building plots for private houses are allocated, embracing gardens of between 0.07 and 0.12 hectare in the *dacha* settlements or recreation areas—as in rural areas in general, or between 0.03 and 0.06 hectare in urban areas [*346*, VIII, 73-74], or else allotments (see below) are allocated which are not subject to the agricultural tax. In union-republic capitals and in many other towns since 1 February 1962, building plots may no longer be allocated to private individuals but must be developed through residential construction and *dacha* cooperatives [*111*, 225]. As of 1 January 1964, this was extended in the Russian Socialist Federal Soviet Republic (RSFSR) to all urban centers down to the *oblast* level, to all resort areas, and to all towns with more than one hundred thousand inhabitants, but this was partly modified by a decree of 21 May 1966, which allowed local organs to grant exemptions [*346*, VIII, 75-76].

The dimensions of the plots for workers and employees living on the countryside were redefined and in many cases enlarged throughout most of the country. This occurred one month after Khrushchev's removal, by a decree of the RSFSR Central Committee and Council of Ministers of 13 November 1964.[25] For all categories other than "service allotments" and "gardens" (at some distance from the house), tenure is for an unlimited time and free of charge. This tenure greatly resembles the kolkhoznik's tenure of his private plot [*111*, 200].

In addition to the quantitative variations (size of plot), there also exist qualitative distinctions for land use by workers and employees. Apart from the plots discussed above (which in fact are sites for privately owned houses), there are the "service allotments" (*sluzhebnyi nadel*), the "haying plots" (*senokos*) which usually accompany them, and the

---

[24] For a definition of "urban" in Soviet legislation, see [*178*, 19-21], and the RSFSR ukaz of 12 September 1957 in [*346*, I, 37-38].

[25] [*346*, VIII, 79-83]; [*390*, 106] gives an indication that comparable decrees were passed in the other union-republics. See also [*72*, 91-96]; [*125*, 48]; [*111*, 197 ff.]. For a recent survey on juridical aspects of private land use by rural workers and employees, see G. F. Iasinskaia, "Zemlepol'zovanie rabochikh i sluzhashchikh, prozhivaiushchikh v sel'skoi mestnosti" [*460*, no. 8, 1971, 84-90].

normal "garden allotments" either planted with vegetables (*ogorod*) or with fruit, berries, or grapevines (*sad*).[26] Both service allotments and gardens (at some distance from the house) are usually allotted for a limited period only. They are registered in the name of the enterprise, local authority, organization, or institution which has issued them to the individual. Before 1961 the gardens could be transferred—under certain conditions—to the permanent, registered use of the individual. The same was true for the "individual and collective gardens" in towns, after the individual concerned had served for five years at the place of employment which had issued the garden or after he had terminated this employment not on his own instigation. But even after 1961—although in principle such garden plots were now to be distributed anew each year—in practice sometimes the same families retained the same piece of land year after year [282, 123]. On the other hand, service allotments are allocated for the duration of the service relationship, which covers also a posting or retirement by virtue of age or invalidity; in the latter two cases, the plot is normally retained for life. Should the holder die in the course of his duties, then the land use rights usually pass to his widow or his parents for life—if they are not able-bodied—or to his children until the age of maturity.[27]

Because the size of plot and land use rights depend upon the social status, occupation, and residence of the individual receiving them, the following categorization of recipients and their families and/or households[28]

[26] For the definition of the *ogorod* and *sad* see the *Bol'shaia Sovetskaia Entsiklopediia*, 2nd ed., vol. 30 (Moscow: 1954), p. 507, and vol. 37 (Moscow: 1955), p. 583; also the *Sel'skokhoziaistvennaia Entsiklopediia*, 3rd ed., vol. 3 (Moscow: 1953), p. 446, and vol. 4 (Moscow: 1955), pp. 368–369. Only since 1949 have private fruit and berry orchards—other than those on private plots and on private building plots—assumed some significance: see the *Bol'shaia Sovetskaia Entsiklopediia*, 2nd ed., vol. 37 (Moscow: 1955), p. 583. This stems from the decree of the USSR Council of Ministers of 24 February 1949 titled "Concerning the Collective and Individual Vegetable Gardens and Fruit Orchards of Workers and Employees" [90, III, 338–341]. This was supplemented by the decree of the RSFSR Council of Ministers of 16 December 1955 titled "Concerning the Further Development of Fruit Orchards and Vineyards of Workers and Employees," of which excerpts were published in [60, III, 368–371], and by two RSFSR decrees of 12 April 1965 and 18 March 1966 on collective gardening, excerpted in [346, VIII, 84–85].

[27] [64, 40–46]; renewed in the RSFSR decree of 20 March 1965; see [346, VIII, 87–88].

[28] The size of plot is, with a few exceptions, unrelated to the size of the family. In other words, although the land use right applies to the individual—unlike the situation with kolkhozniks—the plots are allocated to the family or household as a unit; see [390, 105] and [434, no. 18 (1968), 36].

is appropriate (and employed by several Soviet writers, for example, [*303*, 161]): (a) workers and employees in rural areas who are engaged in agricultural occupations or occupations connected with agriculture; (b) workers and employees in rural areas who are not engaged in occupations connected with agriculture; (c) workers and employees in urban areas.

Workers and employees in category (a) may be given plots from kolkhozes, from state enterprises (especially sovkhozes), organizations, or institutions, or from the general land and forestry fund of the state. If they reside on the territory of a kolkhoz, this allocates them plots within the framework and according to the availability of the fund which is set aside for private plots (see above, p. 22), and within the legal norms for workers and employees (halved in irrigated areas). Only land from the special fund for private plots may be used and under no circumstances social land belonging to the artel. Like the kolkhozniks, the workers and employees in rural areas are given no legal confirmation of their land tenure; this right is merely delegated to them by the kolkhoz or the sovkhoz [*111*, 139, 141].

The most important class of workers and employees in the countryside are those employed by sovkhozes and other state agricultural enterprises. They are granted their plots from the land funds of these enterprises. The plots either adjoin the dwelling houses or are partly or wholly situated some distance away. The plots should not normally exceed 0.30 hectare (0.15 hectare before the decree of 13 November 1964), but the size may extend up to 0.5 hectare, depending upon the region, the type of agriculture carried on, and the size of the family.[29] Furthermore, in sovkhozes which have been wholly or partly based on former kolkhozes, the size of the plots may exceed this norm because former kolkhozniks are permitted to retain private plots of the size laid down for their former kolkhozes. The same privilege is enjoyed by invalid or pensioned kolkhozniks. However, a recent interpretation limits the latter privilege to those who became invalid or who were retired and had no able-bodied members in their households during the period before the kolkhoz in

---

[29] [*125*, 48]; [*111*, 201]; [*434*, no. 18 (1968), 36]. The norm of up to 0.5 hectare is particularly common in both kolkhozes and sovkhozes throughout most of the Soviet Far East (see [*111*, 200]), while in the Ukraine the maximum is 0.4 hectare [*199*, 106]. For the period before the decrees of 1964, see [*64*, 33–34]. The sovkhoz directors or the officials appointed by the sovkhoz ministry are empowered to decide on matters of land tenure and the individual may not take his appeal to court; see Yu. Naumov [*454*, no. 11 (1960), 13–15], cited in [*134*, II, 28].

question was converted [*434*, no. 18 (1968), 36]. When a worker or employee leaves the sovkhoz, unless he is detached, sent for further education, called up for military service, and so on, his plot is reduced to the normal rural size of 0.15 hectare [*111*, 202; *434*, no. 18 (1968), 36]. The norm of 0.30 hectare applies also to workers and employees in other state agricultural enterprises.

Anyone who lives in a kolkhoz and has a private plot there, but works in a sovkhoz, may not be allotted a plot by the latter unless the combined area of both plots does not exceed 0.15 hectare (presumably, 0.30 hectare since 1964). Those who live in a sovkhoz but who are only indirectly engaged in its work are given the same size of plot as sovkhoz workers and employees. If they leave, other than by being transferred or detached, they lose that part of their plot which exceeds the norm of 0.15 hectare. These provisions applied, up to about 1965, only on condition that a dwelling was constructed on the plot or—if a house already stood there—that it was occupied by the user of the land. Otherwise only a garden plot of 0.15 hectare was allocated on a temporary basis. Recently this restriction was lifted as long as the plot was declared to be a *priusadebnyi uchastok* (private plot) and not an *ogorod* (vegetable garden).[30]

Those employed in sovkhozes are, moreover, entitled to graze their livestock free of charge on certain pastures and hay meadows, although the sovkhoz may levy a tax to cover its expenses if it has carried out land improvement work on the areas so used.

Plots of up to 0.25 hectare (or up to 0.12 hectare on irrigated land) are granted to families which have one member employed as a specialist in a kolkhoz, sovkhoz, or any other organization connected with agriculture, or as a teacher, official of the village soviet, or of the rural cultural and club house, the library, kindergarten, day nursery or crèche, trade network or—since 1958[31]—a permanent specialist employed in a Repair and Technical Station (RTS) in *Sel'khoztekhnika* or a similar agricul-

---

[30] [*64*, 34-35, 37-38]; [*111*, 208-210]; for the latest regulations, see [*434*, no. 18 (1968), 36].

[31] The problem of private plots for those mechanizers who did not originally stem from the kolkhoz for which they were working had already become acute prior to the publication of the law of 1958 on the abolition of the MTS; see the speech of Shelepin in *Pravda* of 21 March 1958. Those who had been kolkhozniks before they joined the MTS, and who continued to live in their kolkhozes, were allowed to keep plots of the locally permitted size, even if this exceeded 0.25 hectare; see [*164*, 12].

tural organization.[32] These persons are also exempt from paying the agricultural tax on private plots [*84*, 100]. If they die, are retired because of age or invalidity, are transferred or detached, they or their families retain tenure of their plots at the full size. However, if they leave their jobs for any other reason, their plots are reduced to the normal 0.15 hectare.

The above regulations are valid as long as the necessary land is available and provided that the worker or employee concerned is building or purchasing a house. Otherwise a garden plot with a maximum area of 0.15 hectare is to be allocated for a limited period. This is registered, not in the name of the person using it but in the name of the enterprise from which the individual has received the plot. The workers and employees are not allowed to build houses on these plots nor to plant fruit trees on them.

Workers and employees in category (b), who live in rural areas but who are not engaged directly or indirectly in agriculture, are entitled in general to plots of up to 0.15 hectare (0.075 hectare on irrigated land) either in perpetuity or with short-term tenure. In certain defined oblasts and krais, the plots may be larger, as in Khabarovsk and Maritime krai (0.2 hectare), Kaliningrad (0.3 hectare), and Murmansk (0.5 hectare). When the plots are allocated on a short-term basis and the holders cannot be sure of their tenure beyond one year, there exists the danger that the plots might be poorly tended [*452*, 5 October 1968]. If the territory of a town or city is expanded over land which was formerly rural territory, the private plots there may remain unchanged in size provided that they are still used by the same persons.

Some special regulations[33] are in force for certain categories of workers and employees who live and work in rural areas. These are the regulations concerning the so-called service allotments (*sluzhebnyi nadel*), which were assembled in a decree of the RSFSR Council of Ministers of 20 March 1965 [*346*, VIII, 85–88].

Workers and employees of the railroads and roadworks are granted a service allotment with arable land of up to 0.25 hectare per family, with up to 0.5 hectare in sparsely populated regions of Siberia and the Far East.

---

[32] Decree of the Council of People's Commissars of 2 November 1945, extracted in [*319*, 120]; see also [*64*, 25–28]; for the additional categories qualified in the decrees of November 1964, see [*346*, VIII, 80–81]. The earlier decree of 28 July 1939, conceded plots of only up to 0.15 hectare [*56a*, 149].

[33] For a more detailed discussion, see [*111*, 205–208].

In addition, haying rights are granted over an area of up to one hectare (one to two hectares in sparsely populated regions). Those employed in river transport and pipeline installations are entitled to one hectare of meadow in addition to their usual plots of up to 0.15 hectare. Full-time employees of the postal and communications services in rural areas are given plots of arable land of up to 0.25 hectare and haying rights on up to one hectare. Workers and employees in the timber, forestry, and hunting industries are entitled to up to 0.3 hectare of arable land (0.5 hectare in wooded regions) and haying rights over one to two hectares.

Service allotments are made available from the land belonging to the respective enterprises and organizations. If the latter do not possess adequate land for this purpose, the allotments may be drawn form the general state land fund (*Goszemfond*) or forest fund (*Goslesfond*). Haying rights are extended only to those families which own livestock. The arable land allocated for allotments is meant primarily for the growing of vegetables and potatoes; on irrigated land, the allotment norms are halved. Apart from a few exceptions, such as those for timber felling and flotation enterprises, no private construction is permitted on the service allotments. Any worker and employee who already has a plot elsewhere—for example, as a member of a kolkhoz household—may be granted a service allotment only large enough to bring his total holdings up to the usual norm.

The right of tenure of the service allotment is limited and expires on the termination of the working relationship, although it may be retained while the individual is called into military service or sent away for further training. After five years of service, the right of tenure is retained for life in the event of retirement through age or invalidity. If the holder dies in the line of duty, the right to tenure may be retained by his widow or parents for life or by his children until maturity.

Workers and employees in urban areas, those in category (c), who have no house or building plot and who do not possess a private plot or garden either from their enterprise or from former membership of a kolkhoz, are entitled to the use of "individual and collective gardens" (vegetable and fruit gardens).[34] These gardens are situated on land belonging to the town or on land adjoining the town and belonging to the state land or forest fund; when necessary the gardens may be taken from

---

[34] See [*111*, 213–220] and [*64*, 48–52]; cf. above, n. 26. A comprehensive survey on private land use by urban workers and employees was recently given by V. P. Balezin [*55a*].

agricultural enterprises. Those gardens located inside the town limits may not exceed 0.06 hectare per family, but those outside the town limits may go up to 0.12 hectare.

Collective gardens are, as a rule, connected with—and the necessary land given to—an enterprise or organization for the use of their workers and employees. Some general work on such land is done collectively, through the corresponding "gardeners' society" (*sadovodcheskoe tovarishchestvo*). But usage of the allotments (as a rule, 0.06 hectare) is individual in most cases, and individual summer houses—but not solid buildings—may be erected on them. The right to such an allotment may not be transferred to another person, not even in the same famliy [*434,* no. 3 (1968), 23]. The land granted for collective vegetable and potato growing (*kollektivnoe ogorodnichestvo*) is, as a rule, destined for some other purpose in the long run, and therefore given for only five years or even less [*55a,* 49].

Since the Second World War, particularly large plots of land even in towns have been granted to retired staff officers, generals, and admirals; these may be as large as 1.25 hectares (for retired generals) in the *dacha* settlements and on the countryside. However, this privilege was restricted by the decree of the USSR Council of Ministers of 9 May 1956, and further plots of this type were limited to a maximum of 0.5 hectare. A further limitation was provided by the USSR Council of Ministers decree of 1 July 1958. Since that date, retired staff officers are entitled to 0.15 hectare and generals and admirals to 0.25 hectare in the urban-type settlements (as opposed to actual towns) and then only outside the areas of towns and health resorts. In resorts the limits are fixed at 0.12 hectare. Plots allocated before this date are not to be reduced except in the interests of urban reconstruction.

The building sites granted through residential and *dacha* cooperatives are for perpetual use by the individual member and his family, but may not be sold or bought individually. Most of them are situated in the outskirts of the big cities and are of considerable size—up to 0.3 hectare [*55a,* 44–45].

The limits placed on livestock holdings of urban as well as rural workers and employees are more severe than for the kolkhozniks. The maximum number of animals permitted in the personal possession of each household, as stipulated by the edict of the RSFSR Supreme Soviet of 13 November 1964, are: one cow, one calf (plus those born during the current year), a sow with piglets of less than two months or one pig for fattening, three sheep and goats of over one year together with young animals; if no cows or pigs are kept, the number of sheep and goats may rise to five.[35] However, until 1959 (see below), no official—formal and uniform—legislation appears to have been published concerning the amount of privately owned livestock to be kept by workers and employees. This was apparently the internal affair of the local authorities or of the branch ministries (for example, the sovkhoz ministry). The Soviet press was remarkably reticent on this topic.

A fairly high livestock tax was introduced on 27 August 1956 on holdings in republic, oblast, and krai capitals. These were doubled if the holdings exceeded what was then apparently regarded as the urban norm of one cow *or* one pig (of over six months) *or* two sheep and/or goats. However, some latitude was left—for special regulations concerning the holders and areas—which provided for larger holdings. At present, only a small quasi-tax is levied on urban owners of cows [*339a*, 163].

No formal ban on livestock holdings in towns existed before 1959, as long as the corresponding taxes were paid; the ban was introduced in 1959 only in the larger towns and their environs (see below). As late as 15 January 1961, the First Secretary of the Turkmen Central Committee complained in *Pravda* that there were no officially determined maximum livestock holdings for non-kolkhozniks in his republic and suggested that it was time to correct this.

Livestock belonging to workers and employees are not fed entirely from the plots. As early as 28 July 1939, local authorities were instructed to make available grazing facilities for workers and employees in rural districts "to the requisite degree." This grazing was to be carried out on unused land—in forest clearings and along the edges of wooded areas, the verges of railroad tracks and roads, and so on—and on community land. Where such land was not available, kolkhozes were to permit grazing on their pasture land, for which they were allowed to make a moderate charge; fifteen rubles for the season and per livestock owner was then,

___

[35] [*464*, no. 51 (1964), 782]. Before that, slightly lower norms, and only for rural areas, were given by [*64*, 46]. An indirect stipulation was given in the law of 8 August 1953, "Concerning the Agricultural Tax," Section III: see [*323*, 640]. This provided for taxation at the norms valid for kolkhozniks and not at the double norms for individual peasants (*ibid.*, 651); the norms given by Borodanov and Cherniak [*64*] were treated as maximum limits. The limits for livestock holdings are set separately by each Union republic [*339a*, 159], but presumably do not differ much from those for the RSFSR.

as now, regarded as a fair charge. As the number of sovkhozes grew, in many areas there were just no kolkhozes left; those sovkhozes which had been created from former kolkhozes were also obliged to offer grazing facilities. They were also supposed to offer grazing rights to individuals who were not engaged in the sovkhoz but who lived on its territory, although this concession was to be made only "in exceptional cases" and where "spare land" was available. This behavior of the local authorities reflected the official disapproval, characteristic of the Khrushchev era, of livestock owned by workers and employees. In many instances, local officials forbade the gathering by private persons of hay from unused small swamp and wood meadows [*123*, 91]. Moreover, after 1956, some kolkhozes went so far as to mow grass early on otherwise unused land to prevent workers and employees from so doing, even though the kolkhozes could not then mow their own meadows in time [*97*, I, 23]. This appears to have been inspired from above.

This official attitude manifested itself even more strongly with respect to livestock holdings in nonagricultural settlements; these had reached considerable proportions in view of the scattered building in small towns and on the fringes of the larger towns.

As a rule, pasture and haymaking meadows for urban private livestock owners are to be granted for collective use. For this purpose a "livestock holders' society" (*zhivotnovodcheskoe tovarishchestvo*) of no less than twenty-five owners has to be organized in a form prescribed by a decree of the RSFSR Council of People's Commissars of 17 January 1946. These societies also render services to their members, such as providing breeding bulls, building stables, hiring and paying herdsmen, helping with the sale of animal products, and so on [*55a*, 78–82; see also *111*, 196–197]. Since 1965, the societies may also be organized in rural settlements [*55a*, 20; see also *339a*, 156].

Possibilities for grazing in urban-type settlements—on road verges and on wasteland—exist but do not always suffice, and it is therefore hardly surprising that the inhabitants often feed grain and grain products, which may be purchased relatively cheaply in urban state retail stores, to their livestock. The scale of such purchases could only reach a significant size when these products became freely available in the trade network, especially after the exploitation of the new lands and after the record harvests of 1956 and 1958. A first decree of 27 August 1956 placed a general ban on the feeding of livestock and poultry with grain, grain products, and potatoes which had been purchased in state and cooperative stores. At the same time, the above-mentioned tax as well as meat and milk delivery obligations were introduced upon livestock holdings of workers and employees in the provincial and republican capitals (cf. Chapter VIII).

Three years later, the RSFSR was the first to issue a general ban on livestock holdings in these capital towns and further recommended that local authorities publish a similar ban on holdings in other towns and industrial settlements.[36] This legislation was further strengthened through three edicts of 6 May 1963, which were directed both against the feeding of purchased grain and grain products and against any kind of livestock holdings outside kolkhozes. Furthermore, the edicts reduced the livestock norms in those localities where workers and employees were still allowed to keep animals (cf. Chapter IX). Any inventories above these norms were subject to prohibitive taxation. The only exceptions granted were for people living in desolate regions and for those in the forestry service. Yet all the harsh restrictions were of a temporary nature. Immediately after the removal of Khrushchev, these measures were rescinded and the old norms for livestock holdings were restored by the above-mentioned edict of 13 November 1964 (cf. Chapter X).

---

[36] Edict of the Presidium of the RSFSR Supreme Soviet of 12 August 1959 in [*464*, no. 30 (1959), 600]. Similar edicts followed in other union-republics, for example, on 11 August 1959 in the Ukraine. The Estonian edict of 26 November 1959 was directed generally at "Inhabitants of Towns and Workers' Settlements Who Have Livestock in Their Personal Possession."

4

The Overall Performance

When one tries to extract meaningful data on the private sector from the mass of statistics on Soviet agriculture, the difficulties of the undertaking become gradually apparent. These cannot always be attributed to deliberate concealment on the part of Soviet authorities. The fault sometimes lies with the way in which raw statistical data are collected,[1] with their arrangement into user categories, and with the distorted price system and its various price levels. One should especially note that not all the privately used land area is included in published data on the agricultural area used by the kolkhozniks, and by workers and employees, which are most commonly used by Western observers. Even when allowance is made for the independent peasants, for "small artisans outside the cooperatives," and for similar small population groups, the category would still not reflect reality. This is because plots of land belonging to nonagricultural enterprises and communities and used by workers and employees are excluded from the total agricultural area used by kolkhozniks and by workers and employees. The Soviet rural historian and sociologist Arutiunian complained that the Soviet statistical handbook on agriculture published in 1960 contained only "some" statistical data on the various kinds of subsidiary plots. He also characterized similar data appearing in more recent statistical yearbooks as "obscure" [51, 51].

Capital is of minor importance in the private sector. It totaled some ten billion rubles—less than half the value of the annual gross output—

---

[1] On the gathering of Soviet statistics, see Newth [261, I, 169] and A. Kahan [207, 153–156]. For Soviet treatment of the statistical methodology, see [342]; [126, 46 ff., 108 ff., 203 ff.]. A particularly blatant example is the statistical treatment of the labor force engaged in the private agricultural sector, which is more a rough estimate on an uncertain basis; see, among others, [114, 5], [338, 141, 191, 235].

during 1958 to 1969, and was even less before [*56a,* 59; *339a,* 11]. Labor is paramount, and is almost equaled in importance by land, which has a scarcity value for private agricultural production.

TABLE 1. PRIVATELY USED AGRICULTURAL AND ARABLE LAND OF PUBLIC FARM ENTERPRISES, BY TYPE OF USER, 1950–1969

	Agricultural Land Used by:				*Cultivated Arable Land Used by:*		
Year[a]	*Kolkhoz-niks*	*Workers and Employees* *(thousand hectares)*	*Total in Private Use*	*USSR Total*[b] *(percent)*	*Kolkhoz-niks*	*Workers and Employees* *(thousand hectares)*	*Total in Private Use*
1950	...	...	...	...	...	...	...
1953	...	...	...	...	...	...	...
1955	6,900	1,000	7,900	1.29	6,200	900	7,100
1958	6,100	1,500	7,600	1.25	5,500	1,100	6,600
1959	5,800	1,700	7,500	1.23	5,200	1,300	6,500
1960	5,300	2,100	7,400	1.21	4,700	1,650	6,350
1961	5,000	2,260	7,260	1.19	4,400	1,830	6,230
1962	4,900	2,350	7,250	1.19	4,300	1,860	6,160
1963	4,810	2,730	7,540	1.24	4,200	2,110	6,310
1964	4,700	2,380	7,080	1.16	4,000	1,730	5,730
1965	4,700	2,880	7,580	1.24	4,000	2,130	6,130
1966	4,700	3,300	8,000	1.31	4,000	2,450	6,450
1967	4,700	3,410	8,110	1.33	4,000	2,560	6,560
1968	4,600	3,410	8,010	1.32	3,900	2,560	6,460
1969	4,600	3,500	8,100	1.33	3,900	2,650	6,550

[a] As of November 1, each year. All figures are rounded. [b] The share of total agricultural land is understated, because data in this table do not include agricultural land temporarily made available to private users by nonagricultural enterprises, local authorities, and other government bodies.

SOURCES: For 1950–1965, [*416,* 16, Table 1]; for 1966, [*19,* 127 ff.]; for 1967, [*13,* 342 ff.]; for 1968, [*14,* 330 ff.]; for 1969, [*14a,* 304 ff.].

The available data on privately used agricultural and arable land are presented in Table 1. As is indicated there, these data are limited to land farmed by the kolkhozniks and the agricultural workers and employees. Although these two groups account for the bulk of privately used agricultural (and arable) land, more than one million hectares of agricultural land, used by other (nonagricultural) workers and employees are not in-

TABLE 2. SOWN AREAS OF THE PRIVATE SECTOR
BY TYPE OF USER, 1950–1969

Year[a]	Kolkhozniks	Workers and Employees[b] (thousand hectares)	Total	Total of USSR Sown Area (percent)
1950	5,904	1,563	7,467	5.1
1953	5,453	1,435	6,888	4.4
1955	5,790	1,590	7,380	4.0
1958	5,501	1,828	7,329	3.75
1959	5,320	1,910	7,230	3.7
1960	4,470	2,260	6,730	3.3
1961	4,270	2,470	6,740	3.3
1962	4,200	2,530	6,730	3.1
1963	4,200	2,520	6,720	3.1
1964	…	…	6,270	2.9
1965	4,070	2,530	6,600	3.15
1966	4,080	2,650	6,730	3.3
1967	…	…	6,770	3.3
1968	…	…	6,770	3.3
1969	…	…	6,780	3.2

[a] "Productive spring sown area." Cf. [11, 813]. The data exclude "the possibility of double counting" (resowings in the same year) and covered undercrop sowings. Cf. [228, 171; 117, 41]. Figures for years other than 1950, 1953, and 1958 are rounded. [b] Including areas sown by individuals and made available by non-agricultural enterprises, local authorities, and other government bodies.

SOURCES: As for Table 1, except for kolkhozniks in 1963, 1965, and 1966; these data are derived from those on plot size per household [339, 63] and on the numbers of households [10, 348; 12, 416; 18, 109]. Sown areas of workers and employees is then derived as a residulal.

cluded in the official statistics.[2] On the other hand an additional area of some two million hectares is set aside for private use as part of the household plot fund (priusadebnyi fond). Two-thirds of this part are not actually cultivated for one reason or another, while the remainder is not handed over to individuals [452, 12 February 1969]. The data on sown areas, presented in Table 2, indicate correctly the size and the share of the private sector as a whole, because "sown areas" also include land made available to individuals on a temporary basis by various nonagricul-

[2] For documented calculations, see [416, Appendix A]. The distinction between agricultural land and sown area appears to have eluded C. A. Knox Lovell [183, 52] who, for instance, included fruit gardens in the sown areas.

tural enterprises and government agencies. But these data refer only to sown areas and thus exclude by definition an important part of private land use.

Tables 1 and 2 clearly show that the agricultural land of the kolkhozniks declined after 1955, especially between 1958 and 1961, and their sown areas also diminished (after they had reached their greatest share of 5.8 percent in 1945 [56a, 63] and after a short-lived expansion between 1953 and 1955). Generally speaking, the reverse was true of land farmed by workers and employees, although this area was sharply reduced in 1963 and 1964. These trends reflect the effect of the overall political situation, the conversion of many kolkhozes into sovkhozes (which resulted in a purely statistical shift of land from one user category into another), and the formation of a large number of new farms during the virgin lands campaign (especially in the period from 1954 to 1958). The latest increase in the privately used land, as distinct from sown areas, from 1964 through 1969, is the direct result of the rise in the area of plots of workers and employees in agricultural enterprises.

The continued decline in the private use of land during the period from 1953 to 1965 is also clearly evident. Prior to 1965, that decline was only interrupted once as a result of the relatively sharp increase in the area used by workers and employees during 1962 and 1963. Relative to the overall land areas of the USSR, the share of the private sown area declined more rapidly than that of the agricultural land used privately. This is primarily attributable to changes in the land use in the public sector, where sown areas increased at the expense of other agricultural areas. From 1965 through 1967, the total area of the kolkhozniks' private plots did not decline further, even though the number of kolkhoz households continued to fall. The area used by workers and employees increased at a faster rate than ever, illustrating the growing importance of this part of the private sector. The slower absolute growth of the private sown areas is probably related to the more rapid increase of areas under perennial plants [56a, 60]—such as fruit and berry orchards, vineyards— which continued even after 1967.

Soviet statistics also show data on the structure of private sown areas under the main types of crops. Table 3 shows the dominant position occupied by potatoes and vegetables. Grains, which were very important during and immediately after the war, now are a poor third [373, 186; 153, 54; 275, 75]. About one-half of the total private grain area is under corn. A large proportion of the remaining unspecified sown areas is de-

TABLE 3. STRUCTURE OF PRIVATELY USED SOWN AREAS, 1950–1969
(percent of total private sowings)

Year	Potatoes	Vegetables	Corn	Other Grains	Other Crops[a]
1950[b]	51	4	11	28	6
1952	60	4	13	16	7
1955	63	5	12	13	7
1958	65	6	10	11	8
1959	66	7	10	9	8
1960	74		18		8
1961	67	7	9	9	8
1962	67	7	9	9	8
1963	68	7	8	9	8
1964	69	7	8	8	8
1965	68[c]	8[c]	8	8	7.5
1966	76.5		16		7.5
1967	76.5		16		7.5
1968	76.5		16		7.5
1969	77		16		7

[a] Primarily feed root crops, but occasionally also technical crops. The percentages shown in this column are obtained as residuals. [b] Data for 1950 are not fully comparable with those for other years, because many individual peasants still farmed independently in that year (mostly in the annexed western regions). Cf. [261, II, 161]. [c] The joint percentage for potatoes and vegetables taken together in 1965 came to 76.5.

SOURCES: For 1950–65 as in [416, 17, Table 3]; for 1966–1968, cf. [14, 338–339]; for 1969 [14a, 312–313]. The percentages are calculated from data on total sown areas, including those in certain sectors which appear in the cited sources.

voted to feed root crops, while other crops are relatively insignificant. Substantial regional variations exist. Grains—and especially corn[3]—are

[3] Wädekin in [208, 58]; see also [170, 70]. We have not been able to locate direct evidence of any outright prohibition against growing small grains—or any grains on private plots. Nevertheless, we believe that strong pressure to reduce grain sowing was exercised locally, and that this pressure may at times have taken the form of administrative prohibition, which was locally binding. When the new Model Charter for kolkhozes was under preparation and being discussed, L. P. Khalevina, "Voprosy zemlepol'zovaniia v novom Primernom ustave sel'skokhoziaistvennoi arteli," *Nauchnye osnovy novogo Primernogo ustava sel'skokhoziaistvennoi arteli,* G. A. Aksenenok, S. V. Kuznetsov, eds. (Moscow: 1966), p. 240, proposed the following rule for the kolkhoznik's plot: "By virtue of its purpose it may not be used for growing grains or technical crops." It seems that she gave expression to a prevailing idea. At any rate, as late as 1970, after the new Model Charter had been

considerably more important in the southern part of the European USSR as well as in Transcaucasia than in the other regions of the country. By contrast, potatoes are relatively less popular in these two regions. Special crops become important in different areas; this is true of makhorka, sorgho, and joughara [*339a*, 72] and perhaps even of the forbidden culture of poppies and Indian hemp (*cannabis sativa, var. indica*) grown to yield narcotics.[4]

As a general rule, labor-intensive crops are preferred in the private sector. These are also the crops which usually require almost the same labor inputs per unit of land on the kolkhoz and sovkhoz fields.

Over most of the period surveyed, the share of potatoes and vegetables has clearly grown, while that of corn and other grains has decreased —the latter at an especially fast rate. The share of the remaining crops, particularly fodder root crops, increased before 1958 and then remained constant. Potatoes, of course, are also used for feed.

Meat and animal products represent the most important branch of private sector production. In 1963, the private livestock sector was reported to account for 45.6 percent of total Soviet livestock production.[5] In value terms, private livestock production amounted to 10.4 billion rubles (in 1958 prices),[6] or almost two-thirds of the total value of output of the private sector (cf. Table 6). Percentage data for other years are similar [*209a*, 124; *210a*, 163]. After eliminating double counting of feed and fodder, Ia. B. Lapkes arrives at a figure of 7.03 billion rubles, or 50 percent of total private agricultural output in 1958 [*209a*, 124]. Animal husbandry accounts for an even larger portion of total labor inputs in the private sector: G. I. Shmelev puts it at an increasing (up to 1966) share of 73.1 percent (70.3 percent in 1960) of kolkhozniks' private labor [*339a*,

---

issued without containing such a rule, G. I. Shmelev [*339a*, 73] still deemed it necessary to warn against this tendency. It is at present impossible to say how effective it has been in practice. It apparently never applied to corn. And there is evidence that other grains have also been grown on private plots. This has been (or still is) true for rice in the Kirgiz SSR; see [*140*, 12].

[4] [*68*, 155–156, 159, 161, 167–168, 176]. For a more detailed account, see [*56a*, 65–66]. Where weaving is still done at home—this is increasingly a rare phenomenon—flax is also grown on the private plot [*331*, 216]. The illegal culture of poppies, hemp for the preparation of hashish, and so on, is implied by the wording of the Decree of the Plenum of the USSR Supreme Soviet of 25 February 1966, in [*456*, no. 9 (1966), 29–30].

[5] [*339*, 27]; on the question of such percentages, see [*416*, Appendix B].

[6] Calculated from data in [*12*, 260]; in 1965 prices this was 13.2 billion rubles [*56a*, 54].

53].[7] For the USSR as a whole, labor inputs in private livestock production came to 22 billion hours in 1967 [*176*, 75]. A slight decrease since then may be presumed.

Absolute and detailed data for other animals in private possession became available when this book was already in press. These data shed light on relations hitherto unknown or only partially known. Therefore they must be reproduced here, although very briefly, for horses, donkeys, camels, reindeer, poultry, rabbits, and beehives.[7a]

The number of privately owned horses—roughly two-thirds of them kept by nonkolkhozniks—was 457,000 in 1950 and increased slowly to 511,000 in 1970; in view of diminishing totals, these figures were equal to 3.3 and 6.9 percent, respectively. More than half of these horses are in Kazakhstan, where the meat and milk of horses are widely used for human consumption [*56a*, 72]; another 30 percent are in Central Asia and Transcaucasia. Of donkeys and mules, 98 percent (or 599,000) are kept privately, more than two-fifths of them in Uzbekistan. The number of camels in public herds is decreasing. That is why the private share is now 39 percent, although it was only 15.5 percent in 1950; in absolute numbers, it increased from 47,000 to 94,500. Reindeer numbers illustrate that, for the northern nomads and semi-nomads, collectivization became a reality only between 1940 and 1950 (presumably after 1946). During that decade, the public herds doubled from 0.84 to 1.66 millions; the private herds were reduced to somewhat more than a third—from 1.1 to 0.4 millions. The public sector went on growing to 2.45 millions by 1970, while the private sector decreased further to 0.26 millions at the end of 1963 and then recovered to 0.32 millions.

In poultry growing, the share of the private sector is still large—58 percent, or 376.5 millions, in 1970—although the public sector is expanding rapidly. Twenty years earlier, most poultry (78 percent) was kept privately. In 1960, the figure was still 74 percent, while absolute numbers in private ownership had increased to 380.4 millions (228.9 millions in 1950). Almost one-sixth of the gross animal production of the private sector in 1966 was said to originate from poultry [*339a*, 64, Table 10]. Yet it is clear that statistical accounting for privately owned poultry cannot be very exact in any country. For the Soviet Union, this fact was

[7] For corresponding regional data see [*223*, 24] (Ukraine), [*141*, 51, 109] (Kirghizia), and [*340*, 131] (Rostov oblast).
[7a] The following data are from *Sel'skoe khoziaistvo SSSR, Statisticheskii sbornik* (Moscow: 1971), pp. 272–273, 277, 279–282.

stated as late as the summer of 1970: "Nobody knows for sure how many chickens and geese there are in the possession of the population" [452, 22 August 1970].

Rabbitkeeping still is essentially a private business, although great efforts were made to make it a public issue as well, under Khrushchev and again quite recently. Overall numbers were at a high of 15.1 millions in 1960; of those, 3.2 millions were in public enterprises. Then a precipitous decrease began in both sectors and lasted until 1967. But while the public sector dwindled to 254,000 by that year and then increased to 716,-000 by 1970, private owners fared better, with a 1967 low of 6.4 millions and a recovery to 9.9 millions.

More than half of all beehives (5.2 out of 9.8 millions) were in private ownership by 1970; the share has not greatly changed since 1960.

It is characteristic that the private agricultural sector has concentrated on the production of products for which average production costs are often considerably greater than the corresponding—often subsidized —state retail prices (or where the output in the public sector leads to considerable losses). This was particularly true of animal products. Even in 1966, livestock products and vegetables yielded the narrowest profit margins in the public sector: these products, of course, are both labor- and capital-intensive [106, 53–54].

An additional factor is also relevant to trends in the private sector. This is the more rapid growth of perennial cultures (such as orchards and vineyards) than of sown areas of private plots during the recent years.[8] The exact area planted privately under these perennial cultures is not given in Soviet statistics, but the unreported part must be well over one-half million hectares and thus constitutes a factor to be reckoned with [see 416, 221–230]. Orchards and berry gardens are particularly appealing to urban workers and employees, and their importance may rise with the further increase in the size of urban population or with the more intensive use of land, or with both.

The dominant role of animal husbandry in the private sector can be explained by the following considerations:

1. The upper limits for private livestock holdings—found in the model kolkhoz charter and in the regulations governing such holdings

---

[8] Derived from the difference between agricultural areas and sown areas in [11, 269]; [12, 277]; [19, 127–129]. This residual calculation is not completely reliable because agricultural areas and sown areas are counted at different times of the year and according to differing criteria, but it does provide an adequate indication.

for workers and employees—allow for a number of animals that could not be maintained physically if all their feed and fodder had to be obtained from the output of plots of the size stipulated in these regulations. The bulk of the feed and fodder—some 70 percent, according to Belianov [56a, 10]—for private livestock is obtained by the owners (and particularly by the kolkhozniks) from the public sector. This takes the form of payments-in-kind and of grazing or haymowing rights on lands belonging to the kolkhozes, to the state, or to local communities [373, 185].

2. In contrast with the land of the private plot, privately held livestock is wholly the property of the individual owners. Since 1953, the agricultural tax has been levied uniformly on the area of the plot as such, and this factor, too, favors intensive livestock raising.

3. The supply of animal products in the state and cooperative retail trade network has been particularly inadequate ever since collectivization. Official prices for these products have been and remain high; hence, the incentives to produce for the household's own consumption as well as for free market sales of meat, eggs, and milk have been particularly attractive.

4. The difference between labor productivity on the "mini-farm" of the private sector and that of the kolkhozes and sovkhozes is smaller in animal husbandry than in crop production. This is attributable both to the nature of livestock raising and to the low level of mechanization of this branch of production in the public sector. Labor is *the* means of production most freely available to the Soviet citizen. Once he has fulfilled his obligations to the public sector, there are no limits to the private application of his effort other than those imposed by nature. Moreover, private livestock raising can usually be carried out next to, or even inside, the dwelling house; this work can thus be linked closely to other domestic chores in both time and space. Finally, this type of work is also suitable for juveniles, the aged, invalids, mothers of several children, and other individuals who need not work (or who only work part-time) in the public sector.

As a result, private livestock holdings in the Soviet Union have been and remain large, although the sociopolitical system is not conducive to private ownership, and even though measures aimed at limitation of private livestock holdings have been introduced and implemented from time to time. Considerable regional variations exist here as well: In many regions of the country over 60 percent of total meat output originated in the private sector in 1959, although in other parts (particularly in the Black Soil areas and in Central Asia) that sector's share was less than 40 percent. The Soviet leaders have attempted to emphasize the expansion of the public livestock sector in order to reduce the share of the private in a more positive way. These attempts were to some degree successful, but the share of the private sector in overall livestock holdings remains astonishingly high to date (cf. Table 4, below).

Some caution is in order before conclusions are drawn from the regressive trends in private herds after 1965. We do not wish to suggest that factors discussed in Chapter X supply the entire explanation for recent trends in private livestock holdings. But they indicate that explanations other than those commonly employed in the West are both logical and possible. Of special importance here is the decline in the size of the rural and the kolkhoz populations. Although production on subsidiary plots of the urban population is by no means insignificant, the output on these plots is less geared to livestock raising than is the case in the countryside. Thus, when privately owned livestock holdings remain constant while the rural and the kolkhoz populations decline, this can be viewed as a

TABLE 4. SHARE OF PRIVATE LIVESTOCK HOLDINGS
IN TOTAL SOVIET HERDS, 1950–1969
(percent at the end of the year[a])

Year	Cows	Other Cattle	Pigs	Sheep	Goats
1950	66	36	35	16	53
1952	60[b]	31[b]	34[b]	15[b]	62[b]
1955	58	37	48	20	83
1958	56	28	31	22	84
1959	51	20	26	21	81
1960	47	16	26	21	82
1961	45	17	26	21	83
1962	43	17	23	21	83
1963	41	17	32	20	81
1964	41	19	27	21	83
1965	41	21	31	21	84
1966	42	22	28	21	84
1967	41	20	27	21	84
1968	41	19	26	21	83
1969	39	17	25	21	82

[a] See Table 5, note a. [b] The figures for 1952 may overstate somewhat the actual state of affairs. See Table 5, note c.
SOURCES: Calculated from data given in sources to Table 5.

relative increase in livestock holdings for these two components of the total population.

The generally steady decline in the share of private livestock holdings until 1969 was interrupted on three occasions. The first of these came between 1952 and 1955, when this share began to grow again. The second occurred in 1963, when the share of the private sector in total pig inventories rose drastically as a result of the disastrous decline in the public sector's herds following the poor harvest of that year. The final occasion took the form of a short spurt following Khrushchev's removal. The high proportion of cows is noteworthy. This is primarily attributable to the four factors enumerated above. The kolkhoznik chooses, or is pressured, to slaughter the younger animals and to sell them to the kolkhozes, to sovkhozes, or to other organizations.

Goats are kept almost exclusively in the private sector. In conditions of poverty, and especially in the climatically and economically disadvantaged regions, goats are often kept instead of cows. Just as in Europe the goat was once known as "the poor man's cow," it was called "the Stalin cow" in Russia. One of A. Iashin's female kolkhozniks from the Vologda oblast says [*138*, 14]:

Once upon a time we used to consider the goat as an unclean animal; its milk made one ill and was not considered usable.

But what is the good thing about the goat? It needs little fodder. Give it some aspen leaves or some bark from a spruce—and it is full. She eats posters and newspapers—anything suits her. Nowadays [in 1964] you'll find plenty of goats in the villages.

Conversely (but in the same sense) V. Soloukhin [*349*] cites evidence of the renewed prosperity of his native village: "Suddenly all goats disappeared from the village herds." This remark and the term "the Stalin cow" are only two facets of one and the same phenomenon, which needs no further commentary, and which reappeared once again in a milder form during the last years of Khrushchev's administration [*138*, 14; *200*, 436]. It was no accident that private goat holdings increased significantly during the last Stalin years (cf. Table 5); this was pointed out by a Soviet author, Belianov [*56a*, 71], as well.

The different stages of development of the private livestock herds are clearly shown in Table 5: a decline in Stalin's last years, a sharp upswing from 1953 to 1958, a marked decline in 1959, an uneven performance within an overall declining trend, and a pronounced increase in the first

TABLE 5. PRIVATE LIVESTOCK HOLDINGS
IN THE SOVIET UNION, 1950–1970
(thousand heads at the end of the year)

Year[a]	Cows	Other Cattle[b]	Pigs	Sheep	Goats
1950	16,032	8,777	8,464	12,852	8,636
1952	14,400[c]	7,700[c]	8,400[c]	12,200[c]	10,100[c]
1955	15,915[d]	11,388[d]	16,392[d]	20,885[d]	10,702[d]
1958	18,528	10,678	15,139	28,643	7,776
1959	15,117[d]	7,847[d]	13,815[d]	28,847[d]	6,381[d]
1960	16,317[d]	6,715[d]	15,397[d]	28,100[d]	5,958[d]
1961	16,257[d]	7,619[d]	17,306[d]	29,561[d]	5,815[d]
1962	16,153	8,371	16,093	29,929	5,558
1963	16,002	8,080	13,169	26,549	4,591
1964	16,153	8,962	14,468	25,990	4,512
1965	16,645	11,228	18,202	27,572	4,665
1966	17,125	12,139	16,537	28,638	4,665
1967	17,088	11,355	13,599	28,932	4,672
1968	16,734	10,566	12,779	29,739	4,620
1969	15,895	9,094	13,830	27,441	4,224
1970	15,520	9,433	16,562	33,180	

[a] Soviet statistics report livestock holdings as of 1 January of a given year. We show the same data as reflecting holdings on 31 December of the preceding year. The errors involved must be very small, and we thus indicate more clearly the results of the activity during a given calendar year. [b] Calculated by subtracting cows from total cattle. [c] Data for 1952 are rounded in the original. They are calculated by subtracting public holdings from total herds. While the results are not fully accurate, this method is also used by Soviet writers, e.g., [128, 57]. These figures should be interpreted as upper limits. [d] Calculated by adding holdings of the various groups of private owners of livestock as given in the underlying sources.

SOURCES: For 1950–1964 [416, 20, Table 5]; for 1965–1967, [14, 394–395]; for 1968–1969, [14a, 368–369]; for 1970, [466, no. 6 (1971), 84–87].

year after Khrushchev's removal. The picture is much the same for total herds measured in terms of conventional animal units.[9]

The livestock holdings of the kolkhozniks, which account for the bulk of privately owned livestock, developed in much the same manner as the total private livestock herds (see Table 12). However, herds of workers and employees enjoyed a pronounced recovery later in the Stalin

[9] For the livestock inventories calculated as animal units for every year from 1945 to 1960 (that is, from 1 January 1946 to 1 January 1961), see [261, 414, 429].

period. It was not until 1963 that the upswing began to taper off. There-after, they resumed their growth for a few years in the mid-sixties (see Table 20). This does not mean, however, that livestock holdings per household grew. On the contrary, the number of workers' and employees' households in towns and in the countryside increased at a faster rate. In 1950 there were only 40.4 million workers and employees (annual aver-age). Ten years later their number had grown to 62.0 million; the figure reached a total of 87.9 million in 1969. On the countryside, of course, the greatest impact was exerted by the rise of the number of sovkhoz workers and employees, and the increase in their livestock holdings greatly dis-turbed the political leadership under Khrushchev. The latter often sounded the alarm; he did so most emphatically in his memorandum of 29 Octo-ber 1960, addressed to the Presidium of the Central Committee and again in his "Theses" for 5 January 1961 (cf. pp. 285 ff.), when he added: "This corrupts people, undermines discipline, [and] damages the interests of the state and of the people" [*179*, IV, 177, 248, 249]. Two years earlier, he had stressed that the entire coverage of the country's requirements in animal products had to be secured "on the basis of an accelerated devel-opment of the socialized livestock sector" [*179*, III, 378]. Now his stress was even greater: "The socialized livestock sector was and remains the foundation of foundations" [*179*, IV, 354].

This categorical demand remained unfulfilled. While livestock hold-ings of the kolkhozniks declined—together with the number of house-holds in the kolkhozes—holdings of workers and employees expanded to fill a part of the ensuing void, and against the wishes of the leadership. After Khrushchev's fall, his successors were obliged to call upon the pri-vate agricultural sector for help in overcoming the disastrous state of the livestock sector. Private livestock holdings continue to play a decisive role in agricultural production.

THE SHARE OF TOTAL OUTPUT

"It is known that the personal subsidiary plots play a certain role in supplying the nonagricultural population" [*250*, 175]. This was openly proclaimed after Khrushchev's deposition, but no official statistical data have been published which would allow us to determine to what extent this was true for the urban and the nonagricultural population. A few figures are on hand for the rural population and especially for the kol-khozniks. These show that the kolkhozniks' personal requirements in some products are almost fully met by their own output and that this kind of autarky has persisted. The share of the total consumption of the kolkhozniks' households, supplied by the output of their own plots, was as follows:[10]

	1958–59 average (percent)	1964 (percent)	1966 (RSFSR only) (percent)
Potatoes	93	91	94
Vegetables	85	76	...
Vegetables and Fruit	96	...	...
Meat	100	85	91
Milk and Milk Products	98	91	96
Eggs	100	98	98

The corresponding percentages for the sovkhoz workers are lower but still very large. According to one Soviet estimate for the middle sixties, the figures for potatoes and vegetables ranged between 25 and 50 percent, while those for meat, milk, and eggs were 70 to 75 percent [128, 61]. In 1959, the private plots of sovkhoz workers in Kuibyshev oblast supplied 90 percent or more of their consumption of potatoes, meat, milk, and eggs, and 32 percent of vegetables [56a, 121].

Belianov [56a, 101] estimated that three-fifths of total private agricultural output are for human consumption by the producers themselves, one-fifth for their productive use (as feed, seeds, and so on), and one-fifth is marketed.

On the whole, the share of producers other than the kolkhozniks in the total private agricultural output has been steadily rising, mainly as a result of the absolute and the relative decline in the kolkhoz population. A Soviet estimate for 1967 set the gross output of the kolkhozniks at 13.3 billion rubles, and the gross output of the workers and employees was given as 10.2 billion—or 40 percent of total private agricultural output.[11]

Part of the output of the private sector is used as fodder. In 1969, this use accounted for 54 percent of the kolkhozniks' output of potatoes; the

[10] For 1964: [87, 66]; for 1958–1959: [269, 268]; for 1966 (RSFSR): [435, no. 4 (1969), 50–51]. Cf. for the RSFSR: [230, 60] and [88, 50]. For the Ukraine, see [91, 46].

[11] G. Ia. Kuznetsov, in *Vestnik sel'skokhaziaistvennoi nauki*, no. 9 (1969), 7; see also [56a, 55]. Since then, the share of kolkhozniks' output has decreased, but hardly that of the workers and employees.

corresponding figures for milk and vegetables (incl. cucurbital produce) were 14.5 and 55 percent respectively [*339a*, 102–103]. Most of the kolkhozniks' private output, however, is destined for their own personal consumption, leaving only a small portion (although 28 percent of meat) for sale to the state, the consumer cooperatives, or on the free kolkhoz markets [*87*, 67]. The produce bought by the kolkhozniks from the state and the consumer cooperatives makes up only an insignificant part of their consumption of animal products and vegetables, even though such purchases have increased since 1958 [*87*, 68]. In the RSFSR, the kolkhozniks' private output of milk and meat in 1963 was seventeen times greater on the average than the amounts they purchased from the kolkhozes for cash or the amounts received as payments-in-kind.[12] Apart from sugar, the only basic food obtained from the public sector by the kolkhoz population was grain; this was distributed as payments-in-kind or was purchased from the kolkhoz or from state retail outlets. Sales of bread and grain products by state and cooperative stores to the kolkhoz population rose from 253 kilograms per family in 1958 to 310 kilograms per family in 1964. The increase was attributable primarily to the reduction of payments-in-kind [*87*, 68]. The requirements of the nonkolkhoz population for basic foodstuffs other than grains and sugar are also met to a substantial degree from the output of the private sector; the bulk of potatoes consumed by the nonkolkhoz households come from this source.[13]

Despite its vital significance for the population's diet, the private agricultural sector was significantly curtailed under Khrushchev's administration (cf. Chapters VIII and IX). But trends in output turned upward again after 1964; this was also true of the Kirgiz SSR, where the share of the private sector in output is well below the all-union average [*141*, 50]. As indicated in Chapter X, many Soviet authors now believe that the importance of the private sector will decline relative to that of the public sector, but that the absolute volume of private output will decline "only at a later stage" [*87*, 35].

The private sector's share in total farm output value was even a bit greater in 1940 [*56a*, 53–54] than in 1953 (when it amounted to 45 percent, calculated in 1958 prices, see Table 6). The share of the private sector, of course, has always been much lower in total crop production

---

[12] [*380*, 111]. For the Ukraine, see [*91*, 46].
[13] See below, pp. 93 ff. and [*416*, Appendix D].

than in the total output of animal products. The average for 1960 through 1964 came only to 23.2 percent of Soviet crop output as opposed to 45.7 percent of the output of animal products.[14] For earlier years, the following figures are given by I. Egereva [*210a, 163*]:

	Share of Private in Total Crop Output (percent)	Share of Private in Total Livestock Output (percent)
1953	30.5	56.0
1958	25.8	52.1
1962	22.99	44.9

The discrepancy in the share of the private sector in crop and livestock output is even greater in areas where crops play a foremost role in the output of the public sector as a result of favorable climatic conditions. In the kolkhozes of the Krasnodar krai, the 1965–1967 share of the private plots of the kolkhozniks in crop production was barely 9 percent. The corresponding share for livestock output in 1965–1966 came to 37 to 38 percent; in 1967 it was 32.2 percent [*88, 52*].

Official and other data of this sort allow the construction of Table 6, which shows trends in agricultural output as a whole, as well as those for the two sectors separately, both in terms of 1958 and of 1965 prices.

Data in Table 6 should by no means be taken at their face value. Most data shown in parts A and C of that table are based on official Soviet estimates of gross farm output. Some inconsistencies with Shmelev's data can be stated, but not explained. Gross output data for agriculture must be treated with greater caution than the corresponding data for the other sectors of the economy. Insofar as they describe gross farm output, there is double counting of products used as inputs in certain branches of agricultural production (seeds, feed and fodder, and so on). Some estimates of final farm output in terms of 1958 prices—which exclude the double counting of feed only—have recently been published by the Soviet economist Ia. B. Lapkes. Because these data are of great intrinsic interest, we include them in Table 6 as part B in spite of the fact that the accuracy of these estimates is open to doubt (primarily because Lapkes attributed the *use* of feed to each sector in the same proportion in which livestock products were *produced* in a given sector).

[14] Implied by [*196, 188*]. In addition to percentage figures, absolute figures of total private output are given for the Ukraine in [*173, 64*].

In addition, there are the difficulties of obtaining accurate data for the small units of the private sector. Moreover, nonmarketed output of the public sector is valued at cost of production, while the nonmarketed output of the private sector is valued at average sales prices. In all probability, the share of the private sector indicated by Table 6 (including the shares calculated by Lapkes) is somewhat exaggerated. However, we must keep in mind the possibility that the share of the private sector is understated in official statistics in part for a different reason: These statistics may not cover fully the rapidly growing output of fruit and vegetables on plots of workers and employees. I am inclined to estimate the present true share of the private sector in net farm output at about 25 percent.[15]

Table 6 can be used to illustrate general trends, although other data, not accessible at present, may portray these trends more accurately. But I do not believe that more realistic calculations are feasible on the basis of the available evidence. In any event, the steady if slow growth of the volume of output in the private sector between 1964 and 1968 is unmistakable. (For the most recent trends see Chapter X.) The decline in the output of several main product groups through 1963 is shown clearly in Table 7. The rise in meat production in 1963 is attributable mainly to widespread slaughterings caused by the shortages of feed. Those shortages in turn resulted from a very poor harvest in many parts of the country. The decline also reflects, however, the rigorous measures against private urban livestock holdings. The setback in the following year was correspondingly great.

A significant part of private agricultural output, especially in the southern regions, consists of fruits, berries, and grapes; these yield incomes well above average [87, 92; 116, 72]. Adequate data on these cultures are not on hand, and all-union average trends cannot be determined adequately for a longer period of time. But they would probably show no absolute decline in output even during the last few years of Khrushchev's administration. We do know that the private sector accounted for roughly two-thirds of total Soviet output of fruit and berries in 1961 and 1962 and for about a quarter of wine output at the same time. By 1969, production of these crops in the public sector had increased considerably. Yet, the private sector still produced 35 percent of the total output of fruit and

---

[15] For a further discussion of this topic, see [416, Appendix B]. For a discussion by a Soviet author see [56a, 56–57].

TABLE 6. TRENDS IN GROSS AGRICULTURAL OUTPUT AND ITS STRUCTURE BY SECTORS, 1953–1969

	Unit	1953	1958	1960	1962	1963	1964	1965	1966	1967	1968	1969
A. OFFICIAL GROSS OUTPUT SERIES IN 1958 PRICES												
1. Total value of output	billion rubles	32.3	48.5	49.8	51.9	48.0	54.9	56.0	...	...	...	...
a. Incl. private sector		14.7	18.0	17.3	17.3	16.4	16.6	17.8	...	...	...	...
b. Incl. public sector		17.6	30.5	32.5	34.6	31.6	38.3	38.3	...	...	...	...
2. Share in total value	percent											
a. private sector		45	37	35	33	34	30	32	...	...	...	...
b. public sector		55	63	65	67	66	70	68	...	...	...	...
3. Index of output	1958 = 100											
a. private sector		81	100	96	96	91	92	99	...	...	...	...
b. public sector		58	100	106	114	103	125	125	...	...	...	...
B. LAPKES ESTIMATES OF FINAL OUTPUT[a] IN 1958 PRICES												
1. Total value of output	billion rubles	27.5	40.9	41.7	44.4	41.9	46.8	49.1	...	...	...	...
a. Incl. private sector		9.6	14.0	13.5	13.8	13.6	15.1	14.9	...	...	...	...
b. Incl. public sector		17.9	26.9	28.2	30.6	28.3	34.6	34.2	...	...	...	...
2. Share of total gross output	percent											
a. private sector		35	34	32	31	32	32	30	...	...	...	...
b. public sector		65	66	68	69	68	68	70	...	...	...	...
3. Index of output	1958 = 100											
a. private sector		69	100	96	99	97	108	106	...	...	...	...
b. public sector		67	100	105	114	105	129	127	...	...	...	...

C. GROSS OUTPUT SERIES IN 1965 PRICES:[b]

1. Total value of output[c]	billion rubles	...	61.4	63.0	65.7	60.7	69.5	70.9	77.0	78.1	81.6	78.9
a. Incl. private sector		...	22.8	22.0	22.0	20.8	21.3	22.4	23.3	24.0	23.8	22.7
b. Incl. public sector		...	38.6	41.0	43.7	39.9	48.2	48.5	53.7	54.1	57.1	56.2
2. Share of total gross output (Shmelev)	percent											
a. private sector		...	37.2	34.9	33.5	34.2	30.7	31.6	30.3	30.7	29.0	28.8
b. public sector		...	62.8	65.1	66.5	65.8	69.3	68.4	69.7	69.3	71.0	71.2
3. Official Index	1960 = 100											
a. private sector		...	[104]	100	[100]	[95]	[97]	102	106	109	110	106
b. public sector		...	[94]	100	[107]	[97]	[117]	118	131	132	140	135

[a] Lapkes eliminates double counting of feed. [b] The prices of 1965 tend to raise the share of the public sector. [c] The underlying Soviet source explains that the figures for the years preceding 1965 were obtained not by revaluation of the various components but by applying the index of gross agricultural output (weighted by 1958 prices) to the revalued figure for 1965. Cf. [*13*, *931*].

SOURCES: *A. Official Data in 1958 Prices:* Total gross output, [*12*, *260*]. Percentage shares—for 1953, 1958, and 1962, [*2084*, *163*]; for 1963, [*234*, *10*]. All other percentage data are from [*416*, *22*].

B. *Lapkes Estimates in 1958 Prices:* [*209a*, *125*].

C. *Data in 1965 Prices:* Total gross agricultural output and indices—except for 1958 and 1962–1964 indices, which are derived—are given in [*14a*, *287*, *291*]. The percentage share and the ruble value output of both sectors are derived from G. I. Shmelev's [*339a*, *24*] percentage figures for the private sector; the ruble value output of the private sector in 1969 was given by Shmelev [*339a*, *23*] in ruble terms.

61

TABLE 7. PRIVATE OUTPUT OF SELECTED FARM PRODUCTS, 1953–1969
(million tons except for eggs)

Product	1953	1956	1958	1960	1962	1963	1964	1965	1966	1967	1968	1969
Grains	2.5	...	2.7	2.5	2.8	2.1	3.0	2.4	3.4	2.9	...	...
Potatoes	52.1	64.0	57.0	53.2	48.8	47.4	56.2	55.9	56.3	60.2	63.5	61.5
Vegetables	5.5	6.0	6.7	7.3	6.7	6.1	7.6	7.2	7.5	8.2	7.8	7.3
Meat[a]	3.0	3.6	4.0	3.6	4.2	4.3	3.5	4.0	4.4	4.5	4.4	4.2
Milk[b]	24.3	27.7	31.0	29.1	28.7	27.3	27.0	28.7	30.2	31.1	31.0	30.3
Eggs[c]	13.5	16.9	19.5	22.1	23.0	21.4	19.7	19.6	20.9	21.3	21.1	20.9
Wool	.036	.058	.069	.081	.082	.079	.071	.073	.076	.080	.083	.083

[a] Slaughtered weight. [b] And milk products in terms of milk equivalent. [c] Billions.

SOURCES: [416, 23, Table 7] unless specified otherwise. Data for grains from [56a, 173]. Figures for meat, milk, eggs and wool for 1965 to 1969 are obtained by subtracting production of kolkhozes, sovkhozes, and other state farms from the total output of these products as given in [14a, 373]. The figures for potatoes and vegetables are obtained by applying percentage data from Table 8 to the total output data for these products as given in [14a, 340, 342].

berries and about 20 percent of the output of grapes [*14a*, 351–352]. In the southern parts of the country, many private plots are predominantly under these crops [*339a*, 104; *56a*, 68].

Additional problems result from the aggregation of the underlying Soviet data into various product groups or categories. The grouping of all vegetables into a single product group yields an almost meaningless statistical category which covers the whole range of cheap, mass-produced vegetables (cabbage, turnips) as well as the more expensive items (tomatoes, cucumbers, kitchen herbs, onions). Thus, the increase of the private vegetable crop by one million tons during the decade preceding 1967 [*56a*, 65] may mean even more in value terms, if it is presumed—as seems plausible —that this was accompanied by a further shift toward the higher priced kinds.[16] A similar problem is encountered with respect to wool—the category covers fine as well as coarse wool. But these difficulties in the interpretation of the data do not alter the overall picture.

The private sector's share in the output of the most important farm products is shown in Table 8. The decline of that share during the period from 1958 to 1964 is unmistakable and is about equally pronounced for all products. As is shown in Table 7, only a part of this percentage decline results from an absolute reduction in the volume of private output. Much of it—and practically all of it after 1965—is the result of the growth of output in the public sector.

We should also note that no data are available on such animal products as hides, skins, feathers, honey, wax, and so on. Great quantities of silkworm cocoons are produced by the population and sold to the kolkhozes or directly to the procurement agencies [*339a*, 120]. Most of the honey produced comes from the private sector [*339a*, 119]. An interesting report was published on the production of honey in Armenia. Armenian kolkhozes and sovkhozes virtually ignore beekeeping and do not even bother to include it in their production plans. There are four times as many bee colonies in private ownership as there are in the kolkhozes and sovkhozes. Private yields of 35 to 45 kilograms a year per colony exceed those of the public sector by a factor of ten or more. (This means that some 96 to 98 percent of honey in Armenia is produced privately.) Beekeeping in Armenia is profitable for the private citizen, but it is carried out at a loss in kolkhozes and sovkhozes [*452*, 17 November 1968].

[16] For an example and an explanation of why the cheaper and simpler vegetables are produced by kolkhozes and the choice, higher priced items are grown by individuals, see [*97*, I, 11].

TABLE 8. SHARE OF THE PRIVATE SECTOR IN TOTAL OUTPUT
OF IMPORTANT FARM PRODUCTS, 1950–1969
(percent)

Year	Potatoes	Vegetables	Meat	Milk	Eggs	Wool
1950	73	44	67	75	89	21
1953	72	48	52	67	85	15
1955	...	...	[48]	[60]	[88]	[19]
1958	66	45	52	53	85	22
1959	63	46	47	49	82	22
1960	63	44	41	47	80	22
1961	64	45	46	45	78	22
1962	70	42	44	45	76	22
1963	66	41	43	45	75	21
1964	60	39	42	42	73	21
1965	63	41	40	39	67	20
1966	64	42	42	40	66	20
1967	63	40	40	39	63	20
1968	62	41	38	38	59	20
1969	67	39	35	37	56	21

SOURCES: 1950–1964, [416, 24, Table 8]; for 1965–1968, [14, 321]; for 1968–1969, [14a, 295].

The relatively better quality of output of the private sector should not be forgotten when all these factors are considered.

Growth trends of the private livestock sector (apart from chicken) cannot always be assessed only from figures on meat and milk output, even if other animal products are ignored. Thus, although the number of animals in private ownership grew in 1964, private meat production dropped sharply and milk output declined slightly. The probable explanation for this is not only the overslaughtering during the preceding year (see above), but the combined impact of the excellent harvest of 1964 and the removal of Khrushchev. Fewer animals were slaughtered, and the herds were built up in 1964 after years of neglect. A shift from goats and sheep to cattle raising, with the resulting emphasis on feeding calves, may have accounted for the decline in marketable milk output. This interpretation is supported by the renewed growth of livestock output at the end of 1965, although the share of the private sector in total output dropped as the rate of output of the public livestock sector increased.

The productivity of private livestock per animal, except for milk and wool, is higher than in the public sector. A comparison of the sectoral shares of the overall livestock holdings with the corresponding shares of meat production shows this quite plainly (see Tables 4 and 8), although the private sector's share of total output is probably understated (cf. pp. 236 ff.). The juxtaposition by N. Jasny of the public and the private pig holdings with the relevant data on pork output shows that the private sector is more than twice as productive as the public sector [158, 230–231]. On the basis of data for the Ukraine, A. N. Sakoff established that the slaughterweight of pigs owned by the kolkhozniks in the Ukraine was on the average 50 percent greater than the weight of pigs belonging to the kolkhozes. A similar relationship was reported by a Soviet source for the central Russian oblast of Orel. This applied to beef and mutton as well as to milk, eggs, and wool. More than half of the total meat and milk output in that oblast originated in the private sector. The latter produced nearly twice as many livestock products as did the kolkhozes in that oblast. The reasons for this discrepancy in productivity of herds are the greater proportion of cows, the more rapid turnover of meat animals, the better feeding of animals in private ownership—the greater intensity of livestock raising, and the higher labor inputs per animal. But it must also be borne in mind that some of the young animals for private raising are provided by the public sector.

Much the same is true of crop production. For potatoes, vegetables, berries, fruit, and grapes, yields per hectare of private plot are from one-third to two-thirds higher than in the public sector [56a, 68, 95]. Similar ratios apply in the case of corn, and probably also the feed root crops. The explanation lies again in greater labor inputs, in better cultivation, and in a greater supply of manure to private plots—a result of intensive livestock raising and the proximity of the plots to the livestock sheds.[17] Occasionally, dung from the public livestock sheds finds its way to the private plots after lying unused for years [305, 147]. Furthermore, a portion of the growing supplies of mineral fertilizer for the public sector is somehow diverted to the plots [377, 55].

The productivity per unit of land or per animal is clearly higher in the private than in the public sector, and the productivity of labor in the private sector is not as low as it is at times believed to be. "When comparisons are made of the economic efficiency of the private sector with that of the public, it should not be forgotten that they apply to those products the output of which has hitherto required a large input of man-

---

[17] For the Ukraine, see [173, 62].

ual labor in the kolkhozes and sovkhozes. For this reason, the difference in labor inputs between one [sector] and the other is not large" [*340*, 33]. The productivity of labor for the private sector as a whole is estimated at a level of only 30 percent below that in the kolkhozes by the Soviet writer Lapkes. An attempt to refute this estimate was made by V. Khlebnikov, but this effort is not entirely conclusive. In his review of Lapkes' [*209a*] book, Khlebnikov contends that the productivity of labor in public livestock production in the kolkhozes is almost twice that of the private sector.[18] According to Shmelev, labor productivity in the private sector decreased by 15 percent in 1966 as compared with 1958 [*339a*, 61].

Higher productivity in crop and animal production is thus the joint result of the greater labor inputs, the closer personal concern, and the advantages offered by the proximity of the residence and the work place. The compactness of the mini-farm means that both transportation costs and the related deterioration in the quality of perishable products are very insignificant indeed. In addition, productivity is also affected by the ability of the private producers to concentrate on items in short supply, the prices of which are correspondingly high. "Any assertions concerning the irrationality, the ineffectiveness, or the low labor productivity in subsidiary agriculture have no reasoned basis whatsoever" [*273*, 194, 200]. This, of course, is not true in any absolute sense, but only in relation to the still low efficiency of kolkhoz and sovkhoz production.

I. Vinogradov speaks of the "glaring difference between the kolkhoznik's or urban resident's private plot and the kolkhoz field," and offers an explanation: "Here, on his plot, the kolkhoznik's calculation [with respect to output and income] has a firm, reliable basis, here everything depends on him alone, here he can 'plan,' measure the results of his labor, he can work out what will be left for him after the deduction of the tax. . . . Who can be surprised then that the peasant works quite differently [that is, not as well] on the kolkhoz from on his plot."[19]

This aspect of the population's behavior is caused by bitter necessity.

---

[18] [*176*, 75]. For other Soviet estimates, see, among others, [*190*, 362–363] and [*373*, 187]. Belianov [*56a*, 91–92, incl. n. 1], who puts private labor productivity at 26 to 43 percent lower per employed person, and 17 percent lower per actually worked number of days (on average), also presents a survey of derivations of estimates by some other Soviet authors.

[19] [*402*, 249–250]; cf. *ibid.*, 247. Concerning private onion growing, see, among others, [*67*, 157, 159]. See also [*427*, 58], where figures are offered to show how much more the kolkhozniks derive from work on the plot than from their work in the kolkhoz.

This is especially the case for the kolkhoznik, who must—for the most part—satisfy his own consumption requirements in foodstuffs from the private plot. The required foodstuffs are often not available in the countryside, even when the prospective buyer is well endowed with cash. The supply of foodstuffs in the trade network is often scanty and of poor quality in urban areas as well (cf. pp. 146 ff.). However, prices in the kolkhoz markets are generally higher than in the state and cooperative retail trade, particularly for those products which are produced not only for domestic consumption but also for sales on the market. All these conditions provide incentives for farmers in the private sector to produce both for their own needs and for sales on the market. Increases in the market prices up to 1964, the reduction in taxes on the private plots in 1953 and 1954, and the abolition of compulsory deliveries from the plots of the kolkhozniks and of the workers and employees all contributed to the increase in the material incentive for the continued operation of the private sector. The impact of such inducements persisted even after the Party and the state, in 1956 and again in 1958 and 1959, enacted measures designed to limit the private agricultural sector.

Grigorovskii and Alekseev miss the point when they accuse the "bourgeois economists" of falsely attributing high efficiency to the private plots [128, 41]. The real issue is not that the efficiency of private output is high but rather that the efficiency of the public sector is too low [87, 90–91]. The essence of the matter also eludes Kalinin, who attempts to explain away the superiority of private small-scale production by referring to its inherent advantages. Among these he lists location, saving in transportation costs, greater fertility of the soil (although that is not an inherent, natural phenomenon within a given locality), the monopoly position for some special products or for products of a particular quality, the better use of swill and scraps, a flexible response to growing demand, and the exploitation of advantages of cheaper labor [153, 57–58, 60]. All these considerations are highly relevant. But the crux of the matter is the implication that the public sector is unable to make use of these same features or that the impact of the recognized advantages of the public sector (economies of scale, greater capital inputs) is too small to offset the listed advantages of the private sector.

That the modern large farm unit is more efficient than the traditional small farm is a conviction held widely in the highly developed nations of the West as well as in the Soviet Union. But the nature of the large unit in the West is different. There farms are not as excessively vast as the

Soviet kolkhozes and sovkhozes. There are exceptional circumstances when small-scale production is superior in the West as well—this is a point emphasized by Kalinin [*153*, 59]—but that is a practical matter of the most economically expedient form of enterprise and not a question of ideological concept. It is true that the small peasant's right to survive is often transformed into an ideological construct, especially in western Europe. Yet hardly anyone would support this on the grounds of economic efficiency but rather as a matter of social and political mores or objectives and of the struggle to attain them. If Soviet authors cite social and political concepts (that is, ideology) of a different nature as grounds for preferring their giant kolkhozes and sovkhozes, then this is quite legitimate within the framework of their ideological system. But if they seek to justify this preference on considerations of economic efficiency, their arguments are contradicted by Soviet reality and in particular by the performance of the private sector of their agriculture.

PROCUREMENT FROM THE PRIVATE SECTOR AND ITS INDIRECT CONTRIBUTION TO THE STATE

The performance of the private agricultural sector of the Soviet Union influences state food supplies and living standards of the urban population in two distinct ways. The first consists of direct deliveries to the state and cooperative procurement agencies and of sales on the urban market. The second consists of sales and deliveries to farms in the public sector.

That part of private output which is channeled the first way, together with that channeled the second way—as far as it is accounted for statistically (cf. Chapter VII)—made up 12 percent of all marketed agricultural output in the Soviet Union in 1970 (8 percent of crop and 14 percent of animal production). It had comprised 20 percent in 1953 (14 and 32 percent respectively), and the percentages have steadily decreased since then [*56a*, 177]. The market part, so defined, formed 20 percent of total private output in 1958, and 24 percent in 1962; after that the share decreased again [*56a*, 100, 102]. Two-fifths of private marketed output were sold, in 1967, to state and cooperative procurement agencies, the rest on the free market [*56a*, 101]. But all this does not account for intrarural and illegal or semilegal sales (cf. Chapters VI and VII).

Transactions between private producers and the public sector farms are not clearly defined and are difficult to identify. They are best revealed in a detailed study of the interdependence between the two sectors, and this very specific phenomenon will be dealt with separately in Chapter VII; we only note here that the significance of private activities in the socialized enterprises is generally underestimated. These activities are particularly important in the livestock sector, where private producers enable the kolkhozes and sovkhozes to meet the state demands more adequately than they would otherwise be able to. It seems that Soviet authorities are not only reluctant to disclose the amount of produce which changes hands in this manner, but that they have not been—at least until recently—well informed on this matter.

More than a decade ago, H. Wronski showed that during the first half of the 1950s the state acquired fifteen times as much meat and even more milk and eggs per hectare of privately used land than it procured per hectare of the collectively used areas [422, 207–208]. And these figures exclude that portion which the private producers kept for themselves. Yet it is not just a question of the quantity of output but also of the shortcomings of the socialist state distribution system. R. Dumont was correct in writing: "The present distribution system [in the Soviet Union] is not at the level of a modern civilization, for this sector has been deliberately neglected, especially in the country. The "ideological" price of this neglect is the necessary existence of the private sector" [101, 205].

It would be quite wrong to assume that the private sector could carry out these productive and distributive functions by itself. With all its defects, the improvement of the Soviet transportation system must take much of the credit for the fact that the share of private output destined for the market can in fact reach its destination. Moreover, the task would have outgrown the capacity of the private sector had the state not been able to supply the urban population with virtually all of its requirements in staple grain and sugar, as well as a large proportion of other agricultural products. For this reason, the activity on the free market must be, and can be, concentrated upon particular groups of produce (potatoes, vegetables, fruit, meat, eggs—see Chapter VI).

Compulsory procurements from the private sector became a virtual tax-in-kind during the Stalin era, because only a nominal price of up to one-tenth of the value was paid for the compulsorily delivered produce [373, 189]. During the present stage of the "socialist social order," state procurements from the private sector are only a tolerated, necessary evil, because as long as this practice retains any significance it bears witness to the inadequacy of socialized production.

Such an attitude was evident in Khrushchev's Leningrad speech of 22 May 1957 (see p. 233 below). On that occasion he gave several figures illustrating the share of the kolkhozniks' private farms in total state purchases; these figures indicated shares that were indeed "extremely modest," but his presentation overlooked some facts. After the record harvest of 1956, the share of the public sector must have been particularly high, especially because the Ukraine—where more than a quarter of all kolkhoz private plots were located—had had a poor harvest. Perhaps Khrushchev was not aware of the fact that, in view of the growing number of sovkhozes, the share of the kolkhoz private sector in total procurements had to decline, and so the sovkhoz households would become correspondingly more important. Table 9 shows this share of the private sector in the total procurement (sales) to the state since the death of Stalin. (Data for vegetables are omitted, because weight alone does not tell anything about this produce.)

The figures show a considerable decline in the share of the private sector's contribution to total state procurements of livestock products in 1956 when compared with the average for 1949 through 1953, while the public sector's share grew accordingly. Khrushchev's proposal of 1957 to abolish compulsory deliveries from the private sector appears to have been a rational one. Performance in later years indicates that the private sector's share continued to decline in 1957 and 1958, but this was partly attributable to the bumper harvest of 1958 which enabled the public sector to make a great leap forward. After 1958, the decline continued at a reduced rate.[20]

If, however, we look at the absolute figures rather than the percentage shares, the picture changes dramatically (Table 10). With the exception of milk, the contribution of the private sector in 1956 was considerably larger than from 1949–1953 (average). After the abolition of compulsory deliveries in 1958, the contribution of the private sector to milk and potato procurements became much smaller, but for other products, the volume of private deliveries increased appreciably. A recovery in procurements of milk and wool is to be noted after the disaster of 1963/1964. The new and higher prices introduced in 1965 "created favorable conditions for rising sales to the state of marketable surpluses by owners of subsidiary farms, [a phenomenon] which also strengthened

---

[20] For an appraisal of the influence of prices on private deliveries during these periods, see [416, 162–163].

the market orientation of these farms" [214a, 5]. The irregular but still rising trend in procurements from the private sector appears to have been reversed in 1968, but further observations through 1970 are needed before we can be sure that this is indeed true.

TABLE 9. SHARE OF THE PRIVATE SECTOR IN TOTAL STATE PROCUREMENT OF SELECTED PRODUCTS, 1949–1969

(percent)

Year	Potatoes	Meat and Poultry	Milk and Milk Products	Eggs	Wool
1950	40	31	43	61	15
1953	42	18	29	45	9
1949–1953 average	39	26	38	54	12
1954	...	22	23	46	8
1956	41[a]	19[b]	16[c]	49[d]	11[e]
1957	38	15	15	47	13
1958	23	17	10	42	12
1954–1958 average	32	17	15	47	11
1959	25	18	8	39	13
1960	24	13	7	37	14
1961	18	11	6	34	15
1962	26	14	5	34	15
1963	34	16	5	34	13
1959–1963 average	26	14	6	35	14
1964	29	12	4	30	13
1965	27	10	4	26	14
1966	18	14	4	23	14
1967	20	13	4	19	13
1968	19	13	3	15	13
1969	21	8	3	12	14

[a] The share of procurement from the kolkhozniks only is 16 percent. [b] The share of procurement from the kolkhozniks only is 10 percent. [c] The share of procurement from the kolkhozniks only is 7 percent. [d] The share of procurement from the kolkhozniks only is 19 percent. [e] The share of procurement from the kolkhozniks only is 3 percent.

SOURCES: For years through 1964, as given in [416, 160]; for 1965 to 1967, [14, 326]; for 1968 to 1969, [14a, 300].

The share in total marketed private output of that part which is sold to state and cooperative agencies is increasing. In 1967, it accounted for 60 percent of milk, 56 percent of meat, and 51 percent of eggs; for po-

TABLE 10. STATE PROCUREMENT OF SELECTED FARM PRODUCTS
FROM THE PRIVATE SECTOR, 1949-1969

Year	Potatoes	Meat and Poultry[a] (million tons)	Milk and Milk Products[b]	Eggs (billion)	Wool[c] (million tons)
1952	2.76	0.4	4.3	1.15	0.020
1953	2.27	0.38	3.07	1.18	0.018
1949–1953 average	2.34	0.39	3.5	1.15	0.019
1954	...	0.53	2.6	1.24	0.015
1956	3.78[d]	0.51[e]	2.78[f]	1.6[g]	0.027[h]
1957	3.0	0.45	3.07	2.02	0.037
1958	1.61	0.58	2.21	1.91	0.038
1954–1958 average	2.34	0.48	2.54	1.66	0.028
1959	1.7	0.83	2.0	2.21	0.046
1960	1.7	0.62	1.84	2.39	0.050
1961	1.26	0.49	1.65	2.51	0.055
1962[i]	1.48	0.74	1.46	2.95	0.049
1963	2.72	0.91	1.42	2.95	0.049
1959–1963 average	1.79	0.74	1.64	2.56	0.051
1964	3.22	0.6	1.26	2.49	0.049
1965	2.67	0.53	1.55	2.72	0.052
1966	1.67	0.91	1.60	2.66	0.053
1967	2.34	0.94	1.70	2.45	0.053
1968	2.07	0.96	1.30	2.11	0.056
1969	2.16	0.59	1.30	1.85	0.056

[a] Slaughtered weight. Data for 1954, 1956, and 1957 are obtained from original data in live weight, converted with the coefficients of 60 to 61 percent. [b] Milk products are converted into milk equivalent in Soviet sources. [c] In terms of "accounting weight," which refers to unwashed wool. As a result, and because raw wool sales are not allowed on the free market, procurement figures exceed data on total marketings expressed in physical weight. [d] Including 1.46 million tons from the kolkhozniks alone. [e] Including 0.27 million tons from the kolkhozniks alone. [f] Including 1.23 million tons from the kolkhozniks alone. [g] Including 0.61 billion from the kolkhozniks alone. [h] Including 6 thousand tons from the kolkhozniks alone. [i] Almost the same figures are given in [136, 19].

SOURCES: Calculated by applying percentage data given in Table 9 to the total volume of state procurement as given in [416, 161] for years through 1964 and in [14, 324-325] for 1965 to 1967; for 1968 and 1969 in [14a, 299].

tatoes it was 30 percent, for vegetables 36 percent [56a, 104]. Of fruit and grape procurements, too, a considerable part—from 10 to 44 percent, depending on the kind of produce, in 1968—originated from the private sector [339a, 73]. Private output in the Ukraine in 1964 was reported by

F. Khiliuk to have occupied an "appreciable place" in state and similar purchases [*173*, 64, 66]; he gives detailed sales figures reproduced in Table 11 (some of the rise is accounted for by the increase in prices, of course).

TABLE 11. VALUE OF SALES BY THE PRIVATE SECTOR IN THE UKRAINE, EXCLUDING SALES TO INDIVIDUALS ON THE FREE MARKET
(million rubles in current prices)

Type of Buyer	1955	1958	1963	1964
State procurement agencies	259.6	386.6	520.1	463.0
State farms and other state organizations	53.5	98.9	87.7	81.0
Consumer cooperatives	...	...	244.8	203.0
Organizations buying on the kolkhoz markets	7.6	26.0	16.8	16.0
Kolkhozes and sovkhozes buying livestock	28.8	150.3	85.4	85.0
Total	349.5	661.8	1,054.8	848.0

SOURCE: [*173*, 64, 67].

It should be noted that, as far as milk is concerned, a large proportion of the rural population is not in a position to transport it to the consumer rapidly and in sufficient quantities. Since the small state milk procurement points in the country were abolished, the inhabitants of most villages have generally been obliged to rely upon their kolkhoz or sovkhoz for transportation of their milk to the main procurement points or dairies. Thus the difficulties of marketing milk provide an inducement to consume it on the spot; moreover, the monopoly position of the farm makes it easy for the farm to pour milk from private producers into the communal tank and to transfer the milk to the state as its own output (cf. p. 237).

Other, less important, animal products are also procured from the private sector; these include furs, bones, and skins, feathers, silkworm cocoons, and wax [*339a*, 70]. Some of these products are still subject (wholly or in part) to state deliveries in that the state exercises a processing monopoly for these items.

Among the crops which are not listed in Tables 9 and 10, fruit is the most important item (in value terms), but there are many others of considerable (at times local) importance. Referring to several villages in the southeastern part of the Tambov oblast, K. Bukovskii reports that onions, tobacco, and makhorka are grown not only for local consumption and for the kolkhoz market but also for sale to the state, and in large quantities.[21] Before the plots were reduced, one of these villages had sold or delivered each year from the private plots about six hundred tons of onions [sic], some of which were exported; in addition, each household sold or delivered to the state an average of seven and a half to eight tons of potatoes each year. Bukovskii described the private economic activities in the largest of these villages during the summer of 1965 [68, 177] (it should be added that this is one of the favorably endowed regions of Russia):

The private plots covered a total of 270 hectares here, but in the family budget and even in the market, even for the state, these play a role which, in certain respects, is greater than that of an area of kolkhoz land ten times the size. I saw that now there were almost as many milking cows owned by the inhabitants as by the kolkhoz and that the village [that is, its private sector] provides almost as much milk, meat, beyond that chickens and thus eggs also, and even wool as the kolkhoz itself. Only it doesn't provide grain, it does not provide beetroots, no sunflower [seeds], although sunflowers are planted in the gardens, it doesn't provide groats—groats are no longer to be found in the gardens; it provides hardly any pork, pigs are reared only by the kolkhoz, but it provides everything else and not only for itself but also for my Inzhavino [the raion town] with a population which is almost as large as half of the earlier raion, and even for Tambov [the oblast center of 203,000 inhabitants]. This is all supplied by its two hundred and seventy hectares of private plots. Not only the kolkhozniks supply this but also the doctors [of the local hospital].

Restrictions placed on the private agricultural sector during Khrushchev's administration led to a situation where "the kolkhoznik was converted from the producer of several products into their consumer" [343, 84]. Since 1964, it has been realized that, for the time being, the state cannot dispense with the contribution of the private sector. To do this, it would be necessary to raise the kolkhozes' and sovkhozes' output of potatoes and vegetables, as well as their inventories of cattle, pigs, and sheep, by 50 to 100 percent, not to mention enormous additional investments. Indeed, the private sector is now looked to as a partial means of salvation from the situation which had developed by the end of the

[21] [68, 156, 167–168, 176]. Concerning deliveries of onions from private plots, see [251, 117]. On deliveries of makhorka from kolkhozniks, also in the Tambov oblast, see [331, 162].

Khrushchev era [272, 70]. L. Zlomanov has stated that a more positive policy than a simple extraction of products was required [431, 5–6]:

These administrative limitations have been dropped, but this is not all. The existence of the personal subsidiary farms makes it necessary to perfect their commodity relationships with the kolkhozes and the state. . . . At the present backward state of agricultural production, it is, practically speaking, essential to guarantee the economic conditions for a certain development of the personal subsidiary farms.

The hope for relief of agriculture through greater opportunities for private producers was expressed in a less sophisticated manner by the First Secretary of the Kazakh CP, D. A. Kunaev [295, 103]: "The restrictions upon the citizens' private livestock holdings have been lifted and it is possible to procure a considerable quantity of milk and meat from the population." However, even in 1965, such procurements were not always carried out on a completely voluntary basis, and in many places compulsory sales quotas were fixed for the population or other forms of pressure were applied.[22]

Such expectations of rapid gains, immediately after the lifting of arbitrary restrictions on the private livestock sector, could easily lead again to the well-known procurement methods of old, of which a classic example was provided by the Riazan oblast in 1956. At that time a rural raion was in arrears with its egg deliveries, and so the schools were quite simply given the task of producing fifteen eggs per pupil and twenty per teacher. It was cautiously intimated from above—but quite openly proposed by lower echelons—that the eggs were to be purchased by the inhabitants on the free market out of their own pockets and then brought to the schools: "This is by no means the only case of such a mobilization of the population" [440, 24 May 1956]. That this and similar methods were still applied ten years later is clear from R. Nazarov's words [256, 73]:

Although the personal subsidiary farms have been freed by law from the obligatory deliveries, in many raions the village soviets, the sovkhoz directors,

---

[22] See [452, 4 November 1965]. The purchase of milk and meat from private producers was now the duty of the raion and village soviets; see [182, 46]; cf. P. Strautmanis, in [458, 26 July 1967]; it goes without saying that there were also plans set for these purchases which had to be fulfilled. The physical transfer of this task to the village soviets contradicted the regulations, however. This, in fact, should have been done by the trade and purchase organizations and the processing industries; see [423, 54–57].

and the kolkhoz leaders are illegally laying down tasks for the kolkhozniks and other citizens for the sale of meat, milk, and other products to the state. Those who do not fulfill these tasks are being limited in their rights to the use of grazing or prevented altogether. . . . As is known, it is now categorically forbidden to use the trade reserves of mixed feed and feed grains, which have been made available for sale to the population, for other purposes. It cannot be considered as normal that, for instance, in raions in the Omsk oblast and the Krasnodar and Krasnoiarsk krais, it has been established that feedstuffs are only sold against a counter-delivery of animal products. In these raions, fodder could be purchased under the condition that the livestock owner delivered a certain quantity of meat, milk, eggs, or wool. The inhabitants of these raions were startled and wondered where they should get such products from when they had only just acquired the livestock [once more].

Despite such criticism, a similar attitude toward the private livestock sector appeared to persist—at least here and there. This is shown by another example from the Kostroma oblast in 1966. Similar tasks had been disguised there as "additional commitments in honor of the fiftieth anniversary of the October Revolution" (quite apart, of course, from "normal commitments") and the correspondent of the central Party agricultural newspaper voiced no objection to such practices in his article.[23] An almost identical case to the one cited above from Riazan oblast was reported from Kirghizia in 1967 [452, 15 June 1967]. (For developments up to 1970, see Chapter X.)

However, it should not be ignored that truly voluntary sales by individuals also play a considerable role. An example is a small meat processing plant of the consumers' cooperative, which obtains animals mainly from private producers [452, 1 January 1969]. It probably is relevant that when this is done the consumers' cooperative pays somewhat higher prices than the state procurement agencies and that the latter, especially in recent years, have not always had adequate processing capacities for accepting privately-owned livestock.[24]

In 1957, Khrushchev had declared that the private livestock sector was

---

[23] [452, 21 August 1966]. An illustration of how such obligations are adopted was provided by [459, 6 March 1965]: "Recently there was a village assembly in Chardym. Its inhabitants decided to sell 225 tons of milk and also their surpluses of meat, eggs, vegetables, and other agricultural products to the cooperative store this year." If it is economically advantageous for the population to sell their private output to the cooperatives, then why is it necessary to call a village assembly and to pass a formal resolution? And if it is economically disadvantageous, then doubts must be raised concerning the voluntariness of the "resolution" of the village assembly.

[24] See, for instance, [452, 13 July 1969]; cf. p. 334 below.

almost superfluous. Thereupon, the supply of inputs for this going concern, indispensable for the population's well-being, was severely restricted. Subsequently, as soon as some inputs were restored, the private sector was expected to yield wonders. A real understanding of the possibilities and also of the requirements of a flourishing private livestock sector—which is also of direct and indirect benefit to the socialist state—still did not appear to be commonplace in the Soviet Union. Some open advocates were to be found, and some of these have been cited here. But most commentators limited themselves to the concept that the private output of the future is to be regarded as a bonus in prospective planning and that nothing more needs to be done for the private sector than to avoid artificial hindrances. This was the view expressed by a deputy section head in the USSR Gosplan shortly after Khrushchev's ouster.[25] Only very recently, the official attitude seems to have changed somewhat (cf. Chapter X). Presumably as a consequence of recurring stagnation in agricultural production, the role of the private sector in procurement of animal products was once again being emphasized.[26]

The discrepancy between production and procurement plans for vegetables in some raions of Voronezh oblast was curious. There, in 1967 and 1968, one raion was given a production plan of 10 tons of onions, but a procurement plan of 200 tons, another of 1297 and 9800 tons of vegetables, respectively [435, no. 6 (1969), 17]. Although this action was criticized for being against common sense, one hardly errs in supposing that the local planners knew perfectly well what they were doing. They were simply counting on the private sector to supply most of the vegetables to the state procurement agencies, because this kind of production is considered an unprofitable burden by most kolkhozes and sovkhozes.

The benefits derived from the private agricultural sector by the state and society are not limited to the direct deliveries to the state and to the indirect deliveries via the kolkhozes and sovkhozes. The state is also relieved of certain trade and welfare tasks of which it is not yet capable. One example was the still inadequate provision made for invalids and old people in the kolkhozes; for these people, the private sector represented the chief means of subsistence.[27] It is also worth mentioning that

---

[25] G. Gaponenko, "O demokraticheskom tsentralizme v planirovanii sel'skogo khoziaistva," [448a, no. 1 (1965), 22].

[26] For example, [452, 15 April and 5 July 1969].

[27] [373, 187]; A. Makarov, "Nakanune proshchaniia," [445, no. 10 (1966), 121–124], depicts two widows in a kolkhoz village who live primarily from the proceeds of their private plots.

appreciable quantities of foodstuffs seem to be sent to urban residents by their rural relatives who own plots [*339a*, 52, n. 1]. In most regions of the RSFSR, the total population, including the kolkhozniks, is able to (or wished to) purchase only just over half of its foodtuffs in state stores. As G. Ivanov wrote [*144*, 7]:

The personal subsidiary farm of the kolkhoznik . . . at the present time [1965] fulfills some social functions too: it facilitates the activity of the state trading network in view of the fact that some agricultural products are on sale in inadequate quantities in the state stores.

In this connection, it is fitting to mention that what has been said about the personal subsidiary farm of the kolkhoznik applies to a great extent also to the personal farm of the worker and employee.

The workers and employees referred to are not just those living on the countryside. It will be shown (Chapter V) what quantities of potatoes, vegetables, fruit, and animal products find their way into the population's diet from the urban allotments and livestock holdings. For the time being, the state retail trade network and the consumer cooperatives are not in a position to replace the urban private agricultural contribution: "The small town is inadequately supplied and the subsidiary farm —orchard, sucking pig, chickens—is necessary for the inhabitants."[28] Apart from this, there is the function of the free market in the towns, which will be discussed in Chapter VI. The kolkhoz market has shown itself to be indispensable in practice: "The contraction of the kolkhoz trade took place faster than it could be replaced by the capabilities of the state and cooperative trade. Thus, for instance, the absolute scale of the growing sales of potatoes through the state and cooperative trade in 1963 compared with 1958 did not compensate for the decline in turnover on the kolkhoz market" [*382*, 79]. Especially hard hit were the medium and smaller towns. Altogther, in 1960, the state and cooperative trade network supplied only 60.8 percent of the Soviet population's requirements in foodstuffs: 6.1 percent came from the kolkhoz markets, while 33.1 percent came from the population's own output or from other sources (including the so-called intravillage market; all quantities are valued here at state retail prices).[29]

Even workers' families—primarily urban residents—purchased in 1962 or 1963 only up to 79 percent of the meat and poultry they ate through the state stores [*370*, 5]. At that time they were able to purchase

[28] [*290*, 11]; see also [*230*, 57]; [*258*, 116].
[29] [*382*, 44 (Table 9)]; see also the figures for 1959 in [*44*, 22].

no more than 25 to 30 percent of their potato requirements in state and cooperative stores, buying a further 30 percent from the kolkhoz markets and growing the rest or receiving them from "other sources" [*382*, 71–72]. The supply of potatoes in the southern regions of the country, in Transcaucasia, and in Central Asia, is "completely inadequate," with the result that potatoes on the kolkhoz market there are very dear. The situation with respect to fruit and vegetables will be discussed below (Chapter VI).

The fact that the supply of foodstuffs to the Soviet urban population is still a major problem area is attributable not only to the poor productive performance of the socialized sector but also to the inadequate capacity of the distribution network and retail outlet system. Without the cooperation of the private sector, these difficulties would be incomparably greater, particularly on the countryside.

The Soviet trade network on the countryside is completely insufficient. Against a per capita turnover of 604 rubles in 1963 for the urban population, the rural figure was 195 rubles, less than one-third [*382*, 27]. "The assortment and quantity of products which those employed in kolkhozes and sovkhozes can buy is small" [*427*, 59]. Even though the situation has improved in recent years, the urban–rural differences in this respect remain large. The supply of foodstuffs is especially poor for those who live in the country but do not work in agriculture, such as village teachers.[30] It can be imagined what would happen if the private sector did not assume much of the state's responsibilities in this respect. The situation in the nonagricultural workers' settlements on the countryside would be serious, and this is why private farms are almost as vital to the rural workers and employees as they are to the kolkhozniks.[31]

The reduction in the share of rural earnings paid-in-kind—while overall earnings were rising (cf. Chapter VII)—resulted in an increased demand for foodstuffs from the state and consumer cooperatives, a demand which could not be fully satisfied. Consequently, more and more rural residents were obliged to travel to the nearest towns to buy food. This made things especially difficult for people on farms which were remote from towns and markets. Moreover, "specialization by a number of farms and raions in the production of only a few items [which is being advocated by the policy makers] forces the kolkhozniks to produce on

---

[30] See [*459*, 6 July 1960], as cited by [79, 391, 407]; also the letter from a reader in [*440*, no. 63 (1964)] as cited by [*133*, 31].
[31] [*373*, 187]; see also [*128*, 33–34].

their private plots those crops and to raise those kinds of livestock which are not produced in the public sector" [*452*, 25 September 1969]. This problem is by no means restricted to the kolkhoz population. It also plagues sovkhoz workers, because the sovkhozes are, even more than kolkhozes, specialized in monoculture. For all these people the private plots and livestock holdings are vital.

The problem was particularly acute in many sovkhozes which had been formed on the basis of previous kolkhozes. In 1959, the cashier and the chief of a section in a sovkhoz which had shortly before been a kolkhoz, remarked to the journalist I. Vinnichenko [*401*, 147–148]: "Previously we used to sell food ourselves, but now we too have to buy bread. . . . And the main thing is that even with money you cannot buy anything anywhere. . . . We are not allowed to sell [them] produce from the farm, only through the state organization, for cash. And people don't have any money! What can one do? The earnings are poor. And even these are held back, we don't pay them out. . . . There is nothing in the account, we are operating at a loss!"

If it is accepted that the socialist state, like any other state, has a duty to feed its people on the countryside too, or at least not to impede them from feeding themselves, then it can hardly be disputed that in this respect the private sector has assumed many of the state's obligations. Without the private plots and livestock holdings, a large part of the Soviet rural population could not feed itself, and until now the Soviet state has not been in a position to supply these citizens with enough food.[32]

[32] This is not denied by a number of Soviet authors of recent times; see, for example, [*56a*, 45–46]; [*339a*, 99].

5

Fifty Million
Small-Scale Producers

The actual state of the private sector of agriculture is by no means fully revealed by Soviet media and legislation, and the picture gleaned from a multitude of figures, allusions, and descriptions contains many discrepancies and inaccuracies. This is especially so if, beyond the global figures for the whole sector (for these, see Chapter IV), a breakdown by socioeconomic categories and a picture of the various kinds of the "mini-farms" is wanted.

The clearest picture is obtainable for the kolkhoz population and their private plots and livestock holdings; this covers the most important part of the rural population as well as the most important part of the agricultural private sector. The discrepancy between the legal framework and present reality is illustrated by the fact that the actual average size of the private plots, at 0.3 hectare (see Table 13), is far below the legally permitted norms as described in Chapter III. The average size in 1938, of 0.49 hectare—of which 0.28 represented sown area—was far closer to the permitted norms.[1] (For a discussion of the size and composition of the income from the kolkhozniks' private plots and livestock holdings, see Chapter VII.)

Private plots that exceed the stipulated maxima are not very common, but they do occasionally exist even nowadays and mostly in those parts of the country which became Soviet territory through the Second World War—such as the Baltic republics, West Belorussia, and the Western Ukraine [87, 83]—but also in some other regions.[2] In the poorer kol-

---

[1] [422, 195]. The footnote to [52, 57] makes a specific reference to this state of affairs, which is unusual for a Soviet author; he also confirms that average livestock inventories were always below the permitted norms.

[2] In Nikolaev oblast, they are at present 0.60 to 1.00 hectare: [452, 12 July 1968].

khozes, a simple explanation for this may be the inadequate income in cash and kind from work in the public sector [87, 88].

The kolkhozniks' private livestock holdings are also far below the permitted norms. Data on these holdings and on the total herds are shown in Tables 12 and 13.

TABLE 12. PRIVATE LIVESTOCK HOLDINGS OF THE
KOLKHOZNIKS, 1950–1970
(thousand heads at end of the year[a])

Year	Cows	Other Cattle[b]	Pigs	Sheep	Goats
1950	11,521	18,291	6,317	10,763	5,390
1952	10,400	5,906	5,834	10,104	6,421
1953	10,952	6,593	11,159	12,440	7,617
1955	11,706	8,800	11,668	17,854	7,013
1957	12,302	8,212	10,542	20,219	4,779
1958	12,706	7,564	11,066	22,074	4,417
1959	11,666	5,662	10,036	21,898	3,664
1960	10,379	4,410	10,276	19,468	3,212
1961	9,777	4,890	10,923	19,254	2,994
1962	9,646	5,244	10,063	19,325	2,814
1963	9,476	5,190	8,718	17,508	2,415
1964	9,360	5,237	8,993	16,452	2,273
1965	9,355	6,275	10,553	16,682	2,251
1966	9,534	6,668	9,406	16,784	2,264
1967	9,414	5,951	7,662	16,382	2,246
1968	9,132	5,376	7,367	16,374	2,201
1969	8,579	4,641	8,008	14,506	1,974
1970	8,276	4,773	8,821	14,806	2,008

[a] See Table 5, note a. [b] Calculated by subtracting cows from total cattle.
SOURCES: For 1950, 1953, 1955, and 1957, [16, 266–267]; 1952, [1, 137, 144, 151, 157, 164]; 1958 through 1962, [9, 303–304]; 1963 through 1970, Sel'skoe khoziaistvo SSSR, Statisticheskii sbornik (Moscow: 1971), pp. 246–249.

The overall tendencies are unmistakable from the figures. A marked decline during the latter years of the Stalin period affected all livestock except goats—the so-called "Stalin cows." Then, after Stalin's death, a renewed upsurge brought the figures well over the 1950 levels. This upsurge began to slow down in 1955, and then came a further decline which intensified during the period from 1958 to 1960.

Like the total private livestock holdings (cf. Table 5), those of the

TABLE 13. KOLKHOZ POPULATION, HOUSEHOLDS, MEMBERS, AGRICULTURAL AREAS, SOWN AREAS, AND LIVESTOCK HOLDINGS PER HOUSEHOLD, 1950–1969 (end of the year, except for sown areas)

Year	Households[a] (thousand)	Kolkhoz Population (million)	Members per Household	Agricultural Area per Household (hectares)	Sown Area per Household (hectares)	Livestock per 100 Households			
						Cows	Pigs	Sheep	Goats
1950	20,455	...	...	...	0.29	56	31	53	26
1952	19,900	...	...	...	0.28[b]	52	29	51	32
1955	19,800	ca. 76.6	3.9	0.35	0.29	59	59	90	35
1957	18,869	...	...	...	0.30	65	56	107	25
1958	18,833	65.5	3.5	0.32	0.29	68	59	117	23
1959	18,474	...	3.5	0.31	0.29	63	54	118	20
1960	17,106	60.5	3.5	0.31	0.26	61	60	114	19
1961	16,357	57.8	3.5	0.31	0.26	60	67	118	18
1962	16,255	57.1	3.5	0.30	0.26	59	62	119	17
1963	16,101	56.1	3.5	0.30	0.26	59	54	109	15
1964	15,887	56.4	3.6	0.296	...	...	...	...	...
1965	15,414	54.6	3.5	0.305	0.26	61	61	108	15
1966	15,300	53.0	3.5	0.31	0.265	61	61	110	11
1967	15,261	52.7	3.5	0.31	...	...	...	...	...
1968	15,067	51.6	3.4	0.31	...	58	54	112	14
1969	14,707	...	...	0.31	...	...	...	...	...

[a] Only households in agricultural artels are shown here. We thus exclude fishing and nonagricultural artels, in which the number of households is very small, however. [b] 1953.

SOURCES: 1950–1965: [416, 44, Table 11]. Data on kolkhoz households for 1966 (rounded), 1967–1969 are from [13, 466, 474], [14, 430], and [144, 404]. The figures for kolkhoz population in 1966–1969 are derived from data on total population in [144, 7] and percentage figures in [18, 12], [13, 34], [14, 35], and [144, 30]. Sown area in 1953, 1957, 1963, 1965, and 1966, and livestock in 1965, 1966, and 1969 per 100 households is from [3304, 63], except for sheep in 1969, which is from G. D'iachkov [435, no. 11 (1970), 40]. All other figures are calculated from data on the number of households, agricultural area (Table 1), sown area (Table 2) and—for 1957—[16, 128], and data on livestock holdings (Table 12).

83

kolkhozniks continued to show only a gradual decline up to the end of 1963. Commencing with 1964, the year of Khrushchev's abdication, a new upswing began and continued until 1966 (or 1967). This is also evident from the available isolated data for certain regions in 1963, 1964, and 1965,[3] where the upswing was not offset by a decrease in the kolkhoz population.

Within the overall totals, the changes in the numbers of pigs and goats are particularly noteworthy. The growth in pig inventories during the 1952–1955 upswing was outstanding and its subsequent decline the least marked, while, in contrast with other types of animal, the goats declined steadily from 1953 on. Wherever the numbers of cows, calves, and pigs increase, there is little ground for expecting the goat totals to do likewise.

The animal inventories demonstrate the productive potential of private livestock raising in kolkhozes but not the importance of this sector for the individual kolkhoznik and his household. The number of kolkhoz households also changed during the period from 1950 to 1962 and subsequently. This change resulted primarily from the conversion of kolkhozes into sovkhozes, but also from other causes such as the flight from the land, a change in the family structure, and the dying out of one-person households. These latter developments are evident from the number of persons per kolkhoz household—a statistic which can be derived for the period after 1952.[4] By juxtaposing the agricultural area and the livestock inventories against the number of kolkhoz households, we constructed Table 13, which describes the average size of the kolkhoznik's private plot and livestock holding.

Data in Table 13 show considerable deviations from the absolute figures. When reckoned on a per household basis, the decline in area and animal inventories appears to be far less significant. If reckoned on a per

---

[3] [39, 70–71] (for Belorussia). In the three Asiatic union-republics of Azerbaidjan, Uzbekistan, and Tadzhikistan, no decline was apparent before 1963, but here also the livestock inventories of the kolkhozniks grew markedly in 1963 and after 1964. See [25, 93]; [38, 164–167]; [34, 80–81]; [35, 96–97]. Similar developments occurred in the Armenian and Moldavian SSRs and in the Krasnodar krai, where inventories began growing again after 1961; see [21, 169–170]; [31, 168–171]; and [28, 204–207].

[4] On calculating the total numbers of kolkhoz population, see Karl-Eugen Wädekin, "The Nonagricultural Rural Sector," James R. Millar (ed.), The Soviet Rural Community (Urbana, Chicago, London: 1971), pp. 175–177.

capita basis for kolkhoz population, there was no decline at all between 1955–1957 and 1958 because the average size of family during that period shrank by about one tenth—as did the plot. Livestock holdings on a per capita basis actually grew at a rapid pace to reach a high point at the end of 1958. The decline which set in thereafter was slow and irregular.[5] As far as agricultural area per kolkhoz household is concerned, a modest rise may be detected for 1965 and 1966. That rise was only partially offset by a temporary increase in the average number of household members in 1965.

The fact that the amount of agricultural area per kolkhoz household remained practically unchanged after 1959 contradicts the general tendency of the agricultural policy of these years. It also seems to give the lie to Soviet statements made frequently since Khrushchev's removal that "the average size of the private plot, reckoned on a per household basis, declined each year," and that this was accomplished by "administrative means." [6]

The explanation for this apparent paradox lies in the average size of those households belonging to the kolkhozes which were converted to sovkhozes as well as those households which ceased to exist for some reason. If the converted households had plots which were smaller than the average, then the average could have grown upon their conversion even if the remaining households lost part of their land and livestock holdings. Conversely, if the converted households had plots larger than the average, then the mean of the remaining plots and holdings would thus diminish more rapidly. The general tendencies of Soviet agricultural policy and the individual decrees of the Khrushchev era concerning the private sector (cf. Chapter IX) suggest that the former variant was valid. In other words, the average size of the private plots and livestock holdings remained fairly constant after 1959, because it was the smaller plots and holdings which were, generally speaking, converted or dissolved.

The above is borne out by the evidence of variations in the degree of conversion which occurred in individual regions [412, 114–121]. In the Russian non-Black Soil area and the Russian area east of the Urals, where a good quarter of all kolkhoz households were located in 1958, the decline reached almost 60 percent. Yet the average size of private

<hr/>

[5] This is by and large confirmed by the regional data; see [416, Appendix C].
[6] Thus [427, 63]; similar statements were made by other authors.

plots in these regions was well under the all-union average [see *416,* Appendix C]. Out-migration from rural (kolkhoz) areas also was most marked in these regions.

The disappearance of almost three million kolkhoz households during the period from 1958 to 1964, primarily north of the Black Soil zone and east of the Urals, signified a shift of the center of private agricultural production to those areas where private plots are larger than elsewhere. Thus the all-union average figures give the impression that the reduction of plot size was less than was actually the case in many locations.[7]

The fact that this was also a shift to more favorably endowed regions (with respect to both soil and climate), added to the more intensive labor inputs, helped to account for the small drop in output per household—2 percent from 1958 to 1962—despite the overall 12 percent reduction in sown area and the 8 percent fall in agricultural area. Zaslavskaia refers to this phenomenon, but attributes it merely to better farming and to higher labor inputs [*427,* 63]. This is surely a simplification. It is also possible, although it cannot be proven, that it resulted in part from the increases in prices for animal products which were manifest from 1962 on [see *416,* Appendix F].

The principal cause—as defined by Zaslavskaia—of the reduction in the average size of private plot was the "administrative measures" which were carried out in "certain parts of the country." This reference to "certain parts of the country" may be the usual euphemism employed in Soviet media to conceal a widespread phenomenon. However, it may also signify the actual regional variations among the measures and the degree of severity in their implementation.

A Soviet journalist's account of his visit to a sovkhoz (converted kolkhoz) reveals much about the difference between private and public cultivation. He remarks that the portions of the plots which had been confiscated from the former kolkhozniks appeared to have been left uncultivated and were covered with goosefoot; the head of the village soviet corrected him and told him that the sovkhoz had in fact planted corn

---

[7] An example of such a sharp reduction in the average size of plots while the number of households remained almost unchanged is given by the Moldavian SSR (see Table 25 in Appendix C of [*416*]).

For plot size (sown area and livestock) differentials by union republics in 1965, which are much the same as before, see [*339a,* 65]; unfortunately, these give no breakdown for the huge RSFSR, which comprises most of the Black-Earth as well as of the Non-Black-Earth zones.

there [68, 157–158]. It appears that "in many kolkhozes, the withdrawn portions of private plots were not used at all and became covered with weeds." [8] This was only partly because portions were withdrawn in the middle of the agricultural year. Often private plots were—and are—so situated that the confiscated portions could not be joined up to the main fields of the kolkhoz. For instance, this would occur when there was not a kolkhoz field beyond the rows of houses with their long strips of plots but another row of houses, a river, a lake, a cliff, a bog, or other land which could not be cultivated. The same holds true for plots which were left uncultivated when their previous owners died or moved.

The above instances show quite clearly that the "cutting off" of plots was more a deliberate political-social measure than an economic one.[9] When the reverse policy of "adding on" (*prirezat'*) portions began at the end of 1964, the aim was more economic than political or, to be more precise, it was a political-social volte-face under the pressure of the economic consequences of Khrushchev's agricultural policy with its campaign against the private sector.

The statistical average shows that roughly every second kolkhoz household has a cow, while every household has one sheep or one goat. To say that this works out at half a cow for every household would not be far from the truth because sometimes two households—not infrequently two widows—get together to look after one animal, taking turns, day by day, tending the cow. More important, however, for the correct comprehension of this statistical average are the circumstances, the size of inventories, and their specialization in various parts of the country [416, Appendix C].

A further point to bear in mind is that the size of household may differ: in the Asiatic, non-Slavic regions, for instance, the size of the average family is notably larger than the all-union average. This means that there are more members in a kolkhoz household and thus a smaller per capita livestock holding. Furthermore, the proportion of single persons—and in particular elderly women—is greater in the European regions than in the Asiatic union-republics. In the former, many kolkhoz households consist of one person. For these the possession of a private

[8] [171, 23]; cf. [340, 136]. Zharikov [430, 102] elaborates on this theme by adding that weeds from these portions spread to the communal fields of the kolkhoz.

[9] The Russian word *otrezat'* ("to cut off") is usually employed in Soviet Russia to describe the reduction in plot size.

plot of 0.2 or 0.3 hectare and a whole or half a cow means a great deal
more than it does for a family of five and more. Soviet writers have recently begun to draw attention to this factor. Table 14 is based on sample
surveys of the Central Statistical Administration, published by D'iachkov.

TABLE 14. PRIVATE AGRICULTURAL OUTPUT OF THE KOLKHOZNIKS
PER KOLKHOZ HOUSEHOLD, 1958–1964

Product	Unit	1958	1959	1960	1961	1962	1963	1964
Meat	Kilograms	141	151	127	144	149	149	111
Milk	Kilograms	1,181	1,149	1,110	1,040	1,064	1,011	992
Eggs	Units	682	726	736	753	770	724	690
Potatoes	Kilograms	2,216	2,166	2,285	2,220	2,018	1,891	2,241
Vegetables	Kilograms	624	452	639	568	589	459	675

SOURCE: [87, 66].

The figures show a remarkable stability, and the decline in output
of animal products was slight in view of the pressures applied to the private sector. The explanation for this may well be akin to that for the
similar showings of the per household livestock inventories and agricultural areas (see above). Nevertheless, these figures should be treated with
caution. For instance, if the figures for 1958 are multiplied by the number
of kolkhoz households at mid-1958, the resultant total for vegetables is
far above the total private vegetable output (see above, Table 7). This
may be because the data on which D'iachkov's calculations are based are
not wholly representative, but this cannot be proven.

However, despite the inaccuracies of such calculations, they do indicate that in 1958 the kolkhozniks accounted for about two-thirds of the
meat and eggs and three-quarters of the milk and potatoes produced in
the private sector. By 1964, their share had fallen to about half of the
meat, 55 to 60 percent of the milk and eggs, and somewhat less than two-
thirds of all potatoes produced privately. In total private output their
share was 60 percent by 1965 [56a, 55].

Separate figures have been published for the total and for the marketed output of animal products from the kolkhozniks' private plots.
These show that an appreciable share of the kolkhozniks' production
reaches the market or is delivered to the state or to the consumer cooperatives. Indeed their marketed share is much greater than that of the
workers and employees (see Tables 21, 22, and 23) and thus also larger

than the marketed share of the private sector as a whole. The quantities involved are shown in Table 15.

TABLE 15. MARKET OUTPUT OF LIVESTOCK PRODUCTS
PRODUCED BY THE KOLKHOZNIKS, 1953, 1958, 1962

Product	1953	1958	1962
Meat and fat, slaughtered weight[a]	803	1,090	990[b]
Milk[a]	4,169	3,392	2,600
Eggs[c]	3,390	4,495	...
Wool[a] [d]	21	29	34

[a] Thousand tons. [b] Meat only. [c] Million. [d] Unwashed.
SOURCES: 1953 and 1958, [16, 337]; 1962, derived from the percentage figures in Table 17 from the total marketed output in [9, 233].

The share of marketings (market output) defined as the sum of sales to state and cooperative procurement and other organizations and sales on the urban collective farm markets, in the gross output of livestock products produced by the kolkhozniks, is shown in Table 16.

TABLE 16. SHARE OF MARKET OUTPUT IN GROSS OUTPUT OF
LIVESTOCK PRODUCTS BY THE KOLKHOZNIKS, 1953, 1958, 1964
(percent)

Product	1953	1958	1964
Meat and fat	34	35	46[a]
Milk	24	16	10
Eggs	37	36	27
Wool	70	56	...

[a] Meat only.
SOURCES: 1953 and 1958, derived from data in [16, 334-337]; 1964, [87, 67].

The share of the kolkhozniks' output of meat and fat sent to market does not appear to have altered very much in recent times. According to a sample survey, kolkhozniks consumed about two-thirds of the produced meat and fat as well as 90 percent of their potato output (including potatoes used for feed) [230, 58]. With such quantities, the kolkhozniks account for a considerable share of all marketed animal products, including state puchases (see Table 17).

TABLE 17. SHARE OF THE MARKET OUTPUT OF THE KOLKHOZNIKS
IN TOTAL SOVIET MARKET OUTPUT, 1953–1962
(percent)

Year	All Meat[a]	Pork	Milk	Eggs	Wool
1953	25	...	30	67	11
1956	25	23	20	...	11
1958	23	18	14	56	10
1959	18	11	11	...	14
1960	15	12	9	...	9
1961	15	14	8	...	10
1962	15[b]	18	8	...	10

[a] Including fat. [b] Meat only.

SOURCES: 1953 and 1958, [16, 337] except for the 1958 figure for pork which is taken from [5, 468]; 1956, [2, 182]; 1959, [6, 395]; 1960, [7, 463]; 1961, [8, 392]; 1962, [9, 309].

The bulk of the private marketed output of animal products is attributable to the kolkhozniks, although this share is diminishing with the growing importance of the marketed output of workers and employees (see Tables 21 and 22) and with the declining numbers of kolkhoz households since 1956 and 1957. Higher levels of consumption on the part of the households themselves may have played a role, but to assess this, it would be necessary to know how much they have also supplied to the intravillage trade without having it counted in the statistics for their private production. In this connection, their relatively low percentage share of all marketed milk is noteworthy because the kolkhozniks in the RSFSR have reportedly been consuming only 70 percent of their own milk [230, 58], leaving 30 percent for the market.

However, although the kolkhozniks' share in the market from 1953 to 1958 declined, the absolute totals of their marketed output—other than that of milk—grew until 1962 (see Table 15). The total output of the Soviet livestock sector during those five years grew by more than 50 percent, and a smaller increase was registered by the kolkhoz private livestock sector. The kolkhozniks' private production totals for 1953 and 1958 are: meat and bacon from 2,374,000 to 2,878,000 tons; milk from 17.3 to 20.9 million tons; eggs from 9,217 million units to 12,636 million units; and wool from 30,000 to 52,000 tons [16, 37]. But stagnation set in for this sector thereafter, and with the decline in the number of kolkhoz households, output actually fell. This is evident from trends in livestock holdings (see Table 12) and the fact that milk production is believed to have dropped to a little over 15,000,000 tons by 1962. No data are at hand for other products of the kolkhoz private livestock sector since 1958.

The kolkhozniks still possess the bulk of all privately owned livestock in the USSR, although their share has been much reduced. Expressed in livestock units, the livestock herds of the kolkhozniks fell from 17,000,000 in 1953 to 15,950,000 in 1962. The holdings of workers and employees, on the other hand, grew from 6,000,000 livestock units in 1953 to 10,200,000 in 1962. The relationship of kolkhozniks' animal holdings to those of workers and employees thus changed from 3:1 at the end of 1953 to 1.6:1 at the end of 1962.[10] The production ratios, however, in 1953 were: meat—3.6:1; milk—2.4:1; and wool—5:1. In 1959, these ratios were 2.5:1, 2:1, and 3.1:1. The larger shares of the workers and employees in the total private output of poultry, meat, and eggs [see 16, 355-336] illustrates the relatively greater significance attached by them to the keeping of poultry, although the difference seems to have diminished by 1966 [339a, 64, Table 10]. Cattle and milk play a relatively greater role with livestock holdings of workers and employees [cf. 339a, 64 and 56a, 73], as is also evidenced by the total numbers (see Tables 12 and 20).

Animal products play a more important though decreasing role in the kolkhozniks' private output than crops, making up 66.3 percent of the total value of their production, and 63.6 percent by 1969.[11] This roughly corresponds to the relationship between the private plots and livestock holdings when it is recalled that most of the feed is obtained from outside the private plots (cf. Chapter VII).

THE PLOTS AND LIVESTOCK HOLDINGS OF WORKERS AND EMPLOYEES

Any attempt to assess the scale and the significance of the plots and livestock holdings belonging to workers and employees encounters almost insuperable obstacles resulting from the official information policy and statistics. Data are made available on the agricultural and arable land in the private use of this sector of the population (see Table 1), but these

[10] Derived from Tables 12 and 20 and counting only cattle, pigs, sheep, and goats. For the computation of livestock units, see the footnote to Table 26 in [416, Appendix C]: a cow = 1.0; other cattle (mostly calves) = 0.3; pigs = 0.25; and a sheep or goat = 0.1 units.

[11] See [339a, 64 (Table 10), and 71]; cf. [396, 31].

figures exclude the area under "individual gardens" and "collective gardens." These are included in the totals for sown area, but the areas under fruit, berries, and vines, and possibly other perennial cultures, are omitted [see *416*, Appendix A]. Thus considerable uncertainty exists over the exact area used by workers and employees. Furthermore, it is not known how many workers' and employees' families are engaged in private farming and gardening, how many of these live in towns and how many in the country, and how many of them belong to the agricultural population. Thus no reliable estimates can be made of the average size of their plots and livestock holdings.

Very rough estimates, derived from the residuals of private output after the kolkhozniks' share has been deducted (see p. 88 above), indicate that the plots and livestock holdings of the workers and employees in 1958 accounted for about one-third of all meat and eggs and a little over one-quarter of all milk and potatoes produced in the private sector. By 1964 these shares had risen considerably, to about half of the privately produced meat, 40 to 45 percent of the milk and eggs, and more than one-third of the potatoes. The weight of animal production in private agricultural activities of workers and employees is said to increase further [*56a*, 73].

Soviet specialists also complain about the lack of data in this sphere and its neglect in Soviet literature [for example, *128*, 4–5; *153*, 52]. The following citations are characteristic:

The economic significance of the collective gardening of the workers and employees cannot be overestimated. Unfortunately, neither our state statistics nor the scientific organizations concern themselves with the economic results of collective gardening. . . . There can be no doubt that the fact that the state is relieved (fully or even only by half) of the necessity of supplying such a large segment of the population, be it only with fruit, represents an economically perceptible measure even on an all-union scale [*350*, 191].

And:

We must not close our eyes to the fact that millions of our citizens, after coming home from work [in nonagricultural enterprises], start a second working day: They work in the garden and orchard, they look after the livestock and the poultry and busy themselves with getting in fodder for the animals [*128*, 68].

Moreover, the number of those members of workers' and employees' families who are engaged solely in the private sector has risen greatly in percentage terms [*153*, 53], and thus even more in absolute terms. This is partly due to the conversion of many kolkhozes into sovkhozes as well as to the increased proportion of the population which is over the pensionable age.

Belianov quotes an estimate by E. P. Shubkin saying that from 1959 to 1964, on the average per year, 12 billion working hours (9 percent of the total working time budget) were spent on private subsidiary farming and gardening by the nonkolkhoz population (as against 16.54 billion hours by kolkhozniks) [56a, 79, n. 1]. Presumably, nonkolkhoznik private labor inputs have increased since that time with increasing numbers of rural as well as urban workers and employees.

It is a minority, but not a small one, of the nonagricultural population who in one way or other produce foodstuffs privately. Those who have plots and livestock derive sizable incomes in kind therefrom, though little money income. Even with industrial workers' families, in 1966, 39 percent of their potato consumption was supplied by their private plots, 12 percent of vegetables, 8 percent of meat, 2 percent of milk, 14 percent of eggs, and 18 percent of fruit and berries, not to speak of the quantities bought on the free kolkhoz market [339a, 150-151]. Especially in urban areas, the assortment of foodstuffs produced privately by workers and employees is slowly changing with the improving supply through the state and cooperative retail trade system. The finer vegetables and fruit take the place of potatoes and of coarse vegetables like cabbage and turnips, and in part also of animal products [339a, 152]. Table 18 shows the proportion of own consumption of foods covered by the private output on plots of workers and employees in the RSFSR (the category includes those employed by agricultural enterprises and others who live on the countryside) for individual regions of the RSFSR in 1962.

The persisting importance of private agricultural activities among the nonagricultural population is influenced by the fact that produce like eggs, meat, vegetables, and fruit still are in insufficient supply in the state retail trade system. Often they are to be had on the free kolkhoz market, but at a high price, so that low-income workers and those with big families cannot afford them. For these, own private production is of major importance: in nonagricultural families with an annual income of less than 480 rubles per head the subsidiary income from private plots is four times greater than in families with 900 rubles per head and per year [339a, 161].

There are various reasons for the differing degrees of self-sufficiency in the individual regions. In the Northwestern and Central regions, for

TABLE 18. SHARE OF FOODS PRODUCED ON PERSONAL PLOTS
IN TOTAL FOOD CONSUMPTION OF WORKERS AND EMPLOYEES
IN THE RSFSR, BY REGION, 1962
(percent)

Economic Region	Meat	Milk	Eggs	Potatoes	Vegetables and Melons
Northwestern	5.6	15.8	18.6	53.9	12.5
Central	9.2	16.0	27.6	62.0	24.2
Volga–Viatka	10.0	30.8	46.2	72.2	40.7
Central Black Earth	18.3	40.5	59.3	83.9	35.3
Volga	19.8	33.8	61.3	74.4	41.4
North Caucasus	18.0	28.6	57.0	40.0	20.4
Urals	16.4	31.3	45.2	77.3	32.2
West Siberia	22.4	38.7	58.1	85.0	47.0
East Siberia	19.1	34.5	60.2	79.3	38.7
Far East	13.1	24.8	53.3	77.9	27.7

SOURCE: [380, 110].

instance, the share is related to the degree of urbanization; in the Volga region, a considerable influence is exerted by the very large number of sovkhozes and their labor force, while the favorable soil and climatic conditions in the Central Black Soil and North Caucasus regions produce higher yields. The high degree of self-sufficiency east of the Urals is due both to the larger average size of plot and livestock holding and to inadequate supplies in this area by the state and cooperative food trade. The following view on this topic dates from 1961 [338, 222]:

In the personal use of the workers and employees living in Siberia, the Far East and Kazakhstan, there are (per thousand workers and employees) two to three times as many livestock and one-and-a-half to two times as much garden land as there are for the workers and employees of the central provinces of the European part of the USSR. This explains the great degree of preoccupation of the population with the private sector and with housework.

In spite of the fact that the private sector plays a significantly greater role in feeding those employed in the eastern regions, there still exists a large discrepancy between demand and supply, depending partly on local production. The consumption of many of the most important agricultural products is smaller in the Asiatic part than in the central provinces of the Soviet Union.

In 1966, the inadequate agricultural output of the public sector in Siberia and especially in the Soviet Far East was even more marked than in 1959. This applied above all to produce typically supplied by the private sector such as meat, vegetables, milk, and eggs.

In Appendix A of the original German version of this book [416], I demonstrated, on the basis of Soviet statistics, that private land use covers a markedly greater area than appears at first sight from readily available statistical data. To give just an extract (because the Appendix is not included in this version): The most cited figures for 1962 are 2,530,000 hectares for the sown area or 2,350,000 for the agricultural area (see Tables 1 and 2). How can sown area be larger than agricultural area? The latter figure is a major understatement, because it excludes gardens belonging to enterprises and leased to private persons, formally on a short-term basis. These garden areas are included in the sown area of the private sector, but they are excluded from the private agricultural areas because of differences in statistical practices (the land belongs to enterprises and municipal organizations). The real figures should be about 3,700,000 hectares of agricultural land for workers and employees, including about 310,000 hectares of meadowland and about 860,000 hectares of fruit and berry orchards and vineyards. No such detailed data are available for the other years, but it is quite clear that the amount of land privately used by workers and employees during the period from 1958 to 1965 was greater by well over one million hectares than has been generally supposed. Because the main reason for the discrepancy has been the growth of the urban population and its gardens, the degree of understatement has tended to grow each year.

The appreciable increase in the area under workers' and employees' private plots in 1964 and 1965 (see Table 1) is attributable primarily to the fact that after Khrushchev's removal a size of 0.15 hectare, or more, depending on the occupation, was set for building plots for workers and employees in rural areas [314, 7], and also to the new norms for workers and employees of agricultural enterprises (see Chapter III).

Before discussing individual groups of workers and employees, we present a number of statements and data drawn from Soviet media which shed light on this sector of private agricultural production.

A series of sociological surveys were carried out during the period 1960–1963 in the Novosibirsk oblast and Krasnoiarsk krai. The results[12] indicated that in these regions private agricultural activity in urban areas was of the greatest significance in the small and medium-sized towns and

[12] [350, 235]; see also [308, 150 (the table of West Siberian towns) and 199].

that it was there, and not in the larger towns, that private farming showed little, if any, signs of abatement. The same appeared to be valid throughout most of the country. In the larger towns of these two provinces, out of every 1,000 housewives of working age (evidently including unmarried women) 61 had no occupation; of these only five attributed their lack of a job to private household farming. In the small and medium-sized towns, however, 178 out of 1,000 were not employed in the public sector, and of these 37 gave the private household plot as a reason. At the time of the 1959 census, an average of 10.2 percent of the able-bodied population of the RSFSR were not engaged in the public sector, while in West Siberia the proportion was 17.5 percent. While there is relatively little private agriculture in the big towns—apart from the collective gardens—private household plots are "fairly widespread in the medium-sized and small towns and play a significant role in material income" [*350*, 235]. It will be shown later, however, that private household farming nevertheless has considerable significance on the peripheries of the large towns.

Of the 4,003 able-bodied inhabitants of the small town of Demidov in the Smolensk oblast in 1959, 2,300 were primarily engaged in market gardening, livestock raising, handicraft, and *shabashnichestvo* (semilegal or illegal work) [*172*, 243–244]. This may have been an extreme case, but it was not considered exceptional.

The significant role of private agriculture for part of the nonagricultural population of the Soviet Union is quite evident to any foreign observer who visits small towns and the outskirts of the larger cities, as well as on trips by train when the relatively large plots by each signalman's hut are very evident. The proportion of the urban population engaged in agricultural work is particularly high in the southern regions. In the Moldavian SSR, for instance, it comes to 13 percent and in Tadzhikistan to 10.8 percent [*178*, 44].

On the basis of my own estimates and calculations [see *416*, Appendix D], I submit that in 1963 practically every rural household had a private household plot. In towns and in urban-type settlements, there were 14 to 17 million private house plots and service allotments, individual gardens and individual plots of collective gardens (cf. p. 125).

In his speech of 15 December 1958, Khrushchev did reveal three figures for livestock herds of sovkhoz workers and employees at the end of 1957. These were: 1,700,000 cows, "over" 1,100,000 pigs, and "more than" 3,500,000 sheep and goats [*179*, III, 391]. Since the sovkhoz work force numbered 3,204,000 in 1957 and 3,835,000 in 1958 on an average annual basis, a figure of about 3,500,000 may be assumed for the end of 1957. This would indicate about 2.8 to 3.2 million households. Thus for every 100 sovkhoz households there were: 53–61 cows, 35–40 pigs and 111–126 sheep and goats.

These holdings are not appreciably smaller than those of the kolkhozniks in the same year. The relationship between sovkhoz workers' and employees' livestock holdings and those of kolkhozniks is comparable to that of sovkhoz workers' and employees' plots to the plots of kolkozniks (cf. Table 13 and *416*, Appendix D). Indeed, from the above it would be unjustified to speak of any qualitative difference between the kolkhozniks' and the sovkhoz workers' and employees' private farms. The latter may be about one-fourth smaller, but they have a similar structure.

TABLE 19. PRIVATELY OWNED LIVESTOCK IN THE LIPETSK OBLAST,
PER 100 HOUSEHOLDS, 1957–1966
(heads at the end of the year[a])

| | Kolkhoz Households | | | | | Sovkhoz Households | | | | |
Year	All Cattle[b]	Cows	Pigs	Sheep	Goats	All Cattle[b]	Cows	Pigs	Sheep	Goats
1957	95	67	48	190	16	78.3	58.0	39.6	133.5	16.4
1960	87	67	54	182		63.0	54.6	31.2	125.8	13.3
1963	95	63	43	160		65.0	51.0	18.6	86.1	11.6
1966	114	67	59	142		...	...	...	...	...

[a] See Table 5, note a. [b] Including cows.
SOURCES: For sovkhoz households, [*339*, 30]; for kolkhoz households in 1957, derived from [*29*, 54, 86]; for kolkhoz households in 1960, 1963, and 1966, derived from [*30*, 56–57, 80–81].

No all-union data are on hand to show whether this relationship persisted in later years, although we do have some figures for the Lipetsk oblast. In that province the sovkhoz plots in 1957 averaged 0.25 to 0.28 hectare of cultivated arable land, and the kolkhoz private plots averaged 0.37 hectare (in 1966 these still averaged 0.37 hectare; perhaps they had regained this size).[13] The livestock holdings per 100 households are given in Table 19.

[13] Derived from [*29*, 18 and 86] and [*30*, 22, 80–81].

The average livestock holdings of kolkhoz households in 1957 and 1960 in the Lipetsk oblast were well above, and the sovkhoz household holdings in 1957 were fractionally above, the all-union averages for the respective years (see above and Table 13). As far as private livestock herds are concerned, this oblast can be taken as being fairly representative of the typical Black Soil regions of Russia which are favorably endowed in comparison with the non-Black Soil areas. However, between the end of 1957 and the end of 1960, the number of kolkhoz households in this oblast declined by 50 percent, and the number of sovkhozes grew by a similar percentage.[14] This means that despite the conversion of many kolkhoz (with the greater private livestock holdings) into sovkhoz households, the livestock inventories per sovkhoz household declined. That can only be explained by drastic limitations on private livestock in the sovkhozes.

It appears that trends in the private livestock holdings of sovkhoz households in the Lipetsk oblast up to the end of 1963 were fairly representative of all-union trends, although not necessarily of trends in such regions as Kazakhstan, Central Asia, Transcaucasia, and the Baltic republics.

The growing number of sovkhozes and the increased size of the sovkhoz labor force meant that the privately owned livestock of the sovkhoz population also grew in absolute terms, but this did not necessarily mean that holdings per sovkhoz household also grew. Even where figures for the livestock holdings of workers and employees exist separately for the urban and rural categories, these figures do not enable us to calculate exactly the holdings per sovkhoz household (even though much of the livestock owned by rural workers and employees belongs to the sovkhoz population). Table 20 sets out the available totals. (Beginning in 1963, these include other groups of the population, such as individual peasants, priests, and so on, but their numbers are minimal: 19,000 cows, 14,000 pigs, 50,000 sheep, and 15,000 goats in 1962.)

The table shows the importance of the urban livestock holdings, at least until 1956, and, presumably, since 1964. Most of these animals must have been fed largely from purchased feed and from common land (cf. p. 228), although garden plots in the towns probably helped.

The absolute increase of livestock holdings of workers and employees during the period from 1959 to 1961 and again partly in 1962 (of cows

---

[14] [29, 18, 86]; [30, 22, 80–81]; [32, 290]; [33, 326].

TABLE 20. LIVESTOCK HOLDINGS OF WORKERS AND EMPLOYEES, 1950–1970

(thousand heads, at end of the year)[a]

Year	Cows Urban	Cows Rural	Other Cattle Urban	Other Cattle Rural	Pigs Urban	Pigs Rural	Sheep Urban	Sheep Rural	Goats Urban	Goats Rural
1950	1,803	2,445	489	1,348	1,088	809	408	1,428	1,472	1,647
1952	1,580	2,305	401	1,028	1,278	821	467	1,227	1,652	2,010
1953[b]	1,616	2,464	643	1,786	3,100	2,935	591	1,887	2,027	3,041
1953		3,935		1,762		3,893		2,078		3,690
1955		4,142		2,547		4,671		2,966		3,628
1956[b]	1,440	3,059	780	2,667	2,429	3,541	767	3,479	1,773	2,763
1956	4,064		2,571		4,481		3,235		3,292	
1957	5,430		3,208		4,099		5,461		3,507	
1958	5,776		3,097		4,047		6,508		3,319	
1959	5,471		2,164		3,754		6,896		2,693	
1960	5,911		2,089		5,097		8,577		2,725	
1961	6,457		2,712		6,363		10,253		2,802	
1962	6,488		3,114		6,016		10,564		2,729	
1963	6,526		2,890		4,451		9,041		2,716	
1964	6,793		3,725		5,475		9,538		2,239	
1965	7,290		4,953		7,649		10,890		2,406	
1966	7,591		5,471		7,131		11,854		2,401	
1967	7,602		5,404		5,937		12,550		2,426	
1968	7,602		5,192		5,412		13,365		2,419	
1969	7,316		4,453		5,822		12,935		2,250	
1970	7,244		4,660		7,741		14,013		2,353	

[a] See Table 5, note a. [b] October 1.

SOURCES: [416, 55, Table 15] and, for 1965–1970, *Sel'skoe khoziaistvo SSSR, Statisticheskii sbornik* (Moscow: 1971), pp. 246–249.

and other cattle, but not of pigs, sheep, and goats) was much smaller than the decline in the kolkhozniks' holdings, as far as cattle and cows were concerned, but greater for sheep (see Table 12). But when livestock holdings are reckoned on a per kolkhoz household basis during these years, there was only a slight decline in cow holdings and an increase in pig holdings (Table 13). Hence the change in workers' and employees' livestock holdings may largely be attributed to the conversion of kolkhozes into sovkhozes. Pig holdings were generally not reduced by the conversion, but it appears that many kolkhozniks kept only a few sheep, instead of a cow, when they transferred to a sovkhoz.

If the figures for the fall of 1956 (fall herds are greater than those revealed by the end-of-the-year count due to the winter slaughterings) are compared with Khrushchev's figures for the end of 1957 (see above), it becomes clear how important was the share of the sovkhoz workers' and employees' holdings in the total livestock herds of rural workers and employees. This share must have risen further—because between 1957 and 1964 the size of the sovkhoz labor force more than doubled—and must, by now, make up nearly half of all rural nonkolkhozniks. If the Lipetsk oblast figures are taken as representative, we can assume all-union holdings for 1963 to be 40 to 50 cows, 15 to 20 pigs, and 70 to 80 sheep and goats for each one hundred sovkhoz households. With an estimated total of approximately 7.5 million sovkhoz plots [*339a*, 23], the present total inventories of these in 1969 would thus amount to 2.8 to 3.8 million cows, 1.0 to 1.5 million pigs, and 5 to 6 million sheep and goats, that is, somewhat less than half of all rural nonkolkhozniks' inventories. Thus, the livestock holdings, total and per household, of the estimated [*339a*, 23] 6.5 million plots of rural, nonsovkhoz workers and employees may be said to be roughly of the same size as those in sovkhozes.

Another question is whether the distribution of output between the market and owners' consumption is the same for the different kinds of workers' and employees' private plots—those in sovkhozes, those elsewhere on the countryside, or those in urban areas. In other words, is the marketed share of this output less in the towns than in the country? On the basis of surveys in towns of the central Siberian oblast of Novosibirsk and the Krasnoiarsk krai during the period from 1960 to 1963, Sonin reckoned that the average annual income from the urban private plots amounted to 922 rubles [*350*, 204], or 76 rubles a month. This is no mean sum when compared with the average monthly income of 39 rubles derived from sovkhoz private plots throughout the RSFSR (cf. p. 192 f.), or with the monthly earnings of all Soviet workers and employees which averaged 80 to 90 rubles at that time. (In Siberia the average earnings were higher, 90 to 100 rubles, but were offset by higher living costs.) Moreover, most of the private plots are worked by the more poorly paid, less qualified workers and employees. It is in particular a part of the output of this lower paid category of workers and employees that is said to find its way to the kolkhoz market [136, 24].

However, the conditions in Siberia are especially favorable for urban private farming (see p. 94 and Table 18) and cannot unqualifiedly serve as representative for the rest of the country. Another criterion is offered by Borodin [in 65, 26] on the basis of his earlier research in East and Central Kazakhstan. He found that the cultivation of a plot of one tenth of a hectare took 40 to 50 eight-hour working days each year and yielded 256 to 278 kilograms of produce per head of the family (mostly potatoes).

The required labor inputs are shared among several members of the family and can be easily applied in the evenings, on weekends, or during the vacations. If livestock is kept, this usually demands the attention of a housewife who is not employed outside the home.

The above must also be true for all parts of the country. A marketed share is quite feasible, certainly from plots in rural areas (with dimensions of up to 0.15 hectare outside sovkhozes) and probably also from some of the urban house plots. A marketable surplus is even easier to attain when the family consists of only two or three persons.

Soviet writings indicate that private farming provides an essential part of workers' and employees' incomes in the smaller towns and in certain regions where partial structural unemployment is present. Yet this function also presupposes the marketing of a share of the produce. Sonin refers to the existence of some structural unemployment in small and medium-sized towns in the Western Ukraine, Belorussia, the Baltic states, Transcaucasia, and Siberia [350, 214, 222–226]. E. Manevich further speaks of the Central Black Soil region, the Moldavian SSR, and especially of the Northern Caucasus.[15] L. S. Chizhova [in 220, 149] adds Central Asia to this category. The phenomenon is therefore common to a large part of the Soviet Union [350, 222]:

---

[15] [223, 26]. Markov [236, 6] cites the North Caucasus as an area where, more than anywhere else in the RSFSR, a large proportion of the population is engaged in private farming; on p. 7 he refers to the problem in small towns in the same sense as the other two authors.

The excessive concentration of industrial production in the large towns has a negative impact on the development of the small towns and urban-type settlements and limits their industrial development. As a result, the able-bodied members of the population of small towns encounter difficulties when they seek their desired occupations, and they either move to an area of industrial development or they concentrate upon private farming, making this the main source of their income. The latter is especially characteristic of those members of the population who move from the country into the small towns.

It can be assumed that the residents of larger towns only rarely sell the produce from their private gardens, but the same cannot be said with certainty for those living on the outskirts of the cities and towns. The produce on sale is not limited to foodstuffs; as any observant visitor to the Soviet Union will confirm, flowers are sold by women not just in the markets but also in the street and especially near railroad or bus stations. The sale of flowers has grown greatly with the rising standard of living [56a, 67]; flowers are indeed often transported over great distances by air [442, 12 March 1968]. This is somewhat outside the province of agricultural production, but often the sellers of flowers on the kolkhoz markets have other products to offer as well [281, 168, 174].

Although private gardening in the larger towns serves primarily to augment the amount of produce available for the gardener's own consumption and, in the main, is limited to this function by the modest average size of the plots, the proximity of so many potential customers does offer an occasional incentive to sell the produce. Yet most of the marketed produce from the private plots is found in the medium and smaller towns. Here the prices tend to be somewhat lower (cf. p. 140), because the elasticity of demand is less.

Conversely, it is believed that many rural nonkolkhoz inhabitants have more agricultural produce than they require for their own personal consumption.[16] An unknown share of this produce is delivered to kolkhozes and sovkhozes, to consumer cooperatives, or direct to the state retail stores (see Chapter IV). There is no way of deducing how much of this turnover comes from the private plots of kolkhozniks and how much from those of workers and employees. It is most likely that the intravillage kolkhoz markets (cf. Chapter VI) also account for a sizable portion of the marketed produce of the workers and employees.

---

[16] For example, the sovkhoz worker from Rostov oblast, mentioned in [281, 181], who in 1968 sold six to seven tons (sic) of onions received as premium-in-kind from his sovkhoz.

Soviet statisticians consider only a small part of the turnover on the intravillage market as a part of what they call market output. This must be borne in mind when reading Soviet statements on market output in which a distinction is made between that of the kolkhozniks and that produced by the rest of the population. The share of the kolkhozniks is, on balance, probably not excessively understated, because the payments-in-kind which they receive from the public sector are not included under marketed production either, and form part of what they produce, resell, or both. (Hence, the marketed share of the public sector would also appear greater if the intravillage market were included. Payments-in-kind made by the sovkhozes to their workers and employees, but not those of the kolkhozes, are included in market output.) Yet in all probability the share of the kolkhozniks' private output would still turn out to be somewhat greater than is indicated by Soviet sources. The workers and employees bring only small amounts to the market and their wages-in-kind are generally less significant. Therefore, in relation to their other market output, the quantities which they sell on the intravillage market must be quite sizable. If these quantities were included, they would probably add some 50 to 100 percent to their marketed share.

Data for market output of workers and employees are on hand only up to 1962 and only for the most important animal products. These show an unbelievably low percentage share for eggs when compared with the considerable output figures. Perhaps this is because, outside the regulated markets, the sale of eggs is difficult to control and to estimate. Nevertheless, it is worth noting that in Lithuania, during the period from 1958 to 1962, no less than 1.5 million head of poultry were kept by workers' and employees' households, while the number of such households at the time of the 1959 census was about 470,000. It is highly probable that a considerable part of the eggs thus produced was destined for the market. E. Dorosh mentions a small town one hundred kilometers southwest of Moscow where, in 1961, great numbers of hens were owned privately with an eye on the high market price of eggs (15 kopeks per egg) [97, 20]. A not inconsiderable proportion of all potatoes, vegetables, and fruit reaching the market must come from the private production of workers and employees, especially from those living in rural areas. An example of how milk from the private urban livestock holdings could be formally included in the output from the public sector is provided by the rural town of Ust'-Labinsk (cf. p. 122). Table 21 should thus be viewed with certain reservations.

TABLE 21. SHARE OF MARKET OUTPUT OF LIVESTOCK PRODUCTS
PRODUCED BY WORKERS, EMPLOYEES AND OTHER NONKOLKHOZNIKS
IN TOTAL SOVIET MARKET OUTPUT OF LIVESTOCK PRODUCTS, 1953–1962
(percent)

Year	All Meat and Fat	Pork	Milk	Eggs	Wool
1953	2	. . .	7	1	1
1956	3	3	3	. . .	. . .
1958	4	1	1	5	0.3
1959	4	4	1	. . .	. . .
1960	4	4	1	. . .	4
1961	5	3	2	. . .	5
1962	8[a]	5	2	. . .	5

[a] Meat only.
SOURCES: 1953 and 1958, [16, 337], except for pork in 1958 which is taken from
[5, 468]; 1956, [2, 182]; 1959, [6, 395]; 1960, [7, 463]; 1961, [8, 392]; 1962, [9, 309].

Thus workers and employees in 1958 accounted for about one-tenth
of the total private marketed output of animal products (cf. Table 26);
this share rose by 1962 to roughly one-fifth of the milk and a good third
of the meat. The rest came from kolkhozniks. The increased share can
be attributed mainly to the substantial growth in the number of sovkhoz
households; the proportion coming from kolkhozniks declined accordingly. A further possible source was the increased number of workers'
and employees' households in the towns and country outside the sovkhozes. Be this as it may, the part of private output of livestock products
produced by workers and employees and destined for the market grew
markedly. As can be seen in Table 22, marketings increased several fold
(except for milk).

Table 23 shows that private production of the workers and employees
is mainly oriented towards their own personal consumption.

It may be assumed that the marketed part of the workers' and employees' animal products accounts for the bulk of their total marketed
output of all produce, although the share of fruit and vegetables in this
total has been rising in recent years.

In 1966, an average of two-thirds of their total output was said to be
animal products, more than one-quarter was potatoes and vegetables, and
the rest was mainly fruit [339a, 64]. Thus, the share of animal products
in the total private output of the workers and employees is as large as

TABLE 22. MARKET OUTPUT OF LIVESTOCK PRODUCTS PRODUCED
BY WORKERS AND EMPLOYEES, 1953, 1958, 1962

Product	1953	1958	1962
Meat and fat, slaughtered weight[a]	72	215	530[b]
Milk[a]	934	341	650
Eggs[c]	76	402	...
Wool[a] [d]	2	1	17

[a] Thousand tons. [b] Meat only. [c] Million. [d] Unwashed.

SOURCES: 1953 and 1958, [16, 337]; 1962, derived from percentage figures in
Table 21 and total market output as given in [9, 233].

TABLE 23. SHARE OF MARKET OUTPUT IN GROSS OUTPUT OF LIVESTOCK
PRODUCTS BY WORKERS AND EMPLOYEES, 1953, 1958, 1962
(percent)

Product	1953	1958	1962
Meat and fat	11	19	...
Milk	13	3	6
Eggs	2	6	...
Wool	33	6	...

SOURCE: [416, 60].

that of the kolkhozniks. During the period from 1958 to 1962 it had been
even larger (three-quarters), although their share of the agricultural,
arable, and sown areas (cf. Tables 1 and 2), both in 1953 and in 1961, had
been greater than their share of private livestock inventories.[17] Moreover,
part of their garden plots—and, probably—of their crop produce is not
accounted for in Soviet statistics [see 416, Appendices A and D]. Crop
and garden products must therefore still play a greater role for them than
for the kolkhozniks. Indeed, it is surprising that they do not place even
greater emphasis on nonanimal products in the light of their far greater
share of purely gardening area and the different structure of their earnings—which provides for less in payments-in-kind and, hence, less fodder
from outside their plots. However, the available data are too uncertain
and ambiguous to provide a firm basis for conjecture.

[17] Deduced from Venzher's calculations [396, 31].

Generally speaking, only a small proportion of the workers' and employees' private output of animal products comes to the market (although it may be somewhat greater than Soviet statistics allow), and probably an even smaller share of their crop production is sold. A study carried out in Kazakhstan of 84 workers' and employees' private plots and livestock holdings showed that 3.5 percent of their crop output and 4 percent of their milk products came onto the kolkhoz market [65, 27]. However, nothing was said about the marketed share of their meat production, although the all-union average marketed share for this was appreciably higher (see above).

Nevertheless, Soviet authors are justified in their oft-repeated statements that "the commodity character" of the workers' and employees' private plots "is insignificant," and that "by their nature they represent subsistence-type holdings" [65, 27]. Sonin comments [350, 183]:

The economic significance of the private plots (measured by their specific weight in the real income of the family and in the labor inputs) is significantly greater in kolkhoz families than in the families of workers and employees. . . . Work on the private plots of workers and employees has less grounds for incompatibility with social production than work on the kolkhozniks' private plots.

Nazarov concluded from a study of the workers' and employees' private agricultural output that of these products "the bulk is used for personal consumption and only an insignificant quantity has a commodity character" [256, 69].

On the basis of the foregoing statements and calculations, an attempt will now be made to sketch the nature of the different kinds of workers' and employees' private agricultural activities, insofar as the sources permit. I employ the same categories used in legal descriptions (Chapter III), namely: (a) workers and employees in rural areas who are engaged in agricultural occupations or in occupations connected with agriculture; (b) workers and employees in rural areas who are not engaged in occupations connected with agriculture; (c) workers and employees in urban areas.

Groups (b) and (c) will be treated here in some detail, because their private plots have largely been overlooked both in Western and in Soviet writings.[18] Hardly any comprehensive data about these two categories are available, and so a picture must be built up from many scattered and

[18] Welcome exceptions are provided by B. Kerblay [168, 337–338] and Shmelev [339a, passim].

varying bits of information. On the whole, their combined share of the agricultural area [cf. *416*, Appendix A], and probably also of the total output, is no less than that of group (a) and is generally underestimated.

Group (a) consists in the main of sovkhoz workers and employees together with their families. Up to 1933, private plots and livestock holdings were practically forbidden in sovkhozes. Four years after their introduction, which greatly helped to reduce the fluctuation of the workforce, there were already 58 "personal [potato and vegetable] gardens" per 100 sovkhoz workers and employees [*56a*, 147–148]. They meet most of their own requirements for animal products and cover much of their consumption of potatoes and vegetables from their private plots (see above). Their output made up over 20 percent of the family income as late as 1964 or 1965.[19] It had been 25.6 percent in 1960 and still was 21 percent in 1969, according to Shmelev [*339a*, 102]. Sovkhoz wages increased greatly during those four years, but incomes from private plots also did, by 9 percent, on a per family basis [*339a*, 102]. A smaller proportion of this group is made up of workers and employees of other state agricultural enterprises, of the agricultural machinery and equipment repair and supply points, and other various organizations closely connected with agriculture. Very little is known about their private farms apart from the regulations which permit their existence and stipulate their size.

After mentioning the "insignificant part" of the sovkhoz workers' and employees' private agricultural output which is marketed, Nazarov goes on to qualify this: "A considerable portion of the agricultural products is produced on the plots adjacent to the dwelling houses of the sovkhoz workers and employees. In this respect, those employed in sovkhozes hardly differ, practically speaking, from the kolkhozniks.[20] And he adds a justification for the continued existence of these private plots which is exactly that given for the further existence of the kolkhozniks' private plots, namely the still inadequate supply of the sovkhoz population, for the time being, through the trade network and the level of earnings— which is also much lower in the sovkhozes than in industry. "The existence of private plots is more a common characteristic of the village [as such] rather than a distinctive mark of the kolkhoz peasantry," asserted

[19] [*128*, 64]; cf. below p. 193. In 1959 when incomes from the public sector were lower, private plots accounted for 27 percent of total and for 21 percent of money incomes of sovkhoz workers' families [*56a*, 120].

[20] [*256*, 69]; similarly, as far back as 1961, A. N. Gol'tsov in [*338*, 92].

Arutiunian on the basis of research in a southern Ukrainian village [52, 57].

Thus the prerequisites are the same as for the kolkhoz private plots, the only difference being that the average size of plot and the permitted —as well as actual—livestock inventories per household in the sovkhozes are smaller than in the kolkhozes. The chief crop on sovkhoz plots, as on kolkhozniks' plots, is the potato [357, 24]. Of course the size of plots and animal holdings may differ from one sovkhoz to another, and often they may be smaller in the central village of a sovkhoz than in its outlying villages [ibid.]. In 1963, the average size of a sovkhoz household's plot was about 0.22 hectare [416, 244]. But this had increased by 1964–1965 (see above) and the same is probably true of livestock holdings. The conversion of many kolkhozes into sovkhozes, and the creation of new sovkhozes upon virgin territory, at first led to a growth of the average size of plots and private livestock holdings in the sovkhozes. But in late 1958 a vigorous campaign was mounted against these tendencies, and so two opposing trends interacted (cf. Chapter IX). On the whole, private livestock holdings in the sovkhozes were one-fifth smaller than those of the neighboring kolkhozes in 1957 and 1958, and this differential had increased to about one-third by the end of the Khrushchev era.

Apart from the officially authorized higher norms for private plots (see p. 36), only isolated data are available on the privileged groups in agriculture—normally for the specialists—and these do not permit us to draw any general conclusions. It is perhaps not accidental that these specialists and other leading cadres were singled out for Khrushchev's indignation when he complained of exceptionally large private holdings of livestock in sovkhozes. Among the seven who were then pilloried were a sovkhoz economist, a bookkeeper, and a cart driver. Although the occupations of the others were not specified, this does not mean that they were rank and file sovkhoz workers, and Khrushchev made it clear that the seventh was a party member [179, IV, 248–249, and III, 73]. In any case, a sovkhoz agronomist came in for sharp criticism in 1961 on the grounds that he had developed his private farm beyond the desired bounds, even if within the strictly legal limits [440, 5 January 1961]. Because there is no formal obligation for the sovkhoz to provide fodder and grazing for the private livestock of its workers or employees—in contrast with the guaranteed provision of private plots as such—it may well be that sovkhoz specialists and administrators take advantage of their positions to look after their own interests in this respect.

A somewhat undefined status is held in the kolkhozes by the agricultural technicians. Those under the blanket heading of *mechanizers* who are kolkhoz members are subject to the same regulations as other kolkhozniks when it comes to private livestock holdings. But not all mechanizers rejoined kolkhozes upon the dissolution of the Machine Tractor Stations. Bukovskii [68, 174, 176] tells of one central kolkhoz village—evidently not exceptional—which contained 170 households not belonging to the kolkhoz. Many of these were accounted for by seventy men belonging to the local branch of *Soiuzsel'khoztekhnika*, the successor of the MTS and RTS. Of these seventy, only twenty-five were actually employed, and the others were labeled as *nakhlebniki*—parasites or hangers-on. Says Bukovskii of the real mechanizers: "The tractor drivers and combine drivers of the MTS were always the best off [individuals in the kolkhoz village], they were more devoted [than the others] to that sort of prosperity which comes from the plots." The same may well be true for the remaining parasites who presumably also came from the former MTS or associated organs.

As for group (b), or workers and employees living in rural areas who do not work in occupations connected with agriculture, these people live mostly in one-family houses [239, 100] of agricultural settlements, and their private farms do not basically differ from those of the kolkhoz and sovkhoz population. On the basis of field surveys carried out in a large village of 5,158 inhabitants of the southern Ukrainian raion of Melitopol' which he considered to be typical, one Soviet sociologist came to the following conclusion [52, 56]:

Our findings from the village examined show that the personal [private] farm is common *to all strata* of the village population. . . . The private farm is (contrary to a widely-held opinion) favored by all social groups in the village, including the workers and employees of state institutions and enterprises: 85 to 100 percent of the workers, employees, and kolkhozniks, of the [professionally] qualified as well as the unqualified, have sown areas and a fruit and berry orchard. . . . On the average, the sown area of a kolkhoznik family in 1964 amounted to about 0.4 hectare, while the workers had 0.17 hectare. There was one cow for about every three kolkhoznik families and for every eleven workers' families.

It is by no means true that private farms are primarily run by manual workers. As early as 1963, another Soviet author stated [372, 16, 109]: "Empirical social inquiries have shown that the great majority of the rural intelligentsia of our country have a personal private farm." He accused these members of the intelligentsia of excessive concern with such private farming and wrote that some village teachers had turned themselves into a kind of "farmer." (Here it should be added that the Soviet concept of intelligentsia also embraces many of those who in the West would be termed merely "specialized workers.")

But it has also been said that for most members of the village intelligentsia the private plot and livestock holding is "economically essential for their families' existence." [21] This is especially true for the village teachers, most of whom have a plot and many of whom own a cow, a pig, or other livestock. In the Novosibirsk oblast in 1967, three out of four village teachers of the lower paid category (up to 75 rubles a month) and every second teacher in the higher salary brackets had a plot or livestock of some kind or both; on the average they spent two to three months of their annual working time on the plot [63, 150–152].

Arutiunian [52, 56] confirms that there is far less difference between kolkhozniks and other population groups than between the skilled and unskilled members of both groups, and that the only appreciable difference between the private farms of kolkhozniks and those of workers and employees is in the livestock holdings. He makes an exception for a sizable minority:

An exception consists of the less skilled employees. Both in the state and in the kolkhoz sector, these are relatively worse equipped with personal plots. In the state sector, more than 40 percent of the less skilled employees have neither sown areas nor a fruit and berry orchard. One of the explanations for this may be their relative youth. Evidently, many of them just have not yet had an opportunity to establish a private farm. The question of the extent to which this is connected with the psychological condition of the young person and the extent to which it has to do with economic circumstances is a subject for a special sociological investigation.

A Soviet journalist described another instance which would permit similar conclusions. The village in question was Parevka, in the Tambov oblast, a large kolkhoz village which served as the local center of an agricultural region. According to Bukovskii, 106 households of the total of 1,078 were households of workers and employees. Most of the residents —"mainly employees"—appeared to have nothing to do with the public agricultural sector, and the village had no less than 194 state pensioners. But as a rule the household members were engaged in private farming;

[21] [63, 153]; cf. [443, no. 26 (1969), 10].

the majority had once been kolkhozniks and had retained their former plots. Bukovskii gave a general area of 0.4 hectare per plot and, without differentiating between kolkhoz and other households, added that all private livestock holdings amounted to 971 cattle, 48 pigs, over 2,000 sheep and goats, and more than 8,000 birds [68, 163].

In the neighboring kolkhoz village, in addition to the households of the seventy above-mentioned workers and employees of the local branch of *Soiuzsel'khoztekhnika*, there were one hundred worker and employee households. Their members belonged to the raion hospital (with a staff of seventy, including physicians), to two schools, to a kindergarten which had been set up in a former manor house, to a consumer service combine, to the state tobacco monopoly warehouse, to the local soviet, and to the village store. All of them, "from kolkhoznik to doctor," busied themselves with their private plots and especially with the locally most profitable crop—tobacco [68, 175–176].

Of the total of 52.3 million persons who were working in rural areas at the time of the 1959 census, about 15 percent were employed in industry, construction, and communications, and a further 16 percent or so belonged to the service industries (trade, education, and health). There were at that time in the Soviet Union roughly 80,000 nonagricultural, rural settlements; of these, only 1,550 had more than one thousand inhabitants, and the majority—something like 50,000—had less than ten inhabitants. These settlements may be grouped in the following principal categories:

1. Industrial settlements which are too small to count as urban settlements and which may be either purely industrial or partly agricultural and partly industrial.

2. Settlements connected with the transportation system.

3. Construction settlements at new large building sites.

4. Timber and forestry settlements.

5. Fishing and hunting settlements.

6. Research station settlements.

7. Settlements for health and education services (convalescent homes, sanatoriums, hospitals outside urban areas, children's and invalids' homes, boarding schools, and so on).

8. Settlements of workers and employees who work in the towns (usually located on the peripheries of large towns and including the dacha settlements [see below]).

The most important of these, historically and in respect to the number of inhabitants, are categories 1, 2 and 8. With the passage of time many such settlements qualify for the administrative designation of *urban-type settlements,* and may eventually incorporate as towns.[22] Most of the occupants of these settlements work full-time in agriculture or other branches of the economy, but some change their jobs according to the season. In addition to their production functions, these settlements often play a certain role in economic organization, trade, and distribution as administrative, political, and cultural centers for the outlying villages, even when they are not the formal raion centers.

Of those living on the countryside but not employed in agriculture, an important and numerically very considerable group is composed of those living in the dacha settlements (*dachnye poselki*). As with the spas, it has never been categorically specified whether, administratively speaking, these dacha settlements are urban or rural, and differing interpretations apply in various republics.[23] The word dacha means a country house or a weekend house, originally a one-family house occupied during seasons of the year and usually during the summer. However, on the peripheries of the larger towns, many of these dachas have become the permanent residences of people who work in the town but who live outside it. The largest concentrations of such dachas can be found around Moscow, but they are also to be seen around other large cities. Around Moscow alone, more than 18,000 new dacha plots had been granted during the years preceding 1960 [*55a,* 84]. Then the government put a ban on individual dacha building by a decree of 30 December 1960.

Dacha construction cooperatives (*dachno-stroitel'nye kooperativy*) had not been banned. They greatly expanded during the 1960s, but are not expected to do so in the future. In fact, the cooperative character of these organizations ceases as soon as the plots are divided up and the dachas are built on them. Official control is not efficient [*55a,* 41–43].

"The townsfolk do all they can to get at least a dog kennel, as long as it is out in the fresh air. Just something to themselves, without a neighbor. Have you noticed how many huts like that there are around Moscow or Kiev? Not to mention the proper dacha settlements." In re-

---

[22] For more details, see L. L. Trube, "Ob ekonomiko-geograficheskom izuchenii poselkov gorodskogo tipa," [*122,* 113–121].

[23] [*93,* 130–132]; the rather laconic and still valid definition for the RSFSR of a "dacha settlement" was given in a decree of 14 June 1927 [*346,* I, 39] and is clearly obsolete.

sponse to these observations, which he does not dispute, Stadniuk pictures his hero as thinking: "They have the same frame of mind as those villagers who fear a large communal apartment building the way the Devil fears the holy water" [*364*, VIII, 54].

According to G. M. Lappo, at the beginning of the 1960s there were about half a million people living in the dacha settlements (whether or not so designated officially) around Moscow; formally these counted as rural inhabitants.[24] The transformation of these types of seasonal settlements into year-round dwelling places is called "winterization" by Lappo; this practice was known even before the October Revolution, but became widespread thereafter, especially as a result of the housing shortage in Moscow. A recent picture of such an outlying suburb of Moscow was given by E. Gerasimov [*124*, 7]. This dacha settlement had grown rapidly since the latter part of the 1950s, during "the stormy wave of the postwar dacha and garden construction period," and is surrounded by a large number of allotments with their summer houses. The gardens are well tended. Geese, goats, and many cows (tended in the summer by private cow herds) are kept there. Among the residents are many who came from the land, even if they no longer work there, and some—especially women—who retain a farming way of life and believe "the time has passed when we considered it to be wrong for a working chap to dig a bit in his vegetable plot" [*124*, 7, 11, 13, 17–18, 30–31, 40].

There are many small industrial settlements which rate administratively as villages but which are really half way between rural and urban settlements. Many are to be found in the *Podmoskov'e*, the peripheries of Moscow, but they are not exclusive to this area. Lappo pictures another group of towns—ones which were originally simply villages or rural raion centers and which are gradually becoming urbanized.

Common to all such rural, although nonagricultural, settlements, is their origin as service or industrial enterprises, railroad stations, sanatoriums, hospitals, colleges, institutes, agricultural enterprises, or villages. These lie thickly scattered around Moscow, at an average distance of 1.8 kilometers from one another. Since most of these arose on nonurban territory—and this applies also to those which, in the meantime, have ac-

[24] G. M. Lappo, "Geograficheskoe izuchenie naselennykh punktov, zanimaiushchikh promezhutochnoe polozhenie mezhdu gorodskimi i sel'skimi poseleniiami (na primere Moskovskoi oblasti)," [*122*, 250–255]; see also [*178*, 147 ff., 158–159]; "Les grandes Villes du Monde: Moscou," *La Documentation francaise: Notes et Etudes documentaires*, no. 3493, 24 mai 1968, pp. 43–44.

quired the status of towns or urban-type settlements—the private plots within their confines could usually extend to 0.15 or 0.12 hectare (see pp. 37 ff.). These account for the bulk of the private plots and livestock holdings of the nonagricultural rural population.

In the village earlier described by Bukovskii, a fairly large proportion of the nonagricultural population consisted of teachers, doctors, and technicians, as might well be expected in a rural raion center. However, of the above occupational groups, only those who work in agriculture or who work directly for the rural population (such as a village teacher) have, together with their families as well as after their retirement, the right to a plot of 0.25 hectare. Presumably, the proportion of those who qualify for the above, in the dacha settlements and in similar places around Moscow, is small. Yet in this connection one should not forget the middle and higher ranking state and party pensioners, and in particular retired service officers, who are entitled to somewhat more than the usual size of plot and who received even greater areas before 1958.

An example of the economic significance such a plot can attain, under some circumstances, was provided by *Izvestiia of* 26 May 1962. This told of how a 47-year-old teacher, residing in a rural raion by the Caspian Sea, gave up his profession to devote himself entirely to running a small market garden. On the quarter of a hectare of land, to which rural teachers are entitled, he raised 32 fruit trees, 236 vines and 1,600 tomato plants. With the help of a greenhouse and a mechanical irrigation system which he installed, the ex-teacher grew enough produce to keep a lively business going, both in the local oblast capital of Astrakhan and beyond the borders of the oblast. In seven years, he earned enough to purchase a motorboat for carrying his produce and to build himself a brick house. Of course, this is exceptional, but it does show what can be done, under Soviet conditions, with 0.6 acre of land. Eighteen months before, a teacher who had *not* given up his profession, had been pilloried for systematically trading with the produce from his private plot [*440*, 5 January 1961].

Private agricultural production under category (c)—in urban-type settlements, either as plots next to the house or as separate allotments, and with or without livestock—was boosted by the outset of industrialization [*55a*, 9–10]. Private output grew rapidly because of the inadequate supply of foodstuffs in the newly created towns and industrial areas, and was intensified during the state of emergency prevailing during the Second World War [*128*, 18–19]. But urban private agricultural production was and is not limited to such new residential areas (which include some of the dacha settlements).

More than forty million urban people—"according to the most cautious estimates"—are presently involved in individual land use, especially in small towns and urban-type settlements [55a, 83]. This means some ten million households at least. The most widespread uses of individual urban land are for one-family homes on plots, dachas, and potato and vegetables gardens (other than on housing sites). Although granting of plots for building one-family homes has been forbidden in the big cities, exceptions to this rule were recently allowed again; in medium-sized and small towns the building of such houses on plots continues to be effectuated "on a rather large scale" [55a, 88]. The overall number is still increasing [55a, 13]. (For incomes, see p. 100, above.)

A case similar to that of the ex-teacher by the Caspian Sea was cited in Khrushchev's memorandum of 31 July 1963, to the Central Committee Presidium [179, VIII, 73]. This time it was a 53-year-old man, with higher technical training, who for eight years had not done any "socially" necessary work and had mainly busied himself with the sale of suckling pigs, pork, and milk on the markets. In the town of Skhodnia in the Moscow oblast, he owned a house, a plot of land, three milking cows, sixteen breeding sows, and fifteen meat pigs. Significantly, he was prosecuted under the provisions of the "parasites" law (as was the ex-teacher referred to earlier). This confirms that, before the edicts of August 1963, pertinent legal provisions did not exist in all towns which could be applied to those Soviet citizens who kept a large number of animals and paid the necessary taxes but who did not qualify as members of a kolkhoz or sovkhoz (see pp. 40, 43). For the charge of "speculation" can only be brought against those who sell goods which they themselves have not produced and who thus "exploit" the labor of others. It was also recorded that, in the medium-sized town of Syktyvkar on the northern edge of the country's agricultural zone, private pig holdings and potato-growing played an important role in feeding the population, even though feed was hard to come by [282, 54, 65, 123].

What has been said about the private plots in the settlements which are still formally regarded as rural is also valid for most of private farming in urban residential areas. The character of such farming does not change immediately and automatically when the locality is promoted to the category of urban-type settlement or town. Only after the date of this promotion are all newly-issued plots only half as large (see Chapter III). Yet the number of the older, larger plots is gradually reduced, because these can be withdrawn when so required by urban renewal plans and the private houses on them must then be sold to the state. The collective gardens become important afterwards.

However, when a real town is built from scratch and subsequently expands, the apartment buildings in it spread out from the center to the region of single-family houses with their relatively large gardens. Around the larger cities, or those destined to be large, new outskirt settlements spring up, sometimes on the land already belonging to the town, where small plots are the rule, or else on rural territory which is later incorporated into the city limits.[25] The process repeats itself continuously. State and communal residential construction never kept up with the demand as towns grew and people flocked into them. This promoted the growth of such outskirt settlements with their basic, mainly wood or wattle, one-family houses with private sites or garden plots [178, 157]. Nowadays in large towns like Orenburg, Omsk, and Penza, over 80 percent of the built-up area is occupied by single-storied and mostly privately owned houses; in Novosibirsk, Tula, and Kaluga their share is 80 percent, and in Ufa and Arkhangelsk over 70 percent.[26] Whenever such towns grow rapidly and their demands outstrip the supply of food from the neighboring farms, this provides an extra stimulus for private agricultural production. This was specifically acknowledged and described by a Soviet author in the case of Novosibirsk.[27] In this city of more than one million inhabitants, teachers depend to a considerable degree on private agricultural activities for their livelihood. In 1967, this applied to 27 percent of the teachers of Novosibirsk, and even to 36 percent of those with a monthly income of the head of the household of less than fifty rubles [63, 151–152]. In such towns, moreover, the proportion of the able-bodied population not employed in the socialized sector is especially large [253, 89–91].

This milieu, long neglected in Soviet belles-lettres, was skillfully

---

[25] See, for Khar'kov, [202, 86–87].

[26] [110, 110]; see also the portrayal of life in a Siberian suburb by Viktor Likhonosov [212].

[27] [253, 103] (for a description of the different parts of Novosibirsk see ibid., pp. 149–150). In Novosibirsk the construction of large apartment houses without garden plots is progressing rapidly at present, although the population's demand for vegetables and fruit is only to a minor degree satisfied by the state and cooperative trade, I was told there in September of 1969.

portrayed by the writer V. Semin. The setting of his novel is an outskirt
settlement of the town of Rostov-on-Don (720,000 inhabitants in January
1965, and not to be confused with the ancient small Central Russian town
of Rostov) which forms the center of a growing conurbation around the
mouth of the Don [333, 234].

I haven't far to go to the center. Five streetcar stops in the town itself, then
over a level crossing and then you are in the outer suburb. It stretches and
stretches—you cannot see the end of it. If you go by the electric suburban
train, and not the streetcar, then you can travel for sixty kilometers through
green outskirt settlements like this with their one-storied houses. First comes
the outer ring of our inner town and then the suburbs begin. Our suburbs
overlap with the suburbs of the neighboring raion town, and then follow the
suburban settlements of this raion.

The literary critic Lakshin, who dealt with this novel at great length,
said of this milieu [209, 234]:

Neither town nor village: thus the outskirt settlement lives its own life, perhaps not quite isolated but yet embellished and regulated in its own way.
Those advances and changes for the better in the people's material and cultural spheres which have been registered during the last ten to fifteen years,
do come here also, but slower and later than one would wish.

Another critic had raised the objection that the novel dealt with an
"atypical" part of Soviet life. Lakshin refuted this by citing a letter from
a construction engineer in a forge works in Azov:

That is in Rostov, but doesn't one get the same picture on approaching Moscow or any other town you like, whether large or small? The five-storied
houses replace the outskirt settlements, but these stretch further and take up
the free areas. And these outskirt settlements with their millions of people live
just as Semin described.

There has recently been a great spurt of public construction activity
in Moscow and a few other cities. In these instances, the growth of public
housing of the apartment block variety may well exceed the growth of
single-family housing. This is partly the result of administrative restrictions on migration into such cities. But the description given in the text
holds true for the majority of Soviet towns and most big cities.

"The *dachniki* who illegally use garden plots" are still considered a
problem [452, 21 September 1968]. In the outskirt settlements of Baku
alone, in 1962, some six thousand one-family houses were reported in this
category, with two thousand hectares of garden area [168, 363]. On gar-

den plots, where only insubstantial summer houses and sheds are allowed, there often appear "one-family houses with attics and with concrete floored cellars, surrounded by metal fences." And much of the building material was acquired illegally [*462*, 30 August 1968].

The garden around the house is taken for granted in Semin's novel, and yet it is noticeable that the garden as portrayed here does not assume the same importance as a garden on the countryside. It is, of course, useful and even necessary, but it no longer plays a central part in life and sustenance. Semin pictures a retired officer as "living in Dachnoe [the dacha quarter] on a colonel's plot, there where all the pensioned officers have built themselves houses," and as having made a vineyard which not only keeps him supplied with wine for himself but also with wine "which he sells on the market for a few thousand rubles every year." [28] But this is presented by Semin merely as one of several aspects of existence there and not as the principal one. Nevertheless, given the vast number of these plots, they still represent an economic factor. Although they are essentially urban, part of them seems to be situated on surrounding rural territory.

For urban inhabitants who do not live in the outskirt settlements, possibilities for small-scale private gardening exist in the potato and vegetable gardens (*ogorody*) and the fruit and berry orchards (*sady*), which are granted for a limited term only. The number of people tending such plots has been increasing in the 1960s [*339a*, 156]. In 1962, individual and collective gardens covered an area of some 1.35 million hectares (my estimate, see [*416*, 226, 248–250]).

The number of collective gardens has been and still is growing. In 1969, about 9.5 million people (excluding dependents), with plots of 0.07 hectare each on the average, participated in collective gardening, of which 7.4 million had potato and vegetable gardens and 2.1 million had orchards (fruit and berries) [*339a*, 153]. This adds up to an area of 665,000 hectares. The number of individual gardens (mainly potato and vegetable), other than as part of housing sites, comprises an unknown few more million. Potato and vegetable gardens, individual and collective, had reached a numerical all-time high of 18 million in 1945 [*55a*, 10–11]. Their number has greatly decreased since then, and individually they are granted now only to people who are not working in a big enterprise and are mostly situated in small towns and so-called settlements of an urban type

---

[28] [*333*, 114]; this probably refers to pre-1961 rubles, and thus several hundreds of current rubles are meant.

[55a, 86]. At least this is the general rule. In middle towns and big cities, collective gardening is the almost exclusive form at present [55a, 86]. Individual orchards, which had been propagated and favored by a decree of 24 February 1949, have decreased in number since then [55a, 11]. At present the practice of granting them has virtually stopped [55a, 63]. In 1961, the government found that collective orchards, too, had in many cases become individual gardens for all practical purposes, and tried to prevent their development, but in vain; after the removal of Khrushchev, the benevolent policy, as far as collective gardens are concerned, was resumed [55a, 65–70].

Many collective gardens and orchards are not genuinely collective. They are allowed to be used individually, that is, the collective is the holder of the right of land use, but each member works his own part of the garden and keeps the crop for himself. This form prevails by far at present [339a, 155–156; 55a, 48]. The truly collective form of working together in brigades and dividing—in a rather complicated way—the crop according to each one's work participation is not widespread [55a, 57]. "As the practice shows, the holders of this derived right of land use are at present almost exclusively individual citizens, not their collectives" [55a, 54]. This is favored by the fact that control by municipal and other authorities is not very effective [55a, 52–53]. "Among a certain part of the urban population there exist mistaken ideas that plots in collective orchards may be bought and sold. One can hear about buying and selling orchard plots from people who are being accepted as members of gardeners' societies in the place of other people who end their membership in the societies" [55a, 76].

One Soviet author speaks of the "so-called collective [gardens] which in fact are individual orchards and gardens" [173, 60]. Grigorovskii and Alekseev chose to exclude the "collective orchards" from the category of private plots, considering work there as "active relaxation in the lap of nature" as much as a way of meeting the need for fresh fruit. However, they also conceded that "some of the fruit-growing enthusiasts turn their orchards into a means of extracting considerable additional income, selling fruit and berries on the market" [128, 20].

The great majority of townspeople use their gardens for productive purposes [339a, 153; see also 56a, 67].

When V. P. Rodionov [180, 96] puts the share of money income that the urban workers and employees of the Orenburg oblast derived from the private plots as only 2 percent (with the share in small towns and workers' settlements higher than the oblast average), he excludes these gardens and orchards. Yet they play an important role. In 1959, a total of 8.5 million tons of potatoes (or 9.8 percent of total Soviet potato output in that year) were harvested from the private and collective gardens of the urban population; this works out to 670 kilograms of potatoes from 0.04 to 0.06 hectare for each family which grew potatoes [462, 14 April 1965]. In the central Siberian industrial oblast of Kemerovo, 293,000 tons of potatoes were grown in 1966 on 31,000 hectares of such potato and vegetable gardens, divided among 480,000 workers and employees. The figure thus amounts to an output of 610 kilograms per family [462, 18 May 1967]. Since the total urban population of the oblast at that time was 2,470,000, more than half of the urban families must have worked such gardens. Of course, the number of these gardens in Kemerovo oblast must have been greater than the all-union average (see the degree of self-sufficiency of the Siberian urban population in Table 18 above). At the time of Khrushchev's removal, there were only eight hundred hectares of such gardens around Kiev, used by about fifteen thousand families. Even those gardens which were formally designated as collective merited in fact only the description of cooperative, because only part of the work was performed communally, and the harvesting was carried out individually [173, 62]. This kind of gardening was also criticized under Khrushchev on the grounds that it "promotes the restoration of private property attitudes" [ibid.].

Medium and small-sized towns are the locales of the third major category of workers' and employees' plots. These are here taken to mean towns with up to fifty thousand inhabitants. If urban settlements with less than five thousand inhabitants are excluded, then 41.2 million people lived in the medium and small towns at the beginning of 1970. The population of such towns has grown by nearly a million annually since the 1959 census. This was caused largely by population growth in towns with twenty thousand to fifty thousand residents, many of which are either new towns or towns which used to have less than twenty thousand inhabitants before [220, 141]. In small towns, especially if they are industrially underdeveloped, a considerable proportion of the population is engaged in agriculture—from 5 to 15 percent, and up to 45 percent in extreme cases, of the able-bodied population.[29] In recent years, the problem of the small towns has attracted increasing attention from Soviet

[29] L. L. Trube, "Malye goroda i bol'shie poselki i problemy ikh razvitiia," [122, 151, 163, 165–169]; [254, 179].

sociologists, economists, planners, and writers. This is primarily because of the exceptionally high proportion of individuals in such towns who are occupied with housework and work on the private plots and thus are not available for work in the public sector. The problem is not restricted to isolated parts of the country, but is especially pressing in Central Asia, Transcaucasia, and in the Moldavian SSR. In those areas "a large proportion" of these town dwellers "is employed in personal subsidiary farming, the income from which forms an important component of total family income" [220, 149].

In 1970, the Soviet writer Lev Iudashin wrote of the rather old and not industrialized town Fort Shevchenko (located on the east coast of the Caspian Sea): "The permanent inhabitants of Fort Shevchenko are mostly Kazakhs. Every one has two or three camels, about a dozen sheep —and in part they live on the basis of these animals. Some housewives milk camels right on the street. Cows are also kept here. They are small, hairy, thin, they walk all over the streets, picking up garbage and pieces of paper. This was the first time that I had seen such strange cows, which also eat paper" [445, no. 6 (1970), 151].

The three main problems of the small and medium towns are: industrial underdevelopment, a high birth rate, and the inflow of people from the village. What has already been said concerning the rural settlements and the outskirt settlements (insofar as the latter have spread over the territory of existing small towns) is valid also for the role of the private plots of the workers and employees in small towns. But the real small town with a long history of its own, or one which has grown out of an old, larger village, is different. Characteristic and faithful descriptions of three examples of small towns in differing parts of Soviet Russia are on hand.

The oldest of these comes from the pen of Dorosh and refers to the period from 1957 to 1960. The old town of Rostov makes frequent appearances in other parts of his diary, but it figures most prominently in his "The Raion Center in February" and "Dry Summer." Rostov Pereiaslavskii (not to be confused with Rostov-on-Don) is a town of less than thirty thousand inhabitants. Dorosh makes clear the impact of the private plots on the lives of its residents, many of whom have deep roots on the countryside.[30] A similar situation—arisen from "bitter necessity"

[30] [99, 32–33]; [100, 29] (see also p. 37: "He has a vegetable garden like everyone around here"); [97, I, 10] ("Almost the whole territory which is free of buildings, has been ploughed . . .") and [97, II, 20].

(from scarcity of food)—prevailed in small provincial towns of Siberia as late as 1968 [*443*, no. 6 (1969), 12]. On warmer evenings the women and girls in Dorosh's raion center wait at the crossroads at the entrance to the town for the herds of goats, sheep, and cows to be brought to the main street; then each drives her beast or beasts home through the town. The animals were grazing all day out on the meadows, watched by a herdsman hired jointly by the owners.

This same type of grazing is portrayed by another writer in greater detail. Chernichenko depicts the raion town of Ust'-Labinsk in the Kuban region, "one of the most typical small towns of Southern Russia," and he demonstrates the importance of this kind of livestock raising [*73*, 179–180]:

Until recently [up to the end of the fifties] almost every worker and employee here was given a particular piece of land for vegetables and corn, almost every household kept a cow, a pig, a flock of geese, two or three ducks with their young. . . .

From this there arose a number of economic customs.[31] The town was divided into sectors, each one forming its own herds, and an elected committee dealt with matters concerning the cows. Subordinate to the chairman of the committee was a herdsman, and sometimes also a special bull attendant (before the introduction of artificial insemination). An agreement was reached with a neighboring kolkhoz over meadow areas. . . .

For a given sum, the kolkhoz allotted two or three pieces of land for the herds, and these were usually sown with lucerne or grass and used partly for grazing and partly for haying. Each of the housewives obligated themselves to sell, *on behalf of the kolkhoz* [emphasis supplied] two or three hundred liters of milk a year to the children's homes, hospitals, or maternity homes. It must be said that all the grass in the water-meadows which were overgrown with bushes, on the verge of woods, on the edges of country roads and on the banks [of the river] was cleanly mown, and the output of the urban meadows per hundred hectares was never below that of the kolkhoz. The little town, with its thousands of heads of livestock, was a large-scale producer of milk and meat, fed itself and delivered considerable quantities to the market. . . .

The purchase of cows [by the state or by the kolkhozes] helped to clean up the streets, but it converted the little town from a producer of milk and meat into a consumer [of these products]. It would not have been half so bad if the confiscation of the personal livestock [that is, livestock in private possession] had boosted the output of animal products in the public sector. But the oblast organizations, which had devoted all their energies to the leadership

---

[31] The following two paragraphs dealing with the organization of private livestock describe not only the methods employed in a given, isolated instance but a system officially sanctioned; see above, p. 41.

of the "cow confiscation" movement, did not derive any benefit from the enormous increase in the size of the kolkhoz and sovkhoz herds. And that is undoubtedly a serious economic failure.

Now [1965] the artificial restrictions have been lifted. But time is needed and the workers, employees, and kolkhozniks must be helped in overcoming the consequences of this absurd idea.

In 1964, Bukovskii wrote about the town of Kulebaki in the Gor'kii oblast [67, 192–193]:

This "village-like town" has fifty thousand inhabitants; it has 7,500 houses, with their own plots of 600 to 800 square meters, with 1,400 cows, several thousand pigs, several thousand sheep, over ten thousand chicken and geese, 37,000 fruit trees (there were more before the war, they were cut down but replanted again after the war). . . .
As can be seen, not just several thousand metalworkers live here but also over seven thousand owners of private plots who not only have fruit and vegetable gardens but also keep livestock.

If it is assumed that the average household consisted of three to four members, then this means that half of the residents of this town (which also had industrial trade and cultural facilities) tended private plots with a total area of five hundred to six hundred hectares. The same author was to tell of a much smaller town of 6,687 inhabitants, with very little industry and with extremely few residents working in the public sector [67, 196]:

The Ardatov of today has 1,100 households, 96 communal apartment buildings with 248 apartments and 1,200 residents; 969 people are householders. In recent years the number of householders has risen by 200. . . .
Practically all householders keep livestock. Altogether there are 792 households with livestock holdings, 419 cows (with calves and heifers), 314 pigs, 86 sheep, 342 goats, and 8,000 birds (mostly chicken and geese).

The author of this book gained a quite similar impression during his visits to the small town of Bershad' and to the medium-sized one of Izmailiia in the Ukrainian SSR. The situation is pretty much the same in those parts of the Soviet Union which are inhabited by the non-Slavic races. Thus, V. S. Dzhaoshvili [122, 219], referring to the smaller towns of the Georgian SSR which have mainly administrative significance, states: "Most of the towns of this type are underdeveloped; agriculture plays an important role in some of their economies, according to the number of people working in it." The word agriculture appears often as a branch of the economy in his list of classified Georgian towns. Because of the nature of the region and the preference of its inhabitants, fruit and wine occupy, probably, a principal place (next to corn and vegetables) in the private farming of these urban residents.

It is hard to say just how much of the private produce from urban plots comes on to the market. It is reported that private farming in the old Russian town of Suzdal specializes in cucumber production, and that the cucumbers are disposed of privately in the large industrial town of Ivanovo, one hundred kilometers away.[32]

There is no doubt that the medium- and small-sized towns in the Soviet Union meet their own needs for fresh foodstuffs to an astonishing extent. Per capita of the total Soviet urban population in 1954 (which at that time amounted to 85 millions) the *urban* private plots alone produced 44 kilogram of potatoes (a quarter of the potato consumption), 11 kilograms of vegetables, 4.8 kilograms of meat (other than poultry meat)—of which 3.8 kilograms was pork, and 27 liters of milk (a third of the milk consumed) [*341*, 11–12].

This comes to a total of about 3.74 million tons of potatoes, 935,000 tons of vegetables, 425,000 tons of meat (including 323,000 tons of pork), and 2.2 million tons of milk. These amounts represented a fair share of the private output of *all* workers and employees, given for 1953 and 1956 as 665,000 and 942,000 tons of meat and 7,060,000 and 7,680,000 tons of milk respectively.[33] Particularly noteworthy is the high proportion of total meat output; however, this is supported by the fact that at that time roughly as many pigs were kept by urban workers and employees as by their rural counterparts (see Table 20). It also ties in with some figures for the record harvest year of 1956, when there was more to be bought in the stores. In that year it was estimated that the private plots of the non-agricultural population supplied 14.1 percent of meat, 20.3 percent of milk, 37.7 percent of eggs, 31.1 percent of potatoes, and 18.1 percent of vegetables consumed by that part of the population.[34]

On the basis of the overt and concealed statistics on plot areas and private livestock holdings (cf. *416*, Appendix D), the available output

---

[32] [*74*, 138]; in Suzdal, in summer 1970, I was told that most of the able-bodied inhabitants are employed in the research and experimental state farm there.

[33] [*16*, 334–336]; other comparable data are not available.

[34] N. Ia. Kirichenko, "Raschet produktsii lichnogo khoziaistva nesel'skokhoziaistvennogo naseleniia," *Sbornik nauchnykh rabot* (*Nauchno-issledovatel'skiy institut torgovli i obshchestvennogo pitaniia*) (Moscow: 1959), p. 33 (as cited in [*157*, 332]).

data, the few studies made by Soviet sociologists, and the writings of Soviet authors, it can be concluded that the private agricultural production of the Soviet urban population is far more substantial and proportionately more important than is often assumed.

It seems useful at this point to recapitulate the results of an earlier calculation aimed at an estimate of the total number of privately used land parcels devoted to agricultural production. It may also serve as a justification for the surprising—to some people—title of this chapter. The details of the calculation, including a reconciliation with partial data provided by Venzher [396, 57; 369, 138], are shown in Appendix D of the original German version of this book [416, 243-250].

In 1963, the number of households using land for purposes of private subsidiary farming, in the widest sense of the word, was as follows:

On the Countryside.

16.3 million households of kolkhozniks (including those located on urban territory in the administrative sense of the word).

1.0 to 1.7 million households of workers and employees, residing in kolkhoz villages and/or on kolkhoz land.

6.3 to 7.1 million households of sovkhoz workers and employees, or workers and employees of other state and institutional agricultural enterprises.

About 4 million households with personal land parcels or service allotments of workers and employees.

4 to 5 million gardens in agricultural use by workers and employees.

In Cities, Towns, and Urban Settlements:

About 4 million personal land parcels (including housing sites) and service allotments.[35]

10 to 13 million collective and individual gardens in productive use.

Of the total number of privately used parcels of land in the towns and cities, about five to seven million were located in towns with less than 25,000 inhabitants and seven to twelve million in towns with more than 25,000 inhabitants.

Many of the underlying figures are guesstimates (cf. [416, 249]), and they can only serve our purpose as long as no better and more accurate

---

[35] This figure, which excludes urban garden plots without houses built on them, recently was also indicated by Shmelev [339a, 23].

figures are made public in Soviet sources. Nevertheless, and in spite of the existing uncertainties, I feel that the general order of magnitude of the overall total, as well as of the various components or of the ranges shown for the individual components, are sufficiently reliable to warrant inclusion at this stage.

6

The Kolkhoz Market

As long as private output of food is used only to cover the personal demands of the respective individuals and households, its disturbing impact on the centrally planned economy is only minor. In fact, its existence reduces some pressures within the planned economy as the state and its trading and distribution agencies are relieved of the task of supplying a large part of the population with food. But even so, the existence of private production causes some problems: The kolkhoznik remains partially independent of income received from the kolkhoz, and his interest in work in the socialized sector may be reduced to a minimum. Workers and employees on the countryside as well as in suburban areas can also gain a certain amount of independence from the state (viewed as the employer in a socialist economy). This may in turn lead to income differentials which could well contravene the existing wage policies [87, 85].

But even though private production often corrects the mistakes of planning, it performs a peculiarly disturbing function in this context when products of the private sector appear on the market outside of the state and cooperative distribution and trade network. It is then that "elements of spontaneity [appear] in the movement of goods and in price formation" [142, 225]. The relatively free exchange relationships of supply and demand are unleashed precisely on the kolkhoz market, the foundation of which rests on private subsidiary production of farm products [91, 49]. These relationships indeed play an autonomous role in the planned economy, although more as a complement to, than a competitor of, the state retail trade in food [421, 384; 168, 189–202]. The legalization of this market in 1932 was a concession, related logically to the existence of private subsidiary farming and to the insufficient supply of food for the population, a development that, in turn, resulted from collectivization.

According to a Soviet definition, "kolkhoz trade takes place on the kolkhoz markets, but it also occurs directly in kolkhozes and in the residences of the kolkhozniks, as well as through direct home delivery to the residence of the buyer. Kolkhoz markets are special parcels of land made available for this purpose in towns, at worker settlements, at railroad stations, and on landings, as well as in rural localities. [They] are equipped with [certain] facilities, and this is where the sale of farm products by the kolkhozes and the kolkhozniks takes place" [65, 243]. Another author, Shmelev [339a, 82], further enumerates: "Besides the trade at permanently working urban and rural market places, kolkhoz trade comprises the selling (vynosnaia torgovlia) at railway stations and at ship landings [and, I may add from own observations, at stations of overland buses], at periodical rural fairs (iarmarka) and the sale of produce of the personal plot at homes (at the place of production or at the house of the consumer; for example, the delivery of milk by kolkhozniks situated near towns directly to urban families.)" [1]

The free play of supply and demand is also manifested outside of this framework in the form of illegal, or semilegal, but nevertheless tolerated forms of exchange, in particular in the "so-called spontaneous markets (sporadic gatherings of buyers and sellers, or in flea markets)" [424, 31]. The latter are generally of limited importance and their development is precluded by the provisions of Soviet law as well as by the state monopoly on transportation. The scope of such activity is actually determined by the interpretation of laws and decrees, by local regulations, and by the vigilance and the devotion to duty of various administrative, judicial, and party agencies and officials. There are indications that the number of private sellers on the fringe of the official kolkhoz markets is at times greater than the number within their formal confines [168, 309], even though such trade is no more permitted now than it was in the past (according, f.i., to the municipal regulation for the Moscow markets, dated 4 October 1966 and displayed in the building of the Central Market). I observed marginal cases of such trade. These included a woman who rapidly offered a few hens from her handbag to passersby on a side street of the Shota Rustaveli Boulevard in Tbilisi, and women who sold small cans of milk at a street corner in Bukhara. The magnitude of such "on the side" transactions cannot be determined from statistical reporting. In

---

[1] Shmelev adds in a footnote that the last mentioned form of marketing milk has lost much of its importance and in many towns has wholly disappeared.

general, however, their importance rises when the official kolkhoz trade is forcibly interfered with, when it is restricted in the performance of its functions, or when its full legal development is impeded by administrative measures.

The magnitude of the legal trade in eggs, milk, potatoes, and other products—which brings the consumer into direct contact with the producer at stations, landings, and through home delivery—must also be considerable. Soviet data on the volume of the extrarural kolkhoz trade appear to include an estimate of the volume of this trade,[2] but the nature of the available evidence is such that no really firm conclusions can be reached. In particular, we do not know whether those Soviet estimates are meant to cover all or only a part of these transactions.

Actual statistical reporting was for a long time for trade concentrated in the well-defined markets of 251 towns but now is for 264 towns of the USSR, including some smaller towns of the raion center type.[3] In addition, a part of the intrarural trade (cf. below, pp. 178 ff.) is also covered by statistical reporting. Similar shortcomings apply to the gathering of information on kolkhoz market prices, as reported by S. Levashev [466, no. 2 (1971), 63]. The reported volume of trade thus probably covers the greater part of the organized urban trade, but presumably only a quarter or even less of the total extrarural trade.[4] First-hand statistical data on the volume of the kolkhoz trade in smaller towns or in raion centers are not even available to Soviet writers.[5]

When this trade occurs at sites designated for the purpose, it is sometimes also referred to as "the kolkhoz bazaar trade" to provide an accurate conceptual definition. In most instances, Soviet citizens refer to the trade and to the market place as either "the market" or "the bazaar." The terms *kolkhoz market* and *kolkhoz trade* are generally used interchange-

[2] [155, 19]; [168, 438]. On the varying scope and usage of the term *kolkhoz trade* in Soviet publications, consult [149, 98–99]; [157, 317].

[3] Statistical reporting practices are described in [157, 318–320]; [168, 437–443]; [163, 128–129, 136]. For greater details see [56, 15–49]. The same reporting methods have since 1968 been used in 264 cities [114, 264].

[4] See [157, 324] and [155, 33], as well as the share of the turnover in 251 large cities in the total turnover of the kolkhoz market, given for 1967 as follows [13, 950]: grains—14 percent; potatoes—22 percent; meat—23 percent; milk—17 percent; and eggs—15 percent.

[5] [135, 71]. The same authors later supplied a detailed account of methods used in their estimates of the total turnover of the Ukrainian kolkhoz markets in [274, passim].

ably in Soviet literature to describe the more or less organized [6] free trade in the cities and towns, in urban settlements, and in raion centers. Free trade within the kolkhozes or in rural settlements, as well as the sale of products by the kolkhozes to the kolkhozniks and the sales and premia distributions of products by the sovkhozes to their workers and employees are included in the intrarural turnover (or intrarural trade or market) which is not considered part of the kolkhoz trade turnover and is not reported as such.

Within the limits of its legal and more or less regulated forms, Morozov defines kolkhoz trade as "a form of commodity turnover through which agricultural enterprises and owners of personal subsidiary farms dispose of the produced output in a noncentralized manner [not through the state procurement network] and at prices determined by demand and supply" [250, 257–258]. When so defined, kolkhoz trade would also include sales of products by kolkhozes or consumer cooperatives to buyers other than state agencies.

Most kolkhoz markets are administered by local soviets. A considerable number of them are subordinated to the USSR Ministry of Trade, while a smaller proportion operate under the supervision of the Ministry of Railroads and/or some other communal and other agencies [424, 31]. On the basis of an authorization of the central authorities, kolkhoz markets are established at a particular site by communal authorities. They are more or less adequately equipped with various facilities and fixtures, as well as with some items of equipment which are rented to sellers at a fee collected in addition to the general entrance or market trading fee.[7] The selected sites are not always suitable as market places [130, 37]:

[6] Morozov [247, 58 ff.], however, considers as organized only that part of the kolkhoz trade which occurs through the intermediary of the consumer cooperatives (or the commission trade on the markets). Direct market transactions between producers and consumers are not viewed by Morozov as organized.

[7] The decision of the Council of Ministers of the RSSR, dated 17 April 1965 ("On the Improvement of Trade on the Kolkhoz Markets") sets out the rules applicable in the recent past. The text, which omits some paragraphs described as "valid temporarily," is reproduced in [346, IX, 419–421]. The decision sets out concrete rules on the basis of general guidelines issued earlier by the Council of Ministers of the USSR on 13 March 1965 ("On the Improvement of Trade and Communal Catering in the Country"). Cf. [359, 304–305, 309]. These decisions provide the basis for "The Model Regulations of Trade on the Kolkhoz Markets," approved on 22 May 1965 by the appropriate State Committee of the Council of Ministers of the USSR (referred to in [455, no. 2 (1968), 108]) and for the "Regulations of Trade on the Kolkhoz Markets in the City of Moscow," issued on 4 October 1966 by the Moscow City soviet, which I saw displayed in the building of the Central Market in June 1967 and again in September 1969.

Some employees of state trade organizations and of the city soviets believe that [the kolkhoz market] is a relic of the past, that the markets compete with state trade, and that they should be pushed aside. On the basis of such false assumptions, they usually select sites for the markets in the older, outlying fringe areas of the city, so that townspeople are at times simply unable to get there. Why should we hide the fact? City planners pursuing their activities have frequently forgotten the markets altogether until just recently [1965].

Toward the end of World War II, the Council of People's Commissars of the RSFSR bestirred itself to improve the organizational and sanitary conditions of the existing kolkhoz markets in a decision dated 7 September 1944 [346, X, 427–428]. The total number of markets at that time was somewhat greater than in 1966 (cf. Table 24), especially because a greater number of small, rural markets existed at that time. Further decisions on the increased supplies of products to the markets and the improvement of market facilities were made at the end of 1953 and again a year later [449, 23 October 1953; 346, IX, 422–424].

In April of 1957 a census was taken of 5,697 organized and authorized kolkhoz markets, including 1,809 markets in rural raion centers.[8] Most of these markets were small. Even among the urban markets a full 39 percent reported a weekly turnover of less than five thousand (old) rubles.

Comprehensive data on the number of kolkhoz markets and the conditions in them were released in 1966. These data are reproduced in Table 24, which indicates that about 60 percent of all markets covered an area equal to or smaller than 5,000 square meters (or some 230 by 230 feet). Of all livestock and feed markets, 60 percent were to be found in the Ukraine and the Uzbek SSR; only 16 percent were located in the largest republic, the RSFSR. All these figures probably represent increases since 1964; in that year alone, twenty-two new markets were opened in the Ukraine. In 1969, there were more than 7,500 markets in the country (excluding those at railway stations and ship landings) with about 1.4 million trading stalls [339a, 81].

Additional information on the results of the market census in 1966 was provided in a Soviet statistical journal [424, 32–34]. In ordinary towns and urban settlements, there were 4,083 markets where the average monthly number of sellers per market was 2,500. In addition, there were 960 markets in the oblast (krai) and republican capital cities; the average monthly number of sellers per market in this category was 5,900. Finally,

[8] For greater details on this investigation, see [168, 202–209].

TABLE 24. MAJOR INDICATORS FOR THE KOLKHOZ MARKETS
ON MARCH 15, 1966

Indicator	Food and Mixed Markets	Livestock and Feed Markets	All Markets
Total number of markets, including markets with:	7,014[a]	246	7,260
Daily trade	3,877	6	3,883
Trade 3 days a week	516	5	521
Trade 2 days a week	597	22	619
Trade once a week	2,012	205	2,217
Trade once or twice a month	12	8	20
Area of markets (thousand square meters)	48,636	1,755	50,391
Length of trading tables (thousand meters) including:	1,205	2	1,207
In enclosed buildings	27	0	27
In pavilions	220	0	220
In the open, of which under cover	488	1	489
without cover	470	1	471
Number of trading stalls (thousand)	1,248.8	0.6	1,249.4[b]
Number of sellers (monthly average, million)	17.5	0.2	17.7

[a] Livestock and feed grains are also sold in small quantities on 3,953 of these markets. Cf. [424, 32]. [b] Including 1,055 thousand on urban markets, [424, 32].
SOURCE: [12, 667].

there were 2,207 markets in rural localitites with an average of 800 sellers per market per month. The rural markets are usually open only once a week. Roofed halls covering the entire market area have been constructed on only sixty-seven urban markets; this type of structure first made its appearance at the beginning of the 1950s. Several smaller selling halls (the so-called pavilions) existed on 2,193 markets. The majority of urban markets and almost all rural markets are described as lacking appropriate facilities: "The major bottleneck is to be found in the supply of markets with storage space, and particularly with refrigerators and coolers" [424, 34; see also 56a, 110]. Mechanical devices for loading and unloading are also missing on most markets, and in 1966 there were only 218 trucks, 329 motorscooters, and 732 horses and donkeys for all the markets of the country [*339a*, 90].

The fact that Soviet citizens who are not members of the kolkhozes but who legally produce farm products on subsidiary plots also have the right to trade on the kolkhoz market is not always adequately recognized by Western observers.[9] Actually the kolkhozniks and other working individuals in the USSR do have this right. But no one is allowed to repurchase and resell farm products. Private trade by intermediaries—retail as well as wholesale—is described as speculation and is punishable under Article 164 of the Penal Code [*281*, 175; *129*, II, 1635–1634]. It is also illegal for private middlemen to act as representatives of the kolkhozes; nor is a fictitious relationship of this kind recognized as legal. In spite of these prohibitions, Soviet authorities have not completely succeeded in eliminating the middleman.

In the aggregate, the purely quantitative importance of the kolkhoz trade is only secondary today. A noticeable downward trend was apparent during the 1950s. From 1960 to 1968, the value of kolkhoz trade in food products alone (excluding the cooperative trade) amounted annually to slightly less than four billion rubles. The state and cooperative retail turnover in food, which came to twenty-one billion rubles in 1950, rose to forty-three billion by 1960 and then to seventy-five billion rubles by 1968. The share of the kolkhoz trade in the "turnover of comparable products" reached a maximum of 75.6 percent in 1945 and was still 29.6 percent in 1953. It declined to 17.3 percent in 1958 and to 8.7 percent in 1969.[10] In spite of these trends, the share of the market in total trade of some products (especially potatoes, eggs, vegetables, and fruit) was still more than 50 percent in 1960–1961. Meat and milk do not quite fall into this category. This phenomenon raises some doubts about the actual comparability of the Soviet category of "comparable products." Less than 10 percent of the state retail trade turnover consists of fresh, not processed,

---

[9] Garden products are occasionally sold on the kolkhoz markets even by students in uniform, by teachers and also by members of the upper strata of the Soviet society; see [*442*, 7 January 1966]. On the sales of garden products by recipients of old age pensions, see [*443*, no. 23 (1967), 10].

[10] [*56a*, 182] and, for 1969, [*339a*, 81, 100]. When calculations are made in terms of state retail prices, the shares of the kolkhoz market in 1958 are reduced by roughly one-third and in 1969 by 27 percent (*ibid.;* see also [*12*, 631]; [*14*, 613, 618]). But such calculations yield distorting results, because they neglect the general quality differentials as well as local scarcity conditions. The operation of the kolkhoz markets rests to a considerable extent on these two elements.

products. In 1965, over one-half of all potatoes, 15 percent of vegetables, and 17 percent of all eggs sold to the Soviet population were marketed through the kolkhoz trade. The corresponding percentages are said to be particularly high in the southern part of the country [424, 30]. While the share of the kolkhoz market in overall food purchases by the population, in 1963, accounted for only 3 to 4 percent in Moscow, Leningrad, and Sverdlovsk, the respective percentages in southern cities like Khar'kov, Rostov-on-the-Don, and Odessa were 19.4, 21.3, and 43.8 [56a, 115] (cf. p. 153 below).

Even industrial workers' families, in 1966, bought the following percentages of their consumption at the kolkhoz markets: potatoes—27, vegetables—17, meat—2, milk—3, eggs—18, fruit and berries—23 [339a, 151]. In recent times the share of milk and milk products, of animal fats, and of bread (which now are in better supply in the state retail trade) has been declining. The share of high quality vegetables and fruit has much increased instead, as a consequence of rising urban incomes and demands and of inadequately increasing and improving supplies in state retail shops. These commodities accounted for more than half the total kolkhoz market turnover in 1967 [339a, 83, 139].

Market trade is relatively important in smaller and medium-size towns and in the outlying areas [128, 77–78; 152, 53]. Conversations with individual Soviet citizens lead me to believe that a typical inhabitant of a Soviet town thinks only of the market when he talks about purchases of fresh fruit and vegetables. This is corroborated by Shmelev's statement [339a, 94, n. 1] that 90 percent of all early vegetables are bought on the kolkhoz market. The fact that inhabitants of a small town must nearly always buy potatoes and vegetables on the market was underlined in a Soviet short story as a major factor contributing to a high cost of living in such a town [259, 84].

The quantity of foods supplied by the state and cooperative stores has undoubtedly increased in the last twenty years, and there has also been an improvement in the quality of products sold by these stores. But the continued existence and the very nature of the free market still indicate that demand is greater than supply at the prevailing state prices, the general level of market prices in 1967 was 50 percent above that of the state retail trade.[11] This is particularly true in large cities, where the av-

---

[11] A. I. Levin, *Sotsial'no-ekonomicheskie problemy razvitiia sprosa naseleniia v SSSR* (Moscow: 1968), p. 39.

erage difference between the two price levels ranged between 50 and 70 percent in the years from 1959 to 1963 [*128*, 32] (cf. [*56a*, 112–113]). Shmelev stated, clearly with a defensive undertone [*339a*, 86]:

Moreover, the high price level for certain kinds of produce on the kolkhoz market must not be considered speculative, because this is determined by the unsatisfactory level of production of these products and by the great demand for them. It must be said that kolkhozes and consumer cooperatives, too, are marketing part of their output in the kolkhoz market at "high" prices.

On the whole, three factors are responsible for this development: (1) the rapid increase of urban population (particularly in the large cities) and of the nonagricultural labor force, accompanied by the unsatisfactory performance of the state food trade; (2) an increase in the purchasing power of these groups of the Soviet population; and (3) the conversion of numerous kolkhozes into sovkhozes. (Former kolkhozniks automatically became wage earners who were to obtain at least a part of their supplies from state stores. The conversions occurred simultaneously with a reduction of income-in-kind in the remaining kolkhozes, and this development also necessitated an improvement in the supply of the retail trade network.)

I. I. Lukinov alleges that the state and cooperative trade turnover in the Ukraine (including sales to catering establishments) rose between 1950 and 1962 by a factor of 4.7 for meat, 3.5 for animal fats, 3.4 for lard, 5.2 for eggs, and as much as 10.5 for milk and milk products. In spite of these increases, retail trade outlets were said to be inadequately supplied with these very products [*225*, 324]. This statement illustrates not only the increase in the requirements and purchasing power of the urban population, but also the sad conditions prevailing in 1950. Lukinov's inference, drawn by hindsight, was correct: "As a result, prices of many products on the market registered a rising trend, even though the volume of sales of these same products has also been rising."

The kolkhoz market (or trade) is repeatedly referred to in Soviet writings, but relatively less often than other problem areas of Soviet agriculture or of Soviet trade. Much of what is written appears in rather inaccessible publications.[12] This has been true in spite of Khrushchev's recognition of the kolkhoz market at the Twenty-Second Party Congress.

[12] See the bibliographies in [*168*] and [*157*, 333–334] as well as the sources used later in this chapter. The important book by Iakhnich was unfortunately not available to me.

His words did not, at first, alter the existing situation or the tendency to apply administrative measures. However, concern with kolkhoz trade was again legitimized at the highest level, and this influenced the number of publications on the subject, even though the increase was not rapid at first. Greater consideration was given to these problems only after Khrushchev's fall from office—within the framework of the new agricultural policy which brought greater opportunities for private agricultural production—and the greater number of articles devoted to it resulted in some positive publicity.

Measures designed to give more elbow room and greater opportunities for the development of kolkhoz markets were then introduced. These covered the improvement of market equipment (including health facilities and sanitary conditions), construction of additional structures, renewed admittance of hunters and fishermen as sellers, closer relations between market administrators and socialized farms, and so on. But most important of all, the administrative restrictions on the kolkhoz market, which hampered the free shipment of goods and free price formation by forces of supply and demand, were lifted or branded as illegal.[13] (As it was, the upper limits artificially imposed on market prices were not very effective in practice, see [168, 391]):

The [new] model rules [for the kolkhoz markets] were approved not too long ago. Paragraph 9 states: "The sale of farm products by the kolkhozniks and other Soviet citizens occurs at prices determined at the markets." This was frequently not the case in the past. Without ever being given the reasons for the ruling, the kolkhoznik was often told: Trade, but this is your price: you have no right to exceed it.

This hindered the shipment of products to the markets. For many [producers] it was simply unprofitable to sell [there]. At present [spring 1965], the administrative setting of market prices is forbidden.[14]

The words just cited were immediately accompanied by a phrase stating that one must "conduct a decisive campaign against an artificial increase" of market prices. A book set in type during the summer of 1965

---

[13] The most important decision was that of the Council of Ministers of the RSFSR of 17 April 1965 (cf. n. 7 above). Hunters and fishermen were again allowed on the markets by the decision of the Council of Ministers of the RSFSR of 24 November 1964 [346, IX, 421–422]. See also the interview with the deputy RSFSR minister of trade, V. I. Feofanov, in [459, 13 May 1965] and [440, 14 May 1965]. A summary of the 1965–1966 situation on the kolkhoz markets is given in [83].

[14] Feofanov's interview (n. 13 above). Such price lists are also referred to in [434, no. 37 (1965), 40].

also expressed a hostile attitude towards the market, referring to the period immediately preceding typesetting: "The market turned the people away from work in the kolkhoz, from study, from culture and rest. What is equally important, [the market] was conducive to the renaissance of the spirit of property ownership among the peasants" [*186*, 231]. The feeling of some line-toeing citizens and bureaucrats towards the revival of the market is shown in these words cited by one Tamkevich [*442*, 7 January 1966]:

By its very nature, the market trade is a humming private trade. A streamlined formulation such as "prices determined at the market" is nothing else but an open invitation to speculation. . . . In general, an unveiled speculation exists on the markets. It is fostered by the unwieldiness of our procurement and trade organizations. . . . Market trade, or—to put it bluntly—private trade is also a social evil. We console ourselves with the thought that it is a transitory phenomenon. But how many years has it already existed? . . . And its end is not in sight.

Some special types of trade were again permitted, but they met with opposition in practice:[15]

The prohibition on selling food on markets [located] at stations has long been lifted. But trade at station markets is often handled as a poor relation, either because the force of inertia is too strong or because failure to understand the importance of the problem is particularly pronounced in this area. In some localities, these markets are simply closed. Worse yet, the railroad police, using numerous pretexts, do not allow the kolkhozniks to sell any fruit or vegetables to the passengers. The [situation] is the same in many river ports or at landings.

As late as 1966, N. Kuznetsov, the deputy minister of trade of the USSR, stated that kolkhoz trade was still hampered by authorities in many localities: "As a rule, these restrictions are not approved by anybody, there are no decisions or regulations about them," but they still operate [*452*, 26 April 1966]. A. Gudimov tells us that in 1965, contrary to the existing government regulations, individuals who wanted to travel to the market to sell produce were held back or restrained and their goods were confiscated [*442*, 10 February 1966]. One might conjecture that opposition to the new government policy on the kolkhoz market existed at the middle and the lower levels of the administrative apparatus. Instead of improving their own performance, state trade organizations often tried to bring about various restrictions on market activity in order

[15] Interview with Feofanov (n. 13 above).

to resist this form of competition [*130, 37*]. An official statement, published on 4 November 1965, confirmed that sovkhoz directors and kolkhoz chairmen interfered with the sale of products by the kolkhozniks or by sovkhoz workers. In September of 1969, I talked to an official of the Novosibirsk oblast administration for agriculture who considered the market an atypical, withering phenomenon, and who pretended to be ignorant of the official attitude dating from the spring of 1965 as well as of the related, specific regulations.

A remarkable effort was made in the first two years after Khrushchev's dismissal to revive the kolkhoz markets. In response, the physical volume of food trade rose in 1965 and 1966,[16] but the increase ceased in 1967 (cf. below, p. 329). New, appropriately equipped halls and overnight sleeping accommodations for the sellers were to be constructed. Trading fees and other fees, collected at the existing markets and formerly channeled into the state budget, were to be used to finance this building program.[17]

Besides the foods already mentioned—potatoes, vegetables, eggs, meat, milk and milk products, and fruit (including dry fruit)—we find many other products sold on the free market. Depending on the season and the climatic conditions, one can buy fruit juices, honey, preserves, wines, sugar, fish, game, livestock (particularly young animals in rural areas), grains and grain products, mushrooms (fresh, dried, or marinated), kitchen spices and medicinal herbs, sauerkraut, pickles, marinated tomatoes, tobacco and makhorka, flowers, and flower and vegetable seeds. With wool,[18] we move into the realm of rural handicraft products, which in-

---

[16] [*452*, 3 February 1966]. In the Ukraine the increase in the volume of food trade came to 7 percent, and prices declined 12 percent [*48, 77–78*].

[17] See *inter alia* the decision of the Council of Ministers of the RSFSR of 17 April 1965 (n. 7 above) and [*339a, 89*]. On the construction of new market structures, see [*416, 79* and n. 18]; [*424, 32*]. For more recent developments in Azerbaidzhan, see [*452, 12 August 1969*].

[18] [*331, 163*]; on home processing of wool see *ibid.*, p. 195, [*68, 163*], and [*258, 115*] (knitted goods from goat wool). In 1958, nearly half of raw wool produced in the subsidiary farms of the kolkhozniks and nearly all wool produced in such farms of the workers and employees was not delivered to the state or sold on the market. This suggests that home processing was a widespread phenomenon, especially for production of carpets and blankets from coarse wool in Central Asia. But it is also possible that a large part of the private wool output was not recorded as marketed or delivered to the state, simply because it was acquired by the kolkhozes and sovkhozes in the intrarural trade and then delivered to the state as output of the public sector (cf. below, pp. 235–246). On knitting mohair kerchieves and fulling felt, for making felt boots, for sale, see [*339a, 76*].

cludes pots, barrels, and brooms, painted wooden toys, spoons, boxes from the forest provinces of North and Central Russia, Belorussia, Western Ukraine, and Eastern Russia, and similar products.[19] The sale of hides, unprocessed wool, raw cotton, sugar beets, and special technical products such as tea and volatile oil plants is not allowed. Trade in certain products of private handicraft was allowed by the Moscow market regulations of 4 October 1966, which I saw displayed in June of 1967. But the leadership also wants retail stores to open outlets at the markets to trade in industrial consumer goods. This is partly to raise the turnover of the public retail network and partly to compete with sales of nonagricultural products of private producers. Such outlets frequently occupy a third or more of the total trading area at the markets. They do enjoy a priority, and the individual seller or a kolkhoz representative is left to shift for himself [452, 10 July 1967; 9 October 1968].

In 1950 as well as in 1957, three-quarters of the total trade turnover on the extrarural kolkhoz market were accounted for by potatoes, vegetables, eggs, meat, livestock, and milk [157, 315, 323]. Currently, food still accounts for 90 percent of the turnover on kolkhoz markets, but the share of handicrafts may well be rising. Permission to sell these products directly to consumers on urban and rural markets was given when the development of subsidiary handicraft shops in the kolkhozes and sovkhozes was encouraged in 1966 and 1967.

Iu. Chernichenko reports the following picture of a market in a small town of southern Russia in 1963 as seen through the eyes of an inhabitant [73, 179]:

These are not bazaars today—may my eyes never see them. One can only buy sunflower seeds; at most a Georgian comes with tangerines. Seven years ago these were really bazaars. . . . On the left, as one entered the gate, animals were traded. Cows mooed and kicked, hens clucked, geese honked. Buy! And the milkstands! Lord, what one could find there! Fresh milk, sour milk, *riazhenka* [a type of baked sour milk], sheep cheese, cream so heavy that you could hardly slice it with a knife. Butter folded in cabbage leaves: those who wished so ate it right away on a roll, others took it home. And it was cheap

[19] Cf. [339a, 76–77]. Bukovskii [67, 768] reports that the old handicrafts, producing primarily for the villages, are still quite active in certain areas. He also mentions a village in the Tambov oblast where ikons were still produced at home for private sales in 1965 [68, 174]. M. Volkova lists a number of areas where rural handicrafts are still pursued briskly; these are mostly located in outlying regions and those inhabited by non-Russian peoples [452, 7 September 1966]. I dealt with the matter of the revival of rural handicrafts in [461, no. 25 (1968), 52–58].

—you would not believe it; eight rubles [naturally old rubles, or 0.80 new ruble] for a kilogram of meat. And what fruit, what tomatoes, what wonderful eggplant and small dill pickles were brought in large quantities! And what wine in the fall!

The above quote not only gives a picture of the market but also indicates its decline in the Khruschev era.[20] The abundance was particularly great and prices especially low in this agriculturally blessed Kuban. But the testimony of Bukovskii from the small Russian town of Ardatov and that of Dorosh (below, p. 143) indicate that regional differences were only a matter of degree. All these markets had this in common: they were located in small rural towns whose inhabitants produced products for sale, not only for their own consumption. The supply from the surrounding farm district is especially large in such towns, because larger cities are distant and difficult to reach by poor public transportation. This limits the opportunities for sale, depresses the prices (especially of perishables), and increases the incentive to seek sale outlets in the large city in spite of long distances [308, 198; 168, 232–233, 236, 309]. Thus Dorosh, describing a small town in Central Russia in 1961 [97, I, 30] noted:

I think that the relative material well-being of the contemporary raion center peasant is best explained by the proximity—not so much of the railroad but —of the highway, with its own regular long distance buses and its trucks. It [is the highway that] lets him trade fresh meat in Moscow, not to mention potatoes and onions.

Some sellers come to markets over considerable distances, sometimes over thousands of miles [434, no. 25 (1970), 17]. S. Levashev stated that considerable amounts of produce are thus exchanged between the various parts of the country [466, no. 2 (1971), 63] (cf. [339a, 49]). These long trips are made worthwhile by the climatic differences among the various parts of the country, by price differentials, and by the relatively inexpensive travel—if one is able to buy an air or a rail ticket, or to secure transport in a legal or an illegal manner.[21] "The sons of sunny Georgia" found on many markets from Kaliningrad to Vladivostok are a well known phenomenon [442, 7 January 1966].

When one considers whether sales on the market are really advan-

---

[20] Compare the decline in turnover per inhabitant of large towns in [168, 67, 71].

[21] Cf. [168, 310–311, 316–317, 341]; [449, 3 March 1961]; [101, 210, 212]; [452, 26 April 1966]; [247, 64]; [68, 157]; and [281, 167–168, 177–178, 181].

tageous for the peasant, one often forgets that a seller on the urban market is also able to buy those goods that are not available in his village store or in the stores of his raion center. "It is a strongly implanted tradition of the rural population to buy things in town with revenues obtained from sales of their farm products" [382, 28]. Purchases in town have provided a well-known motivation for trips to the market ever since antiquity. The opportunity for recreation, visits to the theater, and the like may also play a role in this context [452, 9 September 1966].

A Soviet calculation shows that the average daily number of kolkhozniks selling their products on the markets of the country amounted to seven hundred thousand in 1961 and that the annual "unproductive" expenditure of their labor amounted to 250 million man-days [247, 59]. For 1965, the average monthly number of sellers on the market was given as seventeen million [424, 31]. This fits well with the figure of 200 million man-days given as the annual average for recent years [452, 4 January 1970]. The average daily number of sellers in the Ukraine alone was two hundred thousand on an ordinary day in 1965 or 1966 (and twice that many on holidays). This accounts for 80 million man-days a year [83, 20]. But the data on which such calculations are based were described as "by far not comprehensive" [223, 25].

Trading activity should not be described as unproductive, and it is not generally labeled as such in the USSR today. It is certainly true that labor expenditures on the kolkhoz markets are too large relative to the value of market turnover. This has been noted by foreign observers as well. But part of the problem is explained by the regulations governing kolkhoz trade: Every private producer must sell his products personally, no matter how small the quantity. He cannot go to a middleman; the only alternative is a state or cooperative organization where prices or conditions of sale may not be to the seller's advantage. And cooperative organizations have often lacked transportation or opportunities to bring the products to town from the villages. Hence, the chastnik—the private seller—appears either as a "basketman" or a "bagman," bringing in small quantities of his produce to most markets in the suggested manner.

The existence of the free market constitutes not only an economic but also a political and a psychological problem for the Soviet leadership. All the other problems, however, derive from the market's economic function, which cannot be eliminated until the socialized sector is able to take care of the food requirements of the Soviet population. Surely ideologically determined wishful thinking has caused the Soviet leadership steadily to underestimate the importance of private production and of the kolkhoz market until stark reality forced a better understanding of the situation. This happened on every occasion when the food supply acquired a critical dimension as a result of errors in the economic policy of the leadership. We almost find a regular cycle which manifested itself once in the 1930s, again in Stalin's last years, and finally under Khrushchev.

A particularly crude example of the dilettante manner in which Khrushchev approached these problems may be found in his speech of 29 June 1959: "Livestock belonging to workers and employees is no longer of importance from the economic standpoint, that is, from the standpoint of satisfying the requirements of the state for meat and milk" [179, IV, 24]. It was true that relative to the position of the kolkhozniks, the role of workers and employees was subordinate both in deliveries to the state and in market sales. But Khrushchev completely neglected the fact that food supplied by the subsidiary plots of workers and employees was of great value to those who produced it, especially in small towns and on the countryside. When activity on these plots is restricted, the demands of the workers and employees must be satisfied on the market. This places a greater additional burden on the state retail network, which has barely been able to deal with its earlier, similar tasks. It is difficult to imagine anything more revealing than Khrushchev's view that overall economic interests are identical with the economic interests of the state. This type of "economic" analysis makes the blunders of Khrushchev's agricultural policy understandable; it is quite likely that he was not the only Soviet leader who thought in those terms.

Looking back at the period from 1960 to 1963, Morozov wrote [250, 181]:

The reduced volume of sales [on the kolkhoz markets] affected the supply of food of the urban population both through the increased shortage of certain products and through the increased prices of such products. The importance of the kolkhoz market in sales of food to the urban population—particularly with respect to a comparable group of products—is still very considerable.

MARKET CONSCIOUSNESS AND ETATISM

Soviet sources indicate eagerly that the percentage share of the kolkhoz trade in the total sales of consumer goods has declined steadily since 1940 or since 1950. But this is primarily the result of the growing turnover in state and cooperative trade. Actually, state and cooperative turnover rose by 98 percent between 1958 and 1968. By 1968, it was almost four times greater than it had been in 1950. The turnover of the kolkhoz trade (excluding cooperative sales) stagnated between 1958 and 1968 at a level roughly 25 percent below that registered in 1950. Up to 1964, it maintained this level only as a result of annual price increases of some 5 to 6 percent which began in 1960.[22]

Dorosh shows how a small Central Russian town was affected by the restrictions of the private sector and of the kolkhoz trade that occurred under Khrushchev [*100*, 10–11]:

There is a long line in front of the only milk store. I can well remember when this store opened in 1955 or 1956, when milk yields in our district had doubled in relation to 1953. It was not that the store was much needed—the inhabitants of our raion center bought their milk on the market, where one could bargain as well as taste the milk sold by all the women standing near by. Those buying in the retail store were mainly those who did not get up early in the morning and who did not have to care about ten *kopeiki* [one new *kopeika*—market prices were below state prices there at that time]. And yet the inhabitants of the town were very happy about their milk store. . . .

And it could happen that the market and all its adjoining streets were already empty, but two cardboard signs, attached with string, were hung on the door of the store: "Milk available," "Kefir available." And now there is a line in front of it.

You will understand how this came about when you go to the market. Two years ago [1958], it was difficult to count the tables in the row of milk sellers. . . . cans glistened, white aprons, sleeve protectors, and wet rags shone wherever you looked. Measuring cans clattered to the sound of wooden spoons. The smell of fresh milk, just taken out of the cellar, was mixed with that of milk baked in the oven, with those greasy and acid smells of baked or ordinary sour milk, of cream, and of curd cheese. The kolkhoz women, the kolkhozes, and also some town women sold milk. The price level was of course determined by the kolkhozes, but even the kolkhoz women did not drive prices too high up, because they wished to return to work that awaited them at home.

This was the case two years ago.

Today, there is enough room for all; milk sellers stand behind two or three tables with their products spread around. And they know their worth! People push each other in front of every seller. Should one of the women have cream to sell, several hands stretch out immediately after a single, half-a-pint

[22] [*12*, 635, 665]. The increase in the volume of sales more or less offset the decline in prices from 1958 until 1964 (except for meat). Cf. [*230*, 57]. For further details, see [*416*, Appendix F].

can. The inhabitant of the raion center explains it all with a terse sentence: "It was ordered that no cows may be kept."

Venzher expressed the same thought in relation to the entire Soviet kolkhoz market [395, 286]: "The shrinking of milk output on personal subsidiary plots could not be made good by the kolkhozes."

These observations of life under Khrushchev are confirmed by many competent Soviet writers. Their statements also identify the causes of this development, causes related to the relationship between those who rule and those who are ruled in the USSR. Some of the statements are reproduced below:

One of the consequences of these errors in economic policy with respect to the kolkhozes and the kolkhozniks was made clear in the rapid increase in prices on the extrarural kolkhoz market from 1960 to 1963. Shipments of farm products to the market declined in the same period. . . . The development of this trade on the markets of many cities was "regulated" through direct administrative interference. This was often done under the guise of protecting the interests of the urban population. Actually, of course, it was . . . the urban population that suffered immediately.[23]

Lukinov [225, 325–326] states:

The level of regulated state retail prices plays a decisive role in the formation of the market price only on the condition that—given the level of effective demand—the state trade network is able to cover fully the needs of the people. If this is not the case, market prices are no longer controlled by the [level of] state retail prices.

Lukinov and Gudimov point out that the behavior of private producers is consistent with what in the West we call maximizing behavior [225, 326–327; 442, 10 February 1966]:

By that time [the increase of retail prices on 1 June, 1962], market prices for meat and butter exceeded the state retail prices by a considerable margin. This reflected the increased demand of consumers. The kolkhozniks, as well as the other strata of the population, could earn high incomes from the sale of meat on the market, even when they fed their animals with expensive purchased feed [Lukinov].

The level of food prices on urban markets is very sensitive to the impact of our work [the socialized Moscow Motor Transport Enterprises]. In the

[23] [250, 149]. See also *ibid.*, p. 181, where "the restrictions on subsidiary farming of individuals [applied through] administrative measures" and the "regulation" of kolkhoz markets is mentioned as the main cause of the increase in prices in 1962 and 1963.

past year [1964] prices immediately doubled or tripled when no trucks were available to transport potatoes for two or three days. In order to bring market prices back to about the level of state retail prices, we had to send trucks rapidly out to the countryside so that potatoes could be brought here [Gudimov].

Price declines brought about by similar factors were also reported from the Moscow markets in the course of the following year [281, 168, 172, 178].

It would be erroneous to argue that the behavior of the ordinary kolkhoznik is not market-oriented on the alleged grounds of the impact of the "Russian soul" of the traditional *muzhik*. The problems raised by the kolkhoz market for the Soviet command economy can only be understood if we assume that individual members of the Soviet population tend to behave distinctly as economic men. This would hold true even if their private output was used primarily to satisfy a part of their own demand for food and was only secondarily destined for the market. For the structure of private production would still be determined by the scarcity conditions on the market as a whole, including both the state retail and the kolkhoz market (cf. below, p. 216 f. This is apparently also the view of E. Kerblay in [168, 303-305, 309]).

Efim Dorosh, one of the most knowledgeable authorities on the kolkhoz village, commented precisely on the misunderstanding of this issue:[24]

Some bureaucratic agronomist once told me about *muzhik* indolence (*muzhitskaia kosnost'*), and that it is because of this indolence that the local peasants do not adopt the latest achievements of science. He also meant that this was the reason yields were low in many kolkhozes of the raion. What utter nonsense! One only has to look at the household plots to become convinced of the opposite. And how can one speak of indolence? There were no morella cherry orchards here twenty years ago, when hemp was grown on the plots. But then, almost as soon as people heard that one could earn large incomes from morella cherries, they immediately plowed over their hemp and planted morella cherry trees, even though they had to wait two or three years for the first harvest.

Dorosh also indicates that the rural population, as well as that of the small towns, shows little interest in general lectures on the achievements

---

[24] Cited without reservations by Vinogradov [402, 251]. Vinogradov also speaks in a similar vein of the "plans" a kolkhoznik has for his plot (*ibid.*, p. 249). For the rising interest in the planting of fruit trees, see also [331, 162, 177].

and novelties in agriculture. But he states that they show great interest in specific subjects—such as the use of plant-protecting chemicals—that can be useful in the cultivation of private plots. Individual producers are well aware of the relationships among costs, prices, and profit opportunities in their private production [97, II, 16, 24]. Bukovskii notes that "the people are not backward when they see an advantage." [25]

Another writer describes a kolkhoznik's plot in Northern Russia as wholly market oriented [43, 128]. A kolkhoz chairman from the Kaluga oblast complained that former kolkhozniks, who now work in industry, do not ask their parents to move to the city on purpose: the plot remains in the possession of the parents, who can produce food for the bazaar [434, no. 36 (1965), 17]. In Stadniuk's kolkhoz novel, Serioga is shown as a negative type: as soon "as he hears that the market price for dry prunes or for walnuts rose significantly, he stands with a [full] bag on the roadside and waits for a ride from a truck" [364, II, 55]. More frequently, however, we find at the market an ordinary kolkhoznik, a worker, or a low rank employee, who sells only that part of his output which is not needed for the satisfaction of his personal needs, or that which he must sell when he needs cash. In rare cases we also find individuals who are anything but speculators: These are professional activists of the Party and even a deputy of the oblast soviet [97, I, 19].

The quality of the products is very important, and it was well said of a vegetable seller: "Aunt Pasha knows her worth and that of her goods." When a customer complained that her radishes were too expensive, Aunt Pasha replied confidently: "I do not pull you by your sleeve to my stand; wait till they are to be found in the stores" [443, 29 June 1965]. On a different occasion, the answer of another seller was: "You don't like it? Then buy it in the store!" This "sounded like mockery," wrote the reporting writer, because cucumbers, tomatoes, and apples in the stores cannot compete with the market either in price or in quality [452, 9 September 1966]. The classic exchange with a potato seller on a Kiev market is particularly appropriate here: "Auntie, can't you let me have them for less?" "For less you buy from the state!" [442, 7 January 1966].

The trade margin in state and cooperative trading organizations often comes to several hundred percent in relation to the procurement price for

[25] [68, 174]; cf. the expression "trading people" (narod-kommersant) in *ibid.*, pp. 157–158.

fruit, and partly also for vegetables.[26] Under the circumstances, it is hardly surprising that private producers are at times able to charge lower prices. In spite of the high cost of small scale production, they are still able to realize a profit. On the other hand, the public sector output of fruit and vegetables is often produced at such a high cost that even the costs of production are not covered by state procurement prices. And in spite of high trade margins, the public trade often works at a loss.[27] It is also hardly surprising that it was precisely the supply of vegetables to the markets of the reporting Ukrainian towns that rose by 82 percent between 1962 and 1967.

The role played by the kolkhoz market is related not only to the absolute volume of goods available in the country, or to the shortage of particular goods, but also to the inability of the socialized trade to market the available goods at the appropriate time and place in relation to the existing demand. A shortage of some food products in some parts of the country may occur simultaneously with an oversupply of the same products in another area. This is especially true of vegetables, fruit, and eggs. Even the socialized catering establishments in plants, schools, or in the sovkhozes or kolkhozes are not infrequently forced to buy produce on the kolkhoz markets [168, 254–256].

The centralized planned economy that cannot handle such matters within its own framework still makes it difficult for local agencies, local enterprises, and individuals to improve the situation through their own

---

[26] S. Litiagin [452, 28 September 1966] showed the following relationships between the retail and the procurement prices for 1965 in rubles per kilogram (for each, the procurement price is listed in parentheses after the retail price): all fruit —1.30 (0.28); grapes—about 1.00 (0.29); carrots—0.30 (0.13); turnips—0.26 (0.09); and cabbage—0.20 (0.10). In spite of these high marketing margins, the trade organizations often failed to realize a profit in these transactions [226, 70]. N. Mukhametshin argues for the trade organizations that the situation was partly caused by various rules and price regulations that made such trade unattractive (*Sovetskaia torgovlia*, no. 11 (1966), 20–22). An example he cites for the Tatar ASSR indicates that in such conditions the kolkhoz trade may also influence prices in the retail trade. A trade organization purchased potatoes for 0.10 ruble per kilogram from a kolkhoz but had to sell it in Kazan' for 0.10 ruble per kilogram, because it was not allowed to sell at prices exceeding the local market price (*ibid.*, p. 21). On the nature and the deficiencies of price regulations in state trade, see [393, *passim*] and [434, no. 8 (1969), 32–33].

[27] [*Ibid.*, pp. 32–33]; [226, 70]; [274, 67]. On the irrationalities of state retail prices for vegetables in Moscow and Leningrad in 1964 and 1965, see [393] (with detailed price lists) as well as [252].

initiative. This is well illustrated by the following absurd development in the case of a special product.

No bay leaves, for use as spice, were produced in the socialized sector until the end of the 1950s. Small private producers and traders supplied the population with bay leaves; obviously, prices were high because the quantity offered was small. The task of producing and marketing bay leaves was then assigned to the large socialized farms and to the state trade in Georgia. Georgian state farms developed production until the plantings covered 6,400 hectares in 1969. But official estimates of consumer demand were too small and the demand was not fully satisfied. Yet, state and cooperative procurement agencies were unable to bring the total socialized output of bay leaves to the market. The result is that private production and trade continue, at a smaller scale. Simultaneously, however, many producers, both private and socialized, wish to reduce their output because of marketing difficulties [452, 12 September 1969]. Bay leaves are a special and not a very important product. But planning authorities themselves did not wish to leave this product to the private sector. They included it in their plans, and they failed.

Partial failures of planned supplies of more important products also occur. At least through 1964, workers in the important industrial province of Sverdlovsk "experienced many difficulties during seasonal declines in the supply of farm products, and particularly of milk and eggs" [452, 30 August 1966]. In neighboring Siberia, 70 percent of the milk delivered to and marketed by the state at that time was processed into butter. In the USSR as a whole, only 40 percent of the milk is processed into butter or cheese. Even if we recall that Siberia was famous for its butter production before World War I, it is still possible to conclude that the supply of fresh milk there would be insufficient unless supplemented by the output of the private sector.

Special problems arise in the production and the marketing of fruit, marketing not coordinated through the usual planning channels.[28] State procurement agencies buy only a small part of the output, and the amounts they purchase are earmarked almost exclusively for the processing industry [403, 50]. In 1966, the Ministry of Trade planned to procure only 342 thousand tons of fruit for sale to the population. This came to less than three kilograms per head of the urban population on an annual basis.

---

[28] For a good account of production, pricing, and marketing procedures and difficulties with fruit in the public sector of the Ukraine, see I. Kravchenko, "Nekotorye voprosy proizvodstva i sbyta fruktov i vinograda" [437, no. 6 (1971), 26–33].

The procurement target for 1967 was reduced to 294 thousand tons, although fruit output rose by 1 million tons and the urban population increased by 3.3 million. There are no plans to sell fruit to consumers through state retail outlets in some southern union republics. In such cases, the "population relies only on the market. It is not accidental that fruit seldom appears in stores located in the producing regions and that it is expensive on the market." Consumer cooperatives "also establish for themselves the smallest possible plan for the procurement of fruit, berries and grapes." These are almost never procured from the private sector; consequently "many inhabitants of the southern regions transport their output over long distances for the purpose of marketing" [403, 50–51].

As a result of a bountiful harvest in the summers of 1964 and 1965, there was an oversupply of plums and other fruit in the western Ukrainian oblast of Khmel'nitskii. There were no buyers, not only for the fresh fruit but also for dried plums and other dried fruit. After being subjected to press criticism, the leadership of consumer cooperatives introduced an energetic seven-point program for the purchase and the distribution of dried fruit. (No attempts were made to handle the necessarily more difficult distribution of fresh fruit; this was apparently given up as a lost cause.) But this plan did not help much, if at all. In the spring of 1966, the same newspaper received a letter from the same individuals (including kolkhozniks producing fruit privately) who had written a year earlier. Their complaints were identical [452, 9 July 1965; 452, 22 March 1966].

Procurement organizations again faced a flood of fruit in the fall of 1966, and they were again helpless or indifferent. Kolkhozes and sovkhozes with fruit orchards suffered as much in these conditions as did private subsidiary farms. This affected not only individual areas but many provinces in European Russia, in the Ukraine, and in Belorussia.

All this could be better understood if there was an oversupply of fruit or plums in the entire country. This was not the case, and the newspaper added the texts of letters received in the Khmel'nitskii oblast from other parts of the land. Someone wrote from the town of Vyborg near Leningrad [452, 22 March 1966]: "We learn that you have much fruit. For a whole year we had no fruit to contemplate. If you have surplus fruit, please send it to us, and we will send you [in exchange] cash, or food which you do not have, or industrial products."

Similar requests came from the Altai krai and the Iaroslavl' oblast, and a woman wrote from a sovkhoz in the Orenburg oblast: "When the opportunity arises, you could also send us some fresh [plums or other fruit], because I have children. They have not eaten apples to their hearts' content since they were little."

Similar shortages prevailed in the New Land sovkhozes in Kazakhstan [399, 210]. There were shortages of fruit and vegetables in 1965 even in Moscow and Leningrad: at times they also prevailed on the markets [443, 10 February 1966]. In the fall of 1968, and similarly in 1970, the situation in Moscow was described in these words: "Although fruit and vegetables rot in large quantities in warehouses at the respective procurement points, the shelves of the stores are not filled with those products" [452, 18 September 1968; 452, 27 September 1970].

A bountiful harvest of fruit or vegetables creates marketing difficulties, but this happened in several consecutive years. We can only add that the communist media always maintained that such phenomena are typical of capitalism and could not occur in the planned socialist economy. The kind of unproductive organizational confusion that operates within the framework of such a "planned economy" with respect to the supplies of fruit and vegetables for the cities was made abundantly clear by three high employees of Soviet ministries [452, 28 September 1966].

Procurement of fruit and vegetables in the Georgian SSR has been centralized in a single administration since the end of 1964, and the same organizational structure has been suggested for the entire country [53, 16]. But it is questionable whether this would resolve all the difficulties. The heart of the matter is this: farms are obliged by contract to deliver fixed quantities of fruit, vegetables, and potatoes to the procurement organizations. But in general—and contrary to the prevailing assertions—the latter are not always bound to accept the delivered output, and especially that part which exceeds the amount contracted for. The system of contract deliveries has been set up in a heterogeneous and contradictory manner; it leaves many ways out for the procurement organizations [227, passim]. This system still operates today to the disadvantage of farm enterprises, and the latter must bear the greater part of marketing risks. In addition, procurement agencies often use their position of strength. They buy first grade products at second grade prices under the threat that nothing would be purchased otherwise [452, 25 July 1969]. "Problems of marketing vegetables and potatoes have become really chronic. And they increase more than proportionately with the rise in output" [452, 15 October 1968].

When marketing and sales of fresh fruit and vegetables do not function properly, one could—indeed, one should—find a way out through industrial processing and canning. This is described by a Soviet source [74, 62]:

It is generally known that state industry possessing a monopoly of the processing of farm products did not master its task; many products are destroyed year in and year out. According to annual reports of the kolkhozes, the latter fed 364 thousand tons of fruit and berries to animals in 1963. They thus incurred a loss of 120 million rubles. And this happens in a country that imports fruit! In addition, approximately 1.2 million tons of vegetables were allotted for grazing of livestock. This comes to 22 percent of the amount delivered to the state.

These figures do not include the substantial quantity of private fruit and vegetables, or the sovkhoz output of the same products, for which no buyers could be found in the public sector. Since 1966 the establishment of processing plants in the kolkhozes and sovkhozes has been advocated, but the quantitative achievements remain small.

The public sector of Soviet agriculture harvested 12 million tons of vegetables, melons, and pumpkins in 1964. Of these, 1.8 million (or 15 percent) were fed to animals as a result of marketing problems. In spite of a smaller harvest in 1965 (10.5 million tons), the situation remained virtually the same—1.3 million tons (or 13 percent of output) were fed to animals. A figure of 1.5 million tons was mentioned in this context for 1967.[29]

Marketing problems are also a bottleneck for vegetables, potatoes, and grapes, as well as other perishable products. These problems will become more pronounced as output continues to rise [373, 217].

State and cooperative procurement organizations enjoy a virtual monopoly in local marketing, because they are assigned to specific areas. Farms located in those areas have no opportunity to sell directly to industrial firms, to hotels, or other catering establishments, except with great difficulty [142, 149]. At least until recently, only certain enterprises

[29] [449, 6 August 1966]; [142, 263]; [434, no. 8 (1969), 33]. The steadily repeated complaints, published year after year as late as 1969, indicate that marketing difficulties have really become chronic. Cf. [452, 15 October 1968]. Among the selected sources on this topic the reader may wish to consult are [449, 21 July 1965]; [449, 28 July 1967]; [452, 25 May 1967, 17 September 1967, 10 September 1968, 24 July 1969, 5 August 1969, 12 and 14 September 1971]; [434, no. 32 (1969), 18]; and [443, no. 19 (1969), 12].

were not subject to this rule. These were enterprises for which direct delivery from a farm was foreseen in the economic plan. There were not many of these, and the kolkhoz market remained the only alternative for most producers. Ukrainian kolkhozes sold 40 percent of their fruit crop on the kolkhoz markets. But nearby markets are not generally capable of handling large quantities, and transportation difficulties impede marketing at more distant markets. The shortcomings of the transportation system also hinder marketing of fresh fruit and vegetables because of the size of the country [*419*, passim; *452*, 12 August 1969]. The average rate of speed for Soviet freight trains carrying easily perishable fruit and vegetables was only eleven kilometers an hour in 1966 [*452*, 28 September 1966]! There is also a shortage of refrigerated cars and of freight cars designed to maintain a given temperature. The marketing of produce from private orchards is even more difficult [*143*, 16; *452*, 11 August 1968].

In spite of all the problems, the free market could offer at least a partial alternative marketing channel to the kolkhozes and sovkhozes as well as to private producers. But it was and is hampered in the performance of its functions. Market conditions in various parts of the country differ in an unnecessary and an absurd manner.[30] Thus, fruit was rather cheap in the market of the Georgian town of Poti in the fall of 1965, but potatoes and cabbage (which were brought from the Ukraine and from Russia where there is usually an oversupply every fall) sold for 0.30 to 0.50 ruble per kilogram. Although there was an oversupply of watermelons one hundred miles away, watermelons were expensive in Poti, selling for 0.40 ruble per kilogram [*130*, 37].

Kolkhoz markets are also important on a regional and at times even a national scale. But the scope of their activity is too restricted to allow them to function as a truly regional adjustment and compensating mechanism [*168*, 70, 126, 240]. They play a considerably greater part in supplying the Ukrainian population than for the USSR as a whole. The radius of market influence is really great here. About 40 percent of products brought to the markets of the industrial oblast of Donetsk originated in the other oblasts, particularly those of Kursk, Orel, and Belgorod [*135*, 71]. The share of supplies obtained by the Ukrainian workers and employees through the collective farm market in 1958 was as follows:[31]

---

[30] Cf. [*157*, 328, 331] and [*168*, 209–216].

[31] V. A. Shpiliuk, *Tseny kolkhoznoi torgovli i deistvie zakona stoimosti*, Avtoreferat dissertatsii (Moscow: 1961), p. 5, cited after [*155*, 31] and [*168*, 54, 69–70].

Product	Percent
Meat	29.8
Milk and milk products	16.5
Potatoes	55
Vegetables, melons	42.5
Fruit	71.7
Eggs	55.6

From 1959 through 1961, the markets in fifty-three large Ukrainian towns handled more potatoes regularly than were marketed by the wholesale trade organization of the Ukrainian Ministry of Trade for the entire republic.[32] The situation differed even more markedly from one city to another. For example, only 14 percent of the meat and meat products sold at retail in Kiev were marketed on the free markets. The corresponding figures in other Ukrainian cities were: Khar'kov—20.2 percent, Dnepropetrovsk—32.6 percent, and L'vov—37.2 percent (here and elsewhere we refer only to the organized markets). In smaller towns, these percentages would have been been greater still. For eggs, the corresponding percentages of all retail sales were: Kiev—15.1, Khar'kov—57.4, Dnepropetrovsk—65.5, and L'vov—80.9.[33] In 1968, the share of market purchases in total expenditures of workers and employees in the Ukraine had dropped, mainly as a result of much larger supplies through socialized trade. It came to 15 percent for meat, 37 percent for eggs, and 4 percent for milk and milk products [386, 68].

In per capita terms, purchases on kolkhoz markets are greatest in the largest cities [274, 65], because the proportion of families with private gardens or private animal holdings is not as great in the large cities as it is in smaller towns.

---

[32] [225, 287]. An unknown, additional amount of potatoes is shipped directly to the state and cooperative retail trade. On the other hand, the comparison also ignores the kolkhoz markets in the small and middle-size towns in the Ukraine, so that in the end the results of a fuller comparison should be even more favorable for the kolkhoz trade. At the beginning of the 1960s, sales of potatoes at the kolkhoz market also exceeded retail sales in the state network of East Siberia; from the total per capita consumption of potatoes, only 12.7 kilograms were supplied through state retail stores, and 16.7 kilograms were bought on the kolkhoz markets. The rest came from private production of consumers and from distributions in kind of the kolkhozes. Cf. [380, 127].

[33] [225, 326]. A large number of similar examples for other cities and products in the years from 1955 to 1959 is given in [155, 29–32]. Some of those percentages exceed those cited in the text here.

The differences are noticeable even in a small, local environment. The nearness of the city means easy marketing for products of household and subsidiary farms. It also means specialization for the market. This is more pronounced among private producers than among the kolkhozes or sovkhozes, and private producers specialized at a much earlier date. Products such as vegetables and fruits require particular care in the field as well as in transport and trade. In all these activities, the private producers are way ahead of the unwieldy organizations of the kolkhozes, sovkhozes, and trade agencies. Neither the plan quota nor the procurement price contain meaningful incentives for quality production or for early delivery of the product. At any rate, the kolkhozes and sovkhozes bring primarily the cheap, mass vegetables to the market, even in such climatically favored areas as the Abkhaz ASSR. The private producer, on the other hand, supplies the more refined vegetables for which there is greater demand.[34]

Free market prices are not as much influenced by market supply and its seasonal fluctuations as they are by the scarcity relationships in the state and cooperative retail trade [*168*, 47, 228–232; cf. p. 144 f. above]. If the supply in this trade is sufficient, or even moderately so, the prices on the markets fall. But the opposite also holds true.

Anyone who has had an opportunity to compare displays in Soviet food stores with those on the kolkhoz markets can testify to the quality differentials of fruit and vegetables. The same applies to potatoes:[35]

It is advantageous for the consumer to pay higher prices on the kolkhoz markets but to purchase choice potatoes [there]. The individual gardeners and also some kolkhozes [who also sell on the market] take advantage precisely of the phenomenon. They give more care to the choice of planting material and to fertilizing. They sort the potatoes carefully for delivery to the market, and they sell them at prices which are twice as high as those in state retail trade. They always find more than enough buyers.

Very recently, the contrast was again depicted in the following terms [*437*, no. 7 (1970), 48]:

At present [1970], the consumer has every reason to show his discontent with the potatoes offered by the state trade system—in many cases it is small, affected with ring rot and other fungus diseases, and of inferior taste.

[34] [*76*, 110–111]; [*339a*, 74]; [*452*, 9 August 1968 and 19 August 1969]; [*393*, passim]; [*440*, 28 February 1968]; [*173*, 65]; [*443*, 29 June and 23 November 1965]
[35] [*225*, 286]; cf. [*459*, 3 July 1967]; [*452*, 9 August 1969]; [*281*, 173].

Khrushchev once expressed the same thought with bitterness [*179*, IV, 238]: "Choice potatoes are on the market; although they are cheap in the stores, a man has at times no desire to pay [good] money for a rotten thing." Fresh milk is rarely available in the stores; pasteurized milk is found often, but it is more expensive than fresh milk on the market.[36] Even if milk is available in the stores, the free market prices can still exceed state retail prices because of the large demand.

A quality differential of another type appears for meat. Stores are often supplied with frozen meat which finds little approval among consumers,[37] but which sells at almost the same prices as fresh meat. Other quality differentials manifest themselves when there is no longer a great shortage of meat: "The inhabitants of Briansk, Klintsov, Novozybkov, and other towns [Briansk oblast, summer of 1966] cannot complain about the level of stocks in the [state] meat stores. There is enough there. But the quality of the merchandise produces numerous complaints and curses from the buyers. Demand is thus small in the [state] stores" [*452*, 28 August 1966]. This probably causes a corresponding rise in demand on the kolkhoz markets.

By way of summary judgment, G. I. Shmelev notes [*339*, 33; see also *128*, 79]: "The output of crops in the subsidiary farms is in general of better quality than that of kolkhozes and sovkhozes. As a result, it is sold at prices which exceed state retail prices."

[36] 0.28 ruble per liter (plus an additional bottle deposit of 0.20 ruble). I observed this price in several localities during the summers of 1962 and 1963. For Latvia, the retail price for really fresh milk was given as 0.26 ruble per liter in 1968; see [*458*, 30 May 1968] as cited in [*439*, 27–28 October 1968]. In 1963, the price for fresh milk on the kolkhoz markets was 0.16 to 0.17 ruble per liter on the average; cf. [*250*, 288] (Morozov's table heading refers to the year 1961, but the text on p. 289 makes it clear that this must be a typesetting error and that the data refer to the year 1963). In the large cities—where on the whole one can only buy pasteurized bottled milk—the price on the kolkhoz markets is generally around 0.20 ruble per liter, though at times it is higher. Local and seasonal price variations on the countryside may be very large: a price of 0.30 ruble per liter (3 old rubles) was given for a central Russian village in [*251*, 46]. The state retail prices for fresh milk ranging from 0.28 to 0.30 ruble per liter apply to milk with butterfat content of only 2.5 percent; for milk with butterfat content of 3 percent, those prices should be recalculated to nearly 0.40 ruble per liter. See [*69*, 138]. This factor too must be taken into account when comparisons between the state retail and the market prices for milk are made.

[37] This also holds true for Moscow. See [*468*, 1968] as cited by Radio Svoboda (Munich), CIO 221/68. The same applied to fish in the port city of Poti, where the state retail stores offered no fresh fish [*130*, 37]. Tiukov and Lokshin argued that the decrease in the supply of frozen meat and hence a better opportunity for storage and transportation of fresh meat were urgently necessary [*382*, 70].

There is not only less milk and meat and fewer potatoes and vegetables in the eastern regions (Siberia and the Far East) than in Central Russia; the goods sold in the state stores are usually available only in dried or canned form. Prices on the kolkhoz markets are correspondingly higher. In East Siberia during the middle 1960s, kolkhoz market prices exceeded market prices of North Caucasian markets by 130 percent for fruit and berries, 79 percent for vegetables, and 25 percent for meat and lard.[38] "In the northern and eastern parts of the country, where . . . [fruit and vegetables] are not produced, their market prices are exceedingly high. Trade organizations and kolkhozes still do not make enough of an effort to deliver fruit and vegetables to the outlying and disadvantaged parts of the country. Not infrequently, middlemen—speculators—take advantage of this situation" [378, 63].

It is at this stage that the shortcomings of the distribution system and the quality problem overlap. It is immaterial for the functioning of the market whether the price differential is caused by the particularly good quality of the private output or the particularly poor quality of socialized output. It is also immaterial whether the relevant scarcities affect the entire product group or only the items of the best quality. As long as such differentials exist, the market continues to offer a preferred source of income for individual producers [168, 261].

THE ORIENTATION OF PRIVATE PRODUCTION: CONSUMPTION OR THE MARKET?

Quality differentials, insufficient supplies in state and cooperative stores, local differences in the supply and in prices of individual foods—all these factors exert a combined impact on the market. This impact makes the market an important element in supplying the Soviet population and an important source of income for private producers, in spite of the narrow framework within which it is forced to operate. Thus the importance of the market is much greater than is indicated by its share in overall market output (which includes state procurements). According to Soviet statistics, the free market's share in overall market output during the period from 1958 to 1963 was steadily around 15 percent. The corresponding shares for crops and animal products came to about 10 and 20 percent respectively; all these shares are supposed to have declined

[38] [380, 120-121]. For a more detailed discussion of the differences in the supply and in market conditions between Siberia and Central Russia, see [154, 65-69].

since 1964 [*168*, 261]. Three-quarters of kolkhoznik families' incomes from marketing private produce are derived from free market sales [*56a*, 126]. This is more than the share in physical volume of sales (see Table 27, column for 1967) and is indicative of the better quality and/or greater scarcity of products offered there and of the resulting price differential.

Table 25 shows the share of private marketings in total market output of the USSR for individual products. Although this share has been declining, it is not inconsequential for those products which are produced primarily in the private sector.

TABLE 25. SHARE OF PRIVATE MARKET OUTPUT IN TOTAL SOVIET MARKET OUTPUT OF SOME AGRICULTURAL PRODUCTS, 1950–1969[a]
(percent)

Year	Potatoes	Vegetables	Meat and Fat	Milk	Eggs	Wool
1950	61	24	47	50	74	16
1953	65	23	27	37	69	11
1955	55	14	27	28	71	8
1958	49	15	27	16	61	11
1959	52	17	24	12	56	11
1960	51	14	20	10	54	15
1961	50	15	20	10	51	15
1962	56	14	23	10	48	16
1963	50	13	22	9	45	14
1964	46	11	20	8	42	15
1965	45	12	17	7	36	14
1966	41	13	21	6	33	15
1967	39	12	20	5	29	15
1968	41	13	19	4	24	14
1969	43	12	15	4	20	15

[a] Excluding intrarural marketings.

SOURCES: 1953, 1959–1961, [*9*, 232]; 1955, [*6*, 371]; 1961–1962, [*11*, 254]; 1958, 1963–1964, [*12*, 267]; 1965–1967, [*14*, 323]; 1968–1969, [*14a*, 297].

Before 1953, the kolkhoznik was under inordinately heavy pressure to sell as much of his output as possible on the market. Otherwise he would not be able to pay the high agricultural tax, the rates of which were reduced beginning in 1953 [*179*, II, 89]. As Table 25 indicates, the share of the private sector in marketings of all products except wool has declined steadily [for 1950, see *56a*, 107]. Indeed, the rate of decline of the private sector's share in marketings is twice as great as the rate of decline of the private sector's share in output (cf. Table 8). Yet the absolute volume of private produce sold in the extrarural kolkhoz markets in 1967 still amounted to 4.8 million tons of potatoes, 900,000 tons of vegetables, 700,000 tons of meat, 700,000 tons of milk, and 2.4 billion eggs [56a, 107].

Soviet sources characterize private production as production of a "semisubsistence" nature [128, 31]. Kerblay holds correctly that the volume and the structure of private output are not determined primarily by the market demand or by the structure of market prices, but chiefly by the demand for food by the producers themselves. This is true where the access of private producers to the market is limited [168, 299–303]. A Soviet writer declared in 1968: "But given the difficulties connected with marketings, many kolkhozniks are not interested in producing for the market" [170, 72]. This seemingly confirms the view, advanced by such writers as V. G. Venzher and V. A. Morozov, that the output of the private sector is primarily oriented toward the consumption of the producers. "One could assume that the monetization of [kolkhozniks'] incomes from the socialized sector had to lead to the reduction of the market orientation and to the increase in the consumption orientation of the subsidiary plots of the kolkhozniks" [250, 182]. But this was not true, except possibly from 1959 to 1960.

One cannot talk of an increase in the consumption orientation of private production as a whole. There was no absolute decline in the volume of market sales, even though the share of the kolkhoz market in total market output did decline. This decline is the consequence of a rapid increase in the volume of marketings through state procurements by kolkhozes and sovkhozes. The marketed share of the private output did not change noticeably (see Table 27). As late as 1961, Dorosh described subsidiary farming of the kolkhozniks as "commodity production" [440, 8 October 1961]. Only in the light of this statement can we make sense of the following statement, originally made in 1965 by Z. A. Zaionchkovskaia: "The considerable distance from major urban centers and the resulting lack of a developed market is negatively reflected in the welfare of the local rural population, which cannot sell the surplus output of their subsidiary plots on local markets" [308, 198]. One may well speak of a negative influence when the absence of market outlets depresses incomes or when the unavailability of goods in village stores (or the nonexistence of such stores) forces private agricultural production into activities not undertaken in areas with better market facilities.

As long as private production yields produce that is better, or cheaper, or both than that of the public sector (in special labor-intensive branches, such as animal production, vegetables, fruit), the very existence of the private sector is not, or is only marginally, affected by the availability or unavailability of market outlets. Without these, it rests basically on local consumer demand (which is, apart from the producers themselves, that of the intrarural market, a subject I discuss in the last section of this chapter) and on the availability of land and labor. But where extrarural market outlets are given, these create a *raison d'être* for the private sector beyond better or cheaper subsistence. Given a very restricted supply of basic resources (upper limits for private land use and livestock holding) and given ample labor resources (which is not any more the case in all parts of the country, but generally in the south and in suburban areas) market outlets influence, above all, the direction and degree of the private productive effort, that is, the labor input and the product mix. In other words: Market orientation will be mirrored in the type and degree of labor-intensive specialization.

The market orientation—beyond the basic subsistence function—of the private sector thus is a question of circumstances, not of principle. The circumstances are given in the Soviet Union of today: in this rapidly urbanizing society, urban demand for food is growing quantitatively and diversifying qualitatively. The public sector, although improving its performance, has until now not been able to cope with the increasing requirements. (At least so we are told over and over again by Soviet leaders and press media and can see with our own eyes when we are in the country.) Transportation facilities also exert influence and are improving, though too slowly. Thus, the circumstances favor market orientation beyond the immediate vicinity of towns and cities. The potential is becoming a reality in more and wider areas of former subsistence orientation of the private sector. Soviet private producers seem quick to grasp the changing situation. Their specialization, often mentioned in publications (for recent examples, see [*56a*, 99] and [*443*, no. 43, 1970, 10]), is a sure indicator. One of the best Soviet authorities on the subject, G. I. Shmelev, has the following to say [*339a*, 80, 137-138]:

The commodity character [that is, market orientation] of the personal subsidiary farm shows itself, most of all, in raions which are near . . . market outlets for its produce. In the densely populated raions of the Central Black Earth region, which are near to the big industrial centers [still more than a hundred miles away], in areas of the North Caucasus region where there is a great number of towns, a dense network of railways and automobile roads, and a zone of health resorts with great food commodity demand—especially in such raions the commodity character of the personal subsidiary farm is considerably more pronounced than, for instance, in the vast and sparsely populated rural raions of Siberia. Here, product specialization is developed to a higher degree. A number of villages specialize in the production of garlic and onion, others in growing cucumbers . . . In some villages, berries, tomatoes, Bulgarian peppers, grapes, apples, and so on, are the main marketed produce. Part of the personal subsidiary farms, mainly in suburban areas, specialize in growing flower and vegetable seeds and seedlings.

In view of the developed specialization of the personal subsidiary farms, certain kinds of basic agricultural produce for own consumption, such as potatoes or fruit, are bought by rural inhabitants from state retail shops, at the urban kolkhoz markets, or in the intrarural market. [That is, these people prefer to buy some of their food, because they use their plots for other, marketable production.] . . .

In recent years in certain southern raions, the high level of prices for nuts, combined with the fact that these are less perishable, has led to the partial displacement of fruit by walnuts, hazelnuts, almonds, and other nuts. Because of changes in demand, farms with market orientation have shifted their production from lard to bacon, from early to late ripening apples, and in favor of berries and flowers. In some villages, where the personal plots are strictly specialized on but one kind of commodity, this specialization has changed in recent years under the influence of the market. . . . In some villages such a change in specialization has occurred repeatedly under the influence of changing demand or of increasing local market supply and [subsequently] falling prices.

Ia. Liniichuk contends that those who deny the commercial nature of private subsidiary farms do, in fact, encroach upon the activities of these farms [214a, 51]. One of the best authorities on Soviet agricultural prices and the farm market, I. I. Lukinov, states: "It is an inexcusable error to assume that personal plots of the kolkhozniks and of other individual producers are on the whole oriented toward [personal] consumption and that they play no essential role in the money-commodity relations between the village and the city" [225, 25].

Inexcusable errors of this type are not likely to be made by such competent economists as Venzher and Morozov. We can assume that their views on the consumption orientation of the private sector were a concession to the official attitudes, and that they were designed to protect the market from further restrictions. This interpretation is further strengthened when we compare their cited views with the following statement, published in an official textbook during the Khrushchev era: "The orientation of personal subsidiary plots toward the market conflicts with their [very] nature as subsidiary plots." [39] Quantitative evidence on these problems is presented in Tables 26 and 27. These tables are not easy to interpret, but we have no other data on this important subject. In particular, the tables do not contain data on fruit, a very important product.

As defined in Tables 26 and 27, market output refers only to extrarural marketings; intrarural marketings must be shown with consumption of producers. This necessarily distorts the indicated trends in the consumption by producers, because the volume of intrarural marketings increased in recent years (see below).

It will be recalled that the kolkhoz market is not the only marketing channel open to the private sector. A large part of its output is sold more or less voluntarily to state and cooperative procurement agencies. We should also note that almost half of all potatoes shown in Table 26 as "Consumed by Producers" are fed to livestock. This is also true for slightly more than half of the corresponding figures for vegetables and of approximately one-tenth of those for milk [*139*, 383].

It is also impossible to measure how much of the output delivered to the state by the kolkhozes and sovkhozes represents private output (particularly milk) produced in the private sector and purchased by the large socialized farms who then sell or deliver it to the state (cf. below, pp. 235 ff.). Such amounts are treated statistically as part of the intrarural turnover, and are included in Table 26 as "consumption by producers."

In spite of these qualifications, the year 1958 clearly was a turning point. With the exception of milk and eggs, the share of marketings in private output ceased to decline; in some instances it began to rise again (cf. Table 27). The absolute volume of consumption by producers (which, to repeat, includes feed and intrarural sales) has increased in recent years. Part of the explanation may lie in the greater money incomes from work in the public sector of agriculture: People less in need of money may feel less inclined to sell. G. Radov considers this an important factor [*443*, no. 43 (1971), 10].

As noted earlier, feed accounts for about half of the consumption of potatoes by producers. The rapid rise in producers' consumption accompanied by a decline in pig herds is therefore remarkable. One explanation is that the private production of pork did not decline as much as the pig numbers did (the reasons for this interpretation are given on p. 334 be-

---

[39] *Kurs politicheskoi ekonomii*, part II (Moscow: 1963), p. 98, as cited by Shmelev in [*339*, 27].

TABLE 26. TOTAL PRIVATE OUTPUT, CONSUMPTION BY PRODUCERS AND PRIVATE MARKET OUTPUT, SELECTED FARM PRODUCTS, 1953–1969

Product and Type of Output	1953	1955	1958	1960	1962	1963	1964	1965	1966	1967	1968	1969
A. POTATOES (million tons)												
1. Total private output	52.3[b]	...	57.1	53.1	48.8	47.4	56.2	55.9	56.3	60.2	63.5	61.5
2. Consumption by producers including intrarural marketings	44.4	...	50.2	46.1	42.2	41.0	48.9	48.8	50.2	53.2	55.7	55.4
3. Private market output[a]	7.9	...	6.9	7.0	6.4	6.4	7.3	7.1	6.2	7.0	7.8	7.4
B. VEGETABLES (million tons)												
1. Total private output	5.5	...	6.7	7.3	6.7	6.2	7.6	7.2	7.5	8.2	7.8	7.3
2. Consumption by producers including intrarural marketings	4.3	...	5.6	6.2	5.5	5.1	6.5	6.0	6.1	6.7	6.3	5.9
3. Private market output[a]	1.2	...	1.1	1.1	1.2	1.1	1.1	1.2	1.4	1.5	1.5	1.4
C. MEAT AND FAT, SLAUGHTERED WEIGHT (million tons)												
1. Total private output	3.0	3.3	4.0	3.6	4.2	4.3	3.5	4.0	4.4	4.6	4.4	4.2
2. Consumption by producers including intrarural marketings	2.2	2.3	2.7	2.4	2.7	2.7	2.3	2.8	2.8	2.9	2.7	2.9
3. Private market output[a]	0.8•	1.0	1.3	1.2	1.5	1.6	1.2	1.2	1.6	1.7	1.7	1.3
D. MILK (million tons)												
1. Total private output	24.4	26.0	31.1	29.1	28.7	27.5	27.0	28.7	30.2	31.1	31.3	30.3
2. Consumption by producers including intrarural marketings	19.3	21.2	27.0	26.2	25.4	24.5	24.3	25.8	27.7	28.9	29.0	28.5
3. Private market output[a]	5.1	4.8	4.1[d]	2.9	3.2	2.8	2.7	2.9	2.5	2.2	2.3	1.8
E. EGGS (billion)												
1. Total private output	13.6	16.2	19.6	22.1	23.0	21.4	19.7	19.6	20.9	21.3	21.3	20.9

2. Consumption by producers including intrarural marketings[a]	9.6	11.6	14.7	16.4	17.1	16.1	14.9	14.6	15.8	16.4	16.8	17.0
3. Private market output[a]	4.0	4.6	4.9	5.7	5.9	5.3	4.8	5.0	5.1	4.9	4.5	3.9
F. WOOL (thousand tons)												
1. Total private output	36	49	69	81	82	79	71	73	76	79	83	83
2. Consumption by producers including intrarural marketings[a]	13	32	38	33	28	32	24	27	24	24	25	29
3. Private market output[a]	22[e]	17	31	48	54	48	47	46	52	55	58	54

[a] Extrarural marketings only. [b] In order to preserve the consistency of the calculation and thus the comparability of the figures, we ignored the data available in [16, 238, 243, 333–337], including those for 1959 which must be viewed as preliminary in any case. For the same reason Shmelev's [339, 62] and Belianov's [56a, 177–180] data are ignored. Nevertheless, we also indicate in the following notes an alternative figure supplied by [16], but only for those cases where the difference between the two figures was more significant. In general, the small magnitude of the differentials supports the results of our calculations. Thus, the alternative figure for potatoes in 1953 is 52.1 million tons. [c] The alternative figure is 0.9 million tons (see note b). [d] The alternative figure is 3.7 million tons (cf. note b). [e] The alternative figure is 23 thousand tons (cf. note b).

SOURCES: Calculated from data in Soviet statistical abstracts, listed in [416, 98] for 1953 through 1964. Consumption by producers obtained as residual of total private output after deduction of marketings. Minor discrepancies are due to rounding. Gross private output of livestock products in 1965–1969 was obtained by subtracting kolkhoz and state farm gross outputs from total Soviet gross output put of livestock products in 1965–1969 was obtained by subtracting kolkhoz and state farm gross outputs from total Soviet gross output as given in [144, 373]. Gross private output of potatoes and vegetables obtained by applying the appropriate percentage from Table 8 to total Soviet outputs of these crops [144, 340, 342]. Private market output obtained from percentages shown in Table 25 and data on total Soviet market output [144, 296].

163

TABLE 27. SHARE OF PRIVATE MARKET OUTPUT IN TOTAL PRIVATE OUTPUT
OF SELECTED FARM PRODUCTS, 1953–1969

(percent)

Product	1953	1955	1958	1960	1962	1963	1964	1965	1966	1967[a]	1968	1969
Potatoes	15	...	12	13	13	13	13	13	11	12(8)	12	12
Vegetables	11	...	16	14	18	18	15	16	18	18(11)	19	19
Meat and fat, slaughtered weight	27[b]	29	32	33	37	37	33	30	37	37(16)	39	31
Milk	21	19	13[c]	10	11	10	10	10	8	7(2)	7	6
Eggs	29	28	25	26	26	25	24	26	24	23(11)	21	19
Wool	61[d]	35	44	59	66	60	67	63	68	70(...)	70	65

[a] The figure in parentheses indicates the percentage in the free kolkhoz market. [b] An alternative figure is 29 percent (see Table 26, notes b and c). [c] An alternative figure is 12 percent (see Table 26, notes b and d). [d] An alternative figure is 64 percent (see Table 26, notes b and e).

SOURCES: Calculated from data in Table 26, except for free kolkhoz marketings in 1967, which are from [56a, 107].

low). Another possible explanation is that part of the increase in the consumption of producers shown in Table 26 actually represents the increase in intrarural turnover, and particularly the purchases by the kolkhozes and sovkhozes from private producers, purchases then delivered—partly or entirely—to the state as the output of socialized farms.

Marketings of vegetables are obviously a function of the weather conditions in any given year. The amount marketed was amazingly constant until 1963. Since then, it has increased, partly in response to rising demand on the markets or through commission trade, and partly as a result of an increased market supply produced in the gardens of the urban population.

The decline in producers' consumption of wool (except for 1969) should be related to the rapid decline of home processing. The volume of wool sold to state procurement agencies rose markedly, especially after the middle 1950s. At the same time, the rural population bought larger quantities of woolen textiles and underwear in village stores or in nearby cities. As noted earlier, raw wool may not be sold on the markets, but private sales of processed wool and wool products are important in certain areas (cf. above, p. 138, n. 18, and [54, 396]).

Producers' consumption of meat, milk, and eggs has clearly been rising; there was a brief interruption in the last years of Khrushchev's administration, but the upward trend resumed again in 1965. The sharp decline in the consumption of meat during 1964 reflects not only the harvest failure of 1963 but also the restocking of herds—which necessarily reduced slaughterings—after Khrushchev's removal. These developments since 1958 were caused by the joint impact of several factors. A rapid increase in urban population, combined with a decline in rural population, tends to produce an increased incentive to sell farm products. Both phenomena occurred in the Soviet Union and were further strengthened by the rise of market prices (until 1964 and presumably again since 1966, when no more indices were published) and by the availability of purchasing power in the hands of households. On the basis of calculations using different data, Morozov, in 1965, speaks of "an increase in the market orientation of subsidiary plots" after 1958 [250, 184]. He saw as the cause the insufficient remuneration for work on the kolkhozes which raised the importance of income from sales of private output. But he added a further and an important point. To the extent that income-in-kind received by the kolkhozniks declined, or to the extent that the former kolkhozniks on farms that had been converted to sovkhozes received almost no income-in-kind, they were forced to purchase on the market (or in the stores) those products—primarily feed—which they formerly received from the farm. For this they needed cash which could be obtained, in part, by selling other output produced on their plots. In 1963, for example, 26 percent of all sales on the extravillage markets in the RSFSR represented purchases by the kolkhozniks [*380*, 125; see also below, p. 183].

During the last years of Khrushchev's term in office, Soviet agricultural policy achieved the opposite of its goals. Restrictions on the private sector and on the kolkhoz market, implemented through administrative measures, the increased pull of the market resulting from these restrictions, and continued urbanization increased—rather than reduced—the market orientation of private producers.

The share of the public sector in Soviet market output did rise to 84 percent in the period from 1953 to 1958, but it then stagnated at that level for the next five years [*9*, 232; *12*, 267]. It rose again to 87 percent in 1964, largely as a result of the good harvest. It then remained constant through 1967 and rose by one percentage point in 1968 [*14*, 323]. Yet, the volume of private sales did not decline.

Venzher stated, in accordance with other Soviet writers (see p. 56 f. above), that 20 percent of privately produced products take the form of "commodities" [*396*, 51; *180*, 94]. He used this figure to substantiate his view that private subsidiary farming is primarily consumption oriented. N. P. Voloshin declared: "The sale of a part of output of private subsidiary plots does not alter its consumption character, inasmuch as the sale results in the satisfaction of personal needs. These could not have been satisfied by the socialized sector.[40] This is clearly correct in the most general terms. But it misses the essential point as far as one-fifth of output is concerned. That one-fifth is considerable enough to influence the nature of private production significantly. In relative terms, this is more than the middle and the poor peasants used to sell before collectivization as well as before the October Revolution, when the corresponding figures came to 11.2 and 14.7 percent [*214a*, 50]. And the bulk of the produce sold does appear on the relatively free market (in the form of "commodities"); as we have demonstrated, it plays a considerable role there. Sales on the market are a foreign element in the Marxist–Leninist planned

---

[40] [*404*, 47]. For a similar—understandable, but by no means indisputable—argument see [*331*, 177] and the more recent [*180*, 94].

economy, and any characterization of the private sector as a whole must take this into account. Liniichuk shows, "on the basis of concrete data, that the personal subsidiary plot, while retaining its consumption orientation, is also market oriented to a certain extent. [That extent] will increase in the future, particularly as a result of free purchases of farm products by the state at increased state prices" [*343*, 85].

Speaking of private agricultural activity of workers and employees, Nazarov handled the problem carefully: "An insignificant part [of their output] becomes a commodity. This is conclusive proof that private subsidiary farming exists primarily to satisfy personal requirements" [*256*, 69]. Some lines later, however, when dealing with the private plots of the kolkhozniks as well, Nazarov referred indirectly to their importance for the market:

Whoever raises cattle satisfies not only his personal needs in meat, milk, and fat, but also sells a certain part of his output to the urban population. It is natural that the liquidation of a large number of cattle in private ownership led to the worsening of supply for workers and employees.

As it turns out, the private sector is virtually the only supplier of farm products to the urban kolkhoz markets. This is shown by the following percentages, taken from Morozov [*250*, 180]. These figures show the share of output of personal plots in the total value of sales of farm products on urban markets (all products sold were valued at state retail prices):

Year	Percent
1950	87.7
1958	94.1
1960	94.7
1962	97.4
1963	97.2

These data are partly confirmed by corresponding figures for the share of Ukrainian kolkhozes in total market sales. This share came to 15.2 percent in 1950; thereafter it declined almost monotonously to 4.6 percent in 1963 and to 3.4 percent in 1965 [*214a*, 53].

Thus, the importance of the private sector as a source of supplies for the free market has not only been very large, but continued to increase, at least until 1965. At first glance, the figures just cited seem to conflict with the following percentages for the share of consumer cooperatives in the kolkhoz market trade: 1958—16.4; 1960—14.6; 1963—23.9; 1965—27.4; 1968—30.8 [*11, 657; 14, 654*]. The apparent contradiction is easily resolved when we recall that the cooperatives buy the products they ultimately sell on the free market primarily from the private sector, or they act as intermediaries for the private sector in the commission sales. Thus, although the private producers do not appear as sellers in the proportion indicated by Morozov, they do indeed produce the given percentages of output sold.

THE PUBLIC SECTOR ON THE FREE MARKET

The great majority of all retail stores located on the countryside are operated by Soviet consumer cooperatives. In 1954 and 1955, the cooperatives also undertook the important task of supplying farm products to the trade network of the cities. Thus, cooperative and retail stores now exist in towns, and the cooperatives are sellers of farm products on the kolkhoz markets. But the results of their activity were not impressive until 1957.[41]

The importance of the cooperatives increased when compulsory deliveries from subsidiary plots were abolished as of 1 January 1958. The Party Program of 1961 also spoke of further development and improvement of this function. Since 1959, consumer cooperatives have been allowed to purchase farm products in the villages at prices "formed on the spot," but not higher than the corresponding state retail prices. From 1961 on, cooperatives have been allowed to buy locally at prices mutually agreed upon with the sellers and to sell at urban market prices.[42]

Private sales to organizations other than procurement and cooperative agencies are negligible, judging from Ukrainian data for years before 1964 [*214a, 55*].

[41] See [*416*, nn. 177–180, Chap. IV] and the decisions of the Council of Ministers of the RSFSR dated 21 May 1954 ("On the Unsatisfactory Organization of Commission Trade in Farm Products") and 4 December 1953 ("On the State of Commission Trade in Farm Products"), reprinted in [*346*, IX, 409–411]. For a summary of the cooperative and commission trade on kolkhoz markets see [*168*, 368–378]. On rural consumer cooperatives in general and their buying as well as selling functions, see Henri Wronski, "Consumer Cooperatives in Rural Areas in the U.S.S.R.", *Agrarian Policies in Communist and Non-Communist Countries*, ed. W. A. Douglas Jackson (Seattle and London, University of Washington Press: 1971), 159–173, and the "Comment" by Nancy Nimitz, *ibid.*, 174–177.

[42] Cf. [*416*, nn. 184 and 185 to Chap. IV] and the decisions of the Council of Ministers of the RSFSR dated 20 November 1958, 11 March 1959, 4 June 1959, and 27 May 1961, as reprinted in [*346*, IX, 402–403, 406–408, 416].

The value of cooperative sales on the kolkhoz markets rose only slowly at first. The rate of increase accelerated first in 1962 and then again in 1966.[43] In 1962, only 69 percent of their sales on the free market involved products that were either bought from the kolkhozes and the kolkhozniks or accepted from them for sale on a commission basis [292, 51]. The value of cooperative turnover rose again after a decline in 1963, in spite of a decline in market prices. The increase in the physical volume of sales, which was noticeable by 1965, was not very pronounced, but the level of 1962 had not been reached by 1965. Consumer cooperatives have recently been called on to increase and intensify the scope of their activity in order to increase the quantities supplied in the various forms of trade, as well as to "free the kolkhozniks from the necessity of spending time and resources on travel to kolkhoz markets . . . and to give [them] an opportunity to use their labor more efficiently in the socialized sector."[44] A decision of the Council of Ministers of the RSFSR, dated 5 October 1967, which was devoted to problems of trade improvement in general, also contemplated a further promotion of cooperative trade [346, IX, 202].

The volume of cooperative sales on kolkhoz markets in 1965 amounted to [128, 82]: 277 thousand tons of vegetables; 200 thousand tons of potatoes; 171 thousand tons of meat; 52 thousand tons of fat and oils; 75 thousand tons of milk; and 394 million eggs.

The volume of cooperative procurement of farm products exceeds by far the volume of their sales on the market, because products procured by cooperatives are also sold in state and cooperative retail stores. Cooperative procurement plans account for almost one-half of all planned procurements of potatoes, one-third of planned procurements of vegetables, and about four-fifths of planned procurements of melons and pumpkins.[45]

The value of cooperative procurement for 1966, given as 5.2 billion

---

[43] 1957—700 million rubles [6, 708]; 1961—734 million rubles [8, 664]; 1962—1,400 million rubles [10, 564]; 1963—1,200 million rubles [11, 637]; 1964—1,274 million rubles, 1965—1,291 million rubles [12, 665]; 1967—1,529 million rubles, and 1968—1,701 million rubles [14, 654]. All figures are shown in terms of the new rubles. The so-called commission trade accounted for the greater part of these figures. See also [168, 370] and [247, 61, 63].

[44] [452, 12 September 1967]. Cf. [257, passim], where Nazarov also gives a summary account of the activity of, and the problems faced by, the consumer cooperatives.

[45] [468, no. 8 (1967)], as cited by Radio Svoboda, Munich, CIO 520/67.

rubles, included: 11.5 billion eggs, 380 thousand tons of wool; and a "large volume of hides, pelts and furs, mushrooms, nuts, honey and pharmaceutical herbs and other technical raw materials" [*434*, no. 29 (1967), 6–7]. But only a minor part of this came from the private sector. The activities of cooperatives in procuring mushrooms, berries, and nuts (which people gather in the woods) which are then sold—at least in part—on the markets, have been described as unsatisfactory [*452*, 6 August 1968].

Consumer cooperatives avoid the acceptance of easily perishable products where the marketing risk is considerable. As we have shown earlier (p. 168), the share of cooperatives in the market turnover is appreciable but by no means a dominant one.

There is no doubt that consumer cooperatives could give considerable assistance to the kolkhozniks or to sovkhoz workers when these producers are unable to obtain a day off from their large enterprises at times when labor is urgently needed on farms. They could also do so for those producers who are unable to reach the markets of large cities, as is true of producers residing in outlying villages [cf. *170*, 72; *128*, 81–82; *49*, 77]. While the producers themselves would receive somewhat lower prices than they could obtain in direct market sales, they would be spared the costs associated with the market trade. The loss of time, difficulties with transportation, and other markets costs are sometimes so large that the higher prices obtainable in direct trade and the opportunity to purchase industrial goods in town no longer offer sufficient compensation for all these inputs—which include inconvenience.

Indeed, it is also true that the cooperatives often face the same problems as the individual trader—shortages of transportation and storage space or difficulty in obtaining stalls at markets [*128*, 84; *434*, no. 37 (1965), 40; *443*, 23 November 1965]. Some local officials or organizations hinder or purposely interfere with the cooperative purchase of farm products in the villages. On the other hand, cooperatives often do not exert themselves sufficiently: They fulfill their purchase plans by buying goods on the very edge of the town from individuals coming to the market, or even right in front of the market gate. In such instances, the seller is able to drive the price close to the level that he himself could obtain in direct market trade.

Cooperative procurements are destined either for further processing or for sale. The planned procurements are of little interest in our context: it is the amounts procured over the planned target that are primarily sold on the kolkhoz market. In addition, cooperatives should also accept goods from producers for sale on a commission basis (which shifts to the producers the risks associated with marketing). But, to quote Morozov's view of 1962, "the output of the kolkhozniks is poorly marketed in commission trade" [247, 63]; commission trade mainly involves the output of the kolkhozes [214a, 46]. An inhabitant of Kiev stated at the end of 1965 that "the commission trade of the cooperatives is far from perfection" [442, 7 January 1966]. Commission sales from private sources at the Ukrainian kolkhoz markets came to 142.5 million rubles in 1958; they rose to 169.9 million rubles in 1966. The corresponding figures for direct free market sales by the kolkhozniks were 1.5 and 1.22 billion rubles respectively [214a, 54–55]. At the moment, cooperative commission trade appears to be a far more suitable substitute for direct trading of the kolkhozes than for that of private producers.

Since 1961, those activities of the cooperatives which are more than local in nature have also been restricted in ways similar to those applied to the kolkhozes and to individual private producers. There are "many restrictions which bind the hands of the employees of consumer cooperatives" [449, 6 August 1966]. But no general rules or regulations have been issued as yet [128, 83]. Individual representatives of cooperative branches have not generally been allowed to travel to other regions or republics to purchase farm products. This holds true even in many instances where an oversupply in one area occurs simultaneously with pronounced shortages in other regions. Cooperatives are thus unable to benefit from regional price differentials which are often exploited by individual private producers [128, 83]. They were not authorized to pay cash for their purchases, and this was given as one reason why "the rural population is not interested in selling their goods to the cooperatives" [250, 321; 128, 83–84]. A special type of barter operation was frequently established. For example, cooperative stores in the villages sold goods which were in great demand only to those individuals who in turn sold farm products (for example, a given number of eggs) to the cooperative. There were unofficial lists of conversion factors, establishing the value of allowable retail sales to rural people per unit of farm products sold to the cooperatives.[46] This method was apparently increasingly resorted to after the cooperatives were exorted to raise their share of the kolkhoz trade after 1965. Even mushrooms fell into this category of "tied exchange" [452, 4 September 1968].

[46] [256, 73]; Krokodil, 14 May 1966; [452, 20 August 1966]; and [218, 169].

The construction of a special cooperative market in Krasnodar remains an isolated instance. The project was afflicted by the very same difficulties which beset cooperative trade in general. Even in Krasnodar, a rich farm area, the cooperative market was unable to displace the ordinary, flourishing kolkhoz market.[47] Quite recently G. Radov reported that no more fresh foodstuffs are offered at the Krasnodar cooperative market—only industrially processed, nonperishable goods [443, no. 43 (1971), 10].

Less than half of the purchases or commission sales (including those made in stores rather than on the kolkhoz markets) originated in the private sector. This figure apparently rose later to "more than a half" [247, 64; 256, 41]. In the Ukraine, the kolkhozniks alone must have sold, directly or on a commission basis, about 150 million rubles worth of produce to the consumer cooperatives in 1961.[48] But it is impossible to establish exactly how many products bought by the cooperatives originate in the private sector and how many of these products are sold on the market or in the cooperative stores.

Cash obtained by individuals from sales of farm produce, total and through state and cooperative channels, may be obtained indirectly from data given in Soviet statistical handbooks. We show the results in Table 28, but alternative calculations by Morozov (see the note to Table 28) indicate that the margin of error in such calculations may be considerable.

State procurements from the private sector are lumped together with cooperative procurements in Table 28. We have dealt with the state procurement from the private sector in Chapter IV. It is sufficient to note here that it is far more important than cooperative procurement.

Revenues from sales to the state or to cooperative procurement organizations often rose as a result of increases in government procurement prices. This was particularly true in 1953 and 1954 and again in 1962; the physical volume of sales in those years remained virtually constant. By contrast, the volume of sales to state and cooperative organizations rose markedly from 1958 to 1961. The major cause of this increase was the enforced sale of livestock (cf. Chapter IX).

[47] [168, 390–391]. Cf. [449, 18 March 1961] and [240, 9]. A similar account of the kolkhoz market in Krasnodar (which I can confirm on the basis of personal observation in 1967) is given by Eligii Stavskii in [365, 12].

[48] Roughly 50 percent more than their sales to the kolkhozes, which came to about 100 million rubles [214, 39]. See also p. 183 below.

Comparable data are not available for years after 1964, but we cannot assume that sales to the state and to cooperatives, taken together, declined. Indeed, the opposite is more likely under the impact of various measures of agricultural policy introduced after Khrushchev's removal and described in Chapter X.

TABLE 28. MONEY INCOME OF INDIVIDUALS FROM SALES OF
FARM PRODUCTS, 1952–1964
(billion rubles)

Year	Sales to the State and Cooperatives	Sales on the Kolkhoz Market	Total Income from These Sales
1952	0.7	3.9	4.6
1953	0.9	. . .	. . .
1955	0.9	3.7	4.6
1956	1.4	3.4	4.8
1957	2.3	3.3	5.6
1958	2.6	3.3[a]	5.8[b]
1959	3.1	3.2	6.3
1960	3.3	2.8[a]	6.1
1961	3.0	3.5	6.5
1962	4.0	4.0[a]	8.0
1963	4.7	. . .[a]	. . .
1964	3.7	3.6	7.3

[a] [250, 183] supplies the following alternative figures (billion rubles): 1958—3.8; 1960—3.5; 1962—3.8; 1963—3.5. [b] Total obtained from unrounded data for components.

SOURCES: 1952, 1953, 1958, 1960, 1961, [9, 240, 342, 540], [11, 400, 657]; 1955, [7, 383, 496, 736]; 1956, 1957, [6, 325, 427, 708]; 1959, [6, 325, 427]; [9, 342, 540]; 1962–1964, [11, 257, 400, 657].

Not everything sold by kolkhozniks or sovkhoz workers on the market has been produced on their own plots. This must be remembered in an evaluation of the role of the private sector on the kolkhoz markets and of its contribution to the supply of food for the urban population. Sakoff is explicit on this point. He also gives estimates showing that products distributed as income-in-kind and not consumed by the recipients came at most to one-third of the value of all products brought to the market by private producers or by individuals in 1959 [315, 9].

This estimate is probably too high when we take into account the fact that about four-fifths of the value of income-in-kind in the period 1959–1963 was grains. Grains, of course, were either consumed directly by the recipients or their families or were used as feed for the plot animals (primarily pigs and poultry). Because the absolute volume as well as the importance of income-in-kind declined after 1959, it is likely that there was a decline in the direct contributions of the public sector to market sales by individuals.

The relationship might have been different for some special groups of income recipients, such as combine drivers on the kolkhozes and the sovkhozes. These people receive grain premiums determined by their labor contributions at harvest time. Frequently such premiums amount to more grain than can be used in one household or to more than can be used at a given moment—the recipients may be temporarily employed in a different locality and may not wish to take several quintals home.[49] But apart from such exceptions, the most important factor is the decline of grain distributions-in-kind by 50 percent between 1958 and 1964 [395, 283]. The importance of grain sales in the kolkhoz market turnover had become minor in 1963 and 1964 [416, 259]. However, the indirect contribution of the public sector to private livestock raising was considerably greater (cf. pp. 210 ff.). This greater indirect contribution is partly offset by the indirect contribution of the private sector to the volume of output sold by the kolkhozes and sovkhozes to any buyers, including those on the free market. As is shown in Chapter VII, the market performance of the private sector is actually greater than it appears from statistical reports. These do not cover a considerable portion of the intrarural turnover, which consists of sales of livestock and other farm products by private producers to their large socialized farms.

Lukinov indeed says that "given the relatively low cash incomes of the kolkhozniks from the socialized sector, it was not seldom that income paid for the earned labor days appeared on the kolkhoz market" [225, 38]. The expression "not seldom," however, must be understood in a relative sense. It is, of course, true that a low cash income and (by contrast) the high prices obtainable at the market might induce the kolkhoznik to bring a part of his income-in-kind to the market. And yet, he can obtain considerably greater revenues when, instead of selling grain on the market, he feeds it to livestock along with other fodder and then sells meat at the market (cf. pp. 215-219). Only in those terms can we find the real meaning of the statement: "It is more advantageous for

[49] For details on grain premiums, see Wädekin, "Payment in Kind in Soviet Agriculture," *Bulletin—Institute for the Study of the USSR,* (1971), nos. 9 and 11 passim.

the kolkhozniks to take their income from the kolkhozes in kind than in cash and then to sell a part of their produce on the extrarural market at higher prices" [250, 27, 317]. (The same, of course, also applies to the sovkhoz workers.)

The kolkhoznik in particular may be forced to acquire cash in this manner. This is true if he must buy additional food and feed which he could not produce himself or did not receive from his kolkhoz. And he may have received some products as income-in-kind which he requires in small quantities or not at all.

Kolkhozes and sovkhozes may sell products remaining at their disposal after meeting sales quotas and production requirements, either directly or through the intermediary of the consumer cooperatives.

State farms sell products in their own stores or sales outlets, which are located within the sovkhozes or in towns or worker settlements. They charge their own prices in this trade [250, 259]. Part of their produce is used for canteen meals for their workers. But this cannot play a major role, because sovkhoz workers spend, on the average, only 5 percent of their food outlays (per family) in such canteens [339a, 141–142, n. 2]. But sovkhozes were not allowed to trade directly on the real free market until 1965—"this was the case in practice," says Emelianov[50]—but only through another organization. Much of this trade consisted of potatoes and vegetables [250, 42, 275]. There do appear to have been some exceptions to this rule, especially for those sovkhozes recently converted from kolkhozes [168, 261]. The Twenty-Third Party Congress in 1966 encouraged sovkhozes to sell directly to urban consumers, either on the markets or through the stores [375, II, 357]. Beginning in 1967, a government decree of 1967 allowed sovkhozes to sell "part of" their output (that part which was not accepted by the procurement organization) directly on the markets [434, no. 25 (1970), 17; 339a, 89].

The opportunity to go directly to the kolkhoz market is of no great practical importance for present day kolkhozes. "The kolkhozes have this legal right, but in practice they do not make any use of it" [452, 6 August 1966]. Kolkhozes accounted for only 3 percent of total market sales in 1965 and 1966.[51] The trade of the kolkhozes primarily is of perishable products; it is generally disliked by the kolkhozes, but they are at times

[50] In his contribution to *Kollektivnye material'nye interesy pri sotsializme* (Moscow: 1968), p. 248.
[51] A. I. Levin, *Ekonomicheskoe regulirovanie vnutrennego rynka* (Moscow: 1967), p. 11.

forced to undertake it when the state or cooperative procurement organizations refuse to accept their produce [*373*, 216–217]. The share of the kolkhozes in the kolkhoz trade was expected to rise under the Five Year Plan for 1966–1970 [*283*, 17].

The income of kolkhozes from all kinds of kolkhoz trade (including intrarural sales and sales to consumer cooperatives) ranged between 1.2 and 1.6 billion rubles annually between 1953 and 1964. This came to about 27 percent of total gross cash revenues of the kolkhozes in 1953; since 1958, the share of this trade in gross cash revenues has fluctuated around 10 percent. A further downward trend in the share of the kolkhoz market in total gross revenue (though not the trend in the absolute revenue from such sources) seems to have occurred after 1964 [*9*, 342; *11*, 400; *379*, 44]. But regional variations appear to be very large in this context. "Some economically strong kolkhozes, which dispose of large surpluses of products [beyond sales quotas and production requirements], of sufficient means of transportation and of experienced personnel in dealing with kolkhoz trade" appear on the market more frequently than most others and gain as much as 40 percent of their cash revenues from such trade.[52] The same may be assumed of kolkhozes located in the immediate vicinity of large cities or large towns. Many of these, of course, are "economically strong." Kolkhozes in Turkmenia, which were allowed to open their own stands for the sale of fruit and vegetables in Ashkhabad during the spring of 1965, were located in the immediate vicinity of the city. There the quantities sold at the stand were counted toward the fulfillment of procurement quotas for the kolkhozes on the condition that prices charged at the stand did not exceed state retail prices (a policy that would contribute to low market prices) [*442*, 7 January 1966].

For the moment we can ignore the question of whether the kolkhoz system is inconsistent with intensive and resourceful market activity by

---

[52] [*225*, 21, 23]. In the summer of 1970, I was struck by the amount of watermelons offered at northern kolkhoz markets such as in Novgorod and Vladimir by southern kolkhozes—an amount not equalled by other kolkhoz products offered there. See also [*83*, 20] on the direct relations with the market administration which apply only to kolkhozes located in the immediate vicinity of the cities. Iakhnich [*136*, 18–19] gives considerably higher percentage figures for the share of the kolkhozes (including commission trade and seemingly also the sale of products other than foods). He also notes that the share of such sales in the kolkhoz revenues declined in recent years, particularly because many of the kolkhozes located in suburban areas—which formerly sold relatively more goods on the kolkhoz markets—were converted into sovkhozes.

the individual kolkhozes or their leadership. Even if it is consistent, we would be able to find sufficient explanations for the subordinate role of the kolkhozes on the markets. Often they have inadequate transportation to move products over the sometimes considerable distances to the nearest city or even just to the station. Where the kolkhozes are served by the railroads or by state motor transport, the services offered are often too slow, too inefficient, and too expensive. Kolkhozes are allowed on the market only after the fulfillment of their procurement targets. This means that, if they fulfill their plan at all, they are able to sell only when the market is saturated with such products as fruit and vegetables.

There are additional reasons for the subordinate role of the kolkhozes on the market: As a rule, the permission to sell is given only after the fulfillment of the quota operates at the raion level, and kolkhozes are allowed to sell outside of their raion only after all the kolkhozes of the given raion have fulfilled their sales quotas. Furthermore, the kolkhoz seller cannot respond to changing market conditions as flexibly and efficiently as can a private seller. He must at least consult first with the kolkhoz administration. (One rarely gets a quick telephone connection beyond the city network in the Soviet Union.) We also find hindrances consciously imposed on the kolkhozes by the Party and the administration under the slogans of "struggle against the tendency to [revert to] private ownership," or "against squandering kolkhoz output," or "against speculative trends." All such hindrances were meant to hold back the free market, at least until the most recent years.[53] Kolkhozes are supposed to avail themselves of intermediary services provided by the cooperatives, but we already know that the cooperatives are seldom willing or able to provide much assistance in this context. The situation could really be labeled as a prohibition of trade by the kolkhozes on the kolkhoz market [91, 50].

Khrushchev declared on 17 June 1958 [179, III, 250]:

One must create all the necessary conditions for the widening of the kolkhoz trade together with the development of state trade. This is [in order] to give the kolkhozes an opportunity to sell their surplus products on the kolkhoz market. But it does not mean at all that each kolkhoz should trade on the market. The task should first of all be performed by our consumer cooperatives in an organized way, so that [sales] are advantageous for the state, the kolkhozniks, and the consumers.

---

[53] [250, 42]; [373, 217]. See also [168, 264, 274] and [76, 101–102].

The advice to use the consumer cooperatives (which could not contribute significantly to the solution of the marketing problem) had one practical effect. This was the emergence of the idea that independent trade of the kolkhozes on the market was not economical. In turn, this idea helped to create the attitude described by Lukinov [225, 26]:

There are followers of a purely administrative solution to the contradictions of the kolkhoz trade. Some make the error of suggesting that sales of products on the kolkhoz markets should be forbidden. Others believe that unified market prices should be established at a level not higher than that of state retail prices. Still others want to reduce the household plots and restrict private farming of the kolkhozniks. The lack of sufficient clarity in the theory of kolkhoz trade has occasionally led to errors in the management of this trade. Before the Twenty-Second Congress, which brought the appropriate clarity to this question, many local functionaries allowed themselves to employ detrimental administrative restrictions, or they forbade the kolkhozes to sell surpluses of their output on the market. This occurred even in those cases when the consumer cooperatives did not buy kolkhoz output for one reason or another. Even today, we still find a false approach here and there to the problem of the market. The attempts to artificially reduce the sales of products at higher prices on the markets (after the fulfillment of the procurement plans) checks the growth of kolkhoz revenues and is often accompanied by a revival of speculation.

These words contain a remarkable insight into the relationship between the *dirigiste* economic policy and the revival of speculation. Such tendencies could be identified in practice after the Twenty-Second Congress in the fall of 1961 and also after the removal of Khrushchev. The hindrances and prohibitions on the market trade were still visible in the spring of 1966 (cf. above, p. 137 f.). "And yet experience has shown that every restriction or deliberate encroachment upon the kolkhoz-bazaar trade brought nothing but harm and damage" [249, 34]. In spite of this view, others in the Soviet Union still believe that the way to further development of the kolkhoz trade is to enlarge cooperative activity rather than the activities of the kolkhozes themselves [343, 85] (cf. below, p. 362).

THE INTRARURAL MARKET

The authorized Soviet free market for farm products primarily facilitates exchange between the countryside and the town. A considerable part of the cash income realized on this market is used for the purchase of industrial products.

In addition to the urban, or the more inclusive extrarural, trade, exchange of farm products also occurs on the countryside. This includes exchange between individual members of the agricultural population, between these individuals and the large socialized farms, between socialized farms, or between members of the agricultural population and other individuals living permanently or temporarily on the countryside [*214a*, 45]. Together all these forms of exchange are known as the intrarural (*vnutriderevenskii, vnutrisel'skii*) market, trade, or turnover,[54] and that part which involves exchange within the kolkhoz villages is described as the "intrakolkhoz" trade (*vnutrikolkhoznaia torgovlia*). Rural markets are often held on specially designated sites. Of late, this trade has been described as a special "category of socialist market output" [*343*, 85; *214a*, 44].

Reports on the intrarural kolkhoz trade are not collected by official statistical agencies on a regular basis (see p. 130), and official statistics contain no data on this trade. Soviet authors have no possibility of assessing it numerically [*56a*, 100]. But certain changes in trends are noticeable now. The new interest in the intrarural trade is related to the fact that many of the products distributed to the kolkhozniks by the kolkhozes are paid for in cash, or by deductions of the monetary equivalent of the value of these products from the cash income disbursed to the kolkhozniks by the kolkhoz. The magnitudes involved (which some Soviet writers consider as marketings) are no longer seen to be "of no practical importance," as was true until the end of the 1950s.[55] In the summer of 1966, the joint total of kolkhoz revenues from sales of grain to the kolkhozniks and of the cash equivalent of grain distributions-in-kind came to 60 percent of the total kolkhoz revenues from sales of grain to the state [*177*, 46–47].

The intrarural trade is strongly linked to the socialized sector of agriculture through such sales and distributions. It is also linked indirectly to the official retail trade through the activities of consumer cooperatives acting as buyers or as procurement agencies. In 1961 and 1962,

---

[54] Conceptually this trade includes only the sales within the village or within the farm enterprises (or amounts distributed-in-kind but carried in the accounts in terms of the cash equivalent). Cf. *Statisticheskii slovar'* (Moscow: 1965), p. 243. Because the word "turnover" (*oborot*) may also include barter transactions, Morozov introduces the concept of the intrarural trade [*250*, p. 258, n. 1]. For an explanation of the concepts see [*156*, 152–155].

[55] [*126*, 267]. For a more recent formulation see the additional explanation with reference to the kolkhozes which pay wages in cash alone in the revised edition [*127*, 246].

prices paid for live animals in this type of trade were roughly as high as those prevailing on the urban kolkhoz markets. Prices for all other products were lower; they were in fact lower than state procurement prices, except in the case of grain and potatoes [*162, 332*].

It is, of course, debatable whether a "sale" of farm products by the large socialized farm to their own workers or kolkhozniks should be considered as trade in the strict sense of the word. Recent Soviet sources do, in most instances, use the term "sales" in this connection. But when products are handed over only to individual workers or to kolkhozniks at particularly favorable prices, and when the recipient cannot determine either the kind or the maximum quantity of the received product, we are actually dealing with a special form of payments-in-kind. This is true even though such payments are now given a cash value and are no longer calculated in physical terms per labor-day (as used to be the case in the kolkhozes). Such restrictive conditions exist in most instances of intra-rural sales of this kind, although efforts are made to shift to forms of exchange that come closer to genuine sales.[56] It is, of course, appropriate to speak of sales when discussing communal catering in the canteens operated by large socialized farms. Participation in those is voluntary, and individual meals are paid for. This occurs primarily in the sovkhozes. Large kolkhozes seem to record all distributions-in-kind as "sales" in terms of their cash value, because this results in a purely statistical increase of their marketings. Sovkhozes have always followed this procedure as a matter of official routine.

The conceptual problems of intrarural trade are related precisely to the fact that it often involves intra-enterprise trade within large socialist enterprises. These huge farms usually encompass several villages. This very aspect of the Soviet phenomenon differentiates it from what might be considered intra-enterprise use of farm products in Western conditions, characterized primarily by the existence of much smaller farms.

The exchange of products within the relatively homogeneous agricultural population (where the layer of the local middle class is relatively thin) is small and sporadic. Too often many participants offer the same products. Yet, the rural market has always performed a vital function for those people in the rural population who do not operate subsidiary plots. In that group are physicians, teachers, employees of the general adminis-

---

[56] Cf. Wädekin, "Payment in kind . . ." (n. 49 above).

tration, and workers of industrial firms on the countryside. Those who spend their vacations on the countryside should also be included [*168*, 253, 307]. And how are sales to be classified—and accounted for—which occur at the kolkhoznik's door, partly to rural and partly to urban buyers? This kind of private turnover seems to have become popular lately, according to G. Radov [*443*, no. 43 (1971), 10].

The exchange between rural inhabitants could expand gradually as the social differentiation of the rural population increases and as the number of those pursuing nonagricultural occupations grows. But it can hardly acquire major importance as long as the large socialized farms and the consumer cooperatives expand their activities as suppliers in rural localities, or as long as the kolkhozniks receive decreasing quantities of income-in-kind that may be sold or resold later. Illegal production of vodka may be mentioned as a marginal phenomenon which brings large revenues to those who produce and sell it, but the penalties can be correspondingly high. It is also understandable that very little statistical and other information on the direct sales between members of the rural population—agricultural or not—is available and that this subject has not attracted much attention among Soviet writers.

Direct exchange between individual kolkhozes and sovkhozes—which is insignificant at present—could also develop as farms become more specialized and their managers are granted greater autonomy. This could lead to a rational division of labor between enterprises in the Soviet Union, but such developments are yet to come.

Little attention has been paid until just recently to the transactions between the kolkhozes and sovkhozes and their own kolkhozniks or workers respectively, or between the large farms and the other inhabitants of the villages. This was the result of several factors. Distribution of payments-in-kind to the kolkhozniks was considered formally as a cost of production and not as a part of market output. In order to supplement cash wages, the sovkhozes made some distributions to their workers in the form of advances or sales (to a large extent this was handled through sovkhoz stores, bakeries, or canteens). Such transactions of the sovkhozes were always considered a part of their market output, but then, the sovkhozes themselves were not of major importance until 1959. On the other hand, the deliveries of products—mainly animals—from the private sectors to farms in the public sector have been very important since 1958 (cf. pp. 235 ff.). But they were seldom mentioned in Soviet literature because they testified to the partial dependence of the socialized farms on the private sector, and that did not fit well with the ideologically determined image of socialized farming.

The situation changed with the decline of the importance of income-in-kind and the corresponding increase in cash payments in the kolkhozes as well as with the rise in the number of state farms. The agricultural population is now directed more explicitly to purchase from the large public farms the very same products it used to receive as part of labor remuneration. (Such sales are now often added to sales on the extrarural kolkhoz market in the accounts and reports of many kolkhozes [203, 59]).

The abandonment of methods used under Khrushchev led to a discussion of the mutual rather than the one-sided dependence of the private sector and the large socialized sector on each other, particularly with respect to livestock raising. Two articles on commodity exchange on the countryside appeared in the July 1965 issue of an authoritative economic journal. They testify to the newly awakened and growing interest in problems of the intrarural trade.[57] Taking into account the novelty of the subject and the manner in which the authors pushed aside the existing dogmas of Soviet agricultural economics, the editors prudently labeled them as discussion articles (*v poriadke postanovki*). Both writers made it clear that these problems "have never been researched" until 1965 and that they were either "passed over in silence or illuminated in an incomplete and an unsatisfactory way." [58]

Both authors also concentrated their attention on the transactions between the kolkhozes and sovkhozes and the individuals working on either type of farm. Such transactions represent the most extensive, the easiest to grasp, and the most topical part of the problem from the stand-

[57] [249, 23–35]; [214, 36–43]. Morozov published an article on this subject two years earlier [248]. Its title ("On the Prices of the Intrarural Market") obscured the real meaning of his subject matter and the article was printed by the editors of *Voprosy ekonomiki* in the subdivision called "Notes and Communications." In a still earlier article he dealt briefly and marginally with this subject, but he recognized its growing importance and defined it as an "economic phenomenon" [247, 66–67]. A recent book by Ia. U. Liniichuk, *Vazhlive dzherelo pidniseniia narodnoho dobrobutu* (Kiev: 1967), which discusses "intravillage trade" in some detail, was not available to me.

[58] [249, 24]; [214, 36]. The personal consumption of the agricultural population and the intravillage trade were simply shown together in a booklet sent to typesetting as late as August of 1965 [44, 91, Table 15]. See also [437, no. 11 (1968), 90].

point of agricultural policy (cf. Chapter VII). Among other things, we learn that the value of products and livestock sold by the Ukrainian kolkhozniks to their own kolkhozes in 1961 was approximately the same as the value of sales by the kolkhozes to their kolkhozniks (95 to 100 million rubles as opposed to 100.9 million rubles, respectively).[59] In 1958, the Ukrainian kolkhozes and sovkhozes bought 150 million rubles' worth of livestock just from their members and workers. The corresponding figure for 1963–1964 varied between 84 and 85 million rubles [214a, 55]. In 1963, total sales of all kolkhozes in the Soviet Union to the kolkhoz population rose to 548.7 million rubles. Farm products accounted for 466.4 million, and the value of sales of individual products groups was as follows (in millions of rubles): grains—202; hay and straw—15; meat and fat—58; and livestock—62.[60] The volume, as well as the degree of monetization, of the intrarural trade continued to increase [214a, 46]. In 1966, the sales of grain alone by all kolkhozes to the kolkhozniks— sales which in part replaced the income-in-kind—must have come to more than 1.5 billion rubles[61] (the sales, of course, took place at the higher, 1966 prices).

Considering these data and the overall development of sales by the kolkhozes to the kolkhozniks, and taking into account all the remaining sales of a similar kind, the total value of the intrarural turnover of all kinds may be estimated as ranging from 1 to 1.5 billion rubles in the years from 1961 to 1963. By 1966, the corresponding figure might have exceeded 3 billion rubles. One might venture a guess that about half of this total represented sales by private producers. In recent years, the volume of sales by large socialized farms to their own members or workers rose still further.

The rural market is not negligible, even though its turnover is smaller than that of the extrarural market. The latter, it will be recalled, came to

[59] [214, 34]. In 1959, as a result of the enforced purchases of animals from the private sector, the value of purchases of livestock alone was three times greater. It doubled again in 1960. The sales by the kolkhozes to the kolkhozniks were approximately the same in 1959 and 1960 as they were in 1961 (see [225, 42]; these data include the probably small sales of the kolkhozes on the extrarural markets).

[60] [250, 264, 270]. The value of all livestock sold by the kolkhozniks to the kolkhozes in 1963 came to 249.4 million rubles [339, 30].

[61] These came to 60 percent of the sales to the state (cf. p. 179 above). The total value of grain purchased by state and cooperative agencies from kolkhozes and from individuals in 1966 came to 3.5 billion rubles [19, 124]. Kolkhozes clearly accounted for the bulk of these sales.

4.7 billion rubles' worth of food sales in 1961 and to 5 billion rubles in 1964 (including sales by consumer cooperatives).

To estimate the volume of the intrarural trade in relation to the extrarural trade, transactions on the former would have to be revalued in terms of prices obtaining in extrarural trade. The comparison indicates that the volume of the intrarural trade in 1961 came to slightly less than one-half of that of the extrarural trade (excluding sales of consumer cooperatives). For 1964, the corresponding figure would exceed 50 percent. If the comparisons are restricted to sales by individuals alone, then the volume of sales on the intrarural market may have been slightly less than a quarter of sales by private producers on the extrarural market. For 1964 and 1966, the corresponding figure would have been above 25 percent. Although the extrarural market stagnated for most of these years, the intrarural market expanded steadily.

7

The Interdependence
of Private and
Socialized Production

The interdependence of the socialized and private sectors begins in the sphere of production, not during the distribution of the produce. This is one of the most interesting and important aspects of the Soviet agricultural system. The interdependence is generally overlooked by Western observers, partly because Soviet sources have until recently provided only meager materials on this topic. G. V. D'iachkov, in his book which was published in 1968, was the first to concentrate upon this aspect [87, 179]:

The personal plot is personal kolkhoz production. Social and personal farming are not isolated from one another. On the contrary, they are organically and mutually linked and represent both an economic and a socioeconomic unity.

Quite a few years ago, Sakoff [315, 11] showed that if there were no private agricultural sector, the kolkhozes and sovkhozes would have to produce twice as much as they actually do—with the exception of grain.[1] Moreover, he stressed that the claims of the private sector on the kolkhoz manpower are partly offset, for instance, through livestock sales by the kolkhozniks who attain a certain limit of animal holdings. Indeed, many kolkhozes enter into contracts with their members for the fattening of calves. Young saplings and organic fertilizers are also sold to the kolkhoz by the plotholders. On the financial side, the private incomes of its members enable the kolkhoz to distribute less in earnings and to retain about a fifth of its gross income for capital investment.

[1] A Soviet source reported the same relationship for 1966; see [230, 62].

Sakoff's study was one of the rare examples of Western writings which indicated the direct relationship between the socialized and private agricultural sectors. But even Sakoff limited himself to certain assumptions. This was hardly surprising in view of the paucity of information from Soviet sources, which, if anything, became even more scarce under Khrushchev. The topic is no longer taboo in the Soviet Union, but Soviet authors still complain about the dearth of published data. Liniichuk criticized the "lack of data, especially concerning the sale of produce and livestock by kolkhozniks to the kolkhozes" [214, 38], and Morozov declared: "However, until now, no complete clarity exists unfortunately in the [Soviet] scientific literature concerning the nature of the private plot. The dependence of the private plots on social production is usually overlooked as well as their direct connection." He further pointed out that Soviet authors limited their discussion of the theme:

The existence and the "powers of survival" of the personal subsidiary farms are explained in terms of the petty ownership psychology of the peasant and, as a rule, through emphasis on the consumption orientation of the personal plots. The functions of these plots as a material incentive and as a supplementary source of foodstuffs for the urban population are underestimated.[2]

An early stage in the Soviet perception of interdependence was the recognition of the fact that the private sector in the kolkhozes played a vital role in feeding the agricultural work force as well as contributing an indispensable share of the foodstuffs for the rural though nonagricultural population. A. N. Gol'tsov warned at the beginning of the 1960s [338, 94–95]:

Only insofar as the socialized sector of the kolkhoz grows strong and develops, then, when it is in a position to supply the kolkhozniks' families—which at present have personal plots—fully with animal products, with potatoes, vegetables, and fruit, only then is there no longer any objective necessity to keep livestock in the personal holdings and plots for productive crops. . . . At the present time, however, the development of the majority of the kolkhozes has yet to reach a level which would enable them to supply the kolkhozniks with all the produce which they get from the personal farms.

At the same time, a group of writers from the Economics Institute of the USSR Academy of Sciences wrote that: "In kolkhozes with low earnings . . . the reproduction of the labor force is shifted to a large

---

[2] [250, 175]; see also [386, 68, 70]; [70, 87]; [87, 10].

extent to the nonsocialized personal plot and livestock holding of the kolkhoznik" [269, 251]. From his intimate observation of kolkhoz life, Dorosh declared [440, 8 October 1961]: "The diligence of the kolkhoznik in his own garden depends upon how great and how durable is his income from the large kolkhoz field."

These statements tacitly admitted already in Khrushchev's time the dilemma whereby a considerable and indispensable, if not the principal, share of the income of the kolkhoz population originated from the private sector, although this was supposed in fact to have only a subsidiary function: "The socialized sector, to put it bluntly, has ceased to feed the kolkhoznik" [ibid.].

The same is valid not only for the kolkhozes and their members but also for the sovkhozes. Yet this part of the private sector has at least been "legalized," as was indicated by an article in *Kommunist* at the end of 1965 [256, 69]:

In order to do away with the need for sovkhoz workers' and employees' personal plots, at least the following economic preconditions must be attained: First, such large marketable stocks of meat, milk, eggs, potatoes, vegetables, and fruit must be concentrated by the state that those employed in the sovkhozes may be constantly supplied with them. Second, a level of earnings is required which would enable sovkhoz workers and employees to purchase all the foodstuffs and industrial goods they need from the trade network; this means, basically, a wage level on a par with urban residents. Such conditions do not, as yet, hold for certain categories of workers and employees.

Also, the standards of retail trade outlets and industrial consumer services available to the sovkhoz population are still far below those of urban areas. Only recently, Turchaninov observed [386, 70]: "Such conditions [of trade] for certain categories of sovkhoz workers and employees have still not developed. But even if these conditions exist, many workers want to work their subsidiary farm for traditional reasons, and there are absolutely no grounds for preventing them from doing so."

Even in the sovkhozes, the issue cuts deeper than the fundamental conditions set out above. I demonstrate this partly on the basis of the few direct references in Soviet writings and partly by analogy with kolkhoz conditions.

The catastrophic results of Khrushchev's agricultural and social policies forced his successors to recognize this interrelationship and the interdependence. Thus, the following unusual pronouncements were to be read in the early part of 1965 [339, 27-28, 35]:

The private plots are the necessary and, at the given stage of development, the most expedient form for combining the social (state and cooperative) interests with the personal interests of those working in agriculture. This combination (*sochetanie*) is not only evidenced by the fact that personal plots are permitted along with social production; such a procedure shows not a combination but rather only a coexistence of interests (the socialized sector —social interests, the personal sector—personal interests). What is important is something else, namely that social and personal interests are organically combined with each other in socialist production. As the development of the socialized sectors of the kolkhozes and sovkhozes serves social and personal interests, so too do the personal plots serve not only personal but also social purposes by augmenting the inadequate development of output of the social-ized sector. . . . the personal plots . . . are not incompatible with socialized production, but complement it. . . . When the question of the production structure in the private plots is carefully examined, it can be established that a certain division of labor exists between socialized production and the private plot; this is expressed by the fact that most of the private output is devoted to those items the production of which in the socialized sector is insufficiently mechanized, and to those products where the share of the socialized sector in total output is not large.

N. A. Aitov wrote in *Sociology in the Soviet Union* [*354*, I, 364–365], which appeared in 1965:

The personal plot is a piece of property which is at the same time separated and yet not quite distinct from kolkhoz property. The plot of land is allotted by the kolkhoz only for use by a kolkhoznik, and the kolkhoz may reduce its size or confiscate it altogether if the kolkhoznik does not work well in the socialized sector. The kolkhoznik's livestock grazes upon kolkhoz land, and the kolkhoznik receives animal fodder from the kolhoz land. The degree of interest the kolkhoznik attaches to the private plot depends upon whether he gets much in the kolkhoz. The kolkhoz thereby regulates, to a certain extent, the development of the personal economy.

Similar sentiments were recorded by Venzher, Morozov, Zaslavskaia and others. I. F. Suslov pithily observed [*373*, 185]: "The personal sector grew as the socialized sector satisfied less and less the requirements of the kolkhozniks." D'iachkov drew attention to the connection with kolkhoz investment: "The kolkhozniks, growing food on the personal plots for themselves, facilitated the public sector's situation, for it would have been obliged to reduce the accumulation fund in order to increase the consumption fund, if there were no private plots" [*87*, 40].

The function and the significance of the private sector are nowadays beyond dispute. Detailed comprehensive information is still missing, however, as to how the combination—not coexistence—or interdependence actually occurs before the final product appears on the market, be it on the free kolkhoz market or through the state and cooperative trade network.

It was this lack of information which made I. Ia. Matiukha, deputy head of the Central Statistical Administration, enumerate—during a conference on family budgets in April 1970—among the subjects of current topical interest that "of the role of the personal subsidiary farm in the total family income, of the links of this farm with the kolkhoz enterprise at large" [466, no. 8 (1970), 80].

In order to obtain the most complete picture possible from the fragmentary data, the aspects of this interrelationship are examined separately as follows:

(1) labor remuneration system, formation of personal incomes and problems of labor input;[3]

(2) the performance of the public and the private sectors in growing crops;

(3) the contribution of the kolkhoz and sovkhoz toward feeding privately owned livestock;

(4) the contribution of the private sector toward the kolkhoz's and sovkhoz's output of animal products.

INTERDEPENDENCE IN INCOME FORMATION, WAGES, AND LABOR INPUTS

As early as November of 1959, Zaslavskaia gave discreet hints in *Voprosy ekonomiki* that the private plot might, under some circumstances, involve the kolkhoznik in a conflict of interests with the socialist society, but that this might have something to do with his "relatively low pay." Six years later, she was able to speak out far more openly along these lines and to support her statement with figures [427, 62]:

If the kolkhozes wanted to supply the kolkhozniks with foodstuffs and yet were to keep the marketed share of their output at the same level, their public sectors would have to produce 74 percent more milk, 75 percent more meat, 86 percent more vegetables, and they would have to treble their output of potatoes and eggs. . . . For the above reason alone, the complete replacement of the personal plots by socialized production is a matter for the relatively distant future.

Let us suppose that we could manage, within a relatively short space of

[3] For a detailed investigation into this subject, see my recent book, *Die Bezahlung der Arbeit in der sowjetischen Landwirtschaft* (Berlin: 1972).

time, to increase rapidly the kolkhoz's marketed output and to build up a comprehensive trade network in the kolkhoz villages. If the prices in this trade network were to be at the branch average production costs of the items sold, then, in order to be able to purchase their foodstuffs, the kolkhozniks would have to double their income from the socialized sector when compared with the situation prevailing in 1964.

Even experienced and sober Western observers tended earlier to underestimate the average income originating from the private plot and livestock holding and to overestimate the income derived from the public sector.[4] Soviet data on these matters have been made available only recently.

In 1968, D'iachkov published the following table which was based on a sample survey of twenty-six thousand kolkhoz families carried out by the Central Statistical Administration. Personal consumption was valued at state retail prices (which do not necessarily always exceed the free intravillage market prices), but market output was expressed in actually realized prices—the weighted average of state and cooperative purchase prices and of urban or rural kolkhoz market prices. Suslov [373, 188, 193–194], who used the same percentage figures as D'iachkov, gave an average annual gross revenue for RSFSR kolkhoz families in 1963 as 914 rubles; from this he deducted 40 percent for production costs, leaving a net income which does not differ greatly from that given in Table 29. The production costs, also mentioned by D'iachkov, represent depreciation and construction of farm buildings, purchases of livestock, feed, small agricultural implements, seed, transport, and taxes, but not labor costs [373, 196; 87, 71]. Shmelev puts the material production costs to be deducted a bit lower than Suslov, at 38 percent [339a, 103]; this still appears excessive.

In physical terms, the output in 1964 was lower than in 1958, but in value terms this decline was more than compensated for by price increases, especially in 1962 [87, 69]. Of the total average kolkhoz family income in 1964, 43.3 percent was derived from earnings from the kol-

---

[4] For example, Otto Schiller [328, 190–191] (published in the mid-1950s). He calculated the average annual gross income of a kolkhoznik from his plot and livestock holding to be 455 new rubles and his net income at 405 rubles. However, in view of the subsequent price raises, the net figure of 405 rubles is not far from the data set out in Table 29. The discrepancy in the gross income estimates is large. The share of animal products in the gross output—reckoned by Schiller at only 55 percent—is put at a higher amount by Suslov [373, 193] and D'iachkov [87] (see Table 29).

TABLE 29. AVERAGE INCOME OF A KOLKHOZ FAMILY FROM
PRIVATE AGRICULTURAL ACTIVITY
(new rubles per year)

Type of Income	1958	1959	1960	1961	1962	1963	1964
Total net income, including:	689	646	672	659	739	718	773
Income from crops, of which:	287	249	279	268	292	289	354
Potatoes	131	127	131	126	129	145	178
Vegetables and melons	67	51	67	60	64	50	69
Income from animal products, of which:	372	368	366	368	425	406	395
Milk	160	153	158	148	171	163	168
Eggs	34	38	40	41	47	44	44
Breeding of animals and gain in livestock weight	166	166	156	166	195	187	171
Income from other sources	30	29	27	23	22	23	24

SOURCE: [87, 68].

khoz (including payments-in-kind, valued at state retail prices), 43.9 percent came from the private plots and livestock holdings, and 12.8 percent from other sources (such as earnings and other income from other enterprises, pensions, and welfare payments, but excluding state expenditures on culture, education, and health). The respective percentages in 1965 were 44, 42, and 14 percent [87, 69–70]. The proportion of total income from the private sector differed widely from one republic to another. This share was highest in Belorussia, Lithuania, Georgia, Latvia, and Estonia—where earnings from the public sector were relatively low, and lowest in the Kazakh and the Kirghiz republics—where the kolkhoz payments were relatively high [ibid.]. The differences between individual kolkhozes could be much greater, depending on their level of development and on existing opportunities for work outside the kolkhoz; this is generally known, but also evident from figures for four kolkhozes concentrating mainly on "meat and dairy products but with developed vegetable and potato gardening" in 1959–1960 [87, 70].

Another differentiation is that between the various strata of the kolkhoz hierarchy. In addition to giving overall data on income distribution in kolkhozniks' families, Ostrovskii [275, 85–86, 93] reports that, in the Volga region (apparently in 1964 or 1965), average incomes from the private sector averaged 771 rubles a year, but that this covered a range extending from 678 rubles for rank-and-file kolkhozniks to 730 rubles for those working in the livestock sector to 835 rubles for the mechanizers. He went on to explain: "However, the absolute size [as opposed to the relative share] of income from the personal subsidiary farm not only does not decline but even grows with the scale of earnings from the kolkhozes. The mechanizers and livestock specialists, who receive more from the kolkhoz, have more cattle in their private holdings and acquire larger incomes."

In a calculation which included all cultural, social, and welfare payments by the state, M. Sidorova found that of the all-union average kolkhoz family income in 1964–1965, 37 percent was derived from work in the kolkhoz, "over" 35 percent from the private plots and livestock holdings, thus leaving about 27 percent for income from other sources.[5] If one takes into account the appreciable increase in earnings from the public sector and from transfer payments during the years prior to 1964–1965 [see 80, 97], then it is clear that the percentage of its total income that the kolkhoz family received from the public sector as late as 1960 was considerably smaller than that derived from the private sector, even when state social and cultural services are added to payments from the kolkhoz. The discrepancy was even greater before 1958. During the period from 1953 to 1966, the share of the kolkhoz family's total income derived from the private sector fell by only 11.4 percentage points [231, 22]. However, in absolute terms, income from the private sector grew considerably during this period and particularly from 1953 to 1958 and again from 1964 to 1966, although earnings from the public sector grew even faster [56a, 125]. Part of this increase is, of course, attributable to the rise in food prices, which also influences the statistical assessment of the producers' own consumption. From kolkhoz market sales alone, private sellers in 1963 received 1.3 billion rubles more income than in 1960 as a consequence of rising prices [56a, 113], although the physical volume of sales decreased for most products [416, 259].

The relationship between net incomes from the private sector for sovkhoz workers and employees and those for kolkhozniks is illustrated by the following figures for the RSFSR: In 1961, the average kolkhoz family income from the private sector was 628 rubles (similar to the all-

---

[5] [344, 50–51]; cf. *ibid.* for the regional differentiation. Transfer payments received by kolkhozniks in 1965 were estimated to make up 16 to 18 percent of their total income [279, 26]; the proportion for 1964 was said to be 16 percent [66, 13].

union average given in Table 29), and sovkhoz families earned 465 rubles [52, 57]. In 1964, the private sector in the RSFSR accounted for 43 percent of the income of kolkhoz families and for 22 percent of the income of sovkhoz workers and employees [292, 184, n.]. For the whole Soviet Union, the respective percentages were 46 and 26 in 1960, 34 and 21 in 1969.[6]

Of all RSFSR kolkhozniks, those in Central Russia, in the Volga-Viatka region, and in the Central Black Soil region derived an above-average share of their total incomes from the private sector. This was also true for sovkhoz workers and employees in the Central Black Soil region. The lowest proportion in the RSFSR was found in Northwestern Russia for kolkhozniks, workers and employees.[7] In a livestock sovkhoz in Kazakhstan (the Kustanai oblast) which had been formed from eight former kolkhozes, the average family income from the private sector was actually as high as 770–900 rubles (this figure probably refers to gross income) [357, 22]. The private plots and livestock holdings accounted for a smaller than average proportion of the kolkhoz families' total incomes in Uzbekistan and a greater than average share in Belorussia and the Baltic republics.[8]

Only after the removal of Khrushchev did kolkhoz wages become, on the average, the principal source of kolkhoz families' income. In the poor harvest year of 1963, the share of income from the private sector made up 41.9 percent of the total income (including transfer payments, and so on) [344, 51]. In 1964, payments for work in the kolkhoz equaled the income derived from the private sector,[9] and in 1965 income from the public sector at last became the principal source of kolkhozniks' earnings. In 1966, excluding income from work outside the kolkhoz, some 46 percent of the total family income came from the kolkhoz (including kolkhoz transfer payments), 38 percent from the private sector and 16

[6] [339a, 102]. For sovkhoz families in 1966 or 1967, see [231, 21]; about the same shares, for the RSFSR in 1967 or 1968, are given in [205, 38]. In the Orenburg oblast, in 1964, the private sector accounted for 30 to 31 percent of the "individually distributed material goods" (excluding transfer payments, and so on) received by sovkhoz workers; the equivalent share in the Sverdlovsk oblast was 34 percent; for kolkhozniks in both oblasts it came to 43 percent [180, 99]; V. P. Rodionov, "Puti sblizheniia kolkhoznogo krest'ianstva s sovkhoznym otriadom rabochego klassa," Filosofskie nauki, no. 5 (1966), 19.

[7] [128, 63]; [308, 58].

[8] [160, 36]; for the detailed data for Estonia in 1958, 1960, and 1965, see [107, 90]; these figures are well above the all-union averages but display the same trends.

[9] See above and [369, 139, 145].

percent from state transfer payments.[10] This helped to offset the differences in earning levels between kolkhozniks and sovkhoz workers, although the average income of kolkhozniks' families, even with the contribution from the private sector, remained below that of sovkhoz families [231, 21]. Under some conditions, however, the private income of a sovkhoz family could be higher than the average sovkhoz wages; in a wine sovkhoz in the Dagestan ASSR, for instance, the income from private vineyards in 1963 was as high as one thousand rubles a year [215, 76]. Earnings from the private plots and livestock holdings during the period from 1966 to 1970 are believed to have risen only modestly, so that income from the public sector in 1970 is thought to be about double that from the private sector; however, the latter is still of considerable significance.

We will not examine here the question of Soviet wage and income statistics and in particular the sample family budget surveys;[11] the official indications of the proportions for each sector suffice to justify the following observation by a Soviet writer [66, 13]:

Because the private plot still accounts for a considerable weight in the kolkhozniks' income structure, the widespread attempts in 1959–1960 to socialize livestock which was personally owned by the kolkhozniks, to reduce as far as possible the dimensions of the private plots, to reduce the norms of the [private] poultry holdings, and so on, must inevitably have weakened the kolkhozniks' interest in working at their kolkhoz.

"Sheer necessity forced the kolkhoznik to concentrate his efforts on the personal plot," regardless of whether he agreed with Communist ideals or not. "If the kolkhozniks had not had livestock in their subsidiary farms, they would not have been able to keep themselves alive from what they received from the kolkhoz, not even if they had received all their wages in kind." [12]

Just how decisive in this matter is the peasant's attachment to his

[10] M. I. Sidorova, *Obshchestvennye fondy potrebleniia i dokhody kolkhoznikov* (Moscow: 1969), pp. 148–149. For slightly different figures, see [104, 434].

[11] For a discussion of the type and methodology of such samples, see [344, 49] and [239, 34–38, 49]. The latter shows clearly the significance ascribed to the income and consumption from the private sector by the rural population, regardless of the reliability of such samples. Sidorova [344, p. 50, n. 3] makes it clear that income from the kolkhoz is put too high in the allegedly representative household samples.

[12] [427, 177]. This was true, even until recently, in many kolkhozes; see [170, 67].

own piece of land is a subject of much dispute. It may be resolved only if (and when) the kolkhozniks are paid a wage approaching that of a sovkhoz worker and employee, if they are paid this wage throughout the entire year, if the state trading network can provide them with adequate and high quality consumer goods and foodstuffs in return for cash, and finally, if the party and state cease putting pressure on the private sector. Such a combination can only be feasible in the "relatively distant future." Indeed, Soviet writers are inclined to deny altogether that the kolkhoznik has an "attachment to small-scale production" but until now it has been impossible to disprove this motive because of the agricultural policy of the Soviet leadership. Sheer necessity has displaced all other possibilities.

Those who believe that the interest of the kolkhoznik in his private plot is responsible for the shortcomings of the public sector are overestimating the production possibilities of the Soviet agricultural system. We would reverse this chain of causation. The inadequate performance of socialized agriculture and its neglect in favor of the industrial building of "socialism" have made the devotion of the kolkhoznik to his private plot a condition for his survival. It is noteworthy that this realization is expressed by a growing number of voices in the Soviet Union. Whether the matter will be seen in another light, after the performance of the public sector has markedly improved, remains to be seen. Past experience offers little guidance on this matter.

Soviet authorities have had very little real choice as to whether to permit the private sector as long as they have been unable or unwilling to pay to the kolkhozniks wages which permit an adequate "reproduction of the labor force"—a living wage for those who must feed the population—without the contribution of the private sector.[13] Now that kolkhoz wages provide at least a minimum subsistence, the Soviet leadership is no longer in such a desperate situation. However, this does not automatically signify that the private sector can be dispensed with, if only for the following reason cited by Makeenko [230, 66]:

The introduction of guaranteed wages in kolkhozes on the level of the sovkhoz tariff rates does not lessen the significance of the private sector, but merely alters its function: instead of being an essential condition for a normal reproduction of the agricultural labor force it becomes an additional source of income for those employed in the country. . . . As is known, the task of raising the wages of workers and employees by an average of at least 20

[13] [344, 49] and [265, 403].

percent has been set during the current five-year plan period [1966–1970]. The payments in cash and in kind to the kolkhozniks [are to be raised] by an average of 35 to 40 percent. As a result of this, the level of payments of kolkhozniks will be brought closer to the level of wages for workers and employees. If, however, we leave the private sector out of account, the foreseen growth rate of kolkhozniks' incomes from the social sector will not even bring their incomes in 1970 to the level of workers' and employees' pay in 1965. The situation is changed when the possibilities of the private sector are taken into account as a factor in raising the real incomes of those working in the country.

Against this background we must consider very marked differences among the various regions. For instance, the payment for a day of labor in the kolkhozes of the western RSFSR, Belorussia, and Lithuania were only half of the all-union average in 1957–1959 and amounted to one-third of the sovkhoz pay; thus here the private sector must have played an even greater role than in other regions. In Central Asia, on the other hand, if the private sector is included, the income per household was three to four times greater than in the area between Moscow and the Baltic Sea mentioned above. (However, the average household in Central Asia included five persons as against 3.4 to 3.8 persons in the western RSFSR.) Concerning the naturally poorly endowed central and western districts of the RSFSR, the Kostroma oblast party secretary had the following to say at the March 1965 plenum [295, 176]:

In many kolkhozes of the non-Black Soil zone, the private plot remains to this day the principal, the assured basis of existence for the kolkhoz family. Moreover, as a rule, the labor unit applied to the private plot and livestock holding yields a higher return than the unit devoted to socialized production.

A Soviet literary critic cited from Efim Dorosh's *A Village Diary* the following observation made by a kolkhoznik of this same non-Black Soil region: "For the time being, the kolkhoz still finds it difficult to compete with the private plots, with their high level of farming and with their excellent yields." To this Dorosh attached the comment: "Here is the 'criterion' from which he proceeds and by which the kolkhoznik judges the profitability of his work on the kolkhoz field. . . . A true and valid interest of the peasant in the socialized sector can thus begin only in that moment when he says to himself: 'No, I could not have managed that, not even if I had as much land as I could farm with my own labor.'" [402, 248–250]

Iu. Burtin also refers to the discrepancies between the returns from the public and private sectors pictured by Dorosh. In this connection he generalizes: "It would be false to assume that such a relationship between the returns has only a limited, local character" [70, 87].

The differentials in returns can be enormous between individual regions and between individual farms. There are also kolkhozes which can pay good wages, and in these it is often reported that the kolkhozniks are beginning to lose interest in the private plot. The upper limit aspired for was the level of sovkhoz earnings which on the average came to ninety-three rubles a month in 1969 [14a, 539]. Yet it is difficult to see how such an income (barely twenty United States dollars a week in equivalent purchasing power) could preclude the need for a private plot. Private plots are certainly necessary in the vast majority of sovkhozes, as is shown by the determination with which the sovkhoz workers and employees hold on to their private plots and livestock holdings.

In 1937, and again in 1958, a day's work on the private plot was worth, on the average, twice as much to the kolkhoznik as a day's work on the kolkhoz; during many of the years in the interval between these two record harvest years, the differential must have been much larger. The discrepancy has significantly lessened only since 1964, when higher income levels were reached. But even after this turning point, work on the private plot remained more profitable than work in the public sector.[14]

It should not be overlooked that payments-in-kind by the kolkhoz are more advantageous for the kolkhoznik than is suggested by their worth as foodstuffs or by their face value at current prices. These are foodstuffs or fodder that he could hardly acquire elsewhere. Even today, when a minimum wage is guaranteed, it is of the greatest importance to a kolkhoznik how much of his earnings from the kolkhoz will be in the form of payments-in-kind—be it foodstuffs or fodder.[15] The payments-in-kind can bring additional income through market sales because "the kolkhozniks sell on the market not only the surplus of agricultural produce from their own private plots but also the surplus of produce that they received from the kolkhoz as payments-in-kind" [404, 93]. Under some conditions—for example, when markets are within a reasonable distance and there is not an oversupply of the particular produce, the kol-

---

[14] [104, 434]. In the RSFSR, in 1966, kolkhoz families are said to have applied 30.6 percent of their total labor inputs to the private plots and 60.1 percent to the kolkhoz public sector, yet to have received 33.9 percent of their income from the former and 50.4 percent from the latter; see [88, 51].

[15] See the contribution by A. G. Zinochkin in [429, 132]; cf. [87, 34-35].

khoznik can often derive more from selling his payments-in-kind from the kolkhoz than if he were to receive all his wages in cash. As a rule, the prices on the kolkhoz markets in the larger towns are appreciably higher than those at which he receives the produce, and the state retail stores in the smaller towns and villages—which sell these items at lower prices—often just do not have them in stock (see p. 134). Yet the prices on the kolkhoz markets in the smaller towns, where the kolkhoznik can go most easily to sell his produce, are usually lower than in the larger cities, and so the profit margin is not always large.

Some reservations are in order when using Soviet statistics which show the total income of the kolkhoz population and its rapid growth. These incomes include the returns from the private plots (Soviet statistics on the real incomes of workers and employees also include income from the private sector).[16] This feature can produce some rather knotty problems of interpretation, as evidenced by the following example.

In 1964, the annual average income of an able-bodied kolkhoznik from the public sector amounted to 53 percent of the average income of a sovkhoz worker and employee, about 420 rubles. Reckoned on the basis of income per workday, however, it came to 74 percent of the sovkhoz level, because the kolkhoznik was employed an average of only 196 days a year compared with the 280 days put in by the sovkhoz worker [427, 40]. So far so good, even if Zaslavskaia's formulation does not specify whether the kolkhoznik's income included transfer payments by the kolkhoz and the state as well as earnings outside the kolkhoz. Yet from the above, N. Ia. Bromlei of the Historical Institute of the USSR Academy of Sciences, who specializes in the history of Soviet society, draws the astonishing conclusion that [66, 9]: "The average indicators of kolkhozniks' incomes were basically speaking not below those of the urban population." And this when urban earnings were, for the most part, even higher than sovkhoz earnings!

How is such a conclusion possible? In the first place, Bromlei chose to ignore the fact that the kolkhoznik was, on average, employed eighty-four days less than the sovkhoz worker on an annual basis; this brought the monthly pay up to about 52 rubles a month. "And if it is taken into account that the personal plot contributed a sizable income to the village family's budget"—this brings it up to the urban standard. In fact, if one accepts that the private plot brought in 40 to 50 rubles a month per able-

---

[16] [115, 129–130]; [109, 205]; [239, 34–38].

bodied worker (see the household data in Table 29 above), then the total monthly income would rise to nearly 100 rubles. Yet this would not take into account the fact that the urban wage figure refers only to earnings as opposed to all income, that many urban residents also have private plots which bring in a tidy additional income, that the family structure is more favorable in the towns, and that transfer payments and social and urban services (health services, education, subsidized rents, public transportation, and so on) are twice as high on a per capita basis in towns as on the countryside. But this is somewhat beyond the scope of the present discussion. Nevertheless, a remark by Sonin serves as a commentary on Bromlei's contention that the low incomes of the kolkhozniks are justified because they also have earnings from private plots [350, 189]: "Under capitalist conditions, the existence of the private plots of workers' families would be exploited by the capitalists in that they would reduce the [workers'] wages by that amount which they receive from the private plots." It is only necessary to replace "workers' families" by "kolkhozniks' families" and "the capitalists" by "the Soviet state."

Of considerable importance is the fact that the kolkhoznik is employed for eighty-four days less than the sovkhoz worker. Given the climatic conditions throughout most of the Soviet Union and the shortcomings of the kolkhoz system, it really is not possible to provide employment in the public sector for all able-bodied kolkhozniks throughout the year. "The returns from the private plot compensate, to some degree, for that difference in the annual income which the kolkhozniks do not receive from the socialized sector as a result of the incomplete utilization of the annual fund of worktime" [170, 66]. The kolkhoz pays only for those workdays which the kolkhoznik actually puts in, regardless of whether or not he would like to work longer. His labor is thus cheaper than that of a sovkhoz worker, even if he is paid as much per day; the problem of seasonal fluctuations in the need for labor in agriculture is thereby resolved—at the expense of the agricultural labor force. This solution is feasible because the private plots yield not only an additional income but also offer possibilities for labor inputs which are less dependent on seasonal factors as is the public sector.[17] Above all, the private livestock holdings guarantee employment—albeit minimal—and a continuing return throughout the winter. Of course, these holdings require at-

[17] There is some seasonality, of course, for those private activities which are not directly connected with livestock (see [339a, 55, 57]), but on the whole it is less than in the public sector, where crop production plays a greater role.

tention during the summer too, which means that at peak times the public and the private agricultural sectors compete for the kolkhoznik's time. Yet, the existence of the plot simultaneously furthers his readiness to spare every free hour in summer for work on the private sector, including Sundays and holidays. On the whole, work in the private plots is done mainly during the legitimate free time of the kolkhozniks [55, 237–238, 241]. The advantage of the cheap labor provided by the kolkhoznik (cheap because it is not paid throughout the year)—often intentionally ignored by Soviet sources—by far outweighs the disadvantages of the private plots for the kolkhoz system. Otherwise the history of Soviet collectivized agriculture during the past four decades could not have been written.

Bromlei's comparison of incomes, which is particularly crude but which is reflected in other Soviet writings, thus unashamedly includes the private plot as an additional source of income. Soviet authorities do likewise. This attitude legitimizes the private sector as such, the justification of whose existence was theoretically not questioned but was recognized only to a limited extent in Khrushchev's agricultural policy. It also legitimizes the worktime devoted to the private sector by the kolkhoz population. The roughly eighty-four days less per year spent in the public sector by the able-bodied kolkhoznik—as well as the many hours contributed by his less able-bodied relations—are thereby authorized. He needs them for his private plot, his house, and other sources of earnings. And whatever he earns beyond the inadequate kolkhoz wages, he and his relations have earned through honest, additional labor. This much has been conceded recently by Soviet authors as well.[18]

Yet a fundamental work on kolkhoz law, published in 1962 and officially released as a textbook, severely limited this legitimization: "The main attention of the members of a kolkhoz household must be directed to the socialized sector of the kolkhoz; consequently they may work in the private plot of the household only during that time which is not taken up by kolkhoz work."[19] This view was to be repeated, although in a milder form, in a book which appeared even later, in 1965: "The time which the kolkhozniks spend on their private plots may not be called worktime or a second workday. It is free time, needed for farming the private plot by reason of economic necessity" [55, 237]. A year later,

---

[18] For instance, A. M. Emel'ianov, *Metodologicheskie problemy nakopleniia i rentabel'nost' v kolkozakh* (Moscow: 1965), pp. 104–106.

[19] V. K. Grigor'ev in [*165*, 493]; see also [*404*, 12].

Makeenko wrote [230, 63]: "Some economists regard work on the private plots not as socially necessary for a normal reproduction of the labor force but rather as striving after gains, induced by the dark powers of the peasant psychology." Nevertheless, nowadays it is recognized that this private agricultural labor is "socially useful to the community" [104, 291]. "Work in the personal subsidiary farm, as a whole, is not directly social work, but nonetheless appears as productive work." [20]

In all this, it is hard to separate moral from legal discrimination against the private sector. One causes the other, and thus Zaslavskaia rendered a signal service after the fall of Khrushchev when she pointed out the moral legitimacy of the private plot [427, 56–57, 59, 66–67]. She started from an evidently widely held concept, even though she did not agree with it:

The great, and in some instances the decisive, importance of the personal plot in the reproduction of the kolkhozniks' living conditions led to the idea that its excessive profitability justifies the low payment for work in socialized production. The opinion is heard that the low payment for [kolkhoz] work may not be considered separately [from income from the plot] because conformity between work and income is achieved only in the kolkhoz sector as a whole.

From an economic, and possibly sincerely Marxist, point of view, Zaslavskaia is concerned about whether the income from the private plot may be considered as "not derived from labor, speculative." She concludes: "As long as this income, measured per unit of labor, does not exceed socially necessary limits and, even more, if it corresponds with normal pay, then it is labor payment."

She then calculates that the net income from the private plot amounts to a little more than three rubles per workday—below the average sovkhoz daily wage or equal to it only if retail price levels for calculating private output are used. "Consequently (and this must be emphasized) the income which the kolkhozniks thus acquire is labor income, in most cases it contains no surplus product and does not affect the material interests of the other members of the socialist society." Finally, with some interesting, selected data she attempts to demonstrate how, when pay

---

[20] [56a, 77]. Sonin [350, 181] says that work on the private plots "may not be regarded as directly social [that is, it is social indirectly] because it is not organized on a social basis." For further discussions of the subject, see [56a, 76–77]; [339a, 43–45]. From the Communist point of view, the heart of the problem lies in the fact that although work may be useful for the community and economically necessary, as long as it is private and is not socially organized, it is tainted.

from the kolkhoz public sector is low, a reduction in the private plots does not result in any higher labor inputs into the socialized sector. Suslov [373, 195-198] goes even a step further; he concedes that because the kolkhoznik also has production expenses and because he receives few transfer payments from the state or the kolkhoz, he is entitled to a "surplus product" as long as he does not charge excessive prices on the market. Suslov believed that an income of 4.30 rubles for an eight-hour day on the private plot was legitimate in 1964.

Zaslavskaia's argument is interesting in two respects. It reflects the current attitude of the Soviet leadership toward the private sector, and it shows the point when the present indulgent tolerance could change once again into restrictive measures. That is to say, this could occur when the kolkhozniks' earnings reach the level of sovkhoz pay, and if they do not realize that their private plots have become "superfluous."

At present the authorities are confronted with a dilemma: In most parts of the country, every hand is needed for the socialized sector,[21] but the private sector has been legitimized to such an extent that labor may not be forcibly removed from it—especially since so little of the work done there is put in by able-bodied people who are liable for work in the public sector. The doctrine current during the Khrushchev administration was quite different: "As the public sector of the kolkhozes develops . . . the labor applied with low efficiency to the personal plot will wholly be employed in the social economy." [22]

Several Soviet authors assert that 30 percent of the total worktime of the kolkhoz population is spent on private activities.[23] These are, however, only estimates; no reliable statistical surveys have been carried out.[24] In fact, such calculations lump together all the worktime of family members of kolkhozniks, workers, and employees on the private plots and livestock holdings with everything that the able-bodied kolkhozniks do outside the socialized sector, both within and outside the kolkhozes and during the winter.[25] Even so, it is quite clear that the private plots take up very little of the time available for able-bodied kolkhozniks, and especially the men, to work in the kolkhoz.[26] Thus, only part of the 30

[21] Concerning the shortage of labor in the kolkhozes, see [414, passim].

[22] Politicheskaia ekonomiia sotsialisma (Moscow: 1960), p. 475 (cited in [339, 33]).

[23] [344a, 154]; [339a, 48]; 29 percent, according to [80, 47].

[24] [132, 120]; [339a, 47].

[25] [109, 244-246]; [170, 69]; Zaslavskaia, [426, 177-178]; [113, 142].

[26] [51, 58-59]; [340, 138-139].

percent of the worktime cited above related to the fully able-bodied and would be wholly available for work in the socialized sector; moreover, the amount of time which could legally be extracted would not exceed the obligatory minimums which have to be put in on kolkhoz work. The able-bodied men devote about one-tenth of their efforts to the private sector, the women—mostly married, with children—a little more than one-third, and a considerable proportion of work on the private plots and livestock holdings is done by pensioners, invalids, and children.[27]

One solution to this dilemma has a reasonable chance of success. It is not a new concept and, indeed, was vaguely postulated in Article 4 of the 1935 model statute, which read: "The artel leadership may, when necessary, hire out a few horses from the socialized work animals to the artel members at an appropriate charge." Evidently this was intended for personal requirements such as travel and transportation to town, as well as for working the private plot, for transporting feed, fuel, grain, and so on. This was reaffirmed by the CC CPSU in 1954 [275, 84] and, more recently, in Articles 4 and 42 of the new model statute of 1969. In practice, much has depended on the interpretation of these regulations and on the availability of draft animals and machinery; well-equipped kolkhozes should always have some spare transport capacity. At present, many kolkhozes own but few work animals [170, 68], others keep horses mainly for working their members' plots [339a, 12, n. 1]. In this way, kolkhozes can help to reduce the working time spent on the private sector and thereby make more time available for work in the kolkhoz.

This approach was officially recommended after the removal of Khrushchev, and its purpose was made quite clear in an article, by two agricultural economists, which appeared as part of an economic course in the Central Committee's agricultural paper: "Help by the kolkhoz in ploughing the private plots of the kolkhozniks, in harvesting fodder for the privately owned livestock, and in selling the produce also contributes to the acquisition of additional labor." [28] Shmelev's proposal, in 1965, went a little further:

Meanwhile, it would be worth looking into another way of cutting down the work—its partial mechanization. In our opinion, we should start manufacturing motorized universal hand-cultivators, reapers, and so on, which the

---

[27] [170, 66]; [275, 129]; see also the detailed figures in [239, 72] and [80, 110, 132, 134-135, 137-141]; cf. Nancy Nimitz, [262, 86]; Norton T. Dodge and Murray Feshbach, "The Role of Women in Soviet Agriculture," in [158, 279].

[28] [285]; for similar instances, see [272, 71]; [452, 30 September 1966].

kolkhozes and sovkhozes could rent out to the kolkhozniks and sovkhoz workers for a certain sum. . . . The increase in the work done in the social-ized sector can thereby also come from diminishing the labor applied to the private sector by means of mechanization. This is also important because the seasonal shortage of labor in the social sector coincides with the shortage of labor on the plots. To the extent that the kolkhozniks are assisted by tech-nology and work animals in their harvesting and other work on their plots, the possibilities would be created of freeing their labor for social production.[29]

This is certainly an interesting proposal, but its large-scale implemen-tation at present and in the near future is unlikely. It would require not only "a lengthy period of time" but also "large material resources" [*80*, 143]. At the moment, the Soviet agricultural machinery industry is fully occupied. On the subject of simpler forms of easing the work on the plots, another author confirmed that in 1965 such assistance was by no means universally extended [*170*, 68]. Moreover, the assistance—which must normally be paid for—leaves much to be desired; it is usually too late and the equipment used is not designed for small plots [*153*, 62–63].

Nevertheless, complaints were heard during a conference, at the Eco-nomic Research Institute of the USSR Gosplan in October 1965, that problems of the labor force in the private sector were neglected and that no research was carried out into the relationship of this labor with the socialized sector. The participants at the conference were agreed that: "In calculating the labor requirements of the kolkhoz, one must take into account not only the labor requirements of the kolkhoz's public sec-tor but also the requirements of the kolkhozniks' personal plots." [30]

During Khrushchev's administration, it was felt that the labor re-quirements of the private sector could be disregarded; indeed, the pri-vate sector was regarded as a rich reservoir which needed only to be tapped in the right way. The decree of 6 March 1956 (see p. 265 f.) was quite openly aimed at getting the rural population to put more work in on the public sector by threatening to reduce their private plots if they did not. This was a very real and delicate threat for the kolkhoznik and was later described as "the chief scarecrow on the countryside" [*200*, 619]. Yet, this leverage was lost because the state and the party were unmistakably aiming at a reduction of the private plot in any case, and they seized every opportunity to carry this out even when the plotholders

---

[29] [*339*, 35–36]; cf. [*170*, 68]; [*80*, 143]; [*153*, 63]; Keith Bush, "Minitractors advocated for private plots," Radio Liberty CRD 115/67. Shmelev repeated his pro-posal in [*339a*, 112–113].

[30] [*113*, 141–142]; see also [*373*, 201].

performed their duties in the public sector. The kolkhozniks therefore felt that nothing they could do would avert the Damocles sword which hung over them. The threat may have had some effect, at least initially, but this effect is difficult to assess and is still a matter of dispute within the Soviet Union. A Soviet jurist declared that many kolkhoz chairmen regarded "the diminution of the kolkhoz households' personal plots as the principal means of enforcing labor discipline," but that this practice "proved to be a failure." [31] Dorosh described an instance when this threat proved effective, even though it was used quite illegally by the kolkhoz chairman who issued and carried out the threat without waiting for approval from the kolkhoz or plenipotentiary assembly, as happened quite frequently.[32]

Until recently, the private plot represented—for the average kolkhoznik and his family—the principal means of achieving a modest existence. For this reason, the severity of the threat to reduce the size of the plot was in many cases out of all proportion to its real intent. One cannot meaningfully manipulate the "material interest" of a family in such a way that its subsistence minimum is removed. And if it is to be effective, the reduction must affect a sizable portion of the private plot yet still leave enough for a further cut if need be. This is hardly possible in the case of such tiny plots. Moreover, the reduction of the plot was used only in a minority of cases to combat idleness as such. Usually it was a case of a kolkhoznik trying to earn more than the minimal kolkhoz pay and thus devoting too much of his energy to the private plot or to semilegal work outside the kolkhoz. If his private plot was reduced, increased work in the public sector could not make up for the shortfall unless the kolkhoz pay was really commensurate or unless additional payments-in-kind, and especially fodder, were made for good work. Conceivably, it took a long time for a kolkhoznik to get his confiscated portion of land back by working hard in the public sector. This must have been especially true during the Khrushchev period, when the general tendency was to reduce plots.

Dorosh pictured an instance when a kolkhoz chairman used this threat against a woman whose adolescent son had left the kolkhoz in search of work in the industrial region of the eastern Ukraine. The

---

[31] [171, 22-23]. Similarly, [230, 65].

[32] [99, 25-26]; another case was mentioned in [452, 18 December 1967]; concerning the illegality of this procedure, see [171, 23]; for the frequency of cases, see [38, 22].

woman was to persuade her son to return, or else her plot would be "clipped." The following exchange occurred between two observers [94, 53]:

"If he [the son] doesn't come home and live here, the kolkhoz will cut down the plot. That's the message which he [the kolkhoz chairman] sent to Aunty Polya. But can she manage to get by without the plot?"
    "They won't take it all away."
    "But still."

"But still" meant that even if only a part of the plot was taken away, the remainder was inadequate for providing a bare subsistence.

In such instances, the result may be the opposite of what is desired: The owner of the plot just gives up altogether and attempts to leave the kolkhoz, either by legal or by illegal means. "They are now checking the dimensions of the plots which do not correspond with the statute, and the housewife says if they are cut everyone will quit" [95, 77]. Zaslavskaia made the same point [427, 67]:

When the pay is low for work done in the kolkhoz's socialized sector, any reduction of the personal plot under an average level is not appropriate for raising labor inputs. The kolkhoznik's labor, which is thereby freed, does not find its way into the socialized sector of the artel but in other directions, often with the worker leaving the kolkhoz for good.

Thus, such reductions often resulted in a loss of manpower rather than in increased labor inputs into the public sector. This is clearly evidenced by the millions of kolkhozniks who have left the farms since about 1957 in labor-deficit regions.

Another consequence of the negative results of this hard line was the comparatively recent emphasis on "material incentives" offered for better work in the public sector. The private plot was no longer threatened with reductions; instead larger allocations of fodder were distributed to those kolkhozniks who worked well in the kolkhoz. This had the advantages of saving the kolkhoznik time which he would otherwise have spent gathering feed and of freeing him for more work in the public sector. In this connection, Zaslavskaia wrote [427, 6]:

The fact that the [kolkhoz] peasantry are keen on receiving payments-in-kind (especially grain and fodder) should be exploited for the public good for an increase in kolkhoz production. However, the issue and sale of produce from the socialized sector to the kolkhozniks have been reduced during the past [pre-1965] years.

When a guaranteed minimum wage was introduced for kolkhozes in 1966, the sale or free issue of foodstuffs and fodder to the kolkhozniks was also made obligatory. In that year some 50 percent of all kolkhozes still gave out produce as part of payment [340, 44].

Whether these more humane and more rational approaches work in the desired direction without encouraging the "expansion" of the private sector (which so disturbed Khrushchev) is another matter. But it has been proven that the old methods brought no progress whatsoever; they actually produced "the very opposite results" [195, 80].

Soviet writings of the last few years show that the inner relationship between the public and the private sectors in the sphere of pay and labor use has been fully appreciated; indeed, it has probably been appreciated for longer, even if it has not been set down on paper. However, encouragement rather than discouragement of the private sector, with the aim of stimulating labor inputs into the public sector, presents two dangers to the Communist ideal. It can lead to an even greater interrelationship and mutual interdependence between the two sectors, and nobody can say with certainty how it will work out in practice.

The above remarks are directed mainly at the kolkhoz sector, although many of them also apply to the private plots of workers and employees and especially to those of sovkhozes and other state agricultural enterprises; certainly this is so intended by many of the Soviet authors cited. Specific data referring to the private plots and livestock holdings of the workers and employees are few and far between, probably because this area has been comparatively neglected by Soviet authors, but some data will be treated below.

Venzher, a writer who has been concerned with kolkhozes for several decades, occasionally mentions the situation in state agricultural enterprises, especially to draw comparisons with what is going on in kolkhozes. He is quite aware that the private plots in the sovkhozes are usually smaller than in the kolkhozes but also of less significance for this section of the rural population. This is true because sovkhoz workers and employees enjoy higher earnings from the public sector than kolkhozniks. Thus the private incomes of sovkhoz workers and employees are relatively lower—but not wholly dispensable. Even though the level of mechanization in the sovkhozes is far higher than in the kolkhozes, it is by no means up to modern standards. "The large number of manual laborers in the sovkhozes testifies to the existence of a group of low paid workers; this also lies at the bottom of the necessity of retaining personal plots in the sovkhozes" [*396*, 55]. And it is precisely for these lower paid groups that the contribution of the private sector plays such an important role. For a Kazakh livestock sovkhoz, private incomes made up 50 to 60 percent of total earnings in 1967 but contributed only 30 to 40 percent to the earnings of the higher income groups [*357*, 22]. Figures published in 1961 show that the average income from private plots and livestock holdings in RSFSR sovkhozes amounted to only about 25 percent less than the incomes from kolkhoz private plots [*52*, 57], and in 1969 it was 29 percent less for the all-union average [*339a*, 93] (cf. p. 193 f. above).

The seasonal nature of labor seemingly is no problem for the sovkhoz worker, as he is employed—or at least paid a minimum wage—throughout the year. But that holds true only for those who are called permanent workers. Many women and aged people in the sovkhozes are not accepted as permanent workers; their employment is for the peak season only.[33] For them the private plot offers productive employment and some income for the rest of the year. This is also true for some categories of workers in rural processing industries with seasonal employment [*339a*, 28].

R. Nazarov attempted to distinguish clearly between the private plots of sovkhoz workers and those of kolkhozniks but was obliged to conclude that the basic problem is the same for both groups [*256*, 69]:

If only it were possible to satisfy their [the sovkhoz workers' and employees'] requirements of such [agricultural] products through sovkhoz production, then there would of course be no necessity to retain the personal plots of this group of the population. Yet under the present circumstances, when the sovkhozes deliver by far the major portion of their output to the procurement organizations in order to fulfill the state plan, they have too little produce left to feed their own workers and employees. Moreover, the current level of the total income of the sovkhoz worker (the average per family member) is lower than in the urban workers' and employees' families; this also has great significance when dealing with the question of the fate of the sovkhoz workers' and employees' personal plots.

---

[33] For documentation and details, see Wädekin, *Die Bezahlung der Arbeit in der sowjetischen Landwirtschaft* (Berlin: 1972), pp. 221–222, n. 63, and 320–323.

Nazarov concludes: These private plots too are "directly connected with the socialized production, from which the working force receives its pay and its plots as well as part of its fodder and foodstuffs."

DIVISION OF LABOR IN CROP PRODUCTION

Of the two predominant crop products for the kolkhoznik's diet, potatoes and grain, the former is produced on plots and the latter is obtained from the public sector. These facts illustrate the clear and visible division of labor—some Soviet authors also use that word [*128, 37; 339a, 71*]—between the sectors. However, this is also true for other products, such as feedroots (public sector) and vegetables (mainly in the private sector) [*339a, 71*].

About two-thirds of the area under private plots has been taken up by potatoes for well over a decade (see Table 3). The same ratio is also true of kolkhoz private plots alone. Just half of the total area in the USSR under potatoes belong to the private sector, yet these account for almost two-thirds of the total crop; thus the private plots are more productive than the public fields. From these plots, the private sector has marketed seven to eight million tons of potatoes in recent years (or near to half of the total marketed output) and kept fifty to sixty million tons for own consumption and feed (see Table 26). Some kolkhozes have given up growing potatoes altogether, leaving this entirely to the private sector [*69, 139*].

The converse is true of grain. The proportion of the total area in the private sector sown to grain declined from one-quarter in 1955 to one-sixth in 1969 (see Table 3). During the past decade, this amounted to about one percent of the total area under grain and the share of total grain output to come from the private sector has amounted to 1 to 2 percent. In the Ukraine, the share is larger: The 1.1 million tons in 1964 represented some 4 percent of the total harvest [*173, 61*]. This is clearly insufficient to feed the rural population, not to mention livestock feed requirements or a marketable surplus.

More than 90 percent of the rural population's requirement of grain is supplied by the public sector, but about the same percentage of the consumption of potatoes by the rural population and their livestock comes from the private sector.

During the period 1959 to 1963, grain accounted for some 80 percent of the total value of produce sold or issued as payments-in-kind to kolkhozniks; only 3 to 5 percent was accounted for by potatoes and 2 to 4 percent by hay, the percentages for vegetables, dairy products and young livestock being negligible.[34] (Under the heading "Miscellaneous," however, straw, both as fodder and litter, is also of a certain importance.) Today, the share of grain is still "over 70 percent." [35] In 1958, an average of 1.0 to 1.5 kilograms of grain was paid per workday-unit, and in 1964 and 1965, when the general level of earnings was higher, 1.5 to 2.0 kilograms on those farms which still paid by workday-units.[36]

According to Soviet physiological norms, to which Morozov refers [162, 334], human requirements for food grains amount to 130 to 140 kilograms a year, with a further 60 to 120 kilograms of grain a year to cover all the kolkhozniks' requirements (including, above all, animal feed). For the total kolkhoz population of 1964, this comes to seven to eight million tons for human consumption and some ten to fourteen million tons for all requirements, according to Morozov [250, 149–150]. But he added that "in recent years" (that is, until 1963) such a quantity was not made available to the kolkhozniks, while in 1963 not even the required quantity of bread grain was forthcoming, either as payments-in-kind or on sale by the farms. Thus the kolkhozniks were obliged to meet some of their requirements through purchases of bread and other grain products in the towns and industrial centers. Starting from the Soviet physiological norms, the quantities required by the kolkhoz population in 1969 may be estimated at 6.5 to 7 million tons for human consumption, and at 9.5 to 13 million tons for all requirements. This has to be contrasted with the data for actual grain issues.

No direct figures are published by the Soviet authorities concerning the amount of grain supplied by the kolkhozes to their members, but the quantities can be estimated from indirect sources.[37] According to my

---

[34] [250, 145]. For references for vegetable oil, oil-bearing seeds, fruit and honey, see N. V. Tsogoev, *Statistika sebestoimosti sel'skogo khoziaistva* (Moscow: 1965), p. 47.

[35] K. Garipov, "Natural'naia oplata truda v kolkhozakh," [435], no. 1 (1971), 41. In the Ukraine in 1967, it was still 80 to 90 percent, according to T. Kotsiuba, *Garantirovannaia oplata i zakon raspredeleniia po trudu v kolkhozakh* (Moscow: 1969), p. 81.

[36] Estimated on the basis of the figures given in [87, 144].

[37] Nimitz [263, 105] has constructed a valuable series of estimates for kolkhoz distribution of grain during the period from 1932 to 1959 by using sources other than those cited here. However, her estimates for the period since 1953 seem excessively high and do not wholly correspond with the overall picture given by Morozov or with the figures supplied by [44, 116]. Her estimates of the grain fed to livestock in the private sector (p. 101) also appear to be too high; in subtracting kol-

earlier estimates [*416*, 135–136], in 1958 between 17 and 18 million tons of grain were issued to kolkhozniks, and in the early 1960s only 8 to 10 million tons (including sales). On the basis of more recent information, it can be calculated that in 1965 a total of 12.4 million tons of grain was issued, or 810 kilograms per household, but in 1969 only 6.9 million tons or 460 kilograms.[38] From 1966 to 1967 alone, the total amount dropped by 28 percent,[39] after having presumably already experienced a slight reduction in 1966.

The decline per household was less than in the absolute totals because the number of kolkhoz households also declined. But even so, the amount of grain paid out per household in 1962 was only 60 percent of that paid out in 1958 [*395*, 283]. Of course, 1958 was a record harvest year and especially large quantities of grain were issued. This doubtless would explain the frequent warnings found in Soviet journals of the time and later against the issuance of too much grain to the kolkhozniks because this grain would find its way on to the kolkhoz markets. The warnings also referred to the great regional variations in the distribution of grain. However, by 1960 at the latest, the grain allocations had been so reduced that any warning against excessive distribution must be treated as a pretext. The reductions severely affected the privately owned livestock, to which more than a third of the still available grain was being fed [*139*, 383].

The reductions in payments-in-kind were only to a minor extent offset by the increasing amounts of grain sold by the kolkhozes to their members (from 700,000 tons in 1959 to 2,050,000 tons in 1963 [*250*, 265]). According to figures published for the Ukraine, nearly as much grain was purchased by kolkhozniks in 1960 as in 1959, even though the price to be paid within kolkhozes had risen by an average of 30 percent in the interval.[40] This shows the value attached to grain by the kolkhoz population.

---

khoz and sovkhoz feed grains from the total, she does not appear to have taken into account the other state enterprises such as auxiliary enterprises belonging to factories, fattening farms, scientific institutes, and procurement bases.

[38] Percentages of the kolkhoz harvests are given by K. Garipov (as n. 35 above), and figures on the total amounts harvested and the numbers of households in [*14a*, 292, 295, 397].

[39] V. Zhurikov, "Luchshe ispol'zovat' mery material'nogo pooshchreniia kolkhoznikov," [*435*, no. 1 (1969), 10].

[40] [*225*, 40–41]. In 1963, the average price paid for a centner of grain was 9.66 rubles [*250*, 288], so that the kolkhoz population paid a total of about 198 million rubles for the all-union amount of grain sold in that year (see above).

For an average family of 3.5 persons, we arrive at an all-union average of about 230 kilograms of grain issued in 1965—which corresponds to the norms cited above—but only 130 kilograms in 1969. Assuming that 270 to 280 man-days were put in per family per year,[41] in 1965 barely three kilograms and in 1969 hardly over 1.5 kilograms of grain were issued per man-day (as opposed to workday units),[42] including purchases from the kolkhozes. Even taking into account the increase in retail bread sales in rural areas, the amount for 1969 left hardly anything over for feed. In view of the differences prevailing between regions as well as between farms, this meant that while in some places the kolkhoz population was compelled to purchase bread or grain for its own consumption, in others there was enough grain left over for feed.

More or less comparable sets of indices in various Soviet sources, together with the figures given above for 1965 and 1969, give an approximate picture of the entire period from 1953 to 1969.[43] On this basis, it can be said that in 1953, 1954, 1958, 1965, and 1966, barely three kilograms of grain were sold or issued as payment-in-kind to kolkhozniks per man-day, from 1955 to 1957 as much as 3.5 to 4.0 kilograms, from 1959 to 1964 (except 1963) about two kilograms, and in 1968 and 1969 only 1.5 to 2.0 kilograms. Issues of potatoes remained at an approximately equal level up to 1965: they were greater in 1954, 1956, and 1957, and smaller than usual in 1962 and 1963, while during the period 1960 to 1963, issues of hay were only about half those from 1954 to 1958.[44]

Payments-in-kind play a bigger part in wage increments (*dopolnitel'naia oplata*) and premiums than in basic kolkhoz wages. Milk, meat, rice, buckwheat, and millet in particular are issued as increments, while the decree of 16 May 1966, on minimum wages in kolkhozes, mentioned grain and fodder among the products forming part of overall and guaranteed remuneration-in-kind (or which may be purchased on the basis of work performance). Within the totals outlined above, this means that payment-in-kind per ordinary workday is below those averages.

Whenever it is necessary to mobilize as many kolkhozniks as possible—including those not actually obligated to work—for urgent oper-

---

[41] Calculated for 1965 and 1968 from [*14*, 423].

[42] According to N. Nimitz [*262*, 112], in 1953 an average of 1.45 workday units were reckoned per man-day, and in 1958, 1.58, the coefficient being higher the more specialized the activity.

[43] For example, [*427*, 167; *87*, 143; *395*, 283; *269*, 268–269].

[44] Cf. the indices for potatoes, hay and other products in [*87*, 143; *250*, 145; *269*, 268].

ations such as harvesting, additional remuneration is often promised which not only exceeds normal wages as regards monetary value but is in a considerable part in kind or else includes a right to purchase additional amounts of produce. Frequently, a fixed percentage of the harvest is set aside for this purpose, a practice which of late has once more become widespread, for example, in respect to millet, rice, and buckwheat.[45] In areas where little grain is produced, the situation of the kolkhozniks is particularly difficult. The decree of 27 March 1962 enabled the authorities to exploit this difficulty in Central Asia. They made available grain from other parts of the country for issue as premiums to induce kolkhozniks to work harder in the public sector, especially during the cotton harvest. In the summer of 1963, I met a kolkhoznik at one of the kolkhoz markets of Tashkent (Uzbekistan). With his father, he sold grain there which they had received as premia from their kolkhoz. He had come for this purpose from Chimkentskaia oblast (Kirghizia) and apparently was of an above-average educational level.

Any reselling of grain on the free market by kolkhozniks cannot have been in appreciable quantities, because the market turnover would have reflected the additional amounts. The main interest of the kolkhoznik in payments-in-kind was summed up by a kolkhoz chairman in the following words: "He wants to provide the family with bread and other foodstuffs and the livestock which belongs to him with feed" [*221*, 41]. In economically backward kolkhozes, it was a question of survival rather than interest [cf. *249*, 25].

Because of the underdeveloped means of communication and the primitive trade network in the country—only a minority of villages have their own bakery—and of the still relatively low cash earnings in many kolkhozes, grain from the kolkhoz represents the main source of subsistence unless kolkhozniks want to go to the trouble and expense of traveling far afield. Not enough grain can be grown on the private plot to feed a family unless the whole plot is given over to it, and then the family would have to go without other foodstuffs like potatoes and vegetables. Thus the kolkhoznik is totally dependent upon the public sector for his supplies of grain and bread. When, under Khrushchev, the au-

---

[45] For a thorough account of the system of wage increments and premiums, see Wädekin, *Die Bezahlung der Arbeit in der sowjetischen Landwirtschaft* (Berlin: Duncker & Humblot, 1972), Chapter II and IV, and—as far as these are paid in kind—Wädekin, "Payment in Kind in Soviet Agriculture," *Bulletin—Institute for the Study of the USSR,* nos. 9 and 11 (1971)

thorities sought to exploit this dependency, the maneuver certainly had the kolkhoz population worried. But it also contributed substantially to the deterioration of the agricultural situation. The dependence is mutual: In return for the grain, the state and the kolkhoz receive the labor of the kolkhoznik, which they need today more than ever before.

Furthermore, by supplying the grain, the public sector frees the private sector for growing not only all its own potatoes but also half of the towns' requirements as well. With their present crop structure and organization, the kolkhozes and sovkhozes would not be capable of producing enough potatoes or vegetables. Here is a mutual dependence which can only be avoided through a radical restructuring.

"The fact that the kolkhozniks' subsidiary farms receive farm products-in-kind (especially grain and animal feed) has considerable significance under the present circumstances and represents an important incentive for people to concern themselves with the growth of social production" [50, 40]. A close interrelationship also exists between the livestock sector and the provision of fodder; this is examined in the next section. Compared with grain, potatoes, and vegetables, all other crops supplied by the kolkhoz or sovkhoz are of minor importance in the relationship between the private and public sectors. Exceptions might be oilseeds and vegetable oil, but even these are included in the "other produce" which generally accounts for only six to eight percent of the total value of the payments-in-kind [250, 145].

The situation outside kolkhozes and especially in sovkhozes is less clear. The customary view is that the sovkhoz workers and employees obtain any produce which they do not purchase on the market only from their private plots and not as payment-in-kind. This opinion is also advanced by Soviet writers.

The only thing that is certain is that payments-in-kind play a lesser role here than in kolkhozes, due to both their absolute and relative size (the latter in relation to the higher cash earnings). The idea that sovkhoz workers and employees do not receive any payments-in-kind stems largely from a statistical fiction whereby nearly all agricultural products issued by sovkhozes to their workforce, either as sales and payments-in-kind or in canteen meals, count as marketed output and as part of the plan fulfillment [434, no. 43 (1969), 16]. But even where these items are valued at retail prices, they often represent hidden payments-in-kind. This is because the sovkhoz is obliged to issue the products, first because its workers and employees are often unable to acquire these items else-where (or only with great difficulty), and second, because it wishes to retain its labor force. This is particularly the case in remote regions such as the Virgin Lands. As a rule, however, sovkhozes must obtain the per-mission of the oblast and republican authorities before they can make additional payments or pay premiums-in-kind, and upper limits are pre-scribed.[46]

The statistical sleight of hand and its consequent misconceptions were sharply criticized by Morozov [250, 154–155]:

It is generally thought that labor in the sovkhoz sector is paid with cash and that the sovkhoz workers' requirements of agricultural products are met by the consumer cooperatives. In fact, the system of payments in the sovkhozes has no unit like the *trudoden'* (which, as a rule, consists of cash as well as payments-in-kind), but basically the same problems arise concerning labor pay-ment as in the kolkhozes. The same agricultural characteristics hold for sov-khoz production (such as natural and climatic conditions) as in the kolkhozes. The sovkhozes are served by the same cooperative trade network of stores as the kolkhozes [which Morozov had previously described as completely inade-quate].

It is another matter altogether that the pay of the sovkhoz worker is higher than that of the kolkhoznik (although this is not always so). Without doubt, the personal plots in the sovkhozes are somewhat smaller. This unquestion-ably has an influence on the structure of consumption, consumer demand, and so on, but in principle it does not resolve the problem of supplying the workers with foodstuffs and fodder nor, consequently, the problem of the combination of *natura* and money payments for work done (or the issue [of produce] in lieu of money payments).

In [Soviet] economic literature, it is hard to find any statements concern-ing the payments-in-kind of sovkhoz workers. At one time, the issue of grain for work of the sovkhoz combine operators was even abolished. But statistics show that here, too, a certain part of the payment (especially premiums and additional payments) are given in kind.

Morozov cites figures which, although they contain certain discrep-ancies, do indicate that sizable amounts are involved. However, it is clear that these payments-in-kind, including the sales at prices usually below those of the retail trade and the canteen meals, have by no means the same significance as in the kolkhozes. Yet Chernichenko maintains that the sovkhoz worker is just as anxious as the kolkhoznik to receive

[46] [162, 378]; for the detailed regulations, see Wädekin, "Payment in Kind in Soviet Agriculture," *Bulletin—Institute for the Study of the USSR*, no. 9 (1971), 5–18.

grain as payment-in-kind, and as feed [75, 140, 142]. As early as 1966, twice as much grain was issued and sold to the mechanizers (including those of sovkhozes) in the Altai krai as in previous years [*142*, 122–123]. The amounts were laid down for each union republic. An article at the end of 1966 urged the extension of *natura* payments for sovkhoz workers and made it clear that "many categories" of the sovkhoz labor force [that is, not all categories] had no opportunities for getting grain from their farms [*50*, 43]. One explanation may be that many sovkhozes located near large cities are organized for supplying those cities with foodstuffs, and the sovkhoz workers can thus get to the urban stores and markets relatively easily. Nowadays practically every Soviet city is surrounded by several sovkhozes. The issue of *natura* payments "undoubtedly plays a certain role" in sovkhozes, but it is regarded as a "temporary expedient which will eventually outlive itself" [*162*, 378]. Too little is known concerning these matters by both Soviet and Western specialists for any definitive appraisal.

FEED, GRAZING, AND YOUNG ANIMALS FOR PRIVATELY-OWNED LIVESTOCK

According to a "very rough calculation" by Belianov [*56a*, 40], privately-owned livestock in 1965 consumed about 85 million tons of feed units (1 kilogram of oats by Soviet standards), of which only 25 million tons originated from the private plot area. The rest was from wages-in-kind, haymaking and pasture on public land, purchases from state and cooperative agencies, and so on. Feed grain, hay, and pasture were the most important components.

It has been shown that the quantities of grain issued to kolkhozniks in 1963 were below what is deemed necessary for human subsistence according to Soviet physiological norms. This was primarily attributable to the poor harvest of that year, because the shortfall was clearly not a matter of deliberate policy even during the latter Khrushchev years. The authorities did, however, strive to reduce the amount of grain fed by the kolkhozniks to their livestock. That this represented a privation nearly as severe as the reduction of grain for human consumption was evidenced by the flight from the land, by the purchase of bread in the towns, and by subsequent admissions from the authorities themselves. The private ownership of livestock is, for the kolkhozniks, almost as important as their daily bread. In 1963, a kilogram of meat even on the relatively inexpensive intrakolkhoz market cost from 1.70 to 1.90 rubles and a kilogram of milk cost 13.2 kopeks.[47] When it is recalled that average earnings in 1962 amounted to 1.22 rubles in cash and 43 kopeks-in-kind per workday, it is clear that these prices were much too high for the ordinary kolkhoznik with a family to feed. Unless he chose to live on just bread, potatoes, and vegetables, he had no choice but to keep his own livestock, because he received precious little in the way of animal products from his kolkhoz [87, 143].

A second factor must be considered. The private plot and livestock holding can contribute so much to the modest incomes of the kolkhoz population only because meat, milk, butter, and eggs in the Soviet Union are extremely expensive when compared with other foodstuffs (except certain fresh fruits and vegetables), and this makes it disproportionately profitable to concentrate upon the output of animal products. This is best demonstrated by the price relationship between grain and pork. In 1963, kolkhozes were paid an average of 8.41 rubles for a centner of wheat (including premium payments for plan overfulfillment, and so on), and for a centner of pork the average live-weight price was 98 rubles (but it must be stressed that this is live-weight, because the prices above are slaughter-weight prices). Thus the price of pork was about twelve times that of wheat, whereas the normal price relationship of barley to pork in the West is 1:6 or 1:7 and even less for wheat.[48] (The price relationship which obtained in the Moldavian SSR in 1967 was frankly absurd. Against a price ranging from 94 to 130 rubles a centner for pork—depending upon the quality and the season—the price for a centner of soft wheat or rye was 7.60 rubles, for feed barley 5.20 rubles, and for low-grade corn 5.00 rubles a centner [358, 91, 122], giving a grain to meat ratio of about 1:20 against feed barley and corn.) Even assuming unfavorable conditions, a kolkhoznik in 1963, for instance, could purchase a centner of grain from the kolkhoz for about 8.50 rubles. He could then buy a piglet for five or ten rubles (at the most) in the fall, fatten it up for about 40 rubles, and sell it to the state for 100 rubles. This would give him a profit of about 50 rubles, equivalent to one and a half times the average monthly earnings at that time and as much as six

[47] Prices derived from [250, 288 (table)]; meat is reckoned on the basis of slaughter weight without bones. The price of meat may have been unusually low in 1963, as a result of heavy slaughterings resulting from lack of feed.

[48] Naum M. Jasny, "Production costs and prices in Soviet agriculture" in [158, 238].

months' pay in a poor kolkhoz. His profit would be even greater if he sold the meat on an urban kolkhoz market. Since then, piglet prices have risen,[49] as have procurement prices (not consumers' prices) for meat.

This is not the place to consider why, despite this price relationship, livestock raising in the Soviet public sector should have been unprofitable, at least until the price increases of 1970. Yet the pithy statement of Bukovskii tends to confirm our calculations [68, 172]: "Above all, it is a paradox that livestock raising [in the public sector] is unprofitable, but the people make a living from it." However, one essential condition is adequate fodder for the livestock. That is why the kolkhoznik virtually stopped selling grain and severely limited his sales of potatoes in 1963. That year the Party's agricultural policy and the poor harvest combined to cut down his payments-in-kind, and he preferred instead to convert these into meat, milk, and eggs [139, 383–384].

These calculations explain why the kolkhoznik will spare no bother and shies at hardly any price to lay his hands on grain (or bread, flour, or flour products) which will enable him to devote more of his food grains to feeding livestock. In an article which appeared in 1962, Morozov pointed out that the kolkhoznik would still be willing to purchase grain even at the higher retail prices. The amounts sold to each household had to be limited, because: "Practice shows that even at these prices, some kolkhozniks buy up bread and feed grains and feed it to their livestock, selling the resulting product on the extravillage market. Instances are also to be found in the towns where the so-called 'urban kolkhozniks' buy up bread in the state stores and feed their animals with it for sale later on the market. They are not put off by the state retail prices (even when the trade margin is not deducted [in kolkhozes which sell at retail prices])."[50] The general ban since 1956 on feeding grain, grain products, and other foodstuffs from state and cooperative stores to

---

[49] A market price of 2 to 5 rubles in the fall but 20 to 35 rubles in the spring of 1964 in Central Russia is cited in [67, 200]. Dorosh [97, II, 19] mentions ten rubles paid to a kolkhoz in Yaroslavl' oblast for "a good piglet" in 1961. The retail price for young pigs under five kilograms in 1966 in Moldavian kolkhozes and sovkhozes was reckoned on the basis of 2.80 rubles a kilo slaughterweight exclusive of offal; see [358, 143]. The price of 65 to 70 rubles per piglet in the spring of 1969, is an exceptional case [452, 9 July 1969]. I was informed in an Estonian state farm (September of 1969) that piglets had become very expensive on the free market "of late." On the Novgorod kolkhoz market in August of 1970, I was told that a piglet fetched 35 rubles.

[50] [248, 150]; see also [107, 24].

livestock seems to have had little effect upon the kolkhozniks. In any event, there are not many stores in the villages where these foodstuffs are to be found.

The profit margin "through the animal's stomach" is so great, given the Soviet price structure, that it represents an irresistible inducement and also leads to the theft of fodder.[51] For the ordinary kolkhoznik, that profit is more a necessity than an inducement if he wants to earn an income from the private plot which will ensure a subsistence minimum for himself and for his family, plus a few extra rubles from sales on the market and some milk, eggs, and a little meat for Sundays and holidays. After all, official statistics include these proceeds in his total income (see p. 200 above). If his supplies of feed were to be reduced, this would affect his "not speculative," his honest "labor income" (to use Zaslavskaia's words). According to a Soviet calculation, the privately owned livestock during the period from 1961 to 1964 received on average less feed units per livestock unit than did the animals in the public sector;[52] whether this calculation is accurate and what effect resulted from the differences in the quality of feed used in each sector is an open question. In 1965, more bread grain was fed to livestock in the private sector than in 1964 [107, 24].

Kolkhozes help in supplying livestock, primarily young animals.[53] Under the second Five-Year Plan, 1933–1937, they sold 4,540,000 lambs and 16,140,000 piglets to kolkhozniks [204, 9]. Statements and recommendations to this end were often found in the relevant literature at the end of 1964 and again at the end of 1965, this time officially and with

[51] [442, 15 March 1967]; cf. below, p. 231 f.

[52] According to the table in [105, 86].

[53] [404, 17]; [225, 37, 40–41 (table)]; [173, 63]. The public enterprises themselves are interested in improving the breed of animals in the private sector, because they buy from private owners large numbers of animals for fattening [339a, 124] (cf. pp. 236 ff. below). The fact that the kolkhozniks—as well as other sections of the population—have their breeding cows serviced by bulls from the public herds (including artificial insemination, see [452, 5 December 1967]), must have led to an improvement in the privately owned inventories when compared with the early years after collectivization. This fact may help to explain why milk yields of privately owned cows have improved by 50 percent in comparison with prewar figures [56a, 96]; no other grounds are apparent for this improvement (see the doubt voiced by Jasny, [148, 718]). Paradoxically enough, the various campaigns against private livestock holdings together with the subsequent rebuilding of herds may also have exerted a positive influence. The kolkhozniks probably tended to keep the better animals and to get young animals of good stock when rebuilding their herds.

renewed emphasis (see Chapter X). In 1963 the kolkhozes had sold only 62 million rubles' worth of young animals to kolkhozniks (see p. 183). After the removal of Khrushchev, in the Saratov oblast alone, for instance, in December 1964, forty thousand calves, seventeen thousand piglets, and about thirty thousand sheep were sold to the population from the state inventories in addition to sales from the kolkhoz herds [459, 6 March 1965]. Some kolkhozes kept pigs mainly to be able to supply their kolkhozniks with piglets [146, 222]. In the Tatar ASSR in 1965, provision was made for the sale of at least 3.5 million chicks from the incubator stations to the population in addition to an increased number of piglets.[54] Of young cattle, as a rule, only a small number is sold to the population [339a, 16].

In principle, it is generally accepted in the Soviet Union that it is the duty of the kolkhoz to provide the kolkhoznik with opportunities for obtaining animal fodder, beyond the basic payments-in-kind. In the summer of 1969, the editors of the Central Committee's agricultural newspaper, condemning local actions restricting the feed basis for privately held livestock, explicitly stated: "Providing both social and private livestock with fodder is a most important task" [452, 17 July 1969]. This is again emphasized in most recent policy statements (cf. Chapter X). That it was a necessity in recent times becomes clear when we consider that in 1938, on the then considerably larger private plots (0.49 hectare for kolkhozniks' plots, see p. 81 above), more than half of the area was under grass and other feed crops [87, 25]. Since the 1950s, after much pressure had been applied to reduce the size of the plots, feed crops almost completely disappeared from these holdings.[55] Since then, "the keeping of productive livestock by the kolkhoz household largely depends upon the kolkhoz's socialized sector, because the household obtains most of the necessary feed from it: grain, hay, straw, concentrates, silage." [56] In many cases, even up to 1967, cows were not kept because the public sector did not provide enough feed [339a, 115].

However, the emphasis laid upon the duty of the public sector to provide fodder has not always been the same (cf. Chapters VIII, IX).

---

[54] [173, 63–64]; cf. in the same general sense, [91, 48–49]; [386, 70–71].

[55] See the figures in [16, 132–141].

[56] [404, 17]; in the same sense, [331, 177]: "The growth of the livestock inventories (especially cows) of the kolkhozniks is held back by the lack of an adequate feed basis." See also [230, 60, 65].

After the death of Stalin, the decree of 21 September 1953 urged that the kolkhozniks be allowed to retain stipulated amounts of the hay which they had gathered for the kolkhoz; they were to be allocated grazing space for their livestock; when necessary, kolkhoz transportation was to be provided to help them get hay and other fodder in; they were to be permitted to gather hay on areas which the kolkhoz did not use, and so on. This decree was not always adhered to under Khrushchev, but it was never rescinded, and its provisions were renewed after Khrushchev's removal (see Chapters VIII and X).

In 1965, Shmelev proposed that kolkhozniks and sovkhoz workers be helped to acquire feed; the time thereby saved would be put to use in the public sector [339, 36]. This is the same line of argument that Shmelev used in favor of assisting kolkhozniks and sovkhoz workers with farm machinery and implements to work their private plots in less time.

It was also realized that flourishing private livestock holdings are good for the public sector, too, and for the whole economy, and developments up to 1964 have shown what negative consequences can follow if this is not recognized. "And, really, will the kolkhoznik readily help bring in more and better fodder for the social livestock if his own cow is left hungry?" Thus opined a Soviet newspaper correspondent in 1966, after visiting a kolkhoz which had achieved excellent results by paying attention to the interests of its members [452, 28 September 1966].

The law of 11 January 1955, "On the Responsibility for Damage to Crops in Kolkhozes and Sovkhozes," was directed against a special form of "grazing" which was "widespread"—on winter crops and from haystacks—a practice still mentioned in 1970 [339a, 105]—and also in protective forest belts, and in fruit and berry orchards. The law was also aimed at enterprises, authorities, and organizations or their personnel, as well as at damage caused by carts and vehicles. But the threatened money fines bore more heavily on private owners of livestock.[57] On 23 June 1956, Izvestiia once again criticized the frequent instances of damage by livestock to young grain and especially condemned an apparently widespread "liberal attitude toward those guilty of damaging crops." After that a raion administration went as far as to force kolkhozes and sovkhozes to confiscate privately owned livestock grazing on their meadows

---

[57] The collection of such fines was newly regulated by an RSFSR decree of 21 July 1964: see [346, XIV, 594–595].

and fields.[58] The validity of the law of 1955 was reemphasized in 1967.[59]

When Khrushchev started his campaign to reduce the amount of land under fallow, he offered as one of the justifications, in his speech of 25 April 1958: "And you know yourselves that farming can be carried on better without fallow. You keep it just to have space where you can let the kolkhozniks graze their animals." He was subsequently twice to refer to this disguised reason for retaining fallow, as if it were a well-known fact. Khrushchev's allegations were not so far fetched as one might suppose. To kolkhoz chairmen this method offered a possibility of keeping their kolkhozniks reasonably happy and at the same time to avoid the stigma of being too "liberal" toward private livestock holding. By that time the campaign against private livestock holding had already begun. Kolkhozniks also complained when meadows were ploughed up, saying that this deprived their animals of fodder [87, 84].

In the Soviet Union, the stretches of grazing land along the sides of roads, railroad tracks, and high tension cables, on the outskirts of settlements and farms, on the edges of woods and in forest clearings comprise millions of hectares,[60] and have a far greater significance than, say, in central or western European countries. It just is not worthwhile for the kolkhoz with its machines and large groups of workers to mow these numerous and often large patches of meadow, but this is not the case for the individual private livestock owner.[61] The decree of 21 September 1953 had specifically recommended that kolkhozniks be allowed to mow "pieces of meadows on state land, on forest clearings, and on the verges of roads and canals." [62] If there were no private livestock owners who

[58] I. V. Pavlov, *Razvitie kolkhoznoi demokratii* (Moscow: 1962), p. 85.

[59] [376, 12–13]; that author also gives an account of the current application of this law in practice.

[60] S. A. Udachin, in [391, 34], spoke of as much as five million hectares at the beginning of the 1960s, including unused land set aside for the private sector but excluding forest grazing areas; at a session of the Lenin Academy of Agriculture he later gave a figure of four million hectares of unused land along roads and on the edges of settlements and production centers, and of two million hectares of mostly unused land of the so-called personal plot land fund [452, 12 February 1969].

[61] A number of cases when such land was used for grazing or haying by the population is cited from the Soviet press in [103, 124].

[62] In his speech of 25 January 1955, Khrushchev referred to the same practice, speaking of "areas which are not suitable for mowing with a mechanized haymaker, especially in kolkhozes which are short of labor." Where these pieces of meadow do not belong directly to the kolkhoz, their hay yield appears to be credited to the private sector; otherwise it would be inconceivable how 52 percent of the hay requirements of the RSFSR kolkhozniks (according to [230, 60]) could be covered from private production.

had some incentive to mow them, these pieces of land would remain unused: "Some of the hay from road verges, from the slopes of gullies, and from various waste lands, which are not customarily used by the kolkhozes for fodder purposes, drops . . . out of the productive cycle" [225, 42].

The official policy was to change once more. This potential fodder was allowed to go to waste rather than be made available to the private sector.[63] Even one year after the removal of Khrushchev, when this course had been radically reversed with the decrees of October and November 1964 (see Chapter X), it was necessary to issue an official condemnation of an evidently rather widespread practice:

Especially reprehensible are the actions of those farm officials who do not carry out mowing in woods and in other places which are not suitable for mechanized haymaking for the requirements of the socialized livestock, but who also do not allocate these spaces for the use of workers and employees.[64]

Under Khrushchev's administration, the population tried to do what it could. An elderly kolkhoznik, caught gathering hay illegally in a preservation area, shouted at the ranger in desperation: "Well, where can I get hay? Where? The meadows have been ploughed up, the kolkhoz is short of hay. No meadows anywhere, nothing to cut . . . And there's five of us at home, not counting myself and the wife" [264, 81].

Often it is left to old men, who are no longer obliged to work in the public sector, to cut the grass from the minute pieces of meadow—thus no labor is thereby lost to the kolkhoz. Sometimes these old men also gather hay for others in return for payment.

Another way of getting hay is available to kolkhozniks and other members of the rural population; this is the allocation of part of the kolkhoz hay in return for assistance in bringing it in. For the kolkhoz, this practice has the advantage that people take greater care and interest in haying; also, it attracts people who are not obliged to work in the public sector. The decree of 21 September 1953 recommended [90, IV, 92–93]:

That an advance be given to the kolkhozniks and the labor force of the tractor brigades of the machine tractor, the machine livestock and other special stations for the workdays that they put in during hay- and strawmaking of up to 10 percent of the totals of hay or straw which are prepared and registered as brought in and accepted by the kolkhoz direction, and up to 20 percent

[63] See [335, 32]; [123, 91]; [200, 484–485].
[64] [452, 4 November 1965]; an example of the same behavior as late as 1966 is in [452, 9 August 1966].

of the second cut on natural meadows; in kolkhozes which have fulfilled the haymaking plan, 30 percent of the above-plan hay to be issued for workdays. In addition, an advance of up to 5 percent of the gathered hay and up to 10 percent of the straw collected and stacked during the fodder period according to the workdays put in since the beginning of the year.

In practice, the recommendations were not uniformly observed during the subsequent years. Abramov [43, 98, 123] mentions a regulation in force at the beginning of the 1960s in the northwestern RSFSR, where not more than 10 percent of the fodder crop could be distributed. He makes it clear that 10 percent was inadequate to get the kolkhozniks interested in mowing or harvesting, and that many kolkhoz chairmen tried to get around the regulation—so that up to 40 percent was distributed in many areas. A decree of 4 February 1961 of the Ukrainian Central Committee and Council of Ministers recommended up to 5 percent of the hay and 5 percent of the straw as a guideline. A share amounting to 10 to 20 percent was mentioned for the oblast of Tambov around 1955, but here the qualification "only" was added and it was also noted that: "For this reason, feed must be bought for the cow, and it is very expensive to keep her" [331, 162]. Another reference was made to 10 percent for the Tambov oblast, but this time for 1964 [68, 167].

On the basis of such instances, it cannot be stated categorically that a share of only 10 percent—20 percent in exceptional cases—was generally observed. It can only be said that infringements of the official recommendation, as pictured by Abramov, were seldom reported in print. Nevertheless, it is quite clear that a ten percent share is regarded as inadequate by the kolkhozniks. In Abramov's tale, after the magic figure of 30 percent was promised, everybody, including those who were not obligated to work in the public sector, rushed to participate. Another author pictured the following dialogue between two former kolkhozniks in the mid-1950s [251, 117]:

"In any case, half of the meadows go to waste. They never manage to cut all the grass." "No, in our kolkhoz last year they cleaned off every little space. Old men and women too were scything—a third of the hay mown was given to the kolkhozniks."

Dorosh went even further: "Those areas where it is not worth the kolkhoz's while to make hay, where a little bit of hay can be gotten only by one man with a scythe, such places should be made available on a sharecropping basis to kolkhozniks and to towndwellers who keep a cow." [65] The kolkhoz or any other farm or landowner would thus have no expenses of any kind, but the kolkhoznik would have to give up 50 percent of the crop without payment. Indeed, since Khrushchev's removal, this practice has been actually implemented [*123*, 64, 91] although it is difficult to judge whether it is widespread. In 1965, according to Belianov [*56a*, 40], hay was gathered in privately, under the various rules, from a total of 28 million hectares of public land.

In the spring of 1965, a kolkhoz in the Irkutsk oblast was mentioned —apparently by way of approval—which during the Khrushchev era distributed 15 to 17 percent of the hay brought in. "The amount of hay had increased greatly, and now there was enough for the public livestock sector too." [66] The leading article of *Pravda* on 1 July 1965 recommended that the population be assisted in every way to acquire fodder and, in particular, that patches of grass where machine mowing was difficult be made available to them. A correspondent of the Central Committee's agricultural newspaper in the following year spoke warmly of a kolkhoz chairman who advocated the following view [*452*, 28 September 1966]:

For instance, there is still grass growing on the meadows belonging to the kolkhoz, but in the areas overgrown with bushes, where the machines cannot even get started, these can be left to the kolkhozniks to cut. And so we permit it. Besides this, we give out hay for milk, for calves (under a delivery contract), for turning up for work. For one kilogram of milk sold to the state, we give a kilogram of hay; for a kilogram (liveweight) of calf, five kilos of hay; for each day that the kolkhoznik turns up for work, one to three kilos of hay. And what is the result of this? We can keep the calves in good condition, the kolkhoz hay is brought in on time and without waste, and the state profits from it. On the average the kolkhozniks have sold six hundred liters of milk to the state for each cow in private possession. All by themselves!

Shmelev mentions another practice. As early as 1960 or 1961, a kolkhoz in the Novgorod oblast allocated out its pasture land and meadows —which were thickly overgrown with bushes—to its kolkhozniks for clearance; each able-bodied kolkhoznik received a quarter of a hectare. For three years, they could keep all the hay or firewood that they could grow or gather there, and then the kolkhoz took back the again usable

---

[65] [*100*, 29]; during the same year a similar suggestion—which, however, avoided the term *sharecropping*—was made in a letter to *Kommunist*, no. 8 (1961), 119; this proposed the distribution of "a certain part" of the hay brought in.

[66] [*339*, 36]. (The author was probably referring to the article by the kolkhoz chairman, F. Golsitskiy [*452*, 18 November 1964].)

land (123 hectares).[67] A similar practice was mentioned as having been in effect since 1964 in the Leningrad oblast [*339a*, 117]. Of course, such a procedure is open to abuse. Recently, in the Vologda oblast, strips of land between the fields and the forest or undergrowth have been shared out for private haymaking, with the aim of preventing trees and undergrowth from spreading over arable land. Yet often these strips are then extended far into the fields—through illegal agreements with the tractor driver who works the adjacent fields [*452*, 14 August 1968].

The hay distributed in kind by the kolkhozes seems to be almost exclusively issued to those who have helped bring in the kolkhoz hay. According to Morozov, between 1959 and 1963 this made up between 2.8 percent (1962) and 3.8 percent (1959) of the total value of all payments-in-kind. In kolkhozes which have gone over to cash wages, this hay is carried on the books as sold to the kolkhozniks. In 1959 in the Ukraine a total of 100,000 centners were sold, while in the following year, when more kolkhozes had gone over to cash payments, 140,000 centners were sold; the total prices were 263,000 and 365,000 rubles respectively [*225*, 40–41], yielding an average price of 26 rubles a ton. As further kolkhozes went over to cash payments, the amount of hay sold, rather than distributed in kind, rose further. The price cited, which was apparently somewhat lower than the all-union average,[68] suggests that between a quarter and a half million tons of hay were sold in kolkhozes throughout the country in 1963 (judging from the proceeds of hay and straw sales—see p. 183). For 1966, a price for hay of 69 rubles per ton in the RSFSR has been computed.[69]

The difference between this and the market price is noteworthy. In a small town of the central Russian oblast of Gor'kii in March of 1964, hay cost two rubles a pood or 120 rubles a ton [*67*, 201]. The same price was asked in 1955 in a place about one hundred kilometers from Moscow [*168*, 313]. Of course, this was the higher, seasonal price charged in winter and spring, but even when allowance is made for this and a 50 percent discount is allowed for transportation costs, the high free market

---

[67] [*339*, 36]; a similar proposal was aired in [*440*, no. 82 (1965)] (as cited in [*133*, 35–36]).

[68] Compare the prime costs per feed unit for 1964, which were lower for the Ukraine than the all-union average, in [*105*, 96], as well as the conversion into hay, *ibid.*, p. 95.

[69] See the recommendations for the new system of kolkhoz wages in [*434*, no. 34 (1966), 2].

price testifies eloquently to the shortage. The price of 50 to 70 rubles per ton at which the members of a kolkhoz in the Ukrainian oblast of Chernigov were compelled to sell hay to the kolkhoz[70] may well have been halfway between the market price and the kolkhoz price.

The amounts of hay issued in kind varied greatly according to the region, possibly conversely to the amounts of grain. In the northwestern and central RSFSR these were about six times as great, and in Siberia ten times as great as in the north Caucasus. The smallest quantities were distributed in Transcaucasia and in the southern regions of European Russia.

The issue of fodder as part of the wages or against cash was widely referred to again in 1966 in connection with the introduction of a guaranteed minimum wage in the kolkhozes.[71] During the spring of 1968, the issue of feed was once more urged by the authorities of the RSFSR, especially with the aim of getting people interested in bringing in raw and silage fodder quickly and in good condition by giving them a share of it. At this time, mention was again made of sharing out plots of ground for haymaking "where mechanized haymaking is impossible" [452, 16 May 1968] (see also Addendum in Chapter X).

The feed supply for livestock privately owned by sovkhoz workers and employees is much the same as in the kolkhozes, but again detailed information is scarce. The 1965 and 1968 recommendations cited earlier also applied to sovkhozes and to other state agricultural enterprises. The closest similarity to kolkhoz conditions probably exists in those sovkhozes which have recently been converted from kolkhozes. Bukovskii mentions one such sovkhoz where 10 percent of the hay and silage corn was distributed to the workers and employees as had been done formerly. However, grazing facilities were no longer provided by the sovkhoz, which gave rise to the statement cited on page 298: "We graze them, anywhere, but we graze them." Reference is often made to the fact that the privately owned livestock has to be supplied with fodder by the public sector, specifically in sovkhozes too,[72] and in one case the logical deduction was made [50, 43]:

In the sovkhozes, as in the kolkhozes, measures for creating incentives for the workforce by issuing *natura* can play an important stimulating role. The

---

[70] I. V. Pavlov, *Razvitie kolkhoznoi demokratii* (Moscow: 1962), p. 133.
[71] See the decree of 16 May 1966 in [360, 125].
[72] For example, [256, 71]; [339, 29].

creation of possibilities for supplying the sovkhoz labor force with foodstuffs and with feed for their private livestock would certainly enhance their interest in the growth of the sovkhoz economy.

During the summers of 1964 and 1965, a sovkhoz near Leningrad gave out to its workers as a form of leasehold those meadows which were not suitable for mechanized haymaking [392, 127]. A sovkhoz in Northern Russia was said to have distributed half of its hay crop to its workers [445, no. 3 (1970), 47]. This may be related to the acute labor shortage in these areas.

In general, sovkhoz directors are empowered to issue up to 10 percent of the hay and silage and up to 20 percent of the straw to those who take part in the harvesting [452, 25 May 1966]. A decree, which went into effect from 1 January 1958, had, moreover, provided for 5 percent of the corn and potato crop (up to a maximum of five centners of corn, five centners of potatoes, ten to fifteen centners of hay and twenty centners of straw and chaff).[73] However, this earlier regulation was apparently never fully implemented because of Khrushchev's campaign against private livestock holding in sovkhozes. This is evident from the amounts of fodder which were actually distributed in 1962 and 1963. They amounted, according to Morozov, to 251,000 tons and 342,000 tons respectively [250, 156]. This works out to 35 to 50 kilograms per worker and employee and probably a little more when reckoned per sovkhoz household. The quantities of turnips and silage cited by Morozov in the same source are insignificant.

Yet half a centner of hay is only a supplement to the amount of hay required by livestock during the winter and cannot possibly represent all the hay received by the sovkhoz workers and employees from their farms and all other sources. The private livestock inventories in sovkhozes could only be fed if, in addition to fodder issued in kind, sizable quantities of feed were sold to workers and perhaps even greater amounts were "procured" from other sources. The existence of other sources is intimated in some of Khrushchev's remarks:

All honest workers and employees who work in sovkhozes should account for themselves before their consciences and ask themselves: Where does the fodder

---

[73] The decree was published on 22 August 1957 and was entitled: "Concerning the Way in Which Workers of Sovkhozes and Other Agricultural Enterprises of the Ministry of Agriculture Are Paid"; see E. A. Panova, *Pravovoe regulirovanie truda v sovkhozakh* (Moscow: 1960), p. 121 (including n. 4).

for feeding the privately owned livestock come from? Where, just think, comrades! After all, it doesn't fall from the sky! They say that the miller is always covered with flour . . .[74]

These remarks were made during Khrushchev's campaign against private livestock holdings in sovkhozes (see Chapter IX), and he probably exaggerated somewhat; certainly he overlooked the fact that these privately owned animals could graze during the summer on meadows and stretches of grass that were not used by the sovkhoz. His complaints were echoed in a work published after his removal from office. Shmelev hit the nail on the head when he wrote [339, 31]: "Leading officials, who overlook the necessity of providing feed for the livestock in individual possession, thereby themselves involuntarily encourage the theft and squandering of the social fodder reserves."

However, Khrushchev must have been right when it came to stealing, for there is just no other satisfactory explanation for the existence of these livestock herds. As one sovkhoz director in Stavropol' krai put it: "We all know, but you can't put a watchman behind each one's shoulders."[75] But differentiations must be made among the different kinds of sovkhozes —the grain farms on the vast virgin land territories, the grassland livestock farms, the specialized milk and vegetable farms located near towns, the grape-growing farms in the south, and so on. In referring to this variety, Venzher observes that in sovkhozes there are "many hay meadows unsuited for mechanized gathering (gullies, slopes, banks, verges, marsh and forest grasses, small forest clearings, glades, and so on)" [396, 56].

In some places haymaking facilities have been more readily available to the workers and employees of nonagricultural enterprises and in the smaller towns than to sovkhoz workers and kolkhozniks [146, 226]. What is particularly important for urban dwellers who keep pigs is the possibility of purchasing grain products at relatively low prices. In contrast with Khrushchev, who merely forbade the feeding of bread and purchased grain products to livestock in 1956, his successors have taken the more rational step of making feed grains available for sale to private livestock holders in urban settlements (see Chapters VIII and X).

The sale of young animals from the sovkhoz herds to sovkhoz workers must also play a certain role, although the sources are mostly silent

---

[74] [179, III, 391]; cf. [179, IV, 177, and VIII, 76].
[75] Vasilii Rosliakov, "U diadi Timokhi," [445, no. 8 (1971), 178]. Ibid., 179; the stealing of corn for fodder by almost everybody in another sovkhoz. See also the statements in [246, 79].

about it (but see p. 355 above). Yet a sovkhoz which kept sows especially for providing its workers with piglets was praised recently.[76] Another, rather curious piece of evidence comes from a Siberian subsidiary state farm of the lumber industry, where a veterinarian complained to B. Mozhaev:

You see, the subsidiary state farm here sells off the ailing piglets cheaply. That's why the workers complain. . . . Because the piglets then die. You see, it looks better on the farm's accounts if the piglets are registered as sold, even at a low price. This is supposed to be assistance to individual [plot farmers]. What a hoax! [77]

This writer would have been inclined to discount this as an exceptional case had he not been told, in an Estonian model sovkhoz in September of 1969, almost the same story. Only, there the workers were said not to complain, because the piglets were sold so much more cheaply than those on the free market (where the prices have gone up very much recently, see n. 49 above) that even with one dying out of two they were a bargain. And the sovkhoz's advantage was reportedly that its statistical report showed practically no piglets which had died—they were registered as being sold. The story reads like a Soviet edition of Gogol's *Dead Souls*.

As mentioned in the beginning of this section, the privately owned productive livestock in the Soviet Union is supplied with only 30 percent of its feed requirements from the private plots. The statement to the effect that the private sector produces about one-third of the Soviet agricultural product from roughly 3 percent of the sown area, often to be found in Western writings, is therefore false.[78] But can it be said that, because most of the feed consumed by the privately owned livestock originates in the public sector, this livestock raising is thus basically a socialized operation? Certainly not, for the feed is not wholly supplied by the kolkhozes, sovkhozes, state enterprises, organizations, and the authorities. Much of it is procured from places and in ways which are just not accessible or open to the socialist enterprises and organizations. It would be wasted were it not for the application of private labor and initiative. A lot of the labor directed to this task is not obliged to work in the public sector. No exact figure can be put on the amount of fodder thus procured, but it is certainly considerable.

[76] L. Ivanov, "Martovskie vskhody," *Novyi mir,* no. 8 (1969), 191.
[77] B. Mozhaev, "Lesnaia doroga," *Novyi mir,* no. 9 (1969), 137.
[78] For recent restatements of this misleading juxtaposition in the specialized literature, see [*183,* 46], and [*85,* 63].

Fodder is by no means everything. In order to be productive, the animals must be cared for, milked, and so on. This application of labor is supplied by the private sector.

But the appreciable contribution of the public sector to the private livestock sector cannot be denied; indeed, it is absolutely vital in the framework of the Soviet legal and social order. Yet if the matter were to rest there, with this one-sided dependence, it would not be possible to speak of any interdependence of the two sectors. In return, the public sector of the economy derives two main advantages: the first is the produce of the private livestock sector and not only that which is realized through the free market, while the second is the partial renunciation by the labor force of more or less deliberate slowdowns, of intensified private activity in procuring fodder [272, 71], and of direct theft. This is not to say that there are no slowdowns or that theft does not exist, but merely that these are not practiced on a larger scale.

The deputy head of the planning office of the Orel oblast was very open about these relationships:

There is reason to believe that considerably larger quantities of fodder are used in the personal subsidiary farms (in their livestock raising) than is recorded in the annual accounts [of the kolkhozes and sovkhozes]. . . . In fact, the socialized sector represents the main source of fodder for the livestock of the personal subsidiary farms [excluding grazing]. Regardless of whether this is shown in the plans and annual accounts, the livestock of the kolkhozniks' private farms receive their fodder at the expense of kolkhoz production. For this reason, the practice, observed in a number of farms, of impairing the kolkhozniks' interests under the guise of caring for the socialized livestock production, leads to the opposite results—to the squandering of the already limited supplies of feed and to a decline in the output of animal products.[79]

A similar view was more recently expressed by another author in a more abstract form [379, 40]:

The supply of feed to the personal subsidiary farms of kolkhozniks and sovkhoz workers is often written off [as labor cost] against the socialized livestock production and is reflected in the prime costs of meat and milk in kolkhozes and sovkhozes. This also explains how, as shown by the data, kolkhozniks produce meat and milk using half the scientifically based norms of feed expenditures while an overexpenditure [of feed] occurs in the social economy.

[79] [195, 79–80]; see also the expression "struggle against the stealing of kolkhoz produce and fodder," in [186, 253].

In other words: If the kolkhoznik is not given what he vitally needs, then he is forced to steal it; many in authority who perceive this desperate situation tolerate it more or less tacitly. D'iachkov disclosed that theft was widespread. In the L'vov and Nikolaev oblasts in 1964, averages of 85 and 150 kilograms of hay and 110 and 140 kilograms of straw per kolkhoz household were stolen [87, 57]. Thus there was some substance to Khrushchev's allegations concerning the fodder provision for the sovkhoz workers' animals and to his remark that a large proportion of corncobs were probably stolen from the fields.[80] Just how corn was sometimes stolen—not just removed at night from the field—was pictured in an amusing Soviet short story set in the year 1962 [383, X, 21].

A renunciation of theft—albeit probably incomplete—and a renunciation of any go-slow policy cannot, however, count as a really reciprocal contribution to a mutual economic interrelationship. But there is a substantive contribution which is offered by the private sector—private animal production.

PRIVATE LIVESTOCK RAISING FOR THE KOLKHOZ AND SOVKHOZ

This section deals only with the performance of the private sector on behalf of the public sector within the agricultural enterprises, which cannot always be distinguished easily from its contribution to the state and to the kolkhoz market. Other such services rendered—other than labor—to public agriculture (for example, the sale of vegetable seeds [339a, 18]) are of minor importance. Sakoff concluded that data concerning the sale of private livestock to the kolkhozes and sovkhozes represented "the greatest gap in the information on the production of the private sector" [315, 8]. This gap is no longer as great as it once was, but considerably less is still known in the West about this aspect of Soviet private farming than about its other features, and practically nothing is known about the sale of private livestock during the period before 1958.

Sales to kolkhozes and sovkhozes—which are voluntary only to a limited extent—rose appreciably after abolition of compulsory deliveries from all urban and rural private plots (as of 1 January 1958). The reason for, and purpose and extent of, the abolition of obligatory deliveries

---

[80] [449, 12 January 1961]; see Wädekin, "Soviet Agriculture and Agricultural Policy," in [208, 57–58]. See also the reference to a similar incident in Dumont [101, 206], who also related a parallel which he himself observed in Rumania where clover was stolen from a state farm in a silent general conspiracy.

were outlined in Khrushchev's famous speech of 22 May 1957, in which he announced the intention of catching up with and overtaking America in agricultural production [*179*, II, 457-458]:

At the present time, the share of agricultural produce which we get [in the form of private deliveries to the state] is very insignificant . . . we are getting little produce but it causes us a great deal of bother. Giving up the deliveries from the kolkhoz households would bring us one advantage: We would cut down on the hours put in, on all the red tape. In short, it would be worth-while because we would thereby create a better political atmosphere in the villages. . . . This will bring a relief for the kolkhozniks, but kolkhozes must be aware of their responsibilities and take on the part of the deliveries from which the kolkhoz households are freed.

I believe that the items which are produced in the kolkhozniks' farms will not be lost. The kolkhoznik will sell them himself. What else could he do with the milk? Perhaps he will sell less meat, but he will probaby sell some meat. There are kolkhozniks who have such possibilities. After all, you know that in arithmetic the sum is not altered if the components are added in a different order. The output will in any event come to the market, and in this way the requirements of our society, our people, will be satisfied.

Politically speaking, this [policy] will be received very well by our pop-ulation, not only by the kolkhozniks but also by the workers and employees. It will demonstrate the developed strength of the socialist social order. The bourgeois ideologues say: "There, you see, they have carried out the collec-tivization but in a way the kolkhozniks feed the city with their gardens and sell their produce." They thereby emphasized the weakness of our kolkhozes. We will now strike this club out of our opponent's hand.

These words sprang from an optimism based on the record harvest of 1956, which seemed to confirm the correctness of Khrushchev's agri-cultural policy and of his Virgin Lands campaign in particular. He be-lieved that at last, with the adequate volume of deliveries from the socialized sector, the dependency on the private sector—which was so unpleasant and so difficult to justify ideologically—could now be dis-pensed with. The free kolkhoz market, the bazaar, was no longer a danger to the planned economy, and he generously conceded the un-controlled disposal of the produce which no longer had to be delivered. In so doing, he was probably reckoning that most kolkhozniks would not be able to deliver milk—that most perishable of commodities—to the free market with sufficient speed and in sufficient quantities.

The decree, which was published on 4 July 1957 [*321*, 269], evidenced a more cautious appraisal of the situation. It emphasized the organized, rather than the completely free, sale and urged the state and party organs "to improve the work of carrying out the purchases of surplus agricultural products on the farms of kolkhozniks, workers, and employees at [state] purchase prices." It recommended to kolkhozes that they "help the kolkhozniks in every way to dispose of their surpluses of milk, meat, potatoes, eggs, wool, and other products by organizing the reception of these products on the spot and their further transmission to the procurement points, on to the trade network, and to the kolkhoz market." The free markets were thus mentioned in last place. Moreover, procurement prices paid to private producers were thereafter raised to the level of the higher procurement prices paid to the kolkhozes after 1958 [275, 84].

Revealing in this connection is the constant use of the word surpluses (*izlishki*) which, in Russian, has a connotation of superfluous. It bears witness to an official point of view which considers only the interests of the state and not the well-being of the individual. Considering the relative earnings of the kolkhozniks—in 1957 and, to some extent, even today—one can hardly speak of their having surpluses when all they have is a little more produce than they actually need to keep body and soul together. That this has not been fully realized, even after the eras of Stalin and Khrushchev passed, was pointed out by G. Radov [443, no. 43 (1971), 10] and G. I. Shmelev [339a, 84]. The use of this word subconsciously justifies the state's rigorous policy of "skimming off the cream" which for decades left the agricultural population with the bare subsistence minimum.

Shortly before the new decree came into force, in his speech of 24 December 1957, Khrushchev spoke no more of the bazaar and free market sales [179, II, 495]: "Seventeen to eighteen million farms belonging to kolkhozniks, workers, and employees will have the possibility of selling their agricultural produce at higher purchase prices through the state and the kolkhoz and cooperative trade network—instead of handing their produce over under the compulsory delivery system—and thereby will be able to obtain over three billion rubles [old rubles] more."

The new situation brought new problems which Khrushchev mentioned on 22 January 1958. The kolkhozes were now acting as agents for the state procurement and delivery points. Should the kolkhozes be freed from paying the tax upon these merely transitory products if they did not immediately forward the purchased animals but first kept them in their own stalls to fatten them up for slaughter?

The new function of the kolkhoz as an agent of the state purchase organization, the relief for the state, and the additional workload for the kolkhozes were outlined by Khrushchev on 17 June 1958, during a plenary session of the Central Committee. He used the important example of milk deliveries [*179*, III, 249]:

The small state milk delivery points must be liquidated. . . . Things must be so arranged that the kolkhozes and sovkhozes deliver the milk to large collection points. But the kolkhozniks, who have surplus milk, can sell this in an organized fashion through the kolkhozes. The kolkhoz delivers the produce to the state, gets the money, and settles up with the kolkhozniks. In the kolkhoz there are permanent personnel for this—the head of the livestock section and other personnel.

Shortly after this, on 30 June 1958, the republican soviets were empowered to transfer the milk procurement points operated by the dairy products industry to the kolkhozes. Less and less privately produced milk was delivered directly to the state or to the market [*168*, 289–290, 357]. How much private milk thus became classified as kolkhoz or sovkhoz produced milk cannot be determined. But that a considerable quantity was involved is indicated by the marked decline in private milk deliveries in 1958, despite increased private production and other private marketed milk output (see Tables 15 and 26). Furthermore, the relatively low proportion of their milk output which is currently consumed by the kolkhozniks themselves (70 percent in the RSFSR, see p. 90, above), suggests that sales or deliveries of milk did not decline very much.

The increased marketing responsibilities of the public farms and the minimal compensation received by the farms were laid down in an instruction of the Ministry of Agriculture of 27 August 1959 [*362*, 354–355], more than eighteen months after the abolition of the compulsory private deliveries. This instruction applied to both kolkhozes and sovkhozes, covered purchases of all kinds of vegetables, fruit and all animal products, and made provision for the overhead expenses and the resulting transportation costs incurred by the farms—although only at the official unit tariff. Farms were to count these products separately and were not allowed to include the products as part of their own planned deliveries. Instead, they were to treat the products as "fulfillment of plans for purchases from individual farms"—a phrase that revealed that additional plan targets had been introduced.

Kolkhozes and sovkhozes were thus to become more involved in the relationship between the private producers and the state procurement agencies. The outcome of the new situation for public farms was uncertain. At times they might be able to report privately produced output as output produced in their own public sectors. But they could also be held responsible for the underfulfillment of their plans and would have to bear the loss if their new functions brought them more expenditures than revenue. This also affected the general performance indicators of the farms, such as the amount of livestock products per 100 hectares of arable land. These indicators do not reveal actual profits of the farm but are important for the reputation of farm officials in the eyes of higher authorities. As a kolkhoz chairman explained [*449*, 2 September 1959]:

We all collect such receipts [for private deliveries to the state through a kolkhoz or a sovkhoz]. One sells a calf, another a sheep, and a third sells a young pig. By the year's end, just see how many have been collected. Then we balance up, work out per hundred hectares of land, and from this can calculate that we are running neck and neck with the leading kolkhozes in the production of meat. . . . We know very well what we are doing. . . . A receipt for an animal sold—that really represents something!

Embellishment of the farm's performance does not stop there, as the journalist further reported:

We still have leading officials who are not averse to adding the milk delivered by the kolkhozniks, butter purchased from the store, and a sheep reared by someone on the countryside to their own account.

In violation of the regulations, it happened (and it still happens) that farms credit the livestock purchased from private inventories to their own production and plan fulfillment. *Izvestiia* of 12 November 1960 showed in a report from the Moldavian SSR how this can be entered in the books. If only isolated cases were involved, Khrushchev would scarcely have found it necessary to deal with the matter in his memorandum of 29 October 1960, to the Presidium of the Central Committee [*179*, IV, 182]:

Some officials, who have undertaken large [delivery] obligations [in order to distinguish themselves in the eyes of the authorities], concentrate their attentions not on meeting these obligations through organized work in the kolkhozes and sovkhozes or through mobilization of the kolkhozniks and sovkhoz workers in raising output, but on adopting the wrong and basically criminal course of purchasing the missing produce, chiefly meat and butter, to meet the obligations. There are instances when the purchase of meat on the side is even organized on a raion level, that is to say, purchases in other oblasts, inside the same oblast at other kolkhozes, or from the workers and employees. There are even people who purchase butter in the town and then deliver it as part of the fulfillment of their obligations.[81]

A certain semblance of legality is achieved by the manipulations when the farm purchases livestock from private owners and does not deliver it immediately to the state but keeps it for a time for fattening. One year later, a raion statistical inspector discussed this problem. His report was published in the leading Soviet statistical journal, presumably in connection with the decree of 19 May 1961, "Concerning Measures for the Prevention of Cases of Defrauding the Government and for the Strengthening of Control Over the Reliability of the Statement of Accounts on the Fulfillment of Plans and Obligations." This decree applied to other branches of the economy as well and referred to negligent bookkeeping as one of the factors which made such manipulations possible. This report is so informative that it is reproduced here in full [112, 58]:

As is known, livestock sections of the kolkhozes replenish their herds not only from their own breeding but also by purchasing animals from the kolkhozniks. Without doubt, that is a considerable reserve for enlarging herds and for the production of meat. Yet, a widespread practice of purchasing animals from individuals can lead the kolkhoz leaders to devote less attention to the growth of herds on the basis of the reproduction of their own herds. And certain dishonest officials use the purchase and immediate resale of livestock for purposes of deception [v ochkovtiratel'skikh tseliakh], in order to conceal their own omissions and to create the appearance of fulfilled plans for the production and procurement of meat, contrary to the actual situation on their farms.

Sometimes the kolkhozes purchase a great deal of livestock during the last months of the year with the calculated intention of keeping the animals for fattening for only a short period and thus having little feed outlays, and then delivering them to the state. Sometimes the purchased animals even lose weight during this period and are delivered to the state in a poorly fed condition, and the farm suffers great losses.

In this connection, one instinctively asks the question: Is not the "production of meat" obtained by purchasing animals from the kolkhozniks and the immediate or speedy resale [of the animals] to the government a masked form of illegal manipulation (pripiska)?

In my opinion, in such cases only the weight added to the purchased animal in the period during which it is being fattened should be credited to the kolkhozes for output and procurement purposes. The weight of the animal when it was purchased from the kolkhozniks should be shown wholly under

---

[81] On similar practices in the Stavropol' krai, cf. D. S. Polianskii, *Pravda*, 12 January 1961; for Riazan and neighboring oblasts, see the lively description in [200, 438, 452]. The purchases also included live animals.

the heading of "other entries" in the data concerning the procurements of the raion.

It would not be bad to suspend altogether the kolkhozes' purchases of livestock from individuals if this is done for the sake of immediate resale to the government (within a period of up to a month). First, this would free the kolkhozes from their inappropriate function of purchasing for the purpose of resale; second, this would increase the responsibility of the leading officials of the kolkhozes for the extended reproduction of their farm herds; third, the losses which often result from the resale of livestock purchased from individuals would cease.

Of course, it is a different matter when the kolkhozes purchase calves from individuals in order to raise them and thereby replenish kolkhoz herds. Such a purchase is wholly expedient, since it helps the kolkhozes to increase their livestock herds more rapidly and to deliver more livestock products.

The report reveals several ways in which the socialized sector purchases livestock from private owners and the purposes to which these purchases are put. The purchases assumed significance because of the abolition, since January 1958, of the compulsory deliveries by private livestock owners and also because of the campaign aimed at transferring livestock from the private to the public sector. This campaign varied in intensity after it was launched in 1957–1958, and reached a high point in 1959–1960 (see Chapter IX). Such campaigns apart, private livestock holdings are considered a "certain reserve for replenishing the livestock farms of kolkhozes." [82]

When kolkhozniks do not wish to sell their livestock voluntarily or will not respond to the pressure applied, the best tactic had been the manipulation of the top limit of their permitted animal holdings. Thus if the kolkhoz assembly decides to reduce the norms, as was recommended in 1950 and in 1956 with varying degrees of vigor (see p. 23), then some of the kolkhozniks will automatically have more animals than permitted by the new norms and are therefore obliged to sell the excess holdings. It is not explained to whom these animals should be sold, and for this reason Voloshin proposed that the parent kolkhoz be accorded the first option to purchase [404, 76–77]. Apart from this, the kolkhoznik was also obliged to sell off some livestock when the young animals reached a certain (albeit—until 1969—not precisely determined) age, because his holdings then exceeded the allowed limit for mature animals.

Often the kolkhoznik is induced to sell his own livestock to his par-

[82] [340, 130]; for a more recent case, see [452, 27 December 1969].

ent kolkhoz, because the parent kolkhoz pays a higher price—just to fulfill the state procurement plan—than the individual would get from the state himself;[83] this practice explains the losses mentioned by the above-cited statistical official.[84] A sovkhoz in Kazakhstan, mentioned by Khrushchev on 5 January 1961, bought nine pigs from private owners for 18,000 old rubles (that is, for 200 new rubles each) and was thus paying a considerable premium. Even when the kolkhoznik does not receive a favorable price, he may enjoy other advantages, such as an allocation of feedstuffs or permission to graze his animals on a hectare of meadow which the kolkhoz cannot or does not wish to mow. Indeed, this procedure was recommended, at a conference in the Daghestani ASSR in 1967, for "the purchase of young animals from the population for further raising," and was applied to both kolkhozes and sovkhozes.[85] This bears some resemblance to the so-called contract deliveries (see below).

In the rather sparse materials in Soviet publications concerning these kinds of transactions, a clear distinction is seldom drawn between the varying types of purchases within the kolkhozes and other socialized agricultural enterprises. An attempt is made here to evaluate the sources and to differentiate between deliveries to the state itself (either directly or with the farm acting purely as an agent) and sales to the farm either with the aim of a later resale to the state on the farm's account or to replenish the public livestock inventories. A third arrangement is the sale to the farm in the form of a contract delivery (*kontraktatsiia*). It is very difficult to draw a clear line between these different kinds of transactions. For instance, if a kolkhoz delivers a large quantity of its bulls and cows to the state and then replenishes its diminished inventories by buying young animals from private owners, then these purchases occur indeed purely for restocking purposes.[86] But such deliveries to the state can take place only because of this indirect contribution of the private sector. Under which heading of Soviet statistics does one find animals sold by individuals to special feeding lots which have been expanding their activities of late? One such feeding lot—belonging to a kolkhoz—purchased,

[83] [225, 42] (referring to the Ukraine); D. S. Polianskii, *Pravda,* 12 January 1961 (referring to the Stavropol' krai).

[84] The losses incurred in the resale of hundreds of thousands of calves each year in Belorussia alone were subsequently to be greatly stressed by the First Secretary of this republic, K. T. Mazurov; see [295, 74].

[85] Sh. I. Shikhsaidova in the conference report, [217, 122].

[86] See, for instance, the large share of animals purchased "on the side" in 1963 and 1964 by a kolkhoz in a specimen table in [260, 88].

in 1967 and 1968 respectively, 1,222 and 704 head of cattle from the population and 321 and 1,104 from other kolkhozes.[87]

The farms were able to make some profit even when they paid a little more than the state procurement or delivery prices. Possibly to avoid the imposition of an excessively complicated tax on private deliveries through kolkhozes, and to stimulate surplus purchases from private producers, the state granted to the kolkhozes a tax exemption on 80 percent of their proceeds from the sale of meat, livestock, poultry, eggs, and milk products during the period from 1961 to 1965. The declared aim of the state was "encouraging the output of animal products." This was alleged to result in a saving of some 330 million rubles for the kolkhozes.[88]

An even greater inducement to sell privately owned livestock via the kolkhozes and sovkhozes was the price increase for live cattle announced after the removal of Khrushchev [106, 54-55]. (The same inducement prevails after the new price increases of 1970; see Chapter X.) These prices were valid for kolkhozes and sovkhozes but not for individuals, to prevent the latter from profiting from the by now heavily subsidized state purchase prices. Although this incentive was intended to raise the output of the public sector, several instances were reported of kolkhozes and sovkhozes illegally selling the livestock of their members at the higher prices,[89] either with the intention of making a tidy profit or with the aim of passing at least some of the increase along to the private sellers. To qualify for the higher prices, the animals had to be included in the kolkhoz's procurement figures and, even if they brought no profit in terms of extra cash, these sales at least contributed to the kolkhoz's plan fulfillment [107, 24]. Kolkhozes sometimes appeared eager to prevent private owners from selling their animals directly to the state or on the market and even to prevent them from being present while their animals were being resold [452, 27 December 1969].

It is not possible to determine from Soviet statistics how many purchases from private owners were effected through the kolkhozes and sovkhozes as agents of the state procurement organizations and how many were realized directly. According to the 1958–1959 regulations cited above, both categories should have been recorded as originating from the private sector. It is equally unclear how many kolkhozes and sovkhozes

[87] [452, 4 June 1969]. In Kurgan oblast, fattening farms belonging to sovkhozes were doing much the same; see [452, 2 August 1969].

[88] [179, IV, 253]. This concession was not renewed after 1965; see [378, 60].

[89] [131, 13]; Partiinaia zhizn', no. 24 (1967), 64.

purchased livestock purely as agents and how many resold them to state agencies as part of the output of the public sector.

A figure for 1960 gives some idea of the total amount of livestock and meat purchased at that time by both the kolkhozes and sovkhozes: "Altogether, during the first ten months of this year, the kolkhozes and sovkhozes have purchased about eight million head of cattle, while at the same time actually enlarging the socialized inventories" [255, 61]. Nazarov makes it clear that he described only those purchases made by the public farms on their own account, not just for the replenishment of the socialized herds but also for the fulfillment of delivery obligations,[90] practices denounced subsequently by Khrushchev and the raion inspector (see above). Otherwise these purchases, insofar as they exceeded the normal quantities, would have had to be recorded in the statistics as increases in the state purchases from the private sector. That this was not the case is evidenced by the figure for 1960, which is about two hundred thousand tons less than the preceding year.[91] In 1959, when the decline in private herds had been two and one half times greater,[92] state purchases from the private sector grew by only two hundred thousand tons.[93] (The corresponding totals in slaughterweight are given in Table 10; the fluctuations shown for 1959 and 1960 are much smaller than might have been expected from the excessive purchases.) Even if only half of the purchases had been above the usual amount appearing in the statistics as originating in the private sector, this would have been recorded in the statistics as an increase in 1959 over 1958 of between one-half million and one million tons and between one-quarter and one-half million tons during the period from 1958 to 1960.

The cattle herds in the public sector increased considerably (about 18 percent) from the end of 1958 to the end of 1959, and again by about

[90] As was specifically stated for the Ukraine by [225, 42] and for some oblasts of the RSFSR by Polianskii, *Pravda*, 12 January 1961.

[91] [11, 367] (the difference between the total procurements and purchases and those of the kolkhozes, sovkhozes and other state agricultural enterprises).

[92] See the inventory figures in Table 5. Nazarov [255, 61] gives no all-union purchase figure for 1959, but for Kazakhstan alone he cites an above-plan purchase of 120,000 tons (130,000 tons instead of 10,000 tons). Similarly, Lukinov [225, 42] refers to the total purchases for Ukrainian kolkhozes in 1960 and especially in 1959 as abnormally high, resulting from "distortions committed" in agricultural policy; see also Liniichuk [214, 39], who discloses a further decline in the totals purchased in 1961 compared with 1960. Cf. Khiliuk's data for the Ukraine in Table 11 above.

[93] The totals for 1958 and 1960 were 1.1 million tons, and for 1959, 1.3 million tons [11, 367].

8 percent from the end of 1959 to the end of 1960. Meat deliveries grew faster, by about 38 percent and 10 percent respectively.[94] Such a rapid growth in herds, accompanied by an even greater increase in meat deliveries—and thus slaughterings—can only be explained by the fact that most purchases from the private sector were counted as deliveries from the public sector. Thus the private herds supplied both the animals for build-up of public herds *and* the extra deliveries of the public sector. And although overfulfillment of the meat and milk delivery plans in 1959 and 1960 was greater than ever, the plans were not fulfilled in 1961–1963.[95] It can safely be asserted that the depletion of private livestock herds in 1959 and 1960 was one of the main reasons for the subsequent trends.

The performance of the private livestock sector during years when purchases were not unusually great can thus be determined. During the first ten months of 1960, eight million cattle were purchased from the kolkhozes and sovkhozes (see above), which means that the annual total must have been somewhat greater.[96] Most of the animals purchased must have been calves and heifers. In the same year, the total number of cows in private ownership declined by only eight hundred thousand, and the number of privately owned calves and heifers declined by only a million or so (see Table 5).

Thus the private sector could have sold at least six million calves and heifers and a relatively small number of cows to the kolkhozes and sovkhozes without having to reduce its reputedly normal indirect deliveries through the kolkhozes and sovkhozes and its own herds (see Table 10). Anything over these totals would have affected private herds. But at the same time, "at least five million" heifers were slaughtered each year for

---

[94] [*11*, 367]; the improbably large jump between 1958 and 1959 is partly due to inflation caused by a change in the weight accounting in the statistics; see [*156*, 162–166].

[95] S. V. Rogachev, *Proizvodstvennyi kollektiv i khozaistvennaia reforma* (Moscow: 1969), p. 96.

[96] According to [*382*, 70], about one-third of the annual state purchases are normally carried out in September and October, while another third is purchased during the period from January through April. Thus it is reasonable to suppose that the purchases in the late fall are about on the same level as during the summer and that at least 16 percent of the total is purchased in November and December. However, it is not certain that the purchases from the private sector in November and December of 1960 followed the customary pattern. In 1961, 64 percent of the meat purchases were made during the second half of the year and 26 percent during the last quarter, so that hardly more than 15 percent could have been purchased in November and December; see [*159*, 165].

the kolkhozniks' own consumption or for sale on the kolkhoz market, and the possibilities for purchasing animals from the kolkhozniks were still regarded as inadequately exploited [269, 32–33]. In 1957, Khrushchev [179, II, 468] estimated that some ten million calves belonging to kolkhozniks, workers, and employees were slaughtered every year; this is derived from his figures on the additional amount of meat which could be obtained from purchasing and fattening up these calves. At a later date, "hundreds of thousands" of calves were reportedly purchased annually from the kolkhozniks in Belorussia alone and then resold by the kolkhozes to the state, and similar practices were reported from various parts of the country as late as 1967.[97]

These data give us some idea of the private sector's performance in this area. In the late 1950s and early 1960s, the private sector sold about six million cattle a year (on the average) to the kolkhozes and sovkhozes (mainly calves and heifers), plus an unknown quantity of other livestock. This was more than during the prewar period and in wartime.[98] In 1969, kolkhozes bought 4.2 million head of cattle from private owners for a total of 834 million rubles (65 percent of all animal purchases by kolkhozes during that year) [339a, 18]. The price indicates that these were, on the whole, young cattle but not small calves. If the unknown number of purchases by state farms is added, the figure fits in with the above six million. In view of the state's growing demands upon the kolkhozes and sovkhozes, it is clear that the private sector's contribution is as indispensable as ever for the socialized farms. And the private owners have to slaughter or sell their calves and heifers anyway, because no more than one cow per household is permitted.

In retrospect, Shmelev confirmed this indispensability of the private livestock sector in the context of the disastrous effects of the agricultural policy in the Khrushchev era:

The unjustified limitations upon the personal subsidiary farms of the kolkhozniks and sovkhoz workers not only influenced the growth of the welfare of the rural working class but also had a negative effect on the development

[97] Mazurov in [295, 74]; V. Elin, "Kuplia radi prodazhi," [468, no. 12 (1967), 34–35] (as cited by Radio Liberty CRD 87/68).
[98] The kolkhozes of the then smaller USSR (sovkhozes played a minor role at that time) in 1940 bought 400 thousand pigs, 2.8 million sheep, and 2.9 million head of cattle from the kolkhozniks (and thereby enlarged their public cattle herds by 2.8 million); in 1941 and 1942 they bought 300 thousand pigs, 3.2 million sheep and goats, and 3.7 million head of cattle, according to [275, 24–25, 30].

of the socialized sector. The reserves for restocking the livestock sheds of the kolkhozes and sovkhozes shrank; additional obligations were prematurely imposed upon the public sector to supply the kolkhozniks and sovkhoz workers with necessary foodstuffs which these had previously produced in their subsidiary farms; these obligations were too much of a burden because output did not grow rapidly enough. This had an inevitably negative effect on the growth of the marketed production of the kolkhozes and sovkhozes, on the shape of the all-union balance of agricultural products as regards both socialized production and the personal subsidiary farms, and on the whole process of reproduction in agriculture [*339*, 30; cf. *87*, 58].

The same author shows that, as late as 1963, the kolkhozes alone purchased 249.4 million rubles' worth of livestock from private owners for fattening up and for restocking.[99] This refers to actual purchases and not just to kolkhoz purchases in their capacity as agents for state organizations. That an element of free trade in animals is not altogether excluded was illustrated by a small scene related by S. Vorob'ev. In a prosperous kolkhoz, which had no debts to any state organizations and could thus use its credit balance, a woman kolkhoznik told the journalist [*405*, 63–64]: "And now we have twice as much of everything as our neighbors [neighboring kolkhozes]. They keep on bringing calves from other kolkhozes to sell to us. We can be choosy when we buy." And another confirmed this: "Yes, they bring them. There is nothing you can do about it—the kolkhoznik needs money. His own kolkhoz could well use the heifer, but it has no money to pay straight away." There are also kolkhozes which send special buyers to private owners—and not only to the members of the respective kolkhoz—to contract (illegally) with them [*314*, 6–7]. It is not coincidental that most of the reported purchases from private owners are of calves and heifers, for these make up the bulk of the sales. A few cows are also sold, but young pigs usually move in the opposite direction and are sold by the farms to the population.[100] (Cf. p. 219 above.)

Most references to the sale of livestock in Soviet writings relate to kolkhozniks and sovkhoz workers together and to kolkhozes and sovkhozes together as contracting agents; no data are given for sovkhozes

---

[99] [*339*, 30]. Also after the campaign of 1959 and 1960, the kolkhozes were still encouraged to purchase livestock from private owners, at least in certain parts of the Soviet Union: see the decree of the Central Committee and Council of Ministers of the Tadzhik SSR of 9 February 1962 "Concerning the Results of the Livestock Count in the Republic," in [*322*, 197].

[100] [*225*, 37]; concerning young pigs from kolkhoz inventories, see also [*331*, 163].

alone in this connection. The conditions of sale appear to be much the same in both kinds of farm. When dealing with the intravillage trade as a whole (not only in livestock), Morozov wrote [250, 259]: "The same may be said for those employed in sovkhozes."

There is very little information on sales based on a fixed delivery contract (*dogovor kontraktatsii*), although it is known that these play a certain role. They are usually mentioned in connection with kolkhoz conditions.[101] This form of sale was described as follows in an officially approved textbook on kolkhoz law [165, 492-493]:

> The kolkhoz household is the contracting agent of the delivery contract on young cattle which belong to it in accordance with the law of personal property. The kolkhoz household seals such a contract with the kolkhoz. On the basis of this contract, the kolkhoz household assumes the obligation to raise young cattle and to sell them at the appropriate price to the kolkhoz; the kolkhoz must accept these young animals and pay the agreed price. Moreover, the kolkhoz may issue grain and rough fodder as part of the purchase price and also incur and fulfill other obligations.
>
> Because the property right to the young animal, the object of the delivery contract, is transferred to the kolkhoz at the moment when the contract is signed, the kolkhoz household is not entitled to sell this animal to another person or to keep it beyond the agreed time on its own farm. Otherwise the kolkhoz may demand the surrender of the young animal through legal processes. Or, if the possibility of receiving it in kind is excluded, the kolkhoz may demand the restitution of the value of the animal which has not been surrendered at the market price.
>
> The delivery contracts on young cattle do not possess the quality of law, and their conditions will be determined by mutual agreement.[102]

No figures are available on the volume of these contract sales. Ostrovskii does not make it clear whether he includes contracts with state agencies or with cooperative trade organizations, when he gives a figure of 584 rubles of contract sales per family for 1940 and 11.8 percent of a kolkhoz household's average total income in 1950 [275, 74, 82].

Until recently (end of the 1960s?) in the Baltic republics a practice was widespread which bears some resemblance to contract deliveries: kolkhozniks obligated themselves to raise purebred calves and piglets for the kolkhoz; in exchange they were given concentrate feed and field plots for growing feed near their private plots, and received wages as if they had raised the animals in the public sheds [339a, 120].

---

[101] For a case in a sovkhoz, see [452, 13 July 1969].
[102] See also [404, 77, 95-96].

The gaps in the available data affect Western research, but Soviet writers also complain about these problems (see p. 182). This means that the sales themselves are to a large extent uncontrolled and—until now—also uncontrollable. It is hardly surprising that socialized agricultural enterprises, which are constantly under pressure to fulfill difficult plan targets, try to exploit this situation by making their performance look better than it really is with the help of purchases from their employees which are then counted as the output of the public farms.

8

Policy Toward the Private Sector, 1953–1958

After the deposition of Khrushchev in the fall of 1964, one of the first actions taken by the new leadership was the termination, indeed the reversal, of the restrictions on the private sector of agriculture which had been applied with increasing severity by Khrushchev since 1957. But the success of this change of policy did not meet expectations: After a short-lived recovery, the product of the private sector showed signs of contraction beginning in 1966–1967.

The economic environment had been different after Stalin's death, and this may have been one of the reasons for what were apparently too high expectations in 1964. In the summer of 1953, a similar switch in official policy had been manifest; immediately the output of the private sector rose and contributed significantly to the improved food situation. Soon thereafter, in 1956, most regions enjoyed a good harvest (in the Ukraine this occurred in 1955), and shortly after these first relaxations and successes the reins were drawn tight again. From Soviet data and publications which have since been made available, it is possible to reconstruct a fairly good picture of what happened. We can see how the private sector blossomed beyond the limits envisaged by the party and government, causing alarm and turning Khrushchev—held by many to be a liberal—into the champion of an ever more restrictive policy.

THE UNEXPECTEDLY RAPID RISE, 1953–1954

The new attitude of the Soviet leadership toward the private agricultural sector after Stalin's death was a very important change in domestic and economic policy.[1] But to what extent did it represent a real

[1] Soviet policy toward the private sector of agriculture since collectivization has not been an object of special research among Soviet nor among Western scholars.

change of attitude on the part of the "collective leadership" of 1953 and to what extent pure opportunism? For example, it is difficult to discern anything but opportunism in Khrushchev's espousal of the private sector only two or three years after he had been vigorously advocating the amalgamation of kolkhozes and the distant goal of agrogorods—both of which indirectly, at least, limit the private plots.

It is also surprising that in this struggle for power, L. P. Beria appears to have gone further than his rivals in granting latitude to the private sector. But this accords with the fact that he was quite openly trying to court popularity—a commodity in which he was conspicuously lacking—and therefore made a play for the general public and the non-Russian nationalities rather than the Party cadres. Beria was later credited by the press with having intended to increase the size of the private plots. And he appears to have succeeded, at least among some segments of the population, in gaining the reputation of being a proponent of the relaxation of the kolkhoz system.

During the summer of 1953, G. M. Malenkov also appeared to favor a realistic assessment of the dangerous state of agriculture, advocating a better deal for the kolkhoz population and a relaxation of the taxes and limitations on the kolkhozniks' subsidiary plots. His speech before the Supreme Soviet on 8 August 1953 gave a foretaste of the measures to be implemented during the following two years. Directly connected with Malenkov's speech was the "Law on the Agricultural Tax," passed on the same day and made retroactive to 1 July: This reduced the total tax on the subsidiary plots by some 43 percent. In contrast with earlier legislation, its provisions encouraged the intensive use of the private plots; the basis of taxation was now to be solely the land area, not the use that was made of the plots. The raising of private livestock was stimulated by a levy of only 50 percent of the full tax on plots with no livestock holdings in 1953; this was raised to 70 percent in 1954 and to 100 percent in 1955. In addition, a whole range of tax exemptions were announced for invalids, agricultural specialists, and leading officials.

Three weeks later, with his speech of 3 September 1953 and subse-

---

To my knowledge, the present is the first in Western writings, and it deals with the time since Stalin's death only. Two Soviet scholars, quite recently, were the first to each devote a special chapter in a book to the policy aspect: G. V. D'iachkov [87, 68–92], and V. A. Belianov [56a, 137–162]. For the time up to Stalin's death, the reader is referred to these two authors—with a *caveat* because of Communist bias, of course. For a chronicle of the legislation on urban land use, see [55a, 6–14].

quent decrees, Khrushchev seized the initiative and leadership in agricultural policy which he was largely to retain until the end of his administration. Thereafter, in all of his speeches and measures, he clearly endeavored to relegate Malenkov's role in the inauguration of the new agricultural policy to obscurity as, for instance, in his speech at Kiev on 26 April 1958. Many Western observers and authors were only too ready to accept Khrushchev's version of events, and it is therefore appropriate to draw particular attention to this distortion of history. Yet even if Khrushchev's claim to originating the change is open to dispute, there is little doubt that Soviet agricultural policy bore his stamp from September 1953 onward.

A long time may elapse before it becomes clear which of Stalin's successors initiated the change in agricultural policy and, in particular, the new approach to the private agricultural sector; indeed, this may never be revealed. Such a change does not seem to tie in with the previous actions or statements of Beria, Malenkov, or Khrushchev. That such differing rivals—indeed, opponents—effected this change while apparently competing for power, tends to confirm that an urgent necessity for change existed and was acknowledged at that time. In the contest, and later in the open struggle, for Stalin's succession, each contender sought popularity and support among the masses with measures that met popular demands. These demands can be summarized by the following: the liquidation of terror in the land, an atmosphere of peace, a higher standard of living, and more latitude for the private agricultural sector. The last demand would affect not only the rural population (57 percent of the total population at that time) but also the urban dwellers. The measures initiated during the first months after Stalin's death were directed toward the total or partial satisfaction of these demands.

We are concerned only with the fourth demand. Looking back one can detect a series of indications—if not tangible proofs—that in 1953, throughout the countryside, "a myth arose concerning the benevolence of Stalin's successors" [421, 403].

It is presumably not accidental that the eight volumes of Khrushchev's speeches on agricultural themes, published during his administration and doubtless under his personal supervision between 1962 and 1964, omitted all of his pre-1953 speeches as if he had previously never spoken on agriculture. The volumes begin with his long speech on agricultural policy of 3 September 1953. He was presumably not eager that a review of his earlier, not inconsiderable, agricultural activities and career be made available to the public at home or abroad. Even in the above mentioned volumes many substantial details ultimately had to be revised or omitted, as the following example indicates. As published at the time, his 3 September 1953 speech contained this statement: "We must overcome the prejudice that it is reprehensible for workers and employees to own private cattle" [*449*, 15 September 1953]. This sentence is omitted on page 31 of the first volume of his speeches on agricultural policy published in 1962. It would have contradicted his statements on this topic made after late 1958 as well as the orders and decrees passed after 1959.

His collected speeches on agriculture still contain enough statements to show the Khrushchev of September 1953 as the man who—with less than complete honesty—exposed the inadequate performance of Soviet agriculture and who energetically introduced decisive measures to overcome the shortcomings. The speeches also reveal Khrushchev as one who wanted to give the private sector enough latitude—within the framework of the Soviet system—so that it could contribute to the rise in overall production and to the welfare of citizens who worked in the private sector. At that time he declared the subsidiary plots of the kolkhozniks to be necessary, "as long as the social economy of the kolkhoz is insufficiently developed and cannot meet either the public obligations of the kolkhoz or the personal needs of the kolkhozniks. It has been shown that in many kolkhozes this extremely important principle of the artel economy has been violated. This could only lead, and has led, to the diminution of the kolkhozniks' personal holdings of cows, sheep and pigs" [*179*, I, 12–13].

Khrushchev then pointed out that the kolkhozes and the kolkhozniks would have large surpluses of produce for sale as a result of a considerable reduction of compulsory delivery quotas from the private and the public sector—a measure included in the proposed agricultural decrees. (The reduction had already been announced by Malenkov on 8 August 1953.) He added that the arrears of compulsory procurement of animal products (considered as an outstanding debt-in-kind to the state according to legislation then in effect) were to be canceled. Khrushchev continued [*179*, I, 31]:

It is necessary that—in addition to furthering the growth of public livestock raising—local party, state, and agricultural organizations put a complete stop to their faulty practice of harming the kolkhozniks' interests with respect to their privately owned livestock. Only those who cannot understand the policy of the Party and the Soviet state can believe that the existence of productive livestock in the possession of kolkhoz households—in the amount stipulated by the norms of the kolkhoz statute—presents any kind of danger to socialist order.

It is here that the 1962 version of the speech omits the sentence cited above, concerning livestock holdings of workers and employees.

Khrushchev also said of the new measures:

[They] by no means indicate any lessening of attention to the development of public livestock raising in the kolkhozes and sovkhozes. The time will come when the development of the public livestock sector will have reached such a level that the personal requirements of the kolkhozniks in animal products can be satisfied completely from the public sector. Then it will no longer be advantageous for the kolkhozniks to keep their own animals.

But until we reach such a state, and until the public livestock industry can meet the requirements of the entire population including the kolkhozniks, the personal ownership of livestock by the kolkhoz households is not a hindrance but an aid to the public livestock industry.

The last sentences show some qualification of the concessions; these can be summed up as: the private ownership of livestock represents no danger and socialized livestock raising remains the principal course of development on which the Party and state must concentrate; nevertheless the concessions will be allowed only as long as the requirements of the population cannot be met.

The decree passed by the plenum of the Central Committee after Khrushchev's speech on 7 September contained no such detailed reassurances for the party cadres and ideologists. Perhaps decrees are concerned more with factual measures and go into some detail, whereas Khrushchev's proposals were couched in general terms. But in one point the decree differed noticeably; although it faithfully reflected the first two cited sentences of Khrushchev (albeit somewhat rephrased), it added the following [90, IV, 23].

This situation [violation of "the important principle of the artel economy," decline of the kolkhozniks' private livestock holdings] affects not only the interests of the kolkhozniks but also leads to the distortion of the nature of the artel form of the kolkhoz which represents the only correct form of collective economy during the whole period of socialism.

This raised the official tolerance of private livestock holding out of the realm of purely economic gain to the realm of policy. The private plots and livestock holdings of the kolkhozniks were declared to be irrevocable components of the kolkhoz system and the kolkhoz system was declared to be the only correct form of collective economy during "the whole period of socialism." Because in 1953 there had been no intimation of an imminent "transition to communism," this indicated a more long-term commitment than Khrushchev's speech. It may well be that there were powerful forces in the Central Committee which wanted to go further than Khrushchev in assuring the kolkhozniks and in warning over-zealous ideologists.

The Central Committee also exhorted agricultural officials to build up the public herds and warned them to refrain from doing so by means of the evidently widespread "mass purchases of cattle from the kolkhozniks," a practice which was to manifest itself again only six years later under Khrushchev [90, IV, 26]. Moreover, the Central Committee stipulated more than just tolerance of the restoration of private livestock. It demanded the active assistance of Party, state, and agricultural organs, particularly in supplying kolkhozniks with feed and grazing rights [90, IV, 28, 31–32]. Along with the cited tax exemptions of 8 August, the Central Committee decreed that all kolkhozniks who owned no cattle before 15 June 1953 would be freed from animal products deliveries for the second half of 1953 and for 1954. The decree also confirmed the cancellation of outstanding arrears in deliveries which had been requested by Khrushchev [90, IV, 30]. The concession to the private agricultural sector spelled out in the decree thus went further than the text of Khrushchev's speech as then published. The manner in which the removal of the compulsory deliveries was greeted and exploited by the rural population can be gauged by two observations made later by a Soviet writer concerning the general mood in the summer of 1954 [251, 101, 104].

That the government in its decree of 21 September 1953 issued jointly with the Central Committee followed the lines of the Party's directive goes without saying, since all the important members of the government, from Premier Malenkov down, had cooperated in formulating the provisions of the decree as members of the Central Committee. The decree gave no indication of any opposing viewpoints within the highest circles [90, IV, 62–96].

A comprehensive presentation of the new policy on the private agricultural sector appeared in the authoritative theoretical party journal *Kommunist*, where I. Glotov wrote, *inter alia* [441, no. 1, 1954, 81–83]:

The Party has never denied the need to take into account the day-to-day interests and living conditions of the kolkhozniks, because any encroachment on these interests harms not only the kolkhozniks and the kolkhozes but also the state.

At the same time, Glotov played down the difference between property existing on the private plots, which represents the ownership of the means of production, according to the Marxist definition, and other personal property:

The personal property of the kolkhoznik is linked with the personal plot. But it is also based on labor which is principally applied in the public sector. The plot and livestock holding are only a part of the personal property of the kolkhoznik, a part which is necessary only during the present stage of Soviet society's road to communism.

The time will come when the overall development of social production in all kolkhozes will have reached such a level that it will no longer be advantageous for the kolkhoznik to have his own plot, his own livestock. Insofar as the character of the personal property of the kolkhoznik increasingly approaches that of the worker and employee, it will also lose its specific and special characteristics. *However, this will not happen soon.* [Emphasis supplied.]

Nevertheless Glotov pointed out the dangers (within the Soviet context) arising from such property. He stressed that within the relationships of social and personal productive property it was possible to counter these dangers; the kolkhoz economy could use its economic predominance over the private plots for both controlling and raising production because:

The subsidiary farming of the kolkhozniks is closely bound with and depends on the public sector of the kolkoz. As is well known, the kolkhoznik receives his principal earnings, consisting of cash and payments-in-kind, among them the feed for his livestock, from the public sector in return for labor units. The kolkhoz assists the kolkhoznik's family in tending their vegetable garden, in building or repairing their house, in acquiring livestock, by allocating resources for maintaining nurseries, and so on. Thus together with being able to direct the public sector of the kolkhoz . . . one must . . . also know how and in what direction the personal plots of the kolkhozniks are developing and guide them along the right direction.

The joint party–government decree of 21 September also contained a table showing the increase in livestock inventories planned to October 1954. When these are compared with the actual inventories of 1953 and 1954 (cf. Table 30), it appears, surprisingly, that the authorities must have underestimated the existing private inventories in September 1953, probably because the population took advantage—rather more quickly than

TABLE 30. LIVESTOCK HOLDINGS BY SECTOR ON CENSUS DATES, JANUARY 1953 TO JANUARY 1955, AND PLANNED HOLDINGS ON 1 OCTOBER 1954
(million heads)

Animals	Date	Total	Kolkhozes	All State Farms[a]	Private[b]
Cows	1/1/1953	24.3	8.5	1.3	14.4
	10/1/1953	26.0	9.1	1.4	15.3
	1/1/1954	25.2	8.7	1.4	15.0
	10/1/1954 Plan[c]	29.2	11.5	1.6	16.0
	10/1/1954	27.5	10.3	1.6	16.0
	1/1/1955	26.4	9.6	1.6	15.5
Other cattle[d]	1/1/1953	32.3	21.6	2.0	7.4
	10/1/1953	37.0	22.3	3.0	11.3
	1/1/1954	30.6	19.1	2.9	8.4
	10/1/1954 Plan[c]	36.7	23.5	3.2	9.7
	10/1/1954	37.4	21.6	2.9	12.4
	1/1/1955	30.3	17.5	2.6	9.9
Pigs	1/1/1953	28.5	16.1	4.0	8.0
	10/1/1953	47.6	21.5	5.5	20.2
	1/1/1954	33.3	13.6	4.3	15.1
	10/1/1954 Plan[c]	34.5	21.5	4.3	8.5
	10/1/1954	51.1	22.7	5.6	22.2
	1/1/1955	30.9	10.8	4.2	15.5

Animals	Date	Total	Kolkhozes	All State Farms[a]	Private[b]
Sheep	1/1/1953	94.3	71.9	10.2	11.9
	10/1/1953	114.9	83.2	12.0	18.3
	1/1/1954	99.8	73.7	11.1	14.6
	10/1/1954 Plan[c]	127.4	99.0	13.0	15.0
	10/1/1954	117.5	81.2	12.0	22.4
	1/1/1955	99.0	69.5	10.9	18.1
Goats	1/1/1953	15.7	5.3	0.12	10.1
	10/1/1953	21.0	5.1	0.13	15.5
	1/1/1954	15.7	4.1	0.10	15.3
	10/1/1954 Plan[c]	17.0	5.0	0.10	11.9
	10/1/1954	19.3	3.5	0.10	15.3
	1/1/1955	14.0	2.8	0.08	11.0

a Including sovkhozes and all other farms operated by state agencies and institutions. b Includes individual peasants. c Planned target, announced in September 1953. d Derived by subtracting holdings of cows from figures for total cattle, including cows.

SOURCES: Data for 1 January 1954 and 1 January 1955, [16, 266–267]; planned targets for 1 October 1954, [90, IV, 65]; all other data from [4, 129–130].

was expected—of the new concessions toward the acquisition of live-stock.

Part of the discrepancy may have been attributable to the fact that the statisticians did not appreciate the difference between an October 1 and a January 1 count, especially in the private sector. The difference between kolkhoz and sovkhoz inventories in January and October is considerably less and is indicative of the amount of private livestock sold to the farms, usually in the late fall. (Some of the sales were probably made before October 1 in order to boost the kolkhoz and sovkhoz herds on the census date.)

Table 30 shows that:

1. As far as total livestock holdings are concerned, the planned targets for 1 October 1954 were reached and in part surpassed, except that for cows a rapid restocking was not possible within a single year.

2. The goals for pigs in the public herds of kolkhozes, sovkhozes and other state agricultural enterprises were surpassed by 10 percent. The goals for cows in sovkhozes and other state agricultural enterprises were just reached, but all other planned increases in the public sector remained on paper.

3. The planned target for cows in the private sector was not quite reached, but all other planned increases were easily exceeded. For pigs, the overfulfillment came to 150 percent. In fact, goals planned for 1 October 1954 were reached and in some cases surpassed in the private sector by 1 October 1953—or only a few weeks after the September 1953 Plenum. The planners obviously based their calculations on the extrapolation of the 1 January 1953 livestock count; they evidently had not reckoned with the extent of seasonal fluctuations (that is, private slaughterings and sales) in the late fall. Such fluctuations were much less pronounced in the public sector and were apparently estimated correctly. But here, too, the restocking of pigs by 1 October 1953 was much greater than expected.

Khrushchev later sought to play down his own role in this unplanned development by omitting his September 1953 demand for help to the workers and employees in the acquisition of livestock from the subsequently published, 1962 version, of his 3 September 1953 speech.[2] It is quite possible that he actually uttered these words at that time only at the behest of the Presidium of the Central Committee or had even inserted these words in the text of his speech (which was to be published

---

[2] Compare the originally published text in [449, 15 September 1953, 2] with the text in [179, I, 32].

in *Pravda* twelve days later) only at their wish. In any case, Khrushchev was not the chief instigator of this build-up of private livestock. The Central Committee, not Khrushchev, had warned agricultural officials against "mass purchases of cattle from the kolkhozniks" (see p. 252).

If the population's restocking had begun only after Khrushchev's speech and the resolutions or decrees that followed, then the actual private holdings recorded on 1 October 1953 could never have been attained. The evidence suggests that the build-up of private herds had commenced in the spring of 1953, before the removal of Beria. From the statistical report for the first half of 1954, one can deduce that private pig herds doubled by July of 1953, rising to fifteen to eighteen million [*449*, 23 July 1954]. It would appear that instructions to tolerate or to encourage private livestock holdings might have been circulated internally before that date. Alternatively, the population guessed correctly several months before Khrushchev's speech that the leadership's attitude toward agriculture and toward the private sector was changing. Probably both factors operated.

It should be realized that the increase in private livestock holdings was not only attributable to a normal restocking. Part of the increase was caused by the fact that the population delivered or sold to the state, to kolkhozes, and sovkhozes fewer young animals than usual in 1953 and instead either retained them, slaughtered them for their private needs (or sale), or sold them privately. This made it more difficult for the kolkhozes and sovkhozes to increase their public herds before the census date. (Khrushchev himself mentioned that kolkhozes were obliged at that time—as they are today—to purchase calves from the kolkhozniks in order to reach their planned herds.)[3]

If livestock (other than horses, mules, camels, and other less important animals) is aggregated into a single measure with the aid of Soviet conventional conversion factors,[4] we find that the private sector was allotted a share of 36.5 percent of total planned holdings for 1 October 1954. (The planning, to repeat, preceded the 21 September 1953 decree which listed these targets.) Table 30 shows that the share of the private sector in total livestock holdings so defined came to 38 percent on 1 January 1953 and rose to 40 percent on 1 January 1954. The plan thus envisaged an absolute increase in private herds but their decline relative

---

[3] See [*449*, 15 September 1953]; also [*179*, I, 25].

[4] 1 cow = 1 unit; 1 head of other cattle = 0.5 unit; 1 pig = 0.25 unit; 1 sheep or 1 goat = 0.1 unit.

to total livestock holdings, because an even more rapid growth was planned for the public herds. Yet private herds accounted for 42 percent of the total by 1 October 1953 and 43 percent on 1 October 1954. Thus, the private sector substantially increased its share of total herds, and this increase was contrary to the plan.

The figures for private livestock shown in Table 30 for 1953 and 1954 are based on official data published later. They tally only partially with those released by Khrushchev in his speech before the Central Committee on 23 February 1954, describing the increase during 1953. His data, which must have been based on preliminary reports, understated the actual increase in private livestock holdings. Even his underestimates, however, implied a higher growth rate than was intended for the private sector. It is significant that he released no growth rates for the public sector on this occasion.

Nevertheless, there prevailed a feeling of general satisfaction that the total livestock holdings had grown faster than had been hoped. In the same speech, Khrushchev mentioned that the kolkhozes should lay up enough silage and plant turnips to feed their own public herds and for distribution to the kolkhozniks as payments-in-kind, so that these could feed their animals. In addition he stressed the need to grow more fruit, berries, and grapes to meet the growing demands of the population, and in this connection he spoke positively of the possible contribution from the private sector: "Together with the development of their public orchards and vinyeards, the kolkhozes must assist the kolkhozniks with the development of their private orchards and vineyards."

In this way Khrushchev broached the subject of increasing the production of vegetables, potatoes, and fruit, an area which had already played a considerable role in the planned and implemented overall measures since the summer of 1953. This subject has a direct bearing on the use of private land—not least in the urban areas—and the RSFSR Deputy Minister of Agriculture had previously drawn attention to this in a newspaper article [449, 21 October 1953]:

In several districts of the Central Non-Black Soil region, the areas of the orchards and berry gardens [of the kolkhozes and sovkhozes] have not even been restored to their prewar levels. . . . It is necessary to support and to assist in every way the initiative of the kolkhozniks, workers, and employees in setting up orchards and berry gardens.

Another relevant measure was the decree of 26 March 1954, "Concerning the Hearing [and Settlement] of Petitions by Kolkhozniks and by Workers and Employees who Reside upon Kolkhoz Territory for the Reduction of the Size of Their Private Plots." It was issued three weeks after the Central Committee had called on the kolkhozes and sovkhozes to step up the production of fruit and grapes [*90,* IV, 180 ff.]. The introductory section of this decree stated [*318,* 123]:

In certain districts the private plots of kolkhozniks and workers and employees who live on kolkhoz territory are not satisfactorily utilized. The state and agricultural organs, as well as the kolkhoz authorities of these districts, do not instruct the population adequately how to use their private plots better and more completely.

Of the four articles of the decree, only one stipulates—and then in such a general way as to be almost meaningless—assistance in "using the plots better and more completely." The second deals more specifically with the methods of examining and settling petitions from kolkhozniks, workers, and employees for the reduction of private plots. The third exhorts kolkhozes to exploit fully the plots of land thus freed, and the last article demands that "order be brought within three months" concerning private plots in the land registers. This decree can only be considered as an instrument for the diminution of the private sector.

Such an interpretation seems to conflict with the situation as of the spring of 1954. Nevertheless, the rapid growth of private livestock holdings, contrary to the expectations of the planners, had already become evident. Moreover, three weeks earlier Khrushchev had pushed through his proposed program of cultivating the new lands of southeastern Russia, West Siberia and, above all, Kazakhstan—a program which was to affect every aspect of agricultural policy, including that toward the private sector. It was to lead to a decisive increase in grain output so that in this respect the private sector would become superfluous. Private cultivation was to shift to intensive crops for which smaller plots would suffice, and, finally, the anticipated abundance of feed grains would provide the basis for the development of the public livestock industry so that private livestock holdings could be dispensed with. (On 24 June 1954, the Central Committee plenum ordered the abolition of compulsory grain deliveries by kolkhozniks, workers, and employees.) The then First Secretary of the Kazakh CP, P. K. Ponomarenko, also declared a few months later—after the very good Virgin Lands harvest of 1954—that his republic was to become a principal base for socialist (that is, public) livestock raising [*449,* 27 October 1954]. Furthermore, the measures against the private sector, which were initiated five years later, also followed a record harvest in the Virgin Lands. That harvest gave rise to the impression that the tiresome grain problem was now resolved once and for all.

The decree of 26 March, which seemed to contrast surprisingly with the developments of 1953-1954 and whose purpose can be interpreted in various ways, was not the only signal. From time to time during the spring of 1954, strictures were published concerning the abuse—and by this was meant excessive use—of private plots. This was particularly marked in an extensive *Pravda* article of 20 April 1954. The article stressed that the "personal material interests of the peasants" were to be satisfied primarily through their work in the public sector, and that their private activities were to play a merely subsidiary role. An *Izvestiia* article of 17 April 1954 drew attention to many indications of offenses against the kolkhoz model statute, including the "selling on the side" (*razbazarivanie*) of livestock in the public sector. A month later, an MTS director was pilloried for extending the area of his private plot [*449*, 26 May 1954].

Not long afterward, Khrushchev sounded the alarm over livestock production at the Central Committee plenum of June [*179*, I, 320]: "A marked rise has been manifest in the production of grain, vegetables, and potatoes but not in the livestock sector. Recently the cattle inventories in kolkhozes have not increased, and the number of cows has risen only insignificantly. Sheep inventories have also shown only a slight improvement, and the number of pigs has declined."

As Table 30 shows, the number of cows in kolkhozes actually rose considerably between 1 October 1953 and 1 October 1954. Over the same period, the holdings of calves, heifers, and other cattle and sheep declined somewhat, and the number of pigs in kolkhozes grew. This is probably due to the purchase of livestock by kolkhozes from the population in the summer and early fall of 1954. It is still not clear why the sheep inventories of 1 October 1954 were appreciably less favorable than during the early part of the summer—a decline of two million instead of a "slight improvement." Perhaps the extent of winter losses mentioned by Khrushchev was still not fully known in June? Or did the kolkhozes give out sheep to the population in part payment for the cows?

Four months later, in a memorandum to the Presidium of the Central Committee of 29 November 1954 concerning his journey through the Soviet Far East, Khrushchev touched upon a theme that was later to assume great importance [*179*, I, 407-408]:

The resolution of the CC CPSU and the USSR Council of Ministers on stimulating the expansion of livestock breeding and on freeing the [private] owners
of cows and pigs from taxes has proved to be a powerful stimulus for the ownership of cows and particularly of pigs. Workers and employees have begun to
take advantage of the concessions provided by this resolution. Yet we are not
selling them animal feed, and therefore the people are buying black bread and
feeding this to their pigs, to other domestic animals and to their poultry. . . .
The difficulties in the supply of bread encountered in many places can be
attributed to a considerable extent to the increase in the numbers of pigs and
cows in private hands and to the shortage of feed [especially feed grains]
in the trade network. The increase in bread consumption is also the result of
its use as feed.

Of course, it is a welcome development when the livestock inventories
grow rapidly in our country. This is advantageous for the economy. If we
had enough feed grain, we should sell as much of it as possible to the population. However, it appears that we cannot deliver adequate amounts of feed
grain this year.

In order to cut the consumption of bread, we must increase in the near
future the amount of white bread on sale. This is dearer than black bread and
there cannot be many people who would feed white bread to their pigs. This
will be an indirect constraint on feeding bread to pigs.

At the January 1955 plenary session of the Central Committee,
Khrushchev returned to the subject of the livestock sector. He gave the
figures of inventory increases between 1 October 1953 and 1 October
1954, without distinguishing between the public and the private sector
(as we know from Table 30, the latter had again performed relatively
better). Then he added the following [*179*, I, 439]:

When analyzing the state of the livestock industry, particular attention is due
to the importance and role of public livestock in supplying the toilers with
foodstuffs and industry with raw materials. . . . While developing public livestock, one should not overlook the importance of individually owned livestock
which is raised in accordance with the kolkhoz model statute and in the framework of a personal subsistence economy. The party and the state have encouraged and will continue to encourage the kolkhozniks in expanding their
livestock holdings, because this, it should be recalled, enhances the people's
living standards. But the main task is the growth of the public livestock sector,
which is destined to play a decisive role in creating surpluses of agricultural
produce and of consumer goods.

The Central Committee decree which followed this speech, and
which bore the title "On the Raising of Livestock Production," stated:
"The public livestock sector remains the most backward branch of
agriculture." The decree reflected the recommendations of Khrushchev

(Malenkov had already been maneuvered out and was to hand in his official resignation eight days later) and did not mention the private livestock sector at all. Yet by that time it had become quite clear that the livestock inventories and the milk and meat deliveries of the private sector were growing faster than those of the public sector. Moreover, a significant share of the additional produce was either consumed by the owners, appeared in the kolkhoz markets, or was sold on the side.

In all probability, the Soviet government with Khrushchev at its head was concerned by this development but could not yet bring itself to take decisive steps. It was also quite evident that any constraint would have dealt the recovering agricultural sector a severe blow. All hopes, and particularly those of Khrushchev, seem to have rested on the opening up of the new lands, the success of which would supposedly help the leadership out of the crisis. Thus, for the time being, the situation remained unresolved: No specific measures were undertaken against the private sector, nor was the official policy of encouragement (begun in the summer and the fall of 1953) unequivocally resumed.

FIRST MEASURES AGAINST THE PRIVATE SECTOR, 1955–1957

Official sources in Moscow maintained an almost complete silence concerning the role of the private sector in Soviet agriculture during 1955, but occasional voices were raised in the press—some for and others against the private sector. Those who favored it did not, of course, consider private agricultural activity as an end in itself.

Thus the First Secretary of the Tadzhik Communist Party, B. Gafurov, complained that in his republic "the transfer of the kolkhozniks' work animals had been put off for too long on the excuse of special conditions in the mountains," and that kolkhozniks had been credited with workday units without doing a stitch of work themselves but merely for loaning their animals for work on the kolkhoz [441, no. 6 (1955), 89]. But this concerned a last after effect of collectivization[5] and not a problem newly arisen after the death of Stalin. (Conceivably, however, the problem became aggravated after 1953.)

Considerable interest was also focused on the kolkhoz trade. After 1953 the Soviet government devoted much attention to—and made some tangible investments in—the expansion of facilities for this licensed form

---

[5] See [449, 15 August 1955] and [447, no. 39 (1955), 1509].

of the free market. Trends on this market are, of course, closely related to private agricultural production (cf. Chapter VI). However, a new form of trade was also introduced on this market in 1953 in the form of commission trade. Thus, the semistate consumer cooperatives exercised control over at least a part of this free market. On 30 July 1955, a leading article appeared in *Pravda* under the title "Utilize More Fully the Possibilities of the Kolkhoz Trade." This referred *inter alia* to purchases of farm produce by the cooperatives from individual kolkhozniks in order to bolster the supplies on the kolkhoz markets. At the same time, the article complained that only 38 new kolkhoz markets had been constructed and equipped with proper facilities; the plan for 1955 envisaged the completion of 122 new markets.

On 20 September 1955, an *Izvestiia* article under the heading "The Correct Course" urged kolkhoz chairmen to foster the private agricultural activities of the kolkhozniks by, for example, providing feed for their livestock; the argument was based on the premise that what was good for the kolkhozniks was good for the kolkhoz. A *Pravda* article pointed out on 11 October 1955, that the opportunity to own private livestock and a plot—in addition to higher rates of pay for kolkhoz agronomists—could be used as a meaningful incentive to attract and retain qualified personnel on the land. Finally, *Pravda* of 27 November 1955, reported favorably on the fact that following a very good harvest in the Ukraine (in contrast to the new lands) it had been possible to increase payments-in-kind to the kolkhozniks (mostly in the form of grain and animal fodder).

That Khrushchev had not meanwhile forgotten the private sector is shown by his remarks of 31 October 1955, on the occasion of a visit to his native village of Kalinovka and also by the publication of these remarks. He said [*179*, II, 158–159]:

I would like to say a few words about the private plots. Yours are large, about half a hectare per household. Could not each of you give up a quarter of a hectare and put these portions all together in a large area where corn could be grown for the personal needs of the kolkhozniks? The ploughing and sowing would be done communally; then each of you could tend and harvest your own corn. Or perhaps you could plant and harvest the corn communally by machine and then divide the corn among yourselves. . . . We have been talking about raising labor productivity. But this cannot happen on a small private plot. Yet it would be quite different if you could plant a kolkhoz vegetable garden, using the best plot of ground for each type of vegetable. After sowing and harvesting, the members would have everything they need, distributed on a workday basis. Then they would surely give up their own vegetable plots. But no one should be forced, and those who want to go on in the old way should be allowed to do so. Nevertheless, you should set aside a kolkhoz vegetable garden and then people will understand and say, why should we bother with our own vegetable plots when there is a kolkhoz vegetable garden?

Here are some fundamental ideas of the *agrogorod* (agrotown) concept, broached by Khrushchev a few years earlier, then in 1951, put on ice only to be resuscitated later.

An American observer was to comment in a comprehensive and penetrating article on the state of the kolkhoz market at the turn of that year [*421, 403*]: "It would seem that the real hopes of the Party for agriculture lie in programs in which the wishes of the peasants are not reflected but are rather obstacles which the programs must overcome or circumvent." The point of view of the kolkhoz population was later summed up by a Soviet author: He pictured a former kolkhoznik who, in 1954, was wondering whether to return to his farm and whose decision was: "Let's wait a bit and see what happens" [*251, 118*]. With the coming of the new year, 1956, it was soon to become evident which direction the leadership wanted developments to take.

On 11 January 1956, *Izvestiia* dealt with the significance and possibilities of abuse of the private plots. It proposed, on various grounds, a reduction of the private plots to a quarter of a hectare, with a corresponding amendment to the kolkhoz statute. A similar proposal was aired in *Pravda* on 2 February 1956. At the Twentieth Party Congress, these matters were overshadowed by the "destalinization" which monopolized domestic and foreign attention. In his report of 14 February 1956, Khrushchev himself only touched upon the private agricultural sector when he again condemned publicly the feeding to livestock of grain products purchased from state stores. But N. S. Patolichev, a member of the Belorussian Central Committee, attacked the most important and fundamental aspect of the private farms and testified to official disquiet with the course of events since 1953 [*449, 16 February 1956*]: "In addition to the expansion of the public livestock sector, practically all kolkhoz households have their own cows. The further increase in agricultural output will originate mainly from kolkhoz production. In this area a certain lag must be noted."

It is true that the Directives for the Sixth Five-Year Plan [1956–1960] adopted by the congress did contain a stipulation [*189, IV, 172*]:

"The collective [fruit and berry] gardens of workers and employees and the kolkhozniks' plots are to be developed." But a concealed clause also mentioned that although kolkhozniks' total earnings were to grow by at least 40 percent, this should come primarily from the growth of earnings from the social sector; kolkhozniks' incomes from their private farms were not to increase or were to rise only marginally [*189*, IV, 186].

Ten days after the end of the congress, a decree of the Central Committee and the Council of Ministers—entitled "On the Statute of the Agricultural Artel and the Further Development of the Kolkhozniks' Initiative in Organizing Kolkhoz Production and in the Management of Artel Affairs"—opened a new chapter in the history of Soviet kolkhozes and the leadership's attitude toward private agricultural production. Together with another decree of 6 March 1956—"On Kolkhozniks' Monthly Advances and Additional Labor Payments in Kolkhozes"—it provided a framework for the planned increase of incomes received from the public sector.

The first of the two decrees added some fundamental directives which had been omitted in the documents adopted by the congress and declared [*90*, IV, 607 ff]:

The entire experience of kolkhoz development bears eloquent witness to the fact that the most complete satisfaction of the personal requirements of the kolkhozniks can only be met through the greatest possible expansion of the public production of the kolkhozes. The private sector of the kolkhoz household should be of a subsidiary character: It is necessary as long as the public sector of the kolkhoz is not developed fully enough to satisfy both the social requirements of the kolkhoz and also the personal needs of the kolkhozniks. Affairs in each kolkhoz must be so arranged that the public sector is unremittingly expanded. . . . For this reason, the role of the public sector in the incomes of members of all kolkhozes must be enhanced. All the kolkhozniks' needs are to be satisfied in the main from the public sector. The income which kolkhozniks receive in return for their participation in the public sector is to form the major part of their total income. The private plots, however, and the incomes drawn from them, are of subsidiary importance and are primarily there to satisfy the personal needs of the kolkhozniks for fresh vegetables, fruit, and berries. Fruit and berry gardens are to be created on the private plots in order to beautify the life of the kolkhozniks.

This did not necessarily imply a reduction of the private sector if the earnings from kolkhoz work were raised so that the amount of income from the public sector in total earnings of the kolkhozniks rose, even though the size of income derived from the private sector remained constant. But when this condition was not or could not be met, local authorities were faced with the following Hobson's choice: should the share of total kolkhoznik earnings emanating from private agricultural activity remain constant or even be allowed to rise, or should pressure be applied to reduce this proportion to let earnings from the public sector assume the dominant role—even if total earnings of the kolkhozniks from both sectors did not increase? Kolkhoz chairmen and other officials adopting the first alternative would be considered ideologically and politically incompetent, because their decisions would reveal inability to follow directives of the Central Committee. This course of action would also testify to their economic incompetence or to their inability to raise sufficiently the revenues of the kolkhoz and hence also the remuneration of the kolkhozniks' labor from the public sector. Chairmen and officials choosing the second alternative would of course testify to their economic incompetence for the same reason. But their action would at least be politically and ideologically sound, even though the living standards of the kolkhoz population would clearly suffer.

It is not difficult to guess which course the majority of chairmen and officials would feel compelled to adopt under Soviet conditions. There was, it is true, a third possible course. This was to plead that in the given context of purchase prices, compulsory deliveries, obligatory plans, and the lack of farm autonomy, it was impossible to raise incomes from the public sector, and that the condition for the implementation of the directive could thus not be established. But such a course of action was hardly realistic in the Soviet context during Khrushchev's administration. It would have required great personal courage, with virtual certainty of dismissal and possibly even punishment. Thus this directive bore the seed of all subsequent measures against the private sector—measures which were to be applied with particular emphasis during periods of economic hardship and especially after poor harvests.

The decree on the statute of 6 March 1956, also contained specific provisions for reducing the size of private plots in some cases. Citing "numerous letters" from kolkhozes and kolkhozniks, the decree declared that one of its principal concerns was the problem of the sizes of private plots, livestock holdings, and grazing rights subject to participation in the work of the kolkhoz. "Kolkhozniks correctly point out that the allocation of private plots to kolkhoz households independent of their able-bodied members' participation in the social sector, as provided for in the model charter, runs contrary to the tasks of the organizational and economic strengthening of the kolkhoz." The Central Committee and the Council of Ministers [90, IV, 607, 609] thus deemed it "necessary to recommend to the kolkhozes that in accordance with their primary task they should ensure a rapid growth in crops and livestock products and that they therefore should, depending upon local conditions, perfect and amend certain provisions of the model statute of the agricultural artel." Attention was to be paid to the following [90, IV, 609–610]:

To determine the size of private plots belonging to kolkhoz households in accordance with the labor contribution of the able-bodied members of the kolkhoz family to the public sector of the artel. When establishing the size of the private plot, a smaller area is to be given to kolkhoznik families containing kolkhozniks who did not work in the kolkhoz or who participated inadequately in the public sector than to kolkhoz families who worked conscientiously in the kolkhoz. In allocating private plots, *no increase in the area destined for private farming [whether utilized or not] at the expense of public lands is to be allowed: on the contrary, a reduction in the private area is to be sought*, since the utilization of the public lands with the availability of large-scale mechanization through the MTS is incomparably more advantageous and will eventually yield the kolkhozniks a significantly greater income. [Emphasis supplied.]

Thus it became quite clear that the size of plot was to depend on work in the public sector; the plot was to be reduced when labor inputs into that sector were deemed insufficient and only rarely to be enlarged. Since it was at the same time indirectly but unequivocally stipulated that work norms and the required annual quota of labor days were to be increased, this meant that the private plots would remain at their previous size only if their holders not only met their former norms but also stepped up their labor contributions. The obligatory minimum of workdays per person and per year were to be laid down "depending on the requirements for labor" (that is, not according to what was possible and reasonable for the individual kolkhoznik) and the work norms. The size of the labor unit was to be established "in accordance with the level of mechanization, the factually achieved performance of the conscientiously working kolkhoznik, and the need for economic crediting of work units." [6]

Alterations were also suggested with respect to the number of animals permitted for each kolkhoz household. These proposed reducing the higher holdings allowable under the earlier rules in some regions to the lowest or lower permitted levels. Finally, it was declared appropriate for

[6] [90, IV, 610]. One of the many examples of the increased obligatory minimum of labor days to be put in is given in [440, 10 July 1956].

kolkhozes to consider whether those persons—"especially in kolkhozes situated near towns"—who were not working at all either in the kolkhoz or in state or other cooperative enterprises and organizations, should enjoy any right whatsoever to a private plot, to grazing rights, or to hay [*90*, IV, 610–611].

The remarks and commentaries in the Soviet press which followed this decree left no doubt that it was meant in the above sense.[7] Five years later a Soviet jurist made the following statement concerning the observance of these "recommendations" of the party and state [*404*, 17]: "Generally speaking, the upper limits of the plot norms were decreased," often without the kolkhozes utilizing or being able to utilize the land thus made available. At the same time, in many regions new surveys were undertaken of the existing private plots to discover any previous secret enlargements and to eliminate them [*440*, 25 June 1957]. Gross excesses occurred in the paring down of private plots, some of which were later partially restored (cf. below, p. 319 f.).

On 17 May 1956, at a conference held by the Central Committee, Khrushchev once again referred to this general topic in a connection which clearly showed the inherent contradiction between the striving for a better market supply of agricultural products and the campaign for the limitation of the private sector. He said [*179*, II, 226]:

I would like to express my opinion concerning the individual suppliers of meat and milk whom Comrade Mazurov, the Secretary of the CC of the Belorussian CP, has talked about. I must say openly that, if we rely mainly on the individual supplier, then this would mean that we are testifying to our own impotence. If this "theory" is supported, it will work against the kolkhozes, against the kolkhoz system.

We must now embark on the course of renouncing in time the supply of meat and milk from individual producers and transfer the task to the kolkhozes and sovkhozes. That will be the correct solution to the problem which will be confirmed in theory and in practice by the undeniable advantages of our great socialist enterprises over the individual farms. One cannot constantly pressure the kolkhozniks into developing their individual farms and demand that they deliver animal products to the state. Above all and most importantly, the public sector must be developed.

These words show clearly that the decree of 6 March 1956, faithfully reflected Khrushchev's own thoughts. The same idea was expressed at the end of the year by the then Minister of Finance, A. Zverev [*448a*,

---

[7] Compare, for instance, [*278*, 121–124].

no. 3 (1957), 28]. He disclosed that the state budget for 1957 was compiled on the assumption of reduced revenue from the agricultural tax "in connection with the reduction of the kolkhozniks' private farms in line with the decisions of the kolkhoz assemblies."

Ten years later, after Khrushchev had been deposed, the Soviet author Grigorii Baklanov described the spirit of the 6 March decree with words which went to the heart of the matter, quite apart from whether larger or smaller private plots were desirable in principle. He wrote [*440*, 28 April 1966]:

We know that this decree was not favorable to the display of the kolkhozniks' initiative and to everything that the decree should have stimulated. For what is a decree after all? It is a summary. A scientific generalization, a summary of intense concrete research carried out on the spot. But sometimes we try to start from decrees. We are not able to see life as it really is, or we cannot find the necessary patience, and then it can happen that we try forcefully to dictate to life how it should develop. . . . Of course, administrative measures, which we are criticizing today, bring quicker results than economic measures. Economic measures must be well thought through, they need allocations of money, and it is not enough just to allocate the money—you must also know where to invest it. And after all that you must wait and wait for results. Administrative decisions can be made quickly. But they are not always of much use.

However, during the immediately subsequent period from October 1955 to October 1956, not only did the kolkhozniks' private livestock herds continue to grow considerably [*1*, 137, 144, 151, 158, 164], but the reduction in the size of the private plots was not carried out to any decisive extent.

There are many gaps in Soviet statistics for 1956 and 1957 on the area and distribution of agricultural land, and there are only two key figures relating to the private sector. The private plots of the kolkhozniks comprised a total area of 6.9 million hectares on 1 November 1955 and 6.1 million hectares on 1 November 1958 (cf. Table 1). Yet it remains unclear how much of this reduction (10 to 13 percent allowing for rounding) occurred during the first twelve to eighteen months after the decree of 6 March 1956. On a per household basis, the decline is smaller—from 0.35 to 0.32 hectares—because between 1955 and 1958 the number of kolkhoz households and the size of the kolkhoz population declined. During the same period the sovkhoz population grew, and the area of private gardens belonging to workers and employees expanded from one million hectares on 1 November 1955 to 1.5 million hectares on 1 November 1958. Figures of sown areas are available for each year, but these do not give a clear picture. On the whole the sown areas of the private plots in kolkhozes declined less than their agricultural area, probably because of increasingly intensive utilization of the latter. The total sown areas on the kolkhozniks' private plots in the spring of each year were: 1955—5.79 million hectares; 1956—5.65 million hectares; 1957—5.53 million hectares; 1958—5.50 million hectares [16, 128–129; 3, 114–115].

Data for the Ukraine, which accounted for about one-third of total area in the private sector, show an even smaller decline. The total private agricultural area shrank from 2,167,700 hectares at the end of 1955 to 2,087,300 hectares—or by only 4 percent—by 1 November 1957, eighteen months after the 6 March 1956 decree [24, 45]. The decline of the private agricultural area during the period from 1955 to 1958 was most marked in the RSFSR (by about 600,000 hectares) and, relatively speaking, in the Belorussian SSR—about 100,000 hectares [4, 111; 5, 385].

Thus it is clear that the actual consequences of the March 6, 1956, decree were less pronounced than one would have presumed. This may partly have been due to a certain passive resistance on the part of the kolkhozes themselves and lower officials and, in the Ukraine, possibly at the union-republic level. But a probable further factor was the first indication a few months later of the record harvest of 1956, especially in the Virgin Lands regions. This harvest was to increase the share of the public sector in total agricultural production, without any artificial reduction of the private plots. Relatively little was said concerning the kolkhozniks' private plots. Khrushchev was preoccupied with many other problems, such as the unrest in Poland and Hungary, the reforms of planning and of the legal systems, of industrial and construction administration, and so on, not to mention the looming power struggle in the Kremlin.

The summer of 1956 brought yet another thrust against the private sector in another area, that of the livestock holdings of the urban population. This too fitted in with Khrushchev's earlier views (cf. p. 260) concerning the feeding to animals of grain products purchased in state stores. But whereas Khrushchev had envisaged almost a market economy approach to the problem at the end of 1954, administrative prohibition against such use of grain was to be employed now. The relevant decree of the Council of Ministers, dated August 27, 1956, and published the next day in *Pravda* was entitled "On Measures in the Campaign Against the Use of Grain and Other Foodstuffs Purchased in State Stores for Animal Fodder." The decree also established compulsory deliveries of meat and milk from private livestock owners in towns. Incidentally, it is quite debatable how one could possibly check whether grain products purchased in stores were used for human or for animal consumption. Presumably those who bought large quantities came under suspicion.

It was mentioned as justification for this decree that the private ownership of livestock had increased greatly during the two preceding years among workers and employees—among people who could not grow their own fodder and were therefore obliged to purchase it. Greater and greater demands were made upon the state trading network for grain. This hindered the normalization of the relationship between demand and supply at the prevailing state prices and perpetuated the disequilibrium on the state retail market for grain and grain products. Six months later, on 12 March 1957, Khrushchev was to refer in these terms to the related problems caused by price distortions and the existence of separate markets at the retail level [*179*, II, 342]:

We were compelled to adopt a special law [the above-mentioned decree] which was directed against those who did not work in agriculture but who kept livestock with the help of bread which they bought in the stores. Black bread costs, as you know, about a ruble a kilogram [pre-1961 rubles]. Five kilograms of bread cost about five rubles, and if you feed this bread to pigs you get a kilogram of meat. But pork costs eighteen rubles [a kilogram]. That's where the speculation comes in against which we must fight.

This is certainly a valid argument, but as far as the increase of live-stock in towns is concerned, the justification for the decree is contestable to say the least, especially as regards the number of pigs. Trends in live-stock herds in the possession of urban workers and employees since 1953 are shown in Table 31.

This development could not be termed alarming in the summer of 1956, particularly because a record harvest was nearly in when the decree was published, and there could be no question of livestock holdings placing additional demands upon the state grain reserves. Moreover, obligatory deliveries of milk and meat cannot be justified by such a minimal increase in these animal inventories. Neither can the higher rates of tax on such livestock, which were established by an edict of the same date (cf. p. 40) and which were doubled when a specified quantity of beasts per household was exceeded [*323*, 671 ff.].

It was clear that these measures were aimed primarily at reducing the private ownership of livestock in towns and urban settlements, and

TABLE 31. LIVESTOCK HOLDINGS OF URBAN WORKERS
AND EMPLOYEES, 1953, 1955, 1956

	October 1, 1953	October 1, 1955	October 1, 1956	Index (1953 = 100) October 1, 1955	October 1, 1956
Animals		(thousands of heads)			
Cows	1,616	1,601	1,440	99	89
Other cattle	643	794	780	123	121
Pigs	3,100	3,197	2,429	103	78
Sheep	591	796	767	135	130
Goats	2,027	1,920	1,773	95	88
Total in terms of animal units[a]	2,974	3,069	2,691	103	91

[a] For definition of animal units, see n. 4 to this chapter.
SOURCE: [1, 210, 217, 224, 231, 238].

this was achieved. As Table 31 shows, privately owned livestock inventories shrank appreciably, apart from sheep and calves, and even declined below the level registered in the fall of 1953.

Of course, these decrees were directed not only against the urban workers and employees but also explicitly against those kolkhozniks who resided in urban areas or whose kolkhozes were situated within city limits. The ban on all purchases for feed purposes was also aimed against all other rural residents who lived close enough to the towns to be able to purchase grain products in the urban state stores. This is where the real problem and the true direction of the 27 August 1956 decree lay. Insofar as bread and grain products were available in more ample quantities and at all times in urban retail stores, even in the smaller towns, there were more opportunities for rural inhabitants who lived within easy reach of the towns to stock up. These possibilities must have been enhanced by the record harvest of 1956. Moreover, the kolkhozniks who journeyed into town did not need to purchase bread and grain products for feeding to their livestock; it was sufficient for them to satisfy most of their own food requirements. Previously the kolkhozniks had covered their requirements of grain almost entirely through the payments-in-kind received from the kolkhoz and from their own private farms, and they had baked their own bread. Now those who were able to use the state stores for their own consumption requirements could devote a greater part of their payments-in-kind and their own produce to feeding their animals. This could lead to a really considerable additional burden on the state trade in bread and grain products and was profitable because of disparities between grain and meat prices.

It is difficult to judge just how far these possibilities had turned into realities or had remained threats by the summer of 1956. The problem would have become more acute if the kolkhozniks' payments-in-kind were reduced. This was a development which did materialize later but which Khrushchev might have been toying with at the time. Perhaps he was already intending to stop the state sales of concentrate or other fodder to individuals. These averaged between 700,000 and 750,000 tons a year from 1953 to 1956, then were apparently reduced in 1957 and were finally completely stopped in 1958 [256, 72].

It was doubtful from the very beginning whether the prohibition alone was adequate to deal with the prevailing situation and with expected developments. That it had little effect (apart from the reduction of privately owned livestock in the towns) and, indeed, engendered undesirable side effects was retrospectively confirmed by a Soviet source after the removal of Khrushchev [256, 71-72]:

However, one of the reasons for the increased demand for bread and grain products in state and cooperative trade during the past few years must be considered to be the purchase of bread, groats, and flour in stores for feeding to livestock and poultry. An effort was made to combat this with administrative measures: Feeding livestock and poultry with bread and grain products from market stocks destined exclusively for human consumption was forbidden. But the indisputable fact that appropriate economic provisions should have been made in order to deal with such a negative phenomenon was ignored.

The general euphoria of the fall harvest of 1956 appears to have pushed these problems into the background. How encouraged Khrushchev was by this success and how optimistically he now assessed the agricultural situation was demonstrated by his 22 May 1957 speech in Leningrad. There he announced the target of catching up and overtaking the United States in the per capita production of milk by 1958 and the per capita production of meat by 1960 or 1961 [449, 24 May 1957]. Ten days later, in Moscow, he gave 1962 as the final date by which to overtake the United States in meat production [449, 3 June 1957]. (In the face of the evident failure which followed, the text printed in the volume of Khrushchev's agricultural speeches which appeared in 1962 avoided any specific target dates and merely said, "in the near future" and "it is not worth naming any specific year" [*179*, II, 446, 448].)

Everything points to the fact that Khrushchev himself at that time really believed that it was possible to reach this target, even though it appeared utopian from the very beginning to sensible and competent observers.[8] It makes no difference that his pronouncements were being made by this time against the background of a power struggle. They concur with the sequence of his preceding and succeeding pronouncements and also with subsequent agricultural measures, and it seems to have been precisely his political opponents who rejected them.

In his speech of 22 May Khrushchev announced a new measure affecting the private agricultural sector—the abolition of the compulsory deliveries from private livestock holdings.[9] This also was justified by his optimistic appraisal of the agricultural situation [*179*, II, 445]:

Before, the deliveries of produce from the kolkhoz households assumed a fairly important role in total deliveries and that was a very unpleasant phenomenon for the socialist economy. Now you can see what a recovery the agriculture of our country has made. The kolkhozes and sovkhozes have taken the leading place in supplying the country with agricultural products.

The decree on the abolition of compulsory deliveries was passed and published immediately after the end of the power struggle from which Khrushchev barely emerged as the victor. It was thus without doubt a creation of Khrushchev, but it was not his alone, by any means. The outcome of the 1957 power struggle showed that, apart from Khrushchev, other influential authorities shared his views and were prepared to support him.

[8] This applies also to Soviet experts, whom Khrushchev ridiculed in his 22 May speech. On this topic, see, *inter alia*, Naum Jasny in [*152*, 99–102].

[9] On this occasion the obligation for urban private livestock owners, introduced in August 1956, was also apparently lifted. This is implied by a subsequent remark of Khrushchev [*179*, IV, 25]. The obligation seems to have fulfilled its special purpose by 1957.

9

Policy Toward the
Private Sector,
1958–1964

The year 1958 represents a clear cleavage in Khrushchev's economic and social policy. He was able to implement his ideas without any serious opposition from the leadership, now that the "antiparty group" consisting of previously influential political opponents had been disposed of. The outstanding measures passed in that year were the reorganization of the machine tractor stations (MTS), the working out of the Seven-Year Plan (1959–1965) which replaced the prematurely terminated Sixth Five-Year Plan, and the preparation of the educational reform.

THE GREAT CAMPAIGN, 1958–1960

It is incorrect, however, to believe (as does John De Pauw) that a change in the "government's acquiescent attitude" toward the private sector occurred only in 1958 [86, 65]. Such an attitude no longer prevailed. The initial measures introduced in the preceding two or three years were further developed, and the struggle against this sector of agriculture was sharpened with increased administrative pressure. Nor can one ignore the inner mechanics of the Soviet system by putting the blame for the ensuing restrictive measures mainly on the behavior of "individual collective farms" [86, 66–67]. Two Soviet sources concluded in retrospect: "The idea was propagated that private subsidiary farming held back the development of the public sector and hindered the kolkhozniks' work in collective agriculture" [250, 174]. "During the period of the Seven-Year Plan, in particular, there were voluntaristic attempts to reduce such plots, especially the personal plots of the kolkhoz households" [343, 84]. The objective of these moves was by no means merely economic; it was also political in the sense of accelerating "the countryside's advance towards communism." The pushing back of the private sector was to occur "before the end of the current Seven-Year Plan" and thereafter (or from 1965 on) "at an ever increasing rate" [*338*, 96–97]. The very good harvest of 1958 seemed to permit the execution of such an agricultural policy without endangering the population's supply of food. The "Directives" for the new Seven-Year Plan, approved at the Twenty-First Party Congress on 5 February 1959, furnished the justification and the political basis for such a policy with these words: "Insofar as kolkhoz production is developing . . . the kolkhozniks' material necessities of life will be increasingly satisfied from the public sector, and thus the private plots will increasingly lose their significance" [*189*, IV, 443].

In retrospect D'iachkov also established 1959 as the year when a planned campaign was launched against the private sector [*87*, 55]. However, this policy lost its force within two years, when it became obvious —in 1960—that the agricultural plan targets were not being reached by a wide margin and that the whole agricultural sector was experiencing a crisis.[1] The Central Committee plenum on agricultural problems, which was postponed from December 1960 to January 1961, marked the end of the 1958–1960 campaign, which had consisted of the following six main features.

Private ownership of livestock. The main offensive in 1958 was directed against privately owned livestock. The purpose and the significance of the abolition of compulsory deliveries from private producers —which took effect on 1 January 1958[2]—can be fully comprehended only in restrospect. At first, it appeared to be a popular measure which was very opportune for Khrushchev during and after the power struggle of 1957. He had said on May 22: "We would create a better political climate on the countryside," and, "politically speaking, this will go down well with our people, not only with the kolkhozniks but also with the workers and employees" [*179*, II, 458]. At the same time he indicated that the population could now bring more of their private produce to the kolkhoz market; later he evidently changed his mind and spoke only of sales through state, kolkhoz, or cooperative outlets (cf. p. 233 f.).

Except for potatoes, state procurements from private producers did not decline noticeably after 1 January 1958. But they were now conducted through the state purchases (which meant a better price for the produc-

[1] See J. Karcz, "Seven Years on the Farm—Retrospect and Prospect," in [*389*, 415–418].

[2] [*449*, 5 July 1957]. It is hard to understand why C. A. Knox Lovell [*183*, 50] considers this decree of 4 July 1957 to have been a "retroactive" one.

ers). However, abolition of formal procurement obligations from the
private sector reduced the volume of those procurements from *all* sectors
which the state could regard as guaranteed or vouched to itself under
the system of compulsory delivery quotas or of formal (and equally
obligatory) procurement plans. The authorities responded by imposing
additional delivery or sales obligations on the kolkhozes; the latter in
turn reduced payments-in-kind or sales to their own members.[3] In addition, part of the produce formerly procured directly from private producers was now channeled through the kolkhoz, which acted as an
intermediary link in procurement. Although the connection between the
private sector and the state procurement agencies loosened, the links between the private and the public sectors within the kolkhozes tightened;
this was apparently not intended (cf. pp. 235 ff.).

However, the real—one might almost say the strategic—objective of
the 4 July 1957 decree was to make the state independent of deliveries
from private producers; the state was to concentrate entirely upon the
public sector in attempting to sharply increase Soviet livestock production. Only if the state were to renounce these private deliveries could it
afford, materially and morally, to restrict private livestock production
with more or less mild persuasion and, in particular, to withdraw its
fodder basis. Khrushchev was well aware of this relationship, as his criticism of a year earlier (directed against the view of the Belorussian CP
secretary, K. T. Mazurov) had already demonstrated (above, p. 267). The
prohibition on purchasing grain products for feed purposes and the dis-
continuance of the sale of feed grain and concentrates to private individuals [256, 72] fit logically into this strategic plan. The reduction of the
kolkhozniks' payments-in-kind, consisting mainly of grain and fodder,
was presumably delayed because of the very good harvest of 1958.

In a speech given in Kiev on 24 December 1957, Khrushchev reaffirmed his basic concept that the growth of livestock production was
to take place in the public sector, rather than the private sector, of the
kolkhozes and sovkhozes [*179*, II, 489]. Two days later, at a plenary session of the Ukrainian Central Committee, he returned to the same theme.
But this time he made it clear that he was counting on a rapid growth of

[3] This had been envisaged by Khrushchev already on 22 May 1957 [*179*, II,
458]. Thus it is hardly a concidence that from 1957 to 1958, although the production of milk in kolkhozes in almost every part of the land increased [*17*, 35], the
distribution of milk as payment-in-kind per kolkhoz household was reduced by one
quarter; see [*269*, 268].

public livestock herds and also on an absolute reduction in the privately owned holdings. Since this suggestion represented a new train of thought with far-reaching consequences for the coming years, we quote at length from this and other of Khrushchev's statements on this subject [*179*, II, 498].

I would like to tell you about a good measure which the kolkhozniks of the village of Kalinovka put through. At one of their assemblies they decided to build a public cowshed and to hand their own cows over to the kolkhoz. This they did. They built a good cowshed for two hundred head of cattle, and in the fall each one brought his cow into the kolkhoz shed. I advised them to pay [the former private owners] for the cows at market prices, but they agreed to pay [the lower] state purchase prices. Fine fellows! That shows their [socialist] consciousness.

This course was shown to be advantageous. I am not speaking of the political side of the matter at all. As a matter of fact, the kolkhoz peasant woman had gotten one-and-a-half thousand liters of milk a year from her cow, but the same cow in the livestock section [of the kolkhoz] began to give three thousand liters. . . . One can only start purchasing cows in those kolkhozes which have highly developed animal husbandries and are in the position to satisfy the kolkhozniks' requirements for milk and milk products.

Although he warned against such a course of action before the necessary economic conditions of highly developed livestock production existed, Khrushchev nevertheless showed in the same speech that he envisaged a really wide extension of such livestock purchases. He suggested to the Ukrainians that they have a contest with other union-republics and oblasts to see who could produce the highest livestock count and amount of animal products per one hundred hectares of agricultural land. To the question from the audience, "Does this refer only to kolkhozes and sovkhozes?", he answered [*179*, II, 500]:

Yes, comrades, I mean only the public animal husbandry. After some time the kolkhozniks themselves also will not want to be bothered with their own livestock. The best milkmaids have already given up their own cows, because they receive an adequate quantity of milk for the labor days they put in. Why, one wonders, should the individual sector be counted [included in the indices of the competition]? The comparison should be intended only for kolkhozes and sovkhozes.

Just one month later, Khrushchev again returned to the example of the Kalinovka kolkhoz [*179*, II, 526–527]:

The comrades who have appeared here have spoken about Kalinovka. I was a bit disturbed when they told of how they went to Kalinovka [in order to become better acquainted with this model] and when they spoke of how the kolkhozniks of Kalinovka had decided to sell their cows to the kolkhoz. It was I who, two years ago, advised them to do this.[4] . . . After my departure, the kolkhozniks decided to sell all their cows to the kolkhoz, and they did this but first prepared themselves very well for it. . . . At the kolkhoz assembly it was decided to distribute to the kolkhozniks half a liter of milk a day for each member of the family in winter, but one liter each in summer. The milk was to be delivered to the homes at specified times during the day. Further-more, stalls for giving out milk to the kolkhozniks were to be built. In short, the kolkhoz management was to organize the processing of milk on the spot and the kolkhozniks were to receive curds, butter, and other milk products for their labor-units.[5]

Is that a progressive step? Without doubt, and in the future the kolkhoz-niks will arrive at such a decision. But I would not advise you to do so now. When the raion and oblast party secretaries and the kolkhoz chairmen get enthusiastic about it, then one cannot tell where it happens voluntarily and where under pressure.

Khrushchev said this during his speech at Minsk on 22 January 1958. That speech became famous for its disclosure of the reform, or rather abolition, of the machine tractor stations (MTS), the most important event in agricultural policy during 1958. The abolition of the MTS had an indirect effect upon the problem of the private sector, because the pur-chase of the MTS machinery jeopardized the financial situation of most kolkhozes and tended to make them extract whatever was left to be ex-tracted from the private plots and animal holdings.

However, the sale of cows—whether voluntary or compulsory, and probably mostly compulsory—had obviously already started to grow into a mass campaign by the time of the Minsk speech. Just three weeks later there appeared a decree of the Ukrainian Central Committee and Coun-

[4] In the contemporary press coverage of this visit of Khrushchev to his birth-place Kalinovka on 31 October 1955—coverage which was then incorporated into the collection of Khrushchev's speeches on agricultural problems [*179*, II, 156–162] —this theme is not mentioned. If we assume that Khrushchev is telling the truth here—and it is hardly likely that he would let himself be exposed by his one-time village comrades—then one must ask: did Khrushchev himself feel that it would not yet be opportune to air this idea before the general public in the fall of 1955, or were there other forces in the party at that time who did not want it and who were powerful enough to thwart this initiative?

[5] In fact, the all-union average distribution of milk per kolkhoz household de-clined sharply from 1957 to 1958 (see above, p. 276, n. 3), despite the excellent harvest of 1958, despite the not unfavorable previous year in the main milk-pro-ducing areas, and in spite of growing purchases of cows by the kolkhozes from the kolkhozniks.

cil of Ministers "On Mistakes Made in Certain Kolkhozes of the Zapo-
rozhe Oblast in Purchasing Cows from the Kolkhozniks." The decree
clearly was not aimed only at this one oblast; otherwise it would not
have been reproduced in the central press. It stated, *inter alia,* "Under the
pretext of purchasing, the kolkhozniks are being forced to socialize their
personally owned cows" [*449,* 13 February 1958].

In fact, the all-union herd of cows in the private ownership of kolkhozniks grew slightly during 1958, and the same was true of the holdings per kolkhoz household [*16,* 267]. Khrushchev's suggestion was
either quickly neutralized again or else the campaign did not get fully
under way. Khrushchev himself repeated his warning against undue
haste in Kursk on 25 April 1958 [*179,* III, 188], and then left the topic
alone.

But in his speech of 15 December 1958, to a plenary session of the
Central Committee, Khrushchev returned to this theme with great emphasis. It may well be that the good harvest of 1958 and the relatively
poor showing of animal products (with all categories of owners faring
equally poorly—see [*16,* 334–336]) moved him to give a new impetus to
the livestock sector while, at the same time, ensuring that the private
sector did not pull ahead. He probably felt that in view of the good harvest and of the appreciably increased labor payments in kolkhozes, the
economic and psychological preconditions were now conducive to expe-
diting the transfer of large numbers of cattle from private hands to the
kolkhozes and sovkhozes. Khrushchev declared [*179,* III, 376–378]:

As is well known, the kolkhozes and sovkhozes are the main producers of
meat for the market in our country. . . . For this reason, no matter how high
the increase of meat production in all categories [of farms taken together],
if it is low in the kolkhozes and sovkhozes, then it must be said: [*such and
such*] *an oblast is lagging.* . . . In some oblasts the total number of cows is
growing primarily through an increase in the numbers belonging to the kolkhozniks, workers and employees. At the same time the number of cows in
the kolkhozes and sovkhozes either remains on the same level or even declines. . . . *The leaders of these oblasts* have probably made not a few
speeches concerning the growth and the strengthening of the public sector of
the kolkhozes, but they *do not see the direction of the economy, they do not
conduct the necessary struggle* for the expansion of public production.
  From this must be drawn serious conclusions. . . . It is now necessary
to exert all our strength in order to produce, in the *shortest possible time,* in
the country completely adequate quantities of meat, milk, wool, and other
products on the basis of an accelerated development of the *public* livestock
production of the kolkhozes and sovkhozes. . . . It is important for us that

the necessary upswing in the increase of meat production be attained *already in the coming year.* . . . An important means of raising meat production is the fattening of cattle and the raising of young livestock to full slaughter-weight. . . . It is expedient for the kolkhozes to *purchase calves and heifers from the kolkhozniks* and to fatten them up for delivering to the state. [Emphasis supplied.]

Then he turned to the question of cattle owned privately by sov-khoz workers. This was to become a major theme of Khrushchev for several years to come [*179,* III, 391–392]:

In particular we must look into the question of whether, at the present time, sovkhoz workers and employees should personally own livestock and have sizable private plots.

Now that the sovkhozes are strengthened, now that they use their agri-cultural areas better and are able to satisfy the requirements of their work forces and families for agricultural products, *the existence of large personal plots and livestock holdings has become a serious obstacle* to the further de-velopment of sovkhoz production. . . . It is no secret that this livestock is being fed with fodder from the sovkhozes and that the possibilities for growth of the social herds and their attainment of additional quantities of meat and milk for the country and for the people are thereby limited. . . . With this in mind, the sovkhoz workers and employees are correctly raising the ques-tion of *selling their personal livestock to the sovkhozes.* Obviously one must study and *encourage* this. The sovkhozes must gradually, *in the course of the next few years, purchase the livestock from their workers and employees.* Here it will be better looked after and will yield considerably more with less labor inputs. Then *there will no longer be any need for the sovkhoz workers to occupy themselves with a personal subsidiary farm,* the incomes of the fam-ilies will rise by virtue of their earnings from the sovkhoz. [Emphasis sup-plied.]

Khrushchev again cited the example of Kalinovka, and added [*179,* III, 406–407]:

Is this course correct? Of course it is, and *it will be adopted by all kolkhozes* as public production develops.

But this work must be carried out skillfully, not through administrative measures, not with orders from above, but to the extent that the public economy grows, that the kolkhozniks themselves become convinced that their material position will not be harmed but improved by selling the cows. . . . At present, because the kolkhozniks have large private plots, they are obliged to expend much energy and time on them. If a good *social vegetable garden* is set up in the kolkhoz and vegetable growing is mechanized, then much less labor input is needed for the production of vegetables and potatoes than on the private plots. Potatoes and vegetables will become cheaper and it will be more advantageous for the kolkhozniks to get them from the kolkhoz than to apply their labor to growing these products on their private plots. Then the kolkhozniks will . . . *of their own accord give up their vegetable gardens.* Of course, this measure must also be applied only on a voluntary basis, not through compulsion. [Emphasis supplied.]

Thus Khrushchev emphasized that no pressure was to be applied. But this contradicted the inner logic of the Soviet system in general and particularly on the countryside and also the inner logic of Khrushchev's own statements. He made it quite clear that any further progress in the private sector, as long as it was not accompanied by a much more marked improvement in the public sector, would be regarded as a shortcoming or failure on the part of the leading officials at oblast and raion level. Moreover, he was insisting that the "necessary upswing" was to take place in 1959, and for this purpose young animals were to be purchased from the kolkhozniks. If he linked the growth of meat production in the kolkhozes with the purchase of livestock from the kolkhozniks, then he even more openly declared the private ownership of livestock to be "a serious obstacle" to the upswing in sovkhozes.[6]

Here the contradiction revealed itself. On the one hand the livestock was to be sold only when the public sector of collective and state farms produced enough not only to meet the enhanced requirements of the state but also those of the kolkhozniks; on the other hand the sale of livestock was the precondition for this very upsurge. Because Khrushchev made it quite clear that every official must give priority to increasing public livestock production, in practice this meant that the voluntary principle would have to take second place to public requirements whenever there was a conflict of interests. And a conflict of interests was unavoidable in the given circumstances of inadequate output and greatly increased demands upon public production. Moreover, it was clear that the expropriation, under the euphemism of *purchase,* was to be accomplished within the next few years in the sovkhozes, and here there was no mention of voluntary procedures. A similar differentiation applied between sovkhozes and kolkhozes concerning the diminution or abolition of the private plots used for vegetable and potato growing. This objective was not pursued with as much emphasis, but it was made abundantly clear.

In the Central Committee decree of 19 December 1958 which followed, it was emphatically stated [*189,* IV, 368–369, 372]:

[6] Similar terminology was also applied subsequently to the private plots and livestock holdings on kolkhozes; thus, for instance, "a brake upon high rates of growth of the development of kolkhoz production" [*269,* 31–32].

The most important and urgent matter at the present is the greatest possible increase in meat production on the basis of an accelerated development of animal husbandry in the kolkhozes and sovkhozes. . . . The most important prerequisite for the increase of meat production in the kolkhozes and sovkhozes must be the organization of livestock fattening on a large scale, the attainment of one-time farrowing of pigs for slaughter, and also the purchase of calves from the kolkhozniks and their fattening up to full slaughterweight for deliveries to the state. . . . The initiative of workers and employees, in progressive sovkhozes, who correctly raise the question of selling their livestock to the sovkhozes must be supported in every way. . . . It is necessary that the leaders of local party and state organizations and sovkhoz directors are well prepared to carry out these timely measures, so that the sovkhozes gradually purchase the livestock from their workers and employees within two to three years [by 1961], while at the same time ensuring that they are supplied with animal products.

Local officials now knew quite well what was expected of them, and they acted accordingly [*87, 55*]. Just two months later, on 13 February 1959, Khrushchev felt obliged to restrain those who were interpreting his speech and the Central Committee decree with excessive zeal, and he had to warn them against the use of pressure [*179,* III, 497]:

I must say that from letters reaching the Central Committee from certain regions [it appears that] local organs are compelling the kolkhozniks to sell their cows to the kolkhozes. However, if oblasts are competing with each other to see who purchases cows fastest, then this can lead to negative results. People will work poorly, and no progress will be made.

On 5 March 1959, an anonymous—and so especially authoritative—article in *Pravda* entitled "Against Detrimental Haste in Resolving an Important Task" was concerned exclusively with such occurrences and emphatically condemned them. It declared:

Contrary to these clear instructions from the Party, the leaders of certain raions have recently adopted the course of massive purchases of cows from the kolkhozniks without taking into account the level of the kolkhoz's economic development and its capability of satisfying the requirements of the kolkhozniks for milk from social livestock. Violations of the principle of voluntariness in the purchase of livestock have thereby been permitted, and there is administrativeness and pressure upon the kolkhozniks to speed up the sale of their cows.

On this topic, the editorial staff of *Pravda* has looked into letters from Krasnodar, Vinnitsa, Khmelnitski, Kharkhov, and some other oblasts and krais . . . in the Kuban area . . . the krai organizations, and, following them, the raion organizations, have even introduced "operative" reports every five days on the purchase of cows from kolkhozniks. . . . Some kolkhoz leaders are forcing the kolkhozniks to sell their cows. . . . The local leaders declare that it is now forbidden for kolkhoz members to have cattle in their personal possession. . . . The kolkhoz chairman Dachenko declared at a kolkhoz assembly, "From 1959 on no more grazing ground will be allocated for cows belonging to kolkhozniks." . . . It should be said that signals have been coming into local party organizations . . . but that not everywhere are these signals receiving the necessary attention. In a number of cases there have been attempts to conceal such facts."

Thus, for instance, the office of the Krasnodar krai party committee issued a resolution on 16 February 1959 against compulsory purchases of livestock (evidently after Khrushchev's warning of 13 February), but this resolution was not published in the local press [*449*, 5 March 1959].

Despite such warnings, the campaign achieved results. The kolkhozniks' livestock holdings per one hundred households declined during 1959 from 68 to 63 cows, from 40 to 31 other cattle, from 59 to 54 pigs, from 23 to 20 goats; only in the case of sheep were increased numbers recorded, from 117 to 118—presumably because some families now owned a sheep instead of a cow (cf. Table 13). The success would probably have been even more outstanding had it not been for the warnings by Khrushchev[7] and by *Pravda* in February and March of 1959. Only a few kolkhozes were really in a position to fully supply their members with animal products [*373*, 191].

The setback must have been even more marked in the sovkhozes, for the main thrust was aimed at plots of the sovkhoz workforce in accordance with the differentiation in both Khrushchev's speech and the Central Committee resolution. The *Pravda* article warning against excessive zeal had not referred to sovkhozes, and Khrushchev on 29 June 1959 said only: "This process is now going on, but there is no need to force it, and in the meantime we should not relax our vigilance on these important matters" [*179*, IV, 24]. The statistical picture here is not, however, quite as clear, for the sovkhoz population grew considerably during 1959; the average annual figure of employed hands grew by 1.3 million, or 31 percent. Moreover, Soviet statistics give no separate data for livestock in the possession of sovkhoz workers and employees, only a total figure for all workers and employees. Nevertheless, despite the greatly increased total sovkhoz population, which accounted for the major part of the workers and employees who owned livestock, their overall holdings dropped noticeably—again with the exception of sheep (cf. p. 98 f.).

[7] He repeated them once more on 29 June 1959; see [*179*, IV, 33].

Particularly striking were the developments in the new lands. The Virgin Lands campaign in southeast Russia, Kazakhstan, and Siberia had resulted in a tacit tolerance of the efforts of the new sovkhozes' labor force to build up their private subsidiary farms. Every attempt was made to make migration to the new lands as attractive as possible. Because the sovkhozes were the principal vehicles for the Virgin Lands campaign [418, 19-20], a strict policy against attempts to ensure a private supply of food-stuffs would have been illogical. It is true that the ownership of livestock was not specifically mentioned, but every kind of assistance was promised toward the construction of their own one-family houses for all who went to the sovkhozes in new lands, and a subsidiary plot is usually included with such houses. Only when the first hard years on the Virgin Lands were over (especially after the record harvest of 1958) did the material conditions for further growth appear to have been attained. In Kazakhstan, the main area of the Virgin Lands campaign, the private holdings of the workers and employees experienced a great leap forward during 1957, rising from 347,000 to 525,000 cows, from 310,600 to 458,000 head of other cattle, from 129,600 to 251,000 pigs, and from 427,300 to 796,000 sheep and goats. During the same period, however, the work force in the Kazakh sovkhozes grew from an average of 294,000 in 1956 to an average of 479,-000 in 1957.[8] This means that the number of cows and other cattle grew almost as rapidly as, the number of pigs half as fast as, and the number of sheep and goats twice as fast as the sovkhoz work force. During the same period, the number of kolkhoz households declined by 136,000, but livestock holdings of the kolkhozniks dropped generally by much less.[9] Thus, the private herds were, on the whole, stocked up both in the kolkhozes and the sovkhozes. This development continued throughout 1958, with only a slight deceleration. The first reverse came in 1959.

Flushed with optimism because of the harvest results, Khrushchev declared on 15 December 1958, that the sovkhozes were now strengthened and "able to satisfy the requirements of their workers and their families

[8] [22, 158-161]. For figures for sovkhoz workers and kolkhoz households, see *ibid.*, 203, 207. Actually, data on private livestock holdings per sovkhoz household are not available. But changes in the holdings per household of other workers and employees are not believed to have greatly influenced the totals. Hence, a comparison of trends in the sovkhoz work force and in total private livestock holdings other than those of kolkhozniks reflects the trends in private livestock holdings per sovkhoz household with reasonable accuracy.

[9] By 49 thousand cows, 131 thousand calves, heifers and other cattle, 4.6 thousand pigs, and 215.3 thousand sheep and goats.

for agricultural products." He added: "The existence of large plots and of livestock in personal ownership has become a serious impediment on the road to the further development of sovkhoz production." The Central Committee passed the appropriate order on 19 December 1958.

The reaction was especially prompt in Kazakhstan. In the process of meeting Khrushchev's other demand for the accelerated production of livestock, a start was made with the reservoir of the private herds. In Kazakhstan, which had come in for particularly harsh criticism from Khrushchev for poor meat production results, a "massive purchase of livestock from the population" was carried out, *with 130,000 tons being purchased instead of the planned 10,000 tons* [255, 61]. Significantly, the holdings of the kolkhozniks declined only slightly; most purchases were made from workers and employees, whose livestock holdings were severely reduced. This reduction must have applied mainly to sovkhoz workers and employees, who made up a particularly large proportion of the total in Kazakhstan.

Prior to 1959, "We allowed the sovkhoz workers, *especially in the virgin lands,* to own livestock and poultry in small quantities" [emphasis supplied], noted Khrushchev in his memorandum of 29 October 1960 to the Central Committee Presidium. This had led to no infringements of the existing regulations, because the permitted amount of livestock per household had on average not yet been reached by 1958 in Kazakhstan. A remark by Khrushchev, in his speech of 1 February 1961, showed that tolerant concepts had existed, at least in the field of sovkhoz livestock production: "Many people say that, as an incentive for sovkhoz workers occupied in livestock raising, an additional payment-in-kind could be used in the form of livestock which would be distributed: a suckling pig for the swineherd, a lamb for the shepherd, and so on." Khrushchev rejected this idea, but he would surely not have mentioned it if it had not been suggested by a number of the officials who were concerned with sovkhozes.

By the beginning of 1961, the attack against the private plots and livestock holdings in sovkhozes had long since been launched on a broad front. Khrushchev himself gave it fresh impetus in his letter to the Central Committee Presidium of 29 October 1960: "It is reported that gross irregularities are occurring in the new lands areas concerning sovkhoz workers' livestock. Horses, several cows, pigs, and a few hundred poultry are in personal use. Evidently great liberties have been permitted here. This must be put right wherever necessary." In the "theses" to his speech of 5 January 1961, at the plenary session of the Central Committee, he cited examples of such "liberties" in Kazakhstan, cases in which a single person owned several cows, calves, horses, and dozens of smaller animals. However, our data show that these were exceptional cases. According to our estimates, the average livestock holdings in sovkhozes (not for all workers and employees in Kazakhstan) come to one cow, one calf, less than one pig, and two sheep or goats at the most, even in 1957–1958.

But, the renewed broad hint was heeded by the local officials. While the average number of sovkhoz workers and employees in Kazakhstan rose by 202,000 from 1960 to 1961 (and that of other workers and employees by 151,000), the total of cows owned privately by all workers and employees in Kazakhstan grew by only 125,600, the number of calves, heifers and other cattle by 54,300, pigs by 77,100, and sheep and goats by 151,000. As a recompense, sovkhozes in the Virgin Lands were permitted, after about 1960, to use part of their crop and animal products output "for improving the supplies of their workers and employees" [397, 64]. During the same period, the number of kolkhoz households diminished by a further 133,400, and yet the livestock holdings of the kolkhozniks declined only about proportionally; this indicates again that the campaign was not aimed at the kolkhoz sector [26, 242–246, 261, 283].

The First Party Secretary of another important Virgin Lands area, Altai province, also reacted to Khrushchev's Central Committee letter; this indicates that the campaign was directed not at Kazakhstan alone but basically at the private sector in all new sovkhozes. In an article in *Pravda* of 30 November 1960, K. Pysin took sharp exception to conditions in the sovkhozes of his province and blamed the flourishing private sector for the shortage of effective hands in sovkhoz production. He disclosed that, in one particularly reprehensible sovkhoz, the privately owned livestock alone yielded an average monthly income of 370 old (that is, 37 new) rubles, which was between one-half and three-quarters of the sovkhoz wage. When added to probable additional revenue from crop growing, this was a fair, but not an excessive amount—compared, for example, with the 76 new rubles earned from an urban plot (cf. p. 100). It did not greatly exceed the average monthly income from sovkhoz private plots in the RSFSR during 1961, which amounted to 39 new rubles [52, 57].

As we have shown, the campaign of 1960–1961 was "successful," even if not completely so. A critical review published after Khrushchev's ouster characterized the tendency of the post-1959 years thus: "Voices were raised for the abolition of livestock belonging to sovkhoz workers and employees, although the economic preconditions for this [measure] had not been created" [*256*, 69; cf. *352*, 39]. And "the private plots and livestock holdings—especially those of sovkhoz personnel—were underestimated and ignored" [*339*, 29].

In addition to the above, one must also take into consideration the fact that measures against private livestock holdings in urban areas were intensified in 1959. On 12 August, the Supreme Soviet of the RSFSR issued a decree "On the Prohibition on Keeping Livestock in the Personal Possession of Citizens Who Live in Towns and Urban Settlements [*465*, no. 30 (1959), 600]. This forbade, with few exceptions, the keeping of livestock in the capital cities of autonomous republics and oblasts and their environs, effective 1 October 1959, and implied a future prohibition for other towns and urban settlements. The other union-republics followed this example. This measure also stemmed from the initiative of Khrushchev, who suggested on 29 June 1959, that the necessary law be passed; he mentioned then the disparity between prices of meat and of grain products in state retail trade [*179*, IV, 25–26].

From the official livestock counts alone, it is not possible to determine what quantities were purchased from private owners, because these data only show holdings at the beginning of the year. They give no indication of how many animals were raised from spring onward in the private sector and then in the fall slaughtered for domestic consumption, sold on the kolkhoz markets, disposed of on the side, or sold or delivered to the state or to the public sector. Holdings at the beginning of the year represent only a residual basis from which the private sector each year repeats its production performance. Moreover, the Soviet production figures do not give a full picture of this performance, because an unspecified—albeit considerable—amount of annual production is attributed to the kolkhozes and sovkhozes which in reality originates in the private sector (see pp. 236 ff.).

In the light of these considerations we can reconcile some seemingly conflicting trends during the year 1959. A relatively mild decline in private livestock herds (reported on census dates), a large volume of livestock purchases from the private sector—which took place throughout the year and were reported by Soviet sources, and the remarkably rapid growth of herds and production in the public sector are all mutually consistent.

At the Central Committee plenum at the end of 1959, the Ukrainian party leadership referred to the "example of the Kalinovka kolkhoz" and announced with satisfaction that the purchases of livestock from workers and employees as well as from the kolkhozniks on a "voluntary basis" had made great progress.[10] The purchases of livestock in Ukrainian kolkhozes alone rose to the value of 311 million rubles during 1959 [225, 42]; the bulk of this sum represented the purchase of 635,000 cows which was mentioned by Khrushchev [179, IV, 205]. The cited "mass purchase of livestock from the population" was organized in Kazakhstan in 1959. The prime minister of the RSFSR, D. S. Polianskii, reported to the Central Committee plenum with notably little enthusiasm about the "successes" of the purchasing campaign. But he, too, hoped that additional meat production in the kolkhozes and sovkhozes from this source alone would come to around one million tons during 1960 [449, 23 December 1959].

Although the 1960 purchases turned out to be somewhat less than in 1959 for the USSR as a whole, they did reach about eight million head of cattle alone during the first ten months of 1960.[11] The campaign lasted during 1960 and into 1961, although on a lesser scale. It was directed, in the main, against the livestock holdings of the sovkhoz population (see above). As for the kolkhozes, further warnings against over-hasty measures appeared in Soviet writings during 1959.

One of the most notable unofficial warnings was that of Zaslavskaia, who, in a cautiously involved formulation, pointed out that this concerned a basic problem of the kolkhoz system which could not be resolved with such methods [425, 60]: "That an important part of the incomes [of the kolkhozniks] originates from the private plots in those kolkhozes where remuneration for work in the artel [kolkhoz] is relatively low contains an inner contradiction, in that it opposes the personal interests of the kolkhoznik to those of the total socialist society."

In other words, it was not just a question of the kolkhoznik receiving produce from the kolkhoz as a substitute for giving up his own small private production, but also of the socialist society ceasing to exploit him through inadequate payment for his labor, thus obliging him to look for

[10] See Podgornyi's speech in [449, 23 December 1959].

[11] In the Ukraine, where conditions were basically not very different from the all-union picture, the 1960 deliveries to the kolkhozes amounted to 203.7 million rubles and were thus at least one-third less than in 1959; cf. [225, 42]. Some 359,000 cows were included in these sales [179, IV, 205]. For the all-union trends, see [255, 61].

additional income wherever he could. The problem was not the faulty comprehension of the kolkhoznik but a basic contradiction within the system.

Just how far the political leadership under Khrushchev comprehended this complex interrelationship and how far it was motivated by pragmatic necessity must remain an open question. Livestock holdings of workers and employees continued to grow, but not as fast as the sovkhoz work force. The number of animals per household continued to decline, at a slower rate, and a considerable part of the absolute growth was accounted for by the livestock of kolkhozniks whose farms were being converted into sovkhozes. The absolute figures of kolkhozniks' livestock declined correspondingly, [9, 303] but the per household figures diminished less rapidly and then increased slightly again because the number of households also declined (cf. Table 13).

When Khrushchev renewed his attack against the private ownership of livestock in sovkhozes in a letter of 29 October 1960, to the Presidium of the Central Committee, he referred to the authority of Lenin [179, IV, 177]: "I would like to recall that V. I. Lenin, when he raised the question of sovkhoz organization, said that the worker should not have any livestock for his personal use. And that was absolutely right. We have deviated from this principle."

In the "Theses" of 5 January 1961, written for his appearance before the Central Committee (and published only two years later), Khrushchev wrote of the sovkhozes [179, IV, 248–249]:

The question of the livestock in the personal possession of sovkhoz workers and employees must once again be raised.
Obviously, the measures adopted up to now have been shown to be inadequate. Certain workers and employees are expanding their personal farms excessively and are making them objects of speculation and enrichment. . . . *Many workers are demanding an edict which strictly limits the number of animals belonging to workers and employees. That is a proper demand.* [Emphasis in original text.]

As far as the kolkhozes were concerned, Khrushchev merely pilloried the unsatisfactory development of the public livestock production and chose to warn against excessive purchases without making himself absolutely clear [179, IV, 205–206]. And it is noteworthy that, in the speech which he gave twelve days later on 17 January at the plenary session of the Central Committee (and which was published at once), he contented himself with the following sentences [*179*, IV, 354]: "*Public live-stock production was and remains the basic foundation.* The kolkhozes and sovkhozes have now become the chief suppliers of meat and milk." [Emphasis in the original.]

Who or what led him to this short and far weaker formulation? It seems that it had been made clear to Khrushchev some time before 17 January what harm had been caused by the purchases. In January of 1961, livestock purchases made under pressure were sharply condemned at the plenary sessions of both the CPSU Central Committee and the Ukrainian Central Committee, although only with respect to kolkhozes. On the other hand, it was said of some union-republics in the south that many of their kolkhozes [that is, kolkhoz leaders] were not sufficiently combating those kolkhozniks whose livestock holdings exceeded the stipulated upper limits [*165*, 494]. In fact, the campaign against kolkhozniks' private livestock holdings in the Transcaucasus and in Central Asia appears to have been mounted on a limited scale.[12] However, Khrushchev's statement before the Ukrainian Central Committee on 28 January 1961 sounded half like an accusation and half like a defense, as if he was placing the blame on the subordinate organs:

Comrades: It is very unpleasant and grievous for me that distortions have taken place in the Ukraine in the purchase of cows from the population despite the warnings of the republican leaders.

I have formerly advised my fellow citizens from Kalinovka to sell their cows to the kolkhoz and to receive milk from the kolkhoz. The people of Kalinovka supported this suggestion and sold their cows to the kolkhoz. . . . In time all kolkhozes will adopt this course. But before this course is decided on, all kolkhozes must be raised to the level of the most advanced farms. This is not understood in many regions of the Ukraine. [There] cows were purchased from the kolkhozniks even though provisions were not made for keeping them; in many kolkhozes, there were not enough buildings and feed. The kolkhozes were not in a position to supply the kolkhozniks with milk.

If someone buys the kolkhoznik's cow but does not sell him any milk, then this means committing a grave error. Only enemies [of socialism] can behave like this, but not Communists.

Those who compel the kolkhozniks to sell their cows must be strictly punished.

[12] Note the regional figures in [*416*, Appendix E, Table 24], the report of a conversation on the railroad concerning the conditions in Uzbekistan in [*307*, 32], and Khrushchev's statement aimed at the Georgian SSR at Tiflis on 7 February 1961 [*179*, IV, 469].

The purchase of cows from kolkhozniks should not be rushed, it should not be hurried too much.[13]

When Khrushchev spoke six weeks later, on 14 March 1961 in Kazakhstan at a conference given for workers who had distinguished themselves in farming on the Virgin Lands, he completely evaded the delicate theme of private livestock holdings in the Virgin Lands sovkhozes. And in his letter of 13 March 1961, to the Central Committee Presidium, he alluded to it in a significantly more cautious manner than before [*179, V, 343*]:

In order to provide good and cheap nourishment in the canteens, it is important for each sovkhoz to have a social vegetable garden with the corresponding means of mechanization. If such an arrangement proves to be advantageous and is widely introduced, only *then* should the sovkhoz workers and employees be forbidden to have livestock. *If in such a case* livestock is kept in personal possession, it will unavoidably be fed at the expense of the sovkhoz's own fodder, which induces embezzlement and speculation.

The party and state organs in the Virgin Lands areas and the Union Central Committee of the Trade Unions must *look into this question without fail and submit their recommendations to the government.*

I have been told that certain workers and employees in the virgin lands areas have many cattle, sheep, pigs, and horses in their personal possession. Evidently an edict must be issued which limits the number of animals in the personal possession of the work force in the virgin lands areas. [Emphasis supplied.]

The amount of livestock per household among workers and employees in 1961 declined less than in earlier years. The topic of private livestock holdings was not to reappear in Khrushchev's public speeches until the fall of 1961, that is, until the Twenty-Second Party Congress. The damage caused by the repressive measures, originally encouraged by him, evidently sufficed to keep him away from this topic for some months.

A pamphlet which appeared after Khrushchev's removal reviewed the campaign and its consequences [*237, 50–51*]:

During the period from 1954 to 1958, a considerable growth of livestock holdings in the personal possession of kolkhozniks, workers, and employees was

[13] [*179*, IV, 404]. In fact the purchases of cows from the kolkhozniks in the Ukraine during 1961 did decline in comparison with the previous year and, quite naturally, in comparison with 1959. They amounted to only 95 to 100 million new rubles (including other products) that is, for livestock, less than one-third of the 1959 purchases. See [*214*, 39] and—for 1959—p. 183, n. 59 above.

observed; this undoubtedly enlarged the overall livestock production resources of the country. However, during the first years of the Seven-Year Plan [1959 and on], administrative measures were enacted in many parts of the country to limit the development of livestock production in the personal holdings of the population (the confiscation of cows under the pretext of socializing them, a reduction in the allocations of fodder, a prohibition on the keeping of livestock and poultry in towns and workers' settlements, and so on). But is it not clear that, at the given level of output of livestock products in the country, the personal plots and livestock holdings of the kolkhozniks and other classes of society have not outlived their economic usefulness and must be developed in the near future?

It should be added that inadequate accommodation and lack of fodder decreased the productivity of purchased cattle in many kolkhozes and some animals even perished [91, 52; 128, 51].

The effect on attitudes and labor morale was voiced by a kolkhoz chairman in Abramov's story which was published during Khrushchev's administration [43, 136]: "You know perfectly well and you've known for ages that as long as the kolkhoznik has a cow, just that long will he help to pull the kolkhoz cart along. But without a cow he's kicking off in all directions."

Reports from various parts of the country bear witness to the fact that the "principle of voluntariness" in the sale of cows was very often—if not always—disregarded. Thus indications of compulsion repeatedly came from the Krasnodar krai [73, 175] and from the Ukraine, where it was clearly stated that pressure from above was applied to any kolkhoz chairman who resisted the campaign [364, I, 61; 364, II, 17]. To certain kolkhoz chairmen in the province of Yaroslavl, Dorosh applied the classic formula: "He orders the voluntary handing over" [99, 13]. It is surely no coincidence that Dorosh could publish such a critique in the fall of 1962, while Khrushchev was still in office, but after the great wave of "voluntary" livestock sales had ebbed. But such sales had not completely ceased, and Dimitrashko reckons that they continued into 1963 [91, 52].

Fodder and grazing rights. Not only orders and prohibitions but also the possibilities of fodder in winter and grazing rights in summer are decisive for the private livestock sector under Soviet conditions. This explains the repeated references and citations referring to the fodder and grazing rights problem.[14]

No exact explanation is forthcoming from Soviet sources as to how

[14] The following two paragraphs are a summary of what has been dealt with in greater detail in Chapter VII, fourth section.

livestock belonging to workers and employees on the countryside and in towns is fed during the winter (although some references are made to the purchase of feedstuffs and grain products). In the summer there are many places available for grazing, even in the small towns and in the suburbs. On the countryside, apart from pasture land made available by the farms, an important role is played by the waste lands and unused ground belonging to nonagricultural enterprises, to communities, and to local administrative agencies. In sovkhozes and in farms operated by institutions there are modest payments-in-kind. Tolerated "acquisition" or regular stealing appear to be of great importance during the winter, especially in the sovkhozes where only modest quantities of fodder are distributed as payments-in-kind. Some hay for the winter is gathered by workers and employees from unused public lands. On the whole, a tendency to reduce such opportunities for haymaking and grazing of private livestock became noticeable since 1956 (cf. above, p. 223 f.).

In the kolkhozes, grazing rights are provided for in the kolkhoz statute, and fodder for the winter is an integral part of payments-in-kind for labor inputs of the kolkhozniks. These payments take place through the distribution of grain, potatoes (both for human and animal consumption), hay, straw, silage, and so on. Grain is the major component of payments-in-kind, both in volume and in value. After Khrushchev's dismissal, the following view was expressed in an article by three authors, one of whom was a high agricultural official [120, 69]:

That part of the kolkhoz output which remains for sale and distribution to the kolkhozniks is a very important prerequisite for the strengthening of their material incentives in the development of the public sector. . . . It is thus necessary to bear in mind not only the satisfaction of the personal requirements of the kolkhozniks for grain and other products [for human consumption] but also for provisions for livestock which belongs to the kolkhozniks.

The distribution of payments-in-kind rose steeply between 1953 and 1955. A marginal decline occurred in 1956 and 1957, but the unmistakable turning point took place in 1958 and 1959.[15] A relatively large amount of payments-in-kind was distributed in the bumper harvest year of 1958. But it is significant that the 1958 distributions were barely at the level of 1957, even though a sharp increase in payments-in-kind might have been expected as a result of both the record size of the grain harvest and of the increase in total labor remuneration in the kolkhozes. The decline of

[15] See p. 211 f. above; also [262, 97] and [269, 268–269].

payments-in-kind which took place in the poor harvest year 1959 was thus even more pronounced. This trend continued through 1960. In relation to 1956 and 1957, payments-in-kind per unit of kolkhoznik labor input in 1960 were about 25 percent lower; they did not rise appreciably in 1961 and 1962.[16] The 1964 distributions of hay and straw as payments-in-kind per kolkhoz household were 37 percent smaller than they had been in 1958 [87, 57].

This happened during the very period when demands and efforts were made to raise the incomes of the kolkhoz population through growth of labor remuneration from the kolkhoz rather than by increasing reve-nues from the private sector. A scholarly publication of 1961 warned: "The lowering of the proportion of kolkhozniks' earnings attributable to payments-in-kind should not be sought through their absolute reduction but [rather] through a more rapid growth of cash earnings together with a certain expansion of the distribution [that is, sale] of high grade food-stuffs like milk, meat, fruit, and so on" [269, 268]. But the same source showed that this is precisely what did not happen and that both the share and the absolute volume of payments-in-kind were reduced. Total cash *and* kind income per man day stagnated until 1960 (in comparison with 1956–1957). It rose only in 1961, by about 25 percent [262, 97], and this was partly because many of the economically weak kolkhozes which paid low cash wages were eliminated—that is, were converted into sovkhozes.

This development affected especially the private livestock production of the kolkhozniks. The cited reference to high-grade foodstuffs and other clear expressions found in the publications of the Khrushchev era show that actual trends reflected official intentions. Although human, on-farm consumption was not to be affected,[17] a reduction in the production for the relatively free kolkhoz market was obviously desired [225, 38; 49, 76]. In practice, of course, human on-farm consumption was also affected, because the distribution of grain covered both human and animal re-quirements. This was presumably not intentional and allocations of food-stuffs were reduced, partly because after 1958 and 1959 the excessively raised delivery requirements left many farms no other choice. Years later,

---

[16] See the figures in Nimitz [262, 97, Table B–12] for cash and kind issue per man-day, and see [269, 268, Table 92] for indexes of various types of income in kind per households and [269, 269] (Table 93: indices of issue in kind valued at state retail prices per able-bodied kolkhoznik). See also Venzher [395, 283] for grain distribution per household.

[17] See also [269, 280] and [225, 38].

P. E. Shelest, the Ukrainian First Party Secretary, referring to this at the March 1965 plenum of the CPSU Central Committee, said [295, 38]: "The voluntaristic plans for deliveries without regard for the actual possibilities led to disorganization in the farms and to a reduction in grain distributions to the kolkhozniks per labor-day, and caused the [entire] livestock sector an irretrievable loss." But this relationship has been well known ever since collectivization and was occasionally referred to during the campaign (for example, [269, 273]). The consequences must therefore be considered an integral part of Khrushchev's agricultural policy, even though the secondary effects were not specifically intended.

That it was not really a matter of secondary effects alone but also that of an intended policy emerges clearly from the repeated demands to increase the share of cash payments in total earnings of the kolkhozniks and from the recommendations made after 1958 and 1959 that earnings be paid entirely in cash. This policy was later described by a Soviet source as "the administrative limitation of the distribution of products" [427, 6]. Because, as we have seen, total earnings did not rise before 1960 and did not rise rapidly after 1961, the demands for a greater share of cash in total payments could in practice be fulfilled only at the expense of the payments-in-kind. This aspect of the official policy is further underlined by the reports that mowing of hay or grazing of private livestock on farmlands and in woods or other unused land was often not allowed (even when the kolkhozes or sovkhozes were not in a position to gather hay from these meadows or to let public sector animals graze on such pastures—cf. p. 223).

The kolkhoz population responded to this state of affairs with intensive cultivation and husbandry of whatever land and animal holdings were allowed them and especially with considerable increase in labor inputs. For the period from 1958 to 1962, this development was later stressed by some Soviet sources; it is also appropriately stressed in the major, careful study by Nancy Nimitz.[18]

The size of the private plots. Restrictions resulting from the decree of 6 March 1956 were continued, with the size of the plot and the number of animals dependent upon the amount of work put in to the public sector by the kolkhoznik. Although the reduction, considered on an all-

---

[18] [425, 63]; [262, 24 ff., 52]. See the reservation concerning kolkhozniks' private plots and livestock holdings, which does not however invalidate the overall tendency (above, p. 86).

union average basis, was gradual—from 0.32 hectare per household at
the end of 1958 to 0.31 hectare per household at the end of 1961—this
average is partly misleading. Many kolkhozes were converted into sovkhozes, especially in regions where the kolkhozniks' private plots were
smaller than the all-union average. Precisely because conversions occurred
mostly in the areas where plots were smaller, they tended to raise the
average size of the plots in the reduced kolkhoz sector. This resulted
from shifting the smaller plots to the sovkhozes. Simultaneously, many of
the remaining (and larger) plots of the kolkhozniks were being reduced
in size. In many places the reductions must have been greater than the
cited figures indicate (cf. p. 85 f. and Table 13). In principle, the practice
of "voluntary" reduction of private plots was approved, even by those
Soviet writers who must be considered as moderate (for example, Zaslavskaia [425, 60]).

On a per family basis, the area of privately used land was also
reduced in the sovkhozes, but no exact and comprehensive data are on
hand. Their logical counterpart was a better supply of sovkhoz workers
and employees through communal catering (see Khrushchev's words on
this account, p. 280 above). This was ordered by several decrees in 1959
and 1960 as well as in 1961. In particular the RSFSR decree of 20 November 1959 permitted state agencies setting delivery quotas to take into
account the need of the sovkhozes to supply products for feeding their
own workers and employees [346, IX, 452–456]. Curiously enough, hints
have been made recently that the reduction in the size of private plots in
Virgin Land sovkhozes actually turned out to have been smaller than in
other parts of the country [368, 258]. The contraction of the kolkhozniks'
private plots was apparently even regarded as a form of "convergence" of
the kolkhoz with the sovkhoz, according to a subsequent critical observation of Soviet writer V. A. Peshekhonov [292, 40]. Generally speaking, the size of the private plot is not as decisively important for the
private sector as are the private livestock holdings. Nor can the reduction
of the above-normal house plots of retired officers and generals in urban
and resort areas, ordered in 1958 ([55a, 91]—a decree to that effect was
never published, as far as I know), have had much effect on the total
private plot area. But it is on record as another indication of the general
campaign against the private sector. (For greater detail, see above, Chapters
III and V.)

The effects of the conversion to state farms. Payments-in-kind play
a considerably smaller role in the sovkhozes than in the kolkhozes, but that

role is not quite as unimportant as is often supposed and as the gaps in (and the lack of more accurate) Soviet data might lead us to believe.[19] The fact that the number of sovkhozes and the size of the sovkhoz labor force increased rapidly through the conversion of kolkhozes into sovkhozes (especially during 1960) exerted a significant impact on the private sector. It is only this aspect and not the entire process of conversions which is discussed here.[20]

In principle, and to a lesser degree in practice, the private plot and the livestock holdings of sovkhoz personnel are smaller than those of the kolkhozniks. When a kolkhoz was converted into a sovkhoz, the size of a member's private plot had to remain basically unchanged, because a directive of 3 May 1957 assured the former kolkhozniks that they would be allowed to retain plots of the existing size as long as they remained on the farm [90, IV, 728]. This directive appears to have been contravened often in practice. A major role was apparently played here by Khrushchev's campaign against the private plots in sovkhozes from 1958 to 1961, although no comprehensive data to document this are at hand. It is certainly not by chance, however, that Khrushchev's campaign against the livestock holdings of sovkhoz workers and employees coincided with the second wave of conversions.

Plots were often not touched during and immediately after the conversion of kolkhozes into sovkhozes, but later the former kolkhozniks— now sovkhoz workers—were talked into agreeing to a diminution. This was recommended in an article which appeared during Khrushchev's administration,[21] and such reductions were designated as a common phenomenon of the Khrushchev era by Venzher.[22] In one instance it was considered as something out of the ordinary that the plots remained at their former size for three years after the kolkhoz was converted; nevertheless they were eventually reduced [68, 158]. Private livestock

---

[19] For details on this often obscured subject, see Wädekin, "Payment in Kind in Soviet Agriculture," *Bulletin—Institute for the Study of the USSR*, no. 9 (1971), 9–18.

[20] On the subject of conversions, see [412, 116–125] and [418, *passim*].

[21] V. Nikishov, in *Kolkhozno-sovkhoznoe proizvodstvo RSFSR*, no. 5 (1964), as cited in [439, October 1964, 17].

[22] [396, 55]. See also Sonin [350, 188]. At the beginning of 1965, it was retrospectively reported of a sovkhoz in Moscow oblast that "the reduction of the private plots was done too hastily, for in general the portions cut off were not used in the social economy." Now the old private plot sizes have been partially restored [352, 39].

holdings in this village were also greatly reduced; only every third house-hold still owned a cow and hardly any pigs were left.

In a recently converted sovkhoz visited by Bukovskii, the workers did get some corn silage and hay for overtime work, but no grazing rights for their livestock were granted. To the surprised question by Bukovskii, "How, then?" came the reply, "We graze them, anywhere, but we graze them" [68, 156]. There is so much waste land scattered amid cultivated land everywhere in Russia that such an answer appears not at all improbable; on the contrary, it is characteristic and goes a long way to account for private livestock holdings.

The writer S. Krutilin later pictured the situation as it really existed at the time in a village of the Tula region. He met a woman who tried to conceal the fact that she owned a cow, and he exclaimed astonishedly [200, 459 ff.]: "But a cow isn't an apparatus for distilling moonshine!"

The woman replied: "Worse! Everybody's distilling illicit liquor quite openly now. But the cow, that must be kept hidden. They make lots of trouble over it. They say that the cow is a relic [of the past]. It keeps the women from [working in] the public sector."

"You are presumably in a sovkhoz?"

"Yes, a sovkhoz."

"How is it then—has it got worse in the sovkhoz [than it was in the kolkhoz]?"

"Well, how can I put it? . . . Perhaps it is not worse after all. . . . We have always received a certain wage, it is true, and bread can be bought in the store. One thing is bad: They bother us over the animals. Don't try to keep a cow! The private plots are reduced. That's because you are workers now, they say, and so you must live as they do in the town."

There is another aspect which is hardly mentioned in Western writings. Because payments-in-kind in sovkhozes are smaller than in kol-khozes, the conversion of kolkhozes into sovkhozes meant the elimination of a large portion of the payments-in-kind on the affected farms. This resulted in a larger share of the farm's output being delivered to the state. This share grew further by virtue of the fact that the sovkhozes did not trade on the kolkhoz market, and some of the kolkhozes, and espe-cially those near the towns which were converted, play a role as sellers of surplus produce on this market. Thus in each raion or oblast where kolkhozes were converted, the amount of produce delivered to the state rose automatically without production necessarily rising. In view of the excessive delivery demands imposed after 1958 on raion and oblast administrations as well as on the farms, this factor must have been an added stimulus for conversions for many leading local officials. It also provided an indirect incentive for limiting the private sector, even when that was not the primary motive.

In practice, both motives must have worked together and thus two birds could be killed with one stone. It did not matter that the sovkhoz population still had to be fed, and that the reduction of payments-in-kind was canceled out by greater demand on the market and on state trade. Prominence was given only to delivery plan fulfillment reports. The difficulties entailed for the rural population were overlooked.

The Soviet author Vinnichenko, who made a special investigation into the problems and effects of conversions, cited the following conversation he had in a sovkhoz that had been converted from a kolkhoz [*401*, 147 ff.]:

"Previously we used to sell food ourselves but now we too have to buy bread. It has gotten bad: The worst thing is that even with money you cannot buy anything [food] anywhere. If you had been here before —you should have seen the bazaars [kolkhoz markets]; but if you go there now—it's all cleaned out. You can't help thinking: No market— in such a grain producing region!"

"But how did this come about?" I asked. "The sovkhoz workers have private plots too. And surely there are also cows, pigs, and poultry."

"There was all that once. We have no fodder for our own animals! We do not get grain from the sovkhoz and it is not worth buying it."

And the leader of the local sovkhoz section said:

"The people must be fed. In the kolkhoz that was no problem— there we were our own bosses. Here—no, here the situation's different: We are not allowed to sell [them] produce from the farm, only through the state trading organization, for cash."

This is not the place to discuss whether the kolkhozes are really autonomous and whether the state trading network can supply the villages with enough foodstuffs even when their inhabitants have enough cash to pay for them. In an agriculturally rich area, such as the Stavropol region from which Vinnichenko reported, both of these suppositions may have been true without necessarily having been true everywhere. In our context what is important is that conversions disrupted the self-sufficiency of the farms and curtailed the ability of individuals in the private sector to supply their own needs and to produce for the market.

Once more the agrotown. The process of conversion was interrelated with another tendency of a sociopolitical, ideological, and economic nature which affected the private sector.[23] At the height of the conversion campaign (or from the summer of 1959), a number of references were made in the Soviet press to the topic of *agrogorod* (agrotown). This is an agrarian settlement, consisting not of numerous large or small villages but rather of one central settlement with several thousand inhabitants for each kolkhoz or sovkhoz. These settlements were to consist of "well-appointed, urban-type dwellings with all modern facilities." The ensuing debate was, of course, concerned not only with the question of comfort, but also with the fact that multifamily dwellings "disrupt the old conservative way of life of the peasant household."[24] All these expressions alluded to the still existing rudimentary relationships in the kolkhoz village between the one-family house, the livestock shed and the surrounding private plot—to the connection between the type of rural dwelling and the opportunities for agricultural production by individuals.

Khrushchev had championed the idea of the agrogorod in *Pravda* of 25 April 1950 and again supported it publicly on 4 March 1951. As he saw it, the problem was related to another of his initiatives, the amalgamation of smaller kolkhozes. Whereas the latter proposal was implemented in 1950 (mergers continued in later years at a varying rate), the agrogorod idea was resisted by Malenkov and was indirectly turned down by Stalin. Khrushchev ultimately suffered a public rebuke in *Pravda* of 5 March 1951,[25] but he resumed the plan when he was in power. The first kolkhoz–agrogorod was completed in the Ukraine in the summer of 1958, and by the end of the year the term agrogorod was again being used openly.[26]

In 1959 and again in 1960 Khrushchev discussed the matter of rural settlements and reconstruction on several occasions. Although he originally spoke of two-family houses, he eventually raised his sights to two- and three-story houses and even cited examples of buildings that could accommodate "several thousand people . . . the population of a whole

[23] I deal with this theme at greater length in [410] and [411].
[24] This is the comment in [184, 199] on Khrushchev's suggestions.
[25] [311, 32 ff., 38–41]. Cf. [296, 46–50].
[26] [311, 42] and [401, 163]. Early approaches to village reconstruction in 1957 and 1958 in Belorussia were cited by V. Sokolovskii in [452, 9 December 1967].

kolkhoz." [27] The subject was then discussed in the central daily press and in a special session of the Latvian Supreme Soviet.[28]

The matter was obviously controversial—particularly in view of the limitations of available resources. Khrushchev referred to these on a public occasion in 1961, but about two months later he made clear his basic commitment to the idea in a then unpublished memorandum to the Central Committee Presidum [*179*, IV, 345–346; *179*, V, 335].

As Luba Richter has correctly pointed out, curtailment of the private plot was closely related to the agrogorod concept. A reduction in the area under private plots could not really be compensated for by the envisaged allocation of additional plots outside the proposed new settlements. She also stressed the connection of the agrogorod with the formation of the new sovkhozes, particularly in the new lands [*311*, 34, 42 ff.]. This was clearly illustrated by a description of plans of the new settlement for a sovkhoz in the Amur oblast, published about six months after Khrushchev's removal. The inhabitants obviously preferred an alternative location, partly because that would be more suitable for their livestock. But they received the stern reply: "No fussing about the animals! It is going to be an agrogorod" [*443*, 18 May 1965].

Although some experimental construction began in 1961,[29] the very use of the term experimental suggested that no widespread implementation of the agrogorod idea was as yet envisaged. Toward the end of 1961, the Twenty-Second Party Congress referred to the "urban type settlements" in the new Party program at the end of a related section, but without using the word agrogorod and with no specific directions or time limits [*374*, III, 291]. Nevertheless, the revival of public discussion and Khrushchev's own publicly aired views strongly suggest that the agrogorod and the related reduction of privately operated land areas were a part of a broader vision of the future for him and for some of his colleagues in 1959 and 1960. Later I show that Khrushchev's successors apparently retained this vision of the future, although they have attempted to implement it in a less radical fashion.

The kolkhoz markets. During 1960, more and more voices were

---

[27] [*179*, III, 531, 534, and IV, 157–158]. See also [*449*, 12 May 1959].

[28] [*440*, 12 April, 27 April, 10 June and 13 December 1959]; [*449*, 8 April, 27 May and 22 December 1959].

[29] [*201*, 78, 96–97]. See also the illustrations of the completed houses in this settlement in *Sel'skaia nov'*, no. 12 (1966), 8–9, and of the palace of culture in [*452*, 3 November 1967].

raised in favor of curtailing the relatively free kolkhoz market in one way or another. These were not directed against the institution of the market as such; they asked that an end be put to the activity of speculators and for the introduction of stricter controls.[30] This criticism, which arose at a later date than the measures against the private sector described above, continued beyond the beginning of 1961[31] and was still to be heard up until the fall of Khrushchev. The actual measures undertaken against the kolkhoz market—price regulations, restrictions on supplies, the closure of individual markets [247, 62]—were accomplished administratively or on a local level. They cannot therefore be comprehensively documented and precisely dated, but retrospective critiques in Soviet publications—especially after the removal of Khrushchev—provide ample information (cf. p. 144 f.). The consequences were evident from the decline in total turnover on the kolkhoz markets from 1958 to 1964.[32]

One of the commercial factors affecting the kolkhoz markets and their private vendors was the granting of more competitive flexibility to the consumer cooperatives in the purchasing and selling of foodstuffs and in price formation. This was directed at the kolkhoz market and, in the last analysis, against it.[33] In theory it provided an opportunity for bringing produce from remote villages whose inhabitants found it difficult to travel to the urban markets, but in practice the consumer cooperatives were shown to be incapable of the task (see pp. 168 ff.).

The policy of reducing payments-in-kind to the agricultural population was also directed at the capacity of the kolkhozniks to produce for the free market. A commentary put it euphemistically: "[With the proportion of cash earnings increasing] the kolkhozniks were thereby freed from the necessity of disposing of the surplus produce which they had received in return for labor units" [49, 76]. Far more important, however, was the effect of reduced allocations of fodder on private livestock production, so that less meat, eggs, and milk came on to the market.

The drastic decimation of the private livestock herds, especially in the sovkhozes, and the prohibition on private livestock holdings in the

[30] See [440, 12 July 1960] and [449, 19 December 1960].
[31] For instance, [449, 3 March 1961].
[32] See [416, Appendix F]. Another source [343, 85] indicates an even sharper decline than is inferred from official Soviet statistics.
[33] See Karcz in [389, 417–418]; [449, 18 March 1961].

towns had a devastating effect. Efim Dorosch has pictured, with depressing vividness, how the sales of milk in a small town of Central Russia declined from the abundance of 1958 to a wretched trickle in 1960 (cf. p. 143). It is true that the state and cooperative milk outlets were now supposed to supply more, but they were unable to overcome the shortage.

In addition, when the sovkhoz and kolkhoz population received insufficient payments-in-kind to cover their own needs, they were obliged to turn to the state trade outlets and the free markets and thus increased demand pressure. "Graingrowers had to purchase in town bread and other foodstuffs which they themselves had produced" [221, 41].

In his painstaking inquiry, Lukinov established that the supply of foodstuffs, including state retail trade, in the Ukraine during 1957 and 1958 was considerably better than before, but that thereafter supplies diminished, demand increased, and thus prices on the kolkhoz markets began to rise again [225, 324]. A higher stimulus for private output was thus created, because purchased foodstuffs became more expensive and higher prices were offered for any surplus produce [225, 321, 324, 326–327]. All of this was completely contradictory to the goals of Khrushchev's agricultural policy. The price levels on the kolkhoz markets for most foodstuffs throughout the country showed a slight tendency to rise in 1960 (the rise was probably greatest in the fall), and this became more marked in 1961. The decline in the physical turnover on the markets had already begun in 1955 and 1956, but this had been offset initially by increased supplies in state and cooperative trade, probably originating from the good harvests of 1956 and 1958 [416, Appendix F].

The measures against the kolkhoz market were therefore "sucessful," but their consequences rebounded on their originator, on the state, and on its economy, faster and more obviously than in the other sectors. Developments on the kolkhoz market were a symptom and an alarm signal. They were recognized as such, but their total impact was underestimated. Khrushchev upbraided the zealots who were against the kolkhoz market, declaring, in his speech to the Twenty-Second Party Congress on 18 October 1961 [374, I, 242]:

Some comrades propose forbidding kolkhoz trade, and the most tenacious are even calling for the complete abolition of trade, replacing it by the direct distribution of goods. Is it still necessary to prove that these comrades are running ahead of events? The question of whether there is to be trade is not going to be decided through anyone's wish or by means of an edict. In order to realize the transition to direct distribution, the necessary material-technical

base and a surplus of material goods must be created. As long as these do not
exist, we should not limit Soviet trade but, on the contrary, develop and perfect it. (Applause.) Moreover, kolkhoz trade, which still plays a significant
role in supplying the population with foodstuffs, should not be forbidden. It
is necessary for the kolkhozniks to dispose of part of their produce. Furthermore, the prices on the kolkhoz market should not be determined administratively, as some comrades suggest. A lowering of the prices on the kolkhoz
market should be sought in the first instance by raising the output of agricultural products and not by administrative measures, which should be energetically applied only against speculative elements. At the same time, it is necessary to improve the operation of the [consumer] cooperatives, which should
help the kolkhozniks dispose of their surplus produce.

It is very questionable whether Khrushchev had always held this
view. The words we cite did not appear in the main part of his speech,
but in his closing remarks where he referred to some rejected proposals,
and were therefore not necessarily uttered with great conviction. Perhaps
they represent an after-effect of the relaxation of measures directed against
the private sector, a relaxation already evident by the beginning of
1961. In any case, Khrushchev had by then done nothing to protect the
kolkhoz market. Probably it was still not clear to him that the state of
the kolkhoz market was due not only to the false conceptions of "some
comrades" but primarily to his entire agricultural policy and its consequences.

More specific details of the mood and measures against the kolkhoz
market which had been criticized by Khrushchev were spelled out a few
months later by Soviet writer Morozov who evidently felt himself covered
by the First Secretary's words [247, 62]:

Some practical and theoretical workers came to false conclusions concerning
the necessity of energetically curtailing kolkhoz trade. In some raions and
oblasts, the number of hours and days during which kolkhoz markets were
open was reduced, and materials for building and repairing [market stalls]
were not distributed. In some places the markets were even closed down and
the buildings handed over to organizations and firms which have nothing to
do with trade. Kolkhoz chairmen who used kolkhoz trade to dispose of produce left over after fulfilling their procurement plans were criticized in the
press; it was predicted that kolkhoz trade would cease altogether, that fixed
prices would be introduced administratively on the kolkhoz market, and
so on.

The aftermath, 1961 to 1964. Toward the end of 1960 and at the
plenary session of the CPSU Central Committee in January 1961, Khrushchev had to contend with considerable opposition within the Party lead-

ership, which became known only covertly [*296*, 203-215]. That the policy toward the private sector of agriculture played a role in this became clear when the May 1961 issue of *Kommunist* appeared (with a delay). Its "Correspondence with the Readers" feature carried a review entitled "Some Economic Problems of the Kolkhoz Village." The column surveyed letters, commentaries, and articles, many of which were concerned with the private plots. The critical tone adopted toward Khrushchev's policies of the three preceding years was unmistakable, particularly concerning conversions to sovkhozes. Khrushchev, however, was not directly attacked. The supplementing of public kolkhoz farming by the private plots and livestock holdings was termed "the only possible [course] . . . at the given historical stage." The column warned both against an expansion of the private sector and against any "artificial reduction of incomes from the private plots" [*258*, 114-115]. The reader who had proposed "the abolition of the private plots and livestock holdings of sovkhoz workers and kolkhozniks" received the reply that doubtless the time would come when the private sector would be superfluous, but: "Now the problem is different: Has this time already come? Is it already possible, at the present stage of development of kolkhoz production, to proceed with the task of liquidating the kolkhozniks' private plots?" The journal's answer was: "No, such a moment has not yet arrived and *will not come as soon as some people suppose.*" [Emphasis supplied.] But it is noteworthy that in this resolute defense of the private plots for the present and also for some time to come, only the kolkhozniks were mentioned. Sovkhoz and other workers and employees were ignored, with the possible inference that the campaign against them might continue. Yet a strong condemnation was also aired of the more or less obligatory purchases of livestock from private owners [*258*, 115-116]. Evidently the publication of this issue was a definite public signal for breaking off the campaign against the private sector.

The Twenty-Second Party Congress of the CPSU, which took place from 17 October to 31 October 1961, concerned itself only marginally with the question of the private plots. Its primary task was the passing of the new party program, which embraced economic perspective plans up to 1980. As far as agriculture was concerned, utopian targets were still the order of the day in spite of setbacks encountered since 1958. This must have had a practical effect on policy toward the private sector, but on this topic the program was actually rather cautious, as is clear from the following paragraph [*374*, III, 290]:

Within a certain period, the public sector of the kolkhoz will have reached such a stage of development that it will be able to meet the requirements of the kolkhozniks entirely from its resources. Consequently the individual private plots will gradually become superfluous. When the public sector of the kolkhozes is in a position to fully replace the personal plots of the kolkhozniks, when the kolkhozniks become convinced that it is not advantageous for them to have a personal plot, they will voluntarily give it up.

Apart from the expected reference to the ultimate superfluousness of the private plots, the strong emphasis on the economic preconditions is remarkable. In the light of the actual state of affairs in 1961 and 1962, this must have signified a very long time horizon, but it did not represent an explicit prohibition of the curtailment of the private sector. A great deal depended upon how the statement was to be interpreted and whether priority was to be given to the taut procurement plans or to the living standards of the kolkhoz population.

Moreover, the paragraph of the Party program referred only to the private plots of the kolkhozniks, and no mention was made of the subsidiary farms of the rest of the population—especially of the sovkhoz workers and employees. In any event, the process of conversions to state farms decelerated: The kolkhoz system was declared to be "an inalienable component of the Soviet socialist society," that is, of the stage before the attainment of full communism. On the other hand, during the period from 1971 to 1980, the "material-technical base of communism" was to be constructed, and this also applied to agriculture. The sovkhozes were to play "an ever increasing role in the development of agriculture as the leading socialist enterprises in the countryside" [374, III, 276, 285]. This could be interpreted either as a qualitative enhancement of their role or as a quantitative expansion of the sovkhoz sector.

During the congress, L. F. Il'ichev recalled Khrushchev's 1951 article on agrogorods and termed it "absolutely correct, imbued with the Leninist creative spirit," and he pilloried Malenkov as the chief opponent of the plan at that time [374, II, 183–184]. Nevertheless, the paragraph in the approved Party program was equivocal: "Old-fashioned peasant houses will generally be replaced by new modern houses or, wherever possible, rebuilt so that they offer the requisite comfort" [374, III, 298]. Did "modern" mean one-family and two-family houses with adjacent plots or did it mean multistoried houses with numerous apartments, as Khrushchev had been propagating?

Despite Khrushchev's plea on behalf of the kolkhoz markets late in the congress, these were dealt with in a bare sentence: "Kolkhoz markets will also retain their importance." This gave no indication of any prospective future trends in their turnover. Immediately before this sentence was the stipulation: "The consumer cooperatives, whose task is to perfect trade on the countryside and to organize the marketing of surplus agricultural production, will be further developed" [*374*, III, 298]. This can hardly be interpreted to mean the encouragement of direct marketing by private producers.

On the whole, the new Party program did not particularly encourage further reduction of the private sector. It did not specifically discourage it either, and made no mention of any kind of restitution.

The main problem now was that of stimulating agricultural production, and questions of agricultural policy relating specifically to the private sector were relegated to the background. During the subsequent period, the principal measures adopted were the elimination or a sharp reduction of fallow, the raising of purchase and retail prices for milk and meat, a further extension of corn and root crops, the splitting of the party organization into industrial and agricultural branches, and the increased output and application of mineral fertilizers. Through all these expedients the public sector of agriculture was to be placed in a position to meet the goals set for it.[34]

Khrushchev, whose prestige and position were bound up with the agricultural problem, made more speeches on this topic than ever before; four of the eight volumes of his speeches and writings on agricultural problems cover the period from the beginning of 1961 to the beginning of 1964. Very little of this is devoted to the private sector. A certain reserve is even shown with respect to the purchase of livestock from sovkhoz workers, as in his speech at Tselinograd on 22 November 1961 [*179*, VI, 166]. But in his closing speech at the Central Committee plenum on 9 March 1962, he returned to the subject of private plots, although significantly only with reference to sovkhozes [*179*, V, 469]: "Comrades, in each sovkhoz there should be a communal vegetable garden. Communal in the sense that the sovkhoz workers and employees do not have their own plots next to their houses but meet their requirements for potatoes and vegetables from the sovkhoz vegetable garden."

---

[34] For a good, concise survey, see Karcz [*389*, 420-422].

A decree to this effect was issued in the RSFSR on 26 September 1962 [*346*, IX, 451–452]. The other republics presumably followed at about the same time.

The communal gardens for sovkhoz workers and employees proved anything but successful. They were "unprofitable, did not become widespread," "by far not always rationally solved the problem of providing the families with potaotes and vegetables even in those cases where they became the only source" for such supply, and "at the same time the fertile soil of the personal plots went to waste without benefit" [*339a*, 74–75]. This was admitted much later, though, as well as the fact that usually the measure had been enforced [*339a*].

On 20 April 1962, when Khrushchev was asked by an American publisher, "Do you intend to liquidate the kolkhozniks' private plots?" he conformed to the line of the Party program which, in theory at least, did not run contrary to his own earlier utterances [*179*, VII, 24]:

> No, we do not intend to. This is not the main issue, although I believe that in time the private plots will be liquidated by their owners themselves. But this will happen when the social sector is developed up to a certain level so that it can fully meet all the requirements of the kolkhozniks. . . . For this reason, until the precondition of a surplus is met, the kolkhozniks may keep their private plots. They do not contradict the development of socialism and communism.

As far as the kolkhoz sector was concerned, the predominant approach until 1964 was this: "The withering away of the personal farms of the kolkhozniks will come about gradually" [*391*, 13]. Yet, works also appeared at the same time advocating the reduction of the private sector and scarcely bothering to disguise the methods of compulsion to be used for this purpose.[35] After 1963 in the RSFSR, the rates of the agricultural tax on private plots of the kolkhozniks who did not fulfill their minimum man-day inputs in the public sector were raised by 50 percent. This provision applied only in those kolkhozes which introduced cash wages [*346*, IV, 146].

But Khrushchev could not entirely abandon the propagation of his old views. It is significant that, when speaking to some sovkhoz workers in Turkmenia on 28 September 1962, he returned to the matter of the future layout of villages. Now, however, he contented himself with recommending "two-storied houses or single-storied houses with four to six

[35] See the instances given in [*91*, 52–53].

apartments [*179*, VI, 464]. Nevertheless, agricultural settlements in newly irrigated areas of Central Asia were also planned at that time with diameters of from eight to twelve kilometers [sic] and with five- or six-story houses [*254*, 98].

How closely the process of conversions to state farms was related to the policy toward the private sector and Khrushchev's own awareness of this relationship are shown by his detailed comments on 12 March 1963. This speech was particularly significant for agricultural policy, because he then addressed Party and state officials of the newly created territorial production administrations. Practically speaking, his words amounted to a guideline for the sovkhoz sector [*179*, VI, 424].

The sovkhoz worker of today is an ex-kolkhoznik. [This was true of the majority but not of all sovkhoz workers.] He has his own house and his vegetable garden. He has acquired a cow which he feeds at the expense of the fodder belonging to the sovkhoz. . . . Already in the first years of Soviet rule, *V. I. Lenin* pronounced the warning that *under no circumstance should the sovkhoz worker be allowed to keep his own livestock. We must keep this directive in mind.* [Emphasis supplied.]

The party organizations, the leaders of the sovkhozes must pay attention to supplying the workers with milk and vegetables. Communal sovkhoz vegetable gardens must be laid down, good canteens organized, and foodstuffs supplied at production cost. To sum up: great possibilities exist for supplying the sovkhoz workers. If the sovkhoz director, the Party, and the trade union organization use these possibilities correctly, this will be appreciated by the workers. And then it will not be necessary for the sovkhoz workers to have their own livestock. And a struggle must be waged against those who acquire livestock in order to speculate with meat and milk [that is, to produce in order to sell at the favorable free market prices].

Two months later, legislation followed these words. On 6 May 1963, three edicts were passed by the Presidium of the RSFSR Supreme Soviet [*464*, no. 18 (1963), 444–447]. The first edict renewed the prohibition on feeding animals with grain products purchased in stores and prescribed more severe punishments, threatening sentences of one year's hard labor and prison terms of from one to three years together with the possibility of confiscation of the livestock, for second offenses and for "large scale" offenses.[36] At this time it was reported from Syktyvkar that militiamen were going from house to house, checking on whether bread was fed to pigs [*282*, 54]. The second edict, in effect from 1 July 1963, limited the livestock holdings of all sections of the population other than kolkhozniks

---

[36] This was made a law on 23 December 1963; cf. [*346*, XIV, 584].

—except in a few remote regions—to one cow and one calf of up to four months *or* one goat with young of up to one year plus one meat pig *or* three sheep with young of up to one year. The third edict provided for almost prohibitive taxes on livestock holdings above these norms; the law on the Agricultural Tax was amended accordingly [*464*, no. 16 (1964), 305–306]. These taxes were doubled and applied to all the animals of able-bodied persons who were not engaged in "socially necessary labor."

The second edict appeared to apply to all individuals other than the kolkhozniks, but the third edict on taxes indirectly confirmed that special norms for livestock holdings applied to part of the sovkhoz population, evidently formulated within the earlier sovkhoz ministries and the agencies which replaced them. Although the livestock tax was raised on animals over and above those permitted "in the edict . . . of 6 May 1963," special regulations applied for "those engaged in sovkhozes who own livestock over and above the norms laid down for them," without reference to the other edict.

Thus the problem was not resolved in the eyes of Khrushchev: The smaller union republics still had to follow the example of the RSFSR, but the edicts applied only partially to the sovkhoz population. Therefore he returned to the theme in a more detailed and determined fashion in his memorandum of 31 July 1963, to the Central Committee Presidium [*179*, VIII, 67–68, 72–73]:

Many workers and sovkhoz leaders have been enthusiastic about livestock holdings in personal ownership. This livestock is kept at the cost of sovkhoz fodder, it grazes on sovkhoz crops, destroys the grain. Among those who live in sovkhozes are speculators, layabouts, who plunder sovkhoz property. The leaders of the sovkhoz see all this but behave with complete indifference toward a situation which cries out to heaven and do not look after public property. . . .

The questions connected with strengthening work discipline in the sovkhozes, with the struggle against antisocial elements which undermine sovkhoz production, merit particular attention by the Party, by those active in agriculture. I mean those employed in sovkhozes who expand their personal economy at the expense of the public sector, who acquire a great deal of livestock for their own use, speculate with animal products, and regard their membership in the sovkhoz as a cover for their ugly business. Not a few people have appeared in sovkhozes who do not work but live from speculating in animal products. The parasitic elements get rich through various violations of the established regulations under the very noses of the sovkhoz leaders and the Party organizations, but they receive no rebuff.

Khrushchev next cited several flagrant examples of this type from Kazakhstan and continued [*179*, VIII, 74–75]:

It is characteristic that, in several sovkhozes which have been created on the basis of [former] kolkhozes, the livestock holdings of the workers and employees are considerably larger than the kolkhozniks used to have. . . . The expansion of the livestock inventories in the personal possession of sovkhoz workers seriously harms the interests of the state and of the entire people. In this connection I would like once more to recall the instruction of V. I. Lenin. . . . : "None of the workers and employees has the right to have animals, poultry, and vegetable gardens of their own."

In the same memorandum, Khrushchev warned against excesses in the process of conversions to sovkhozes. He was, however, primarily concerned that many of the kolkhozes being converted were economically weak and thus that their conversions placed a further burden on the state budget [*179*, VIII, 66–67].

The great wave of conversions ebbed in 1961 but did not cease entirely.[37] Together with the campaign against the private plots in the sovkhozes, there was a reduction of the private sector in the converted kolkhozes. By this process a further slow curtailment of the private plots of the kolkhoz sector occurred, quite apart from whether the plots in the remaining kolkhozes were reduced or not.

Shortly before the Twenty-Second Party Congress, a decree was passed, on 18 September 1961, against allegedly collective but in fact individual fruit and berry gardening by townspeople. It was not really effective and was often circumvented by local authorities [*55a*, 66–69]. Another decree, of 1 June 1962, drastically reduced the granting of urban house and garden plots for building one-family homes [*55a*, 8]. That decree seems to have had more effect, but the sources do not permit a precise assessment.

From the published Soviet statistics, it cannot be deduced what effect the overall situation, the decrees, and Khrushchev's admonitions had on the size of the private plots and livestock holdings of workers and employees, especially in sovkhozes. Most data do not cover the total privately used area (see p. 95 above), and they do not differentiate between categories (urban and rural, sovkhoz and other). From several individual indications it is clear that the reduction in sovkhozes was

[37] For details, see [*418*, 39–48].

severe,[38] but precise data and dates cannot be established at this time. The following information indicates that the reduction continued from the end of 1961 to the end of 1964 and was particularly pronounced in the last two years of that period.

The number of sovkhoz workers and employees grew annually between 1961 and 1964, and the total increase during this period came to 697,000 individuals.[39] The private agricultural land area of all workers and employees (including the land of those outside the sovkhoz system and those with house plots in the urban areas) increased by only 120,000 hectares. This increase, however, includes an expansion of 470,000 hectares by the end of 1963 and a contraction of 350,000 hectares in the twelve months preceding 1 November 1964. For arable land, the figures are as follows: An increase of 280,000 hectares by 1 January 1964 was followed by a decrease of 380,000 hectares during 1964—resulting in a net decline of 100,000 hectares between 1961 and 1964 (see Table 1). In all probability, a growing proportion of private plots cultivated by workers and employees was planted with perennial crops rather than being tilled.

Livestock holdings of all workers and employees grew by about 180,000 animal units during 1962, suffered a setback in 1963, and more than recovered the next year (see Table 20). The result was an overall increase of 531,000 animal units from the end of 1961 to the end of 1964. But during that time, 6.7 million new workers and employees, other than those of sovkhozes, joined the workforce [20, 25]. If only 10 percent of these owned 0.5 to 1 unit, this would account for most of the increase of animal numbers and would leave almost nothing for the new sovkhoz workforce. Thus, although the decline in kolkhozniks' land and animals was not relatively much greater than the decline in the number of kolkhoz households (see Tables 12 and 13), the decline per household or family must have been sizable in sovkhozes.

It is true that the overall picture is somewhat obscured, because urban livestock holders were also affected by the edict of 6 May 1963, cited earlier. By that time their once considerable numbers must have been markedly reduced by the 1959 prohibition. If so, a further reduction in urban private livestock holdings in 1963 could not have been the main determinant of the overall development. One can say that Khrushchev's

---

[38] See Appendices D and E in [416].

[39] [20, 127]. The increase slowed down from 322 thousand in 1961/1962 to 159 thousand in 1963/1964.

renewed offensive of 1963 against the private plots and livestock holdings in sovkhozes had an effect, although not to the extent intended.

Not many data are at hand about kolkhozes for the period after 1961, because most Soviet authors writing retrospectively on this topic choose to deal with the whole period since 1958. The head of a raion administration in Belgorod oblast reported at the beginning of 1965 that "last year" the private plots belonging to old kolkhozniks and to small families were "sharply reduced in several farms." In one case, the following rule was added to the kolkhoz statute [334, 34]: "The kolkhoz administration is empowered to confiscate livestock. In cases of compulsory purchase, 50 percent of the state purchase price is to be paid to the kolkhoz household." (It should be noted that state purchase prices in 1964 were considerably lower than free market prices). A Soviet jurist probably also referred to 1964 when she wrote: "Some kolkhoz chairmen regard [threats of] the reduction of the private plots as the principal means of tightening up labor discipline," but in recent years this practice of [making] "numerous reductions" of the kolkhozniks' private plots and also those of workers and employees "has proved a failure" [171, 22-23]. The reduction of payments-in-kind was also continued, partly in connection with the transfer to cash earnings only.[40]

Statistics show that from November 1961 to November 1964 the average size of private plots in kolkhozes declined further from about 0.31 to slightly less than 0.30 hectare, and that during 1962 and 1963 the number of privately owned livestock per kolkhoz household also fell further (cf. Table 13).

The reaction of the free kolkhoz markets to the state's agricultural policy and to the rising demand had already become clear by 1961, and after that year the situation deteriorated rapidly. The turnover of the most important products (grain, vegetables, potatoes, milk, and eggs) declined considerably. For fruit, a different picture obtained, and the curbs on private livestock holdings and the poor harvest of 1963 led to forced slaughterings. These resulted at first in large supplies of meat, but by 1964 they also dropped. The supply situation was mirrored by prices: The overall index rose annually by 5 to 6 percent until 1964. This was also generally true for the individual products until 1963 (no later individual data are available), except that temporarily larger supplies of meat evidently depressed those prices.

[40] See the table of payments in grain per household in [395, 283].

During his last three years in office, Khrushchev evidently did not apply pressure to the private sector in kolkhozes. Yet the campaign of 1958–1960 had its own momentum in kolkhozes too; this must have continued, albeit at a reduced rate. Further problems resulted from the increasing difficulties experienced by Soviet agriculture, especially during the poor harvest of 1963, and delivery obligations remained high and almost unchanged. The 1963 disaster meant a shortage of fodder in many parts of the country. As a result, the number of pigs in the public sector declined by 32.8 percent [*11*, 353]. That disaster also led to the purchase, from the West, of large quantities of grain, and bread remained in short supply. Under such conditions, the squeezing of as much as possible out of the private sector did not reflect any particular policy directed against it. During 1963, the kolkhozniks were given hardly enough grain—as payments-in-kind—for their own human needs and even less grain for fodder. Distribution of grain in part payment to sovkhoz combine operators was also terminated (see p. 215).

Khrushchev's leading position was no longer undisputed by the fall of 1963. While the events of the period from 1958 to 1961 can definitely be attributed to Khrushchev's agrarian policy, this cannot be said with certainty of the latter period. However, no other political force can yet be identified which influenced the Kremlin's policy toward the private sector in either direction. There are some signs, in articles and books published in 1964 and early 1965, that several authors cautiously spoke out for a considerate policy toward the private sector, citing the Party program and some of Khrushchev's statements made in 1961 and 1962.[41]

It also appears that several political functionaries cooperated with Khrushchev only hesitantly and reluctantly; this was shown by his remarks concerning the private plots and subsidiary husbandries in sovkhozes.[42] Subsequently, the First Party Secretary of Estonia was to declare publicly: "To be honest, there were no such reductions of the kolkhozniks' plots in our republic. The personal farms of the kolkhozniks this year [1964] have not, it is true, grown, but there was also no drop in their output." The Lithuanian First Party Secretary made a similar claim [*295, 203, 223*].

[41] These included scholarly books by Karnaukhova, Lukinov, Morozov, and Paskhaver. This trend was felt somewhat earlier in literary publications of Belov, Dorosh, Iashin, and Solzhenitsyn. (Reference is to 1965 books sent to typesetters before Khrushchev's ouster.) See also the correspondence in [*440*, 14 March 1964].

[42] See p. 285 above and also Khrushchev's speech of 1 February 1961 [*179*, IV, 434].

In view of such discrepancies, it is hardly surprising that individual kolkhozes and even sovkhozes formulated their own policy, especially regarding the distribution of fodder for the livestock of their members. In 1964, one sovkhoz in the Leningrad oblast set up a kind of limited lease, permitting its members to keep what they could grow on waste or overgrown land, but this was not reported until 1965 [*392, 127*]. Some kolkhoz chairmen gave out a larger share of the harvested fodder to the kolkhozniks than was officially approved (cf. p. 224 f.).

Thus Khrushchev's administration came to an end, without a change in the official attitude toward the private sector, but with increasing indications of a realization of the serious damage caused by his great campaign of 1958–1960.

10

Policy Toward the
Private Sector,
1964–1971

After Khrushchev's fall, one of the first acts of the new government was the lifting of restrictions on the private agricultural sector. This was initiated by a decree of the CPSU Central Committee of 27 October 1964 (which was not published at the time).[1] The corresponding decrees of the individual union republics followed during the ensuing months [*128, 53; 86, 68*]. On 4 November 1964, the tax on livestock owned by urban residents, introduced in 1956, was repealed [*359, 401–402*]. Other legal restrictions imposed on livestock holdings of the nonkolkhoz population from 1959 to 1963, were lifted.[2] The new regime was undoubtedly taking a serious and positive interest in the private sector in the hope of a favorable public response. There are reports from various parts of the Soviet Union that actual increases in the size of the plots and herds, following the new legislation, exceeded the new legal limits and that the authorities chose to ignore such infringements in 1965 [*246, 69, 72*].

As in 1953, the hopes of the population appear to have been raised even before the change in policy toward private production was publicly proclaimed in Leonid Brezhnev's speech of 6 November 1964. The Soviet writer Krutilin later reported from his native village in Riazan oblast that "in mid-October, when people heard about the plenum, the women began saying that the confiscated plots would be returned." But he also recorded the villagers' mistrust, based on past experience: "Once more the story is: 'We'll give you your plots back and ease up on your live-

---

[1] A very short extract was to be published later in *Resheniia partii i pravitel'stva po khoziaistvennym voprosam*, Vol. V (Moscow: 1968), p. 517.

[2] For the relevant RSFSR edict, see [*464*, no. 51 (1964), 782].

stock' . . . They are all nimble with words, but when it comes to deeds . . ." [*200, 620, 623*]. Similar mistrust was expressed at a later, unspecified, date by a woman in a garden settlement near Moscow. She would have bought a calf from a neighbor had not her husband "suspected that they would once again apply pressure regarding the cow" [*123, 31*].

After the removal of Khrushchev, Soviet writers expressed their views more openly. Among them, Venzher wrote:

The fate of a large part of our country's population—at least one hundred million people,[3] [allowing for three persons to a family] is linked with personal agriculture on the private plots. This problem thus goes far beyond the internal affairs of kolkhozes and sovkhozes and is one of the greatest economic problems of a sociological character. With the solution of this problem are connected the interests of different social strata of our society—the kolkhozniks, the sovkhoz workers and employees, the lower paid industrial workers and government officials, especially those employed in social-cultural establishments in rural areas (schools, hospitals), and others. . . . For this reason, each restriction upon the private sector . . . unavoidably has a detrimental effect also upon the social sphere of production. Agricultural production on the subsidiary plots represents a part of socialist agriculture, and until the latter has reached a certain stage of development, fulfills its special task of providing an important part of the personal consumption requirements of a substantial portion of the toilers in society.

The social-psychological consequences of this state of affairs—that "the kolkhoznik is on the one hand a collective worker and on the other a small owner of the means of production" [*354*, I, 365] and that he "is possessed of a certain duality"[4]—were also spelled out cautiously in a collection of essays on sociology in the USSR sent to press even before the fall of Khrushchev [*354*, I, 461]:

In contrast to the worker's family, the kolkhoz family has several features which bind its members' personalities especially closely with this *kollektiv*. Among these are the existence of the private plot and the domestic economy— however modest—which demand daily attention and care in apportioning the time available. The family life of the kolkhoznik embraces economic functions which are not characteristic of the worker's family.

The same thought was to appear in a similar work published in 1968 [*180, 88*]. It is quite obvious that this is also generally valid for those

[3] This is still an underestimate; see [*416*, Appendix D].
[4] [*258, 114*] and [*440, 8 October 1961*].

workers and employees whose plots approach the size and significance of those of the kolkhozniks. In such families, too, common private production may help to preserve "the birthmarks of capitalism" [253, 22; cf. 340, 128].

Characteristic of the Khrushchev era is a high school textbook of 640 pages which went to the press in 1964. This purported to cover systematically all aspects of the production structure of the socialist agriculture of the Soviet Union and—marginally—of the other "socialist countries," and yet devoted less than a page to the private agricultural activity of the kolkhozniks[5] and totally ignored the rest of the private sector of agriculture.[6] Barely a year later, Zaslavskaia in her book on labor remuneration in kolkhozes [427] did devote a section of thirteen pages to the private sector. Another Soviet author asserted that in 1963 the amount paid by kolkhozniks to the government just in taxes on the private plots was— hectare for hectare—greater than the value of produce grown by kolkhozes on communal land.[7] If this was the case in 1963, it is not difficult to imagine the relationship during Stalin's time, when the agricultural tax levied on kolkhoz households grew to unbearable heights.

Most Soviet learned journals were silent on the subject of the private sector until 1965 [128, 3]. In February of that year, V. Maniakin mentioned casually that more than one-third of total Soviet farm output in 1963 was produced in the private sector [234, 10]. Clear evidence of the turning point came with the publication of Shmelev's article in the April 1965 issue of a leading economic journal, followed later in the year by Nazarov's contribution in the authoritative theoretical journal of the Party.[8] Shmelev passed judgment on the economic significance of the

---

[5] [61, 68]. It is worthy of note that a comprehensive critique of this book, appearing later in a Soviet journal published in December of 1965, also objected to this defect. Cf. [108, 123].

[6] The latter omission can be justified by the title of the book, whereas the output of the kolkhozniks' private plots is nowadays considered as part of the socialized sector, however contestable this may in fact be.

[7] [107, 309]. See also the gross revenue per unit of kolkhoz (public) land in [11, 400] and the provisions of the law on agricultural tax of August 8, 1953 [323, 637–645], as well as the average rates of the agricultural tax by regions of the RSFSR. These rates, fixed by the decree of 28 June 1962, averaged 0.80 to 1.00 ruble per one-hundredth of a hectare. Cf. [346, IV, 143–145].

[8] [339, 23–37] and [256, 68–74]. The change of policy was, of course, reflected earlier in the daily press. Cf. articles by A. Polianskii and F. Golsitskii in [452, 12 and 18 November 1964] and [335, 30–33]

private sector in terms that could not have been printed a few months eariler [*339, 32*]:

Many economists reckon that production on the private plots is of low efficiency. Indeed, much labor is applied on these farms. Nevertheless, it cannot be denied that these plots yield intensively, despite their small size.

This altered assessment opened the way for a broad, objectively based discussion of the private sector. In October of 1965, Makeenko outlined the problem and its hitherto inadequate treatment as follows [*220, 58*]:

What are the objective reasons for the existence of the private plots under socialism, what determines their place and role in extended socialist reproduction? Unfortunately, no exact answer to these questions can yet be found in our scientific literature.

And although he had usually treated the subject with reservations, in his book which appeared in mid-1966 Koriagin wrote with the present and recent past in mind [*191, 57*]:

Under present conditions, it is incorrect to underestimate the role of the private plots. Restrictions on them during the past few years have caused our country substantial losses.

In the Ukraine, the relevant decisions were not only taken but also were made public before Brezhnev's speech. The republican Central Committee and Council of Ministers issued a joint decree recommending kolkhozes "to restore farm plots to their former size and to reinstate the norms for privately-owned livestock which have been subjected to unwarranted reductions since 1955; to extend every assistance to toiling kolkhozniks in acquiring livestock; to provide pasture and feed for their livestock; and to put an end to the arbitrary reduction of personal plots" [*450*, 5 November 1964]. A second decree of the same date rescinded the prohibition of private livestock holdings in towns; and in sovkhozes which had been converted from kolkhozes, the former kolkhozniks who had already passed the age of retirement were to keep or to be given back their original plots, not reduced in size [*450*, 5 November 1964]. What is noteworthy about these Ukrainian decrees, apart from their early date of publication, is their reference to the year 1955. In so doing, they indirectly branded as "unwarranted" the reductions of plots resulting from the decree of 6 March 1956, not to mention the later legislation.

A corresponding decree and an edict of the RSFSR appeared on 13

November 1964. The wording, published at that time in abbreviated form like those of the Ukraine, covered also the regulations for plots of workers and employees and was similar to the above with the significant difference that no mention was made of the year 1955.[9] Thus, although the abrogation of "unwarranted" restrictions was also recommended in the RSFSR, there was no implicit indication as to which restrictions were to be considered unwarranted and which were not. The decree recommended to kolkhozes, and ordered local Party, state, and agricultural organs, sovkhoz directors, managers of enterprises, organizations, and institutions "to render assistance to conscientiously working kolkhozniks, workers, and employees in tending their private plots and gardens, in acquiring livestock and poultry, in making available pasture, and in gathering feed supplies for the winter." In one of the minor republics, the Kirghiz SSR, a decree for the kolkhozes was issued on 19 December 1964, and the corresponding changes in the kolkhoz charters were decided upon by the kolkhozes themselves—as was done in all union republics—during the following months [140, 6-7].

As far as the kolkhozes were concerned, the government clearly wished to avoid stipulating the precise sizes of plots and livestock holdings and to leave a definite regulation of the entire problem to the new Model Charter. This was to be enacted by the Third All-Union Congress of Kolkhozniks, which was initially scheduled tentatively for 1966 but was postponed without explanation until the fall of 1969.

The maximum size of a normal sovkhoz plot was increased from 0.15 to 0.30 hectare, in the Ukraine up to 0.40 hectare, and in some Siberian and Far Eastern districts up to 0.50 hectare.[10] Apparently an increase in the permitted area of the private plots in sovkhozes was now favored even in the Virgin Lands [399, 210, 214]. And the communal gardens in sovkhozes, which were to replace the individual plots under Khrushchev, disappeared in most cases, as they were disliked by people and no more pressure in their favor was exerted from above [339a, 75-76].

For nonfarm workers and employees living on the countryside, the standards remained largely unchanged. But the category of specialists, covered under the existing preferential regulations, was considerably broadened, and under some conditions small strips of 0.03 to 0.05 hectare could be added to the normal plots [346, VIII, 83]. On the other hand,

[9] *Sovetskaia Rossiia*, 14 November 1964, p. 1. The full text of the decree is in [346, VIII, 79-83]; that of the edict in [464, no. 51 (1964), 782].
[10] [346, VIII, 80-81] and [72, 95].

the norms for service allotments (*sluzhebnye nadely*, cf. Chapter III), established for the RSFSR in a decree of 20 March 1965 were, on the whole, somewhat smaller than in 1960.[11] However, it was proposed to return to the railroad workers and employees those service allotments and meadow strips along the railroad tracks which had been confiscated in previous years [*440*, 26 May and 4 December 1965].

Special emphasis was placed on the collective gardens of urban residents [*462*, 14 April 1965]. On 12 April 1965 the RSFSR Council of Ministers, together with the Central Council of the Trade Unions, issued a decree in favor of collective vegetable gardens of up to 0.15 hectare per family to be given to urban workers and employees by their enterprises, organizations, and institutions. Such gardeners were to be supplied with tools, seed, fertilizer, insecticides, and so on.[12] A similar decree for fruit and berry gardens of up to 0.06 hectare per family (0.08 hectare in Siberia) was issued on 18 March 1966 [*346*, VIII, 84].

As far as private livestock holdings were concerned, town dwellers were now given equal rights with nonagricultural rural workers and employees [*303*, 117]. Regulations of 13 November 1964, for the rural as well as urban nonkolkhoz population of the RSFSR [*346*, XIII, 256–257] set the normal limits for each family slightly above the pre-1963 level (see above, p. 39 f.). In other union republics the regulations were apparently similar except for special rules in some national autonomous republics. There were also some exceptions within the RSFSR, especially for the subpolar regions. Under some conditions, even one working animal was allowed [*346*, XIII, 256–257]. For sovkhoz workers and employees there may have been internal directives issued by the authorities responsible for the sovkhozes, but these probably conformed to the basic republican decrees.

Further decrees and official instructions encouraged the private ownership of livestock. On 18 December 1964, the State Bank was authorized to extend loans to those kolkhozniks and sovkhoz workers and employees who did not own a cow and who wished to purchase a cow or a calf [*359*, 296]. State agencies were instructed to resume the sale of fodder and forage to private livestock owners.[13] Several of the measures which were aimed at making livestock raising in general more profitable also benefited private owners. Among these were the increase in the price of milk, the lowering of its prescribed butterfat content, and the payment of meat

---

[11] [*346*, VIII, 85–90]; for 1960 and earlier years, cf. [*64*, 39–46].
[12] [*346*, VIII, 84–85]; for gardening cooperatives, see also [*440*, 2 April 1965].
[13] [*434*, 9 December 1964, 40] and [*346*, IX, 363]

deliveries at retail prices. However, private owners did not benefit from the increase in prices for live animals.[14]

The general outlines for private land use were reaffirmed by the new Land Law of December 1968; this even put slightly more emphasis than its original draft on the use of public land for haymaking by private persons and for grazing by privately owned livestock.[15]

In the matter of payments-in-kind to kolkhozniks, the Ukraine again took the lead. As early as December 1964, official recommendations had gone out to Ukrainian kolkhozes to distribute 15 to 20 percent of their grain and 10 to 15 percent of their potato crop as earnings-in-kind; kolkhozes were also to determine the percentage of raw fodder for distribution according to local conditions [407, 95; 366, 75]. The recommendations seem to have been more detailed than in other union republics and to give more positive support for private livestock raising. In 1966, payments-in-kind in the Ukraine were said to be higher than ever before [214a, 50–51].

Although Brezhnev himself did not go into the matter of payments-in-kind, there were so many favorable commentaries on this theme following the March 1965 plenum [for example, 120, 69] that it was clear that the regime did intend to increase the share of payments-in-kind in overall earnings. Later the decree of 16 May 1966, "On Increasing the Material Interest of the Kolkhozniks in Public Production," represented a fundamental endorsement of the principle of payment-in-kind. The decree stipulated that kolkhozes were to accumulate a "guaranteed fund of produce . . . consisting of a specific part of the grain harvest and other produce" so that the members could receive their portions "and also also fodder for their livestock" within the framework of guaranteed work compensation [360, 125].

Greater consideration was also given to the need for payments-in-kind as a component of earnings in the sovkhozes. In March of 1965, the First Party Secretary of Tambov oblast advised the sovkhozes to "examine the possibilities of paying the workers certain wages-in-kind: of selling them grain, even if in limited quantities, as well as forage, silage, green fodder, piglets, and chicks at purchase prices" [295, 58]. In the spring of 1966, a lengthy article in the agricultural journal of the Cen-

---

[14] Decrees of 16 November 1964 and 1 April 1965; [359, 149 ff., 177 and 188 ff. resp.].

[15] Paragraphs 27, 43 and 45 in [452, 14 December 1968] as compared with the draft paragraphs 26, 40 and 42 in [452, 26 July 1968].

tral Committee reaffirmed and summarized the right of sovkhoz directors to distribute up to 10 percent of their potatoes, vegetables, and fruit
as wages-in-kind. Apparently grain could be distributed, as before, only
to those who took part in the harvest—especially to the mechanizers.
Similarly, workers who owned livestock and who assisted in the harvesting of hay, straw, and silage could receive up to 20 percent of what was
gathered in. Furthermore, special supplementary grain allocations were
permitted in the Virgin Lands, where most of the grain acreage farmed
by sovkhozes is located.[16] How often the directors made use of this right
(especially when the harvest was bad and the delivery plan could not be
fulfilled) is another matter. But viewed as an expression of a guideline,
the percentages cited are still important.

On natural meadows which were not accessible to, or were too small
for, mechanical mowers, a system of sharecropping was in many places
extended to individuals, including members of the nonagricultural population. The intention was to procure additional fodder for publicly—as
well as for privately—owned livestock.[17]

The notion of the agrogorod and the conversion of kolkhozes into
sovkhozes were promoted in a less pronounced and a more differentiated
manner after Khrushchev's removal. The relatively few conversions can
be considered as an indication of the continuing preference for sovkhozes
but not as a vigorous continuation of the conversion campaign. In 1965,
however, the number of conversions was still considerable.[18]

The development and modernization of agricultural villages continued to receive prominent mention in the Soviet press after 1966 and
gave rise to heated discussions.[19] Attention was devoted to both kolkhoz
and sovkhoz villages and to both one-family and multifamily houses.
Frequent mention was made of multifamily, two- or three-story houses
to be erected in the central village of an agricultural enterprise. These
were mainly to house specialists and the cadre personnel, as well as teachers, doctors, and other nonagricultural employees. Most of the ordinary
workers and employees would continue to live in one- or in two-family
houses.

[16] For more details, see Wädekin, "Payment in Kind in Soviet Agriculture,"
Bulletin—Institute for the Study of the USSR, no. 9 (1971), 9-18.

[17] See the general recommendation for the RSFSR in a decree of 1 June 1966 in
[*346,* VIII, 28] and the decision of the Leningrad oblast authorities of 30 June 1967,
as reproduced in an extract by [*128,* 71].

[18] For a more detailed account, see [*418,* 49 ff.].

[19] For a detailed account, see [*410*]; [*411*]; [*417*].

One Soviet writer indicated clearly that contemporary village reconstruction plans and the question of the private sector were closely interrelated [*190*, 47]: "The private plots and livestock holdings of the kolkhozniks and of sovkhoz workers have not yet lost their economic significance. *For this reason,* there still remains the need for building isolated houses with adjoining premises for economic and everyday needs." [Emphasis supplied.] Conversely, this means that there is an implicit intention to reduce the private plots of the villagers wherever and whenever the building of multifamily houses is planned and practiced in a village. Sometimes this intention is quite explicit.[20]

A comprehensive decree on trade matters, issued on 13 March 1965, antedated the meeting of the Central Committee (March 24–26).[21] While the decree dealt primarily with the "improvement of trade and catering in rural areas," it also touched upon the question of the kolkhoz markets. It called for an improvement of trade on these markets, for construction of new market premises, and for better equipment for the existing facilities. The ministries of the union-republics were ordered to increase the supply of privately produced foodstuffs to the kolkhoz markets, to improve facilities there, and to render other assistance. At the same time it was announced that new "model regulations for trade on kolkhoz markets" were being drawn up. Shortly thereafter, union-republics and many cities issued corresponding decrees (cf. p. 130, n. 7). Although the full text of these decrees was not published, their substance was discussed in the daily press. Administrative fixing of prices on the kolkhoz markets was officially discontinued in the spring of 1965. In addition, articles on the promotion of the kolkhoz trade, calling for the removal of earlier impediments, appeared in a wide variety of newspapers. But other articles still warned that kolkhoz markets might give too much scope for speculation, and in some instances local authorities resisted the new instructions surreptitiously or even openly (cf. 137 f.).

CURRENT POLICY AND ITS RESULTS, 1965–1969

Certain restrictions have been lifted and previously confiscated plots were restored, but the actual development of private agricultural production since 1964 has proceeded neither smoothly nor uniformly. The pri-

[20] See the USSR Deputy Minister of Agriculture, A. Dubrovin, in [*443*, no. 16 (1968), 11].

[21] The full text is given in [*359*, 303–314].

vate sector has fared better than under Khrushchev, but its treatment and achievements left much to be desired.

Reservations had already been expressed by certain speakers at the March 1965 plenum. Thus V. P. Mzhavanadze, the Georgian First Party Secretary and a Candidate Member of the USSR Politburo, referred to the suspension of restrictions on the private sector as merely "a secondary question." "The basic and principal question for our Party," he said, "was and remains the problem of the quickest possible development of the public sector" [295, 90]. And the following statement from a book published in 1966 (and presumably written in 1965) by Koriagin is also characteristic [192, 365]:

Today, in some places, private production no longer plays an important role, and it would be wrong to revive it. . . . The fact that the Party and the government have lifted the unfounded restrictions upon personal subsidiary plots and livestock holdings should by no means be taken as an intention of furthering their development.

Most revealing was an official report on a decree—issued by the RSFSR Council of Ministers one year after Khrushchev's overthrow— dealing with the implementation of the decree of 13 November 1964 (see above). The exact wording of this new decree was not published, but the official announcement concerning it states that during the past year there had been considerable local opposition or delay in carrying out measures favoring the private sector.[22] Changes in the statute of one kolkhoz in Orel oblast were still being made—and approved by the raion administration—in April 1965, even though they were in open contradiction to the decree of 13 November 1964 [440, 28 January 1966]. That the new policy toward the private sector was not always taken seriously on sovkhozes was demonstrated by the actions of a sovkhoz director who simply ignored the new instructions [452, 9 August 1966].

The ambivalent attitude of many officials showed itself in a problem arising at a milk processing plant near Kazan'. Private cattle owners had been selling one to two thousand kilograms of milk each year to that plant, although they then received less money than could have been earned in sales on the free kolkhoz market. It was therefore proposed that they be awarded diplomas of honor. But the local raion authorities considered such an honor inopportune for private producers. The matter was brought before the premier of the Tatar ASSR. Although the latter

[22] [452, 4 November 1965]. Part 4 of the new decree is in [346, IX, 302-303].

decided in favor of bestowing the honor, he made it clear that the decision had been a difficult one and that opinions on this issue had been divided [*440*, 16 February 1966].

In that same Tatar ASSR, in 1965 the great majority of kolkhozes wanted norms of 0.25 to 0.30 hectare to be fixed in the new Charter for the private plots of kolkhozniks [*45*, 111]. This would have meant a return to the size prevailing in 1955 and 1959. Yet, by the end of 1965, or one year after the lifting of the "unwarranted restrictions," the average size of the plot was still only 0.23 hectare.[23]

In drafting new kolkhoz statutes, the Ukrainian leadership again appeared particularly liberal in proposing to fix the maximum permissible size of plots for kolkhoz members at 0.6 hectare [*188*, 31]. However, in the neighboring Russian oblast of Rostov, where natural conditions are similar to those throughout most of the southern and eastern Ukraine, a kolkhoznik had this to say in a letter which was published in the Central Committee's agricultural newspaper: "For each kolkhoznik who participates in kolkhoz work, 0.1 hectare is enough. This means 0.1 to 0.3 hectare per family. Some comrades have proposed sizes of 0.5 to 0.75 hectare. I feel that the toiling kolkhoznik, one who is really interested in the output of his kolkhoz, is not in a position to farm such an area" [*452*, 22 January 1966].

As for sovkhoz workers' plots, it was said that in time these would become unnecessary and that in some very advanced and prospering sovkhozes they already were unnecessary. But "it is necessary to be cautious and not to leap prematurely to those forms [of organization] the economic conditions for which are still lacking" [*369*, 94].

By contrast, in May of 1967 the urban and suburban collective gardens for growing vegetables and potatoes again received a favorable mention in the central newspaper of the trade unions [*462*, 18 May 1967]. The area under fruit and berry orchards was to be enlarged by two hundred thousand hectares for the purpose of encouraging a further three million families to take up this form of productive gardening [*254*, 131]. Numerous books and pamphlets containing practical advice for gardeners appeared beginning in 1966, and by 1968 voluntary associations of rabbit breeders had been set up all over the country.[24]

It has been stated repeatedly that additional vegetable gardens,

---

[23] Calculated from figures in [*36*, 41–42]; [*42*, 53, 60]; [*37*, 65, 158 ff.].

[24] See, for instance, *Novye knigi*, no. 18 (1966), pp. 18, 21, and the series of brochures *Bibliotechka sadovoda* issued by the "Kolos" publishing house; see [*437*, no. 4 (1968), back cover].

grouped into one large area outside of the settlement, are to be provided when only small individual gardens are provided next to the new houses.[25] From time to time (although less frequently than in the past), it has also been proposed that privately owned livestock be kept in large communal sheds.[26] Such communal operations could, of course, facilitate some future campaign against the private sector. It has also been suggested that the shed for private livestock be constructed apart from the one-family house on the grounds that "when it becomes superfluous, it can easily be torn down" [400, 180]. (In the traditional Russian peasant house, it is customary to build the shed under the same roof as the living quarters.)

A garden plot which is granted near a rural communal multifamily house and which belongs to the rented flat is a new notion connected with the concentration of rural inhabitants in large urban-type settlements. The "plot near the flat" (prikvartirnyi zemel'nyi uchastok) has already been provided for in a Ukrainian decree of 16 April 1970.[27]

Individuals' building activities are still predominant in kolkhozes, less so in sovkhozes [14a, 562]; but new houses built by the state in rural areas are multifamily houses for the most part, with a little more than two stories, on the all-union average.[28] However, the majority of people do not like to move into them because of the reduced possibilities for private agricultural activities there; often sheds and similar primitive buildings connected with private farming grow up spontaneously around such houses [Stern, loc. cit.]. Up to 1970, village reconstruction was initiated and accelerated without any prior studies and without attention to the socioeconomic conditions and consequences of the process [357, 21]. And where enquiries were made, they often were biased ideologically. Thus, the question put to people was usually formulated in the following way: Do you prefer to live "in a house of two to three stories, with all amenities (waterpipes, central heating, gas, sewage), but without a plot and without a shed for livestock," or "in a one-story house without amenities (heating by a stove, water to be fetched from a street hydrant, toilet in the yard, and so on)?" The possibility of providing technical amenities for one-family houses with plots was not considered at all [Stern, op. cit., p. 97].

Because the topic of rural reconstruction has recently become the sub-

[25] For example, [452, 28 May, 11 June, 14 July, and 17 December 1968].
[26] [452, 16, 28 and 30 April 1966]; [443, no. 13 (1968), 10].
[27] G. F. Iasinskaia, "Zemlepol'zovanie rabochikh i sluzhashchikh, prozhivaiushchikh v sel'skoi mestnosti," [460, no. 8 (1971), 87–89].
[28] V. Stern, "Puti razvitiia zhiloi zastroiki sela," [467, no. 11 (1970), 95].

ject of considerable debate, it could be argued that the option of indirect restrictions of the private sector is being kept open for the foreseeable future. Some of the contributions to this debate seem to indicate that, in the long run, rural reconstruction will lead to a considerable reduction of the private sector.[29]

The vice-president of the Belorussian Construction Administration (*Gosstroi*) wrote in connection with the reconstruction of a Belorussian kolkhoz: "During the first stage of construction, we take into account the fact that private plots and livestock holdings of the kolkhozniks are well developed. When the need [for these plots and holdings] disappears, it will be possible to raise the density of human dwellings by using land currently under [private] farm buildings and household plots" [*452*, 8 June 1968]. In Belorussia generally, the construction of multistory houses was quite openly linked with a reduction of the size of private plots [*443*, no. 34 (1968), 10]. In such instances the desirable size of plots within the residential area of villages was given as 0.08 hectare—which is between one-third and one-quarter of the earlier average size.[30] In an experimental agrotown near Moscow, only plots of 0.03 hectare were provided, and keeping livestock was forbidden [*339a*, 125]. The Armenian First Party Secretary [*452*, 11 July 1968] envisaged not only smaller private plots in the new settlements and the renunciation of all private subsidiary production in prosperous sovkhozes (particularly those located in suburban areas), but rejection of the Khrushchevian concept of five-story houses in the sovkhozes. He did so not on the grounds of principle, but because these were "evidently [started] prematurely."

As for kolkhoz markets, it is characteristic that as late as 1968 a deputy of a city soviet asked whether the soviet was empowered to fix prices on its kolkhoz market. Equally important is the fact that both the inquiry and an answer to it were printed in a central journal [*455*, no. 2 (1968), 108]. The answer was short: No, they have no right. But why should the city soviet entertain such doubts three years after the publication of new regulations on the kolkhoz trade, especially when these regulations clearly forbade administrative fixing of prices? In fact, fixed maximum prices were reintroduced "in a number of cities" in 1969.[31]

---

[29] For example, [*452*, 23 December 1967; 14 June 1968; 7 September 1968]; [*275*, 125].

[30] [*443*, no. 16 (1968), 11] and [*452*, 17 December 1968].

[31] N. Kuz'menkov (USSR Minister of Trade), in *Sovetskaia torgovlia*, 23 July 1970, p. 3.

In 1965 and 1966 the volume of the total turnover on all urban kolkhoz markets rose by 12 percent; at the same time, the overall price
index for these markets registered a decline of 12 percent during the
same period [*12*, 665; *13*, 762]. But then the trend became sluggish; in
1967 and 1968 the value of total turnover increased by 8 percent (4 percent if sales of cooperatives are excluded). Since prices rose by 1 percent
in 1968, the indicated growth in the volume of sales was somewhat
smaller [*14a*, 654]. In Moscow, the growth of the kolkhoz market turnover, which took place in 1965 and 1966, came to a standstill. A decline
occurred in 1967. Although market officials in the capital did their best
to increase the supply of produce, they were hampered by the lack of
promised transportation, by the take-over by outlets of state retail stores
of stalls destined for private and kolkhoz sellers, by the bias of some
party officials, and so on.[32] Truck transport from the Moscow oblast to
the metropolitan markets was found to have diminished from 19,200 tons
in 1965 to 12,500 in 1968. Those market administrations which possessed
their own transportation facilities reportedly did not experience such a
decline [*434*, no. 25 (1970), 17]. The same source added: "In several republics and oblasts, the resources allocated by the state for the development of the kolkhoz markets are being poorly utilized. Materials for the
construction of markets are generally supplied with low priority and in
inadequate quantities. . . . The markets have little storage space and insignificant refrigerator and coolroom capacity. Trade in most of them is
carried out in the open. In addition to the fact that construction is pro-
ceeding slowly, some of the trading facilities on the markets are being
used for purposes other than was intended."

On many of these issues there were clearly conflicting views, but the
leadership did not take sides officially. The latter never left any room for
doubt that the private sector was given leeway only as a temporary measure and within strict limitations. But it did not give any signals to
tighten the reins again—at least not publicly. The prevailing policy was
probably accurately expressed by two authors writing on kolkhoz private
plots in the Party journal *Kommunist* during the summer of 1969: "At the
present stage of kolkhoz development, an underestimation of the importance of private plots and livestock holdings of the kolkhozniks is as completely erroneous as is the attempt to exaggerate its role" [*291*, 79]. There
was also apparently less than full unanimity among the top leadership

[32] [*468*, no. 4 (1968), 20–21]; [*452*, 10 July 1968].

on this subject. In individual cases steps were taken (and statements were formulated) in accordance with pragmatic, day-to-day needs and the inclination of one leader or another.

There was only a brief mention of the private sector in the resolution of the Twenty-Third Party Congress on the Eighth Five-Year Plan. It read: "Personal subsidiary farming, too, must serve as one of the sources of income of the rural population" [375, II, 356]. It was also noteworthy that during the Congress Premier Kosygin said only a few, unemphatic words in favor of the private sector. General Party Secretary Brezhnev did not refer to the subject at all (he was equally silent on the matter two and a half years later, in a major speech on agricultural problems before the Central Committee Plenum on 30 October 1968). The Congress resolution had more to say on the subject of the kolkhoz markets, but its authors chose to stress the role of kolkhozes and sovkhozes on these markets without mentioning the individual private sellers [375, II, 357].

Shortly after the congress, there were again calls for a reduction of the private plots; these calls were, however, comparatively few in number and less radical than the one we cite from the Rostov oblast (cf. p. 326).[33] Toward the end of 1966, similar calls came from the Riazan oblast and were printed in *Pravda* of 24 December 1966. The editors of *Izvestiia* undoubtedly had these views in mind when, on 11 April 1967, they printed an article refuting "some kolkhoz chairmen" (of the same Riazan oblast) who had suggested that the private sector was dying out.

On 8 July 1967, the Central Committee and the Council of Ministers issued a decree "On Measures Concerning the Further Development of the Productive Forces of the Far Eastern Economic Region and the Chita Oblast." To attract settlers, the decree emphasized special advantages for private agricultural activities there. These advantages consisted of credits of four thousand rubles for building a one-family house with outbuildings (only half of the principal had to be repaid) and of four hundred rubles for buying cattle, of grants of private plots and plots for haymaking of the usual, above-average norms for that part of the country, of sale of feed grain to the newcomers, and of an exemption from the agricultural tax for a period of ten years [309, VI, 482–483]. The provisions of this decree clearly show how private agricultural activity—and the important economic incentives it provides—are used by the Soviet leadership in a

[33] See, for instance, the call from a kolkhoz chairman, in [434, no. 20 (1966), 20].

pragmatic manner for special (one is tempted to say, for emergency) purposes. Similarly, in the Pamir region, the private sector has been deliberately used as bait in the effort to resettle the rural population there and to better utilize its potentialities [*121*, 286].

A general emphasis in favor of the private sector was evident in First Deputy Premier Polianskii's words in the fall of 1967 [*297*, 29]:

In the future, personal farming will undoubtedly lose its significance and disappear. But this will not *take place soon nor immediately*. Personal farming of the kolkhozniks, workers, and employees (if conducted within the limits laid down by the law and not used for speculative purposes) does not run counter to the strenghtening of the public sector. [Emphasis supplied.]

He added that the private sector helped to mobilize people who, for reasons of health, youth, or old age, were not obliged to work in the public sector. He further pointed out that as long as the sale of private produce had no "speculative aims," it complemented state retail trade sales. Again, even in this largely benevolent appreciation, one senses a special concern over the influence exercised by the private sector through the free market under conditions of a sellers' market for many better foods.

A draft of "Principles of Land Legislation in the USSR and Union Republics" was published in the summer of 1968 [*452*, 26 July 1968]. It incorporated the existing state of affairs without curtailing the rights of private land use, nor did the final law published five months later [*452*, 14 December 1968]. Agricultural land was to be allocated for "permanent use" to citizens "for conducting personal farming without the application of hired labor," and to nonagricultural enterprises, organizations, and institutions "for the collective fruit and berry orchards and potato and vegetable gardens" of their workers and employees (paragraph 22), as well as to individuals and to housing cooperatives for the construction of houses with garden plots (paragraph 37).[34] Every kolkhoz household, even if it included no able-bodied members, was granted the right to a private plot and to grazing rights for its livestock (paragraph 25). The duty of the sovkhozes to give their workers and employees plots was also laid down (paragraph 26) in more detail than in the draft,[35] as was the

---

[34] Some of the former restrictions on individual house building with adjacent garden plots in urban areas had already been lifted by an RSFSR decree on 21 May 1966; see [*346*, VIII, 76–77].

[35] See also the speech by F. A. Surganov, in [*452*, 14 December 1968].

right of other rural residents (paragraph 27) and of certain categories of state workers and employees to service allotments (paragraph 42). Moreover, it was deemed possible for nonagricultural enterprises to grant their land to citizens for "temporary use" (paragraph 41).

Data on gross agricultural output in 1965 showed a stagnant public sector, although the private sector increased its output by a surprising 6 to 7 percent (cf. Table 6). In 1966 and 1967, the private sector recorded a steady although smaller increase, and the public sector experienced a sharp growth in 1966, mainly—but not entirely—as a result of favorable climatic conditions for crops. In the less favorable year of 1967 the public sector virtually stagnated again, with the result that the share of the private sector was the same as in 1964. In absolute terms, the output of the private sector surpassed its earlier peak and thus made good the ground lost under Khrushchev. But trends in the public sector were even more favorable after 1965. In 1968 the output of the private sector declined in relation to total output (see Table 6).

The share of private holdings in total livestock herds began to drop again after the end of 1966. During 1965, a significant rise was recorded only for pigs and calves (cf. Tables 4 and 5). But after a marked increase in the number of privately owned calves and a somewhat smaller rise in private holdings of cows in 1965 and 1966, the growth of private herds came to a standstill in 1967 (except for sheep). (The widespread epidemic of the foot-and-mouth disease of the Asian-Iranian type, which had already abated in 1966, seems to have exerted no decisive influence on the size of herds.) The decline during 1968 was more pronounced in the private than in the public sector. The upward trend in pig herds had already been reversed in 1966 in both sectors.

It would be misleading to ascribe these trends to deliberate political and administrative pressures, even though such pressures may have played a role in some cases—as, for example, in parts of the Ukraine [386, 69]. Forced mass sales of privately owned livestock—such as those that occurred in 1959 and 1960—are disapproved today, but voluntary sales are still viewed favorably (cf. pp. 355 ff.). The voluntary nature of these sales is determined by local conditions at the given time. Through the fall of 1969 they may well have been voluntary, at least for the most part. And it is an open question to what extent pressures may be applied within kolkhozes and sovkhozes to the kolkhozniks and to workers and employees to induce them to sell some of their animals to the farms (so that the latter can then sell meat to the state and report it as part of the public production). The new prices, paid to kolkhozes and state farms only, offer an inducement for such practices. It seems premature (although this has been done by some Western observers) to exclude entirely the possibility that hidden or local pressures or both, still exist. It is difficult to decide whether the much reduced payments-in-kind (fodder, cf. p. 212 above), resulting from, among other things, the shift to cash wages, can properly be considered as evidence of deliberate indirect pressure. We may have to deal only with a peripheral effect of these reductions. But it is beyond doubt that, in practice, the impact of reduced payments-in-kind bears down on private animal husbandry. Soviet press comments point out that at least some kolkhoz chairmen and other officials act deliberately in this manner [for example, *452*, 15 April and 17 July 1969].

The official attitude favored issuing feed for privately owned livestock, and where kolkhozes or sovkhozes had not enough grassland to provide haying grounds and pasture, such stretches were granted out of the state land fund for private use; the practice of giving out overgrown public land (described on p. 225 f. above) became more common [*339a*, 116–117]. But still, in 1967, there were also complaints to the effect that cows could not be kept because not enough fodder and pasture was provided [*339a*, 115]. The withholding of fodder by the public sector in the Ukraine was given by First Party Secretary Shelest of Ukraine as a cause of declining private pig herds [*450*, 16 November 1969].

While pressures of one kind or another cannot be excluded, a number of other explanations for the reversal of the growth of private herds are possible, even though the accelerating decline in 1968 and 1969 might have been an evil omen. First, it is significant that there was almost no decrease in the number of cows until the end of 1967, and that their numbers declined only slowly thereafter. The more marked decrease in the number of calves (which rose sharply in 1965 and 1966) may indicate that the buildup of private cattle herds had reached a saturation point, given the existing regulations and the availability of feed. The overall decline in private pig holdings in 1966 and 1967 was too marked to be explained away solely in this fashion, but it should be borne in mind that it was accompanied by a parallel, although relatively smaller, decrease of herds in the public sector, and that it was reversed in 1969. Perhaps the main reason was that the procurement organizations and the slaughtering and processing industries were not able to cope with the increased deliveries of livestock and milk.[36] In the Soviet context, preference is given in such a situation to purchases of livestock and animal products from public farms. And in fact many instances were cited in which procurement agencies and the food processing industry refused, at least on occasion, to accept livestock products from private sellers.[37]

In this connection, it should be pointed out that an increase of meat production,[38] accompanied by a decline or stagnation of pig herds and calf holdings, need not necessarily be nefarious. It is partly explained by a growth in the average weight of animals delivered for slaughter.[39] As far as the private sector is concerned, even greater importance might be attributed to a more rapid turnover of pig herds. As long as the kolkhoznik or worker can feel sure that he will be able to purchase piglets in the spring (cf. above, pp. 219, 230), there is no need for him to keep—and feed—a sow throughout the winter. In this event, pig holdings at the time of the official count in January "do not reflect the real state of affairs" [128, 46].

The otherwise surprising increase in on-farm consumption of privately produced potatoes since 1965 (see Table 26) is possibly a hint in this direction: it suggests that more pigs may be fed throughout the year than can be estimated from the numbers in the 1 January count. For the same reason, the voluntary autumn sales of pigs to the kolkhozes and sovkhozes could be larger than before, provided that these farms, in turn, sell a sufficient number of piglets to private livestock holders in the spring. It appears that Soviet authorities are eager to gain further insights into these intersectoral transactions. V. N. Starovskii, head of the Central Statistical Administration, stated recently that sample livestock counts for the private sector will now take place on a quarterly basis [466, no. 8 (1970), 84].

In theory, the private sector could have no pigs at all at the time of the winter count and still produce large amounts of pork between the spring and late fall—as long as the breeding base of the public sector provided it with a sufficient number of piglets. For the public sector too, a quicker turnover of pig herds—as distinct from cattle—might

[36] See Brezhnev's speech in [452, 31 October 1968]; Matskevich's speech two years earlier in [452, 9 October 1966]; [107, 7]; [106, 55]; [394, 40].
[37] [107, 7]; [106, 55]; [455, no. 6 (1968), 19–24] as cited in [439, no. 20 (1968), 27]; [452, 15 April, 6 July, 13 July 1969].
[38] See the data in [466, no. 8 (1968), 95–96].
[39] See the leading article in [452, 19 November 1969].

imply a growth in the production of pork consistent with a decline in the number of pigs at the winter count. But the growing concern of the authorities over the declining pig numbers suggests that this was not true generally (or at least only to a limited degree).[40] It seems that a reduction or, at times, an eradication of pig herds in some kolkhozes and sovkhozes also curtailed the sales of piglets from these public sector farms to individuals. Prices of piglets on the free markets rose accordingly.[41]

An additional impact may also be exerted by changes on the Soviet market for pork. The demand for fat pork is falling, but the breeders' response to trends in the demand for lean pork is inadequate.[42] This is a widespread phenomenon in many parts of the world. It is difficult to imagine that Soviet private livestock holders would adapt production to this change more rapidly than, say, the small farmers of West Germany, although such adaptation is mentioned by Shmelev [*399a*, 137]. In any case, the renewed rise of pig numbers in 1969 (and even more so in 1970) is striking.

Another factor which should not be overlooked is that the rural—and particularly the agricultural—population is aging. It is also decreasing, and most private livestock holders are members of the rural population. Hence, the per capita or per family holdings declined somewhat less than the absolute size of private herds. Moreover, livestock holdings decreased at different rates in different regions of the country [*466*, no. 8 (1968), 92–94]. Cattle herds declined most in those union republics where the outflow of rural residents has been the greatest. This is the case for the RSFSR, Belorussia, the Ukraine, Lithuania, and Latvia. Except for the Ukraine, pig holdings declined at less than the average rate in these same republics, possibly because urban dwellers there raise more pigs than cows. The number of pigs decreased by more than the all-union average in Tadzhikistan, Turkmenia, and Armenia, where pork is generally popular only with the immigrants (or residents) of European origin. Here again, reasons other than pressures from above may account for much of what has happened in private animal husbandry through 1968. Goat numbers did not change significantly and are of minor im-

---

[40] See, for instance, the report on a session of the Supreme Soviet committees in [*452*, 11 November 1968] and the leading article in [*452*, 19 November 1968].

[41] Thus, for Vladimir oblast, [*452*, 15 April 1969] and, for Moscow oblast, [*452*, 9 July 1969]. Cf. Chapter VII, n. 49, above.

[42] [*452*, 20 November 1968]; cf. [*271*, 72].

portance anyway. Private holdings of sheep have increased steadily since
1964 (except for 1969), particularly in the Asian republics.[43] An increase
also occurred in some regions where the public sheep herds declined.[44]

At least during the first year following Khrushchev's ouster, we
nevertheless find clear evidence of both covert and overt warnings and of
some resistance against inordinate relaxation of policy toward the private
agricultural sector. This is especially true of the free kolkhoz markets (see
also p. 137). Here violations of the planning principle become evident,
more than elsewhere, and they represent a particularly irksome aspect
of private production for the economic bureaucracy. This negative reaction was in fact only one conspicuous symptom of a more general
phenomenon, namely, a lack of unanimous support among the middle
and lower strata of the party and government for the leadership's more
liberal attitude toward the entire private sector. As late as 1969 the
Ukrainian local authorities were denounced for creating "all kinds of
difficulties" for private producers who wanted to sell on the collective farm
market [386, 71].

The three percent increase in the average size of a kolkhoz household's plot, which was registered between November 1964 and November
1965 (see Table 13), was too small to have any decisive effect. There has
been practically no further increase. Admittedly, the area of sovkhoz
and nonfarm workers' and employees' private plots has risen much more
sharply: the increase, up to 1966, came to almost one million hectares or
to two-fifths of their 1964 area (see Table 1). But as far as sovkhoz
workers are concerned, the best that can be said is that a good start was
made toward the implementation of the new regulations. The new
norms for sovkhoz workers' plots, combined with their increasing number
as a result of the continued conversion of kolkhozes into sovkhozes and
the creation of new sovkhozes,[45] should have resulted in an increase of

---

[43] Indirect evidence of this are the rising overall numbers, while in the RSFSR
and the European republics there is no rise, or not a marked one (see the statistical
volumes for the RSFSR and other union republics). There is clear evidence for
Tadzhikistan, an Asian union republic with increasing rural population. The numbers of goats and sheep in private ownership there rose from 668 thousand (of
which 502 thousand sheep) on 1 January 1964, to 765 thousand (31.5 percent of
total) on 1 January 1966, and to 951 thousand on 1 January 1968; see [34, 81]; [41,
95]; [363, 241]. For the most important of Central Asian republics, Uzbekistan, see
Narodnoe khoziaistvo Uzbekskoi SSR v 1969 g. (Tashkent: 1970), 127–128.

[44] Thus, for Kalinin oblast, [452, 18 July 1969].

[45] For a treatment of this process from 1964 to 1967, see [418, 51 ff.].

more than one hundred percent in the total area of these plots. This clearly did not happen.

PUBLIC DEBATE ON THE PRIVATE SECTOR

Since 1966 the legitimacy of the private sector, especially in kolkhozes and in the form of collective gardens in urban areas, has been stressed again and again, but with varying degrees of emphasis. Of particular interest were some of the published contributions to the "nationwide discussion" of the draft for the new Land Law, where voices for and against the private plots were heard [for example, *452*, 19 October 1968]. In this context it was pointed out that the land-surveying agencies were short of trained personnel to check whether the land was being used in accordance with the regulations and laws [*198*, 57]. Thus, at a spot check in one of the Central Asian oblast, it turned out that [*198*, 55]:

In the kolkhozes and sovkhozes of the Khorezm oblast of the Uzbek SSR, lands were leased out in an illicit or negligent way, private plots were illegally enlarged and were rented out to individuals, and so on. When landholding checks were carried out in 1966, enlargements of the areas of private plots were uncovered in all [sic] the kolkhozes of the oblast. It was established by the staff of the public prosecutor's office that in several kolkhozes land set aside for feed crops is being leased to individuals for rice growing. . . . For example, the chairman of the kolkhoz "Communism" in the Iangyaryk raion, Comrade Iakubov, leased 7.5 hectares of land to three residents of the town of Urgench. This area did not appear in documents of the land register.

Whether the above practices are typical for the whole country is open to doubt. But they were alluded to on another occasion in relation to "some kolkhozes, especially [those] in the southern regions" [*452*, 23 August 1969], and in 1965 some kolkhozes near Moscow were said to lease land to their members. The latter were obliged to sell 60 percent of the output from leased land to the kolkhoz at state procurement prices and were allowed to keep the remaining 40 percent [*246*, 69, 72]. Another contributor to an important journal issued a call to combat such abuse, qualifying it as a crime and asking for punishment under criminal rather than the economic code by means of a new decree, similar to the infamous measures of 27 May 1939 [*47*, 18].

Because Hungarian experiences were discussed in the Soviet Union during the final phase of Khrushchev's administration, it is interesting to note that rentals of kolkhoz land (including rentals to outsiders) bear some resemblance to the practice of sharecropping in Hungarian agriculture. This practice is frowned on in Hungary but is not considered illegal [*92*, 30–31]. The Estonian practice of contract animal raising (mentioned at the end of Chapter VII, above) also bears some resemblance to recent Hungarian practice.

Newspapers received many letters on the subject of the private plots in the course of the "nationwide discussion," [46] but they did not give the matter much prominence. Some of the correspondents pleaded for stricter control over the use of private land or for collective gardens in kolkhozes in place of the individual plots of the kolkhozniks [*440*, 22 and 29 August 1968]. But their proposals were not reflected in the final text of the Land Law. Neither did opposing views or proposals, such as that of a land surveyor who suggested that untended lands overgrown with weeds be given to the kolkhozniks [*440*, 15 August 1968]. From two kolkhoz assemblies came proposals to grant the right to a private plot "once and for all" to a given kolkhoz household [*452*, 4 September 1968]. One A. Karsiev wanted the kolkhoznik's rights to hay gathering, as well as pasture, to be explicitly stipulated in the law [*452*, 31 August 1968].

The public debate on the private sector in general continued apart from the discussion of the new Land Law. P. I. Simush informed the public of the results of an opinion poll among 853 kolkhozniks in the Voronezh oblast: the overwhelming majority declared in favor of keeping the private plots and livestock holdings; 13.4 percent of those polled wanted the plots to be enlarged and only 4 percent were willing to give up private farming [*345*, 6]. In a sample study for northern Kazakhstan, it was shown that it is primarily single persons and small families with relatively high incomes who are willing to move into two-story houses (not to speak of larger ones), whereas the majority of rural residents want to live in one-family homes and are opposed to any reduction of their plots and livestock holdings [*357*, 25–26]. Past "attempts to abolish and to be 'free' from the personal subsidiary plots of the kolkhozniks as soon as possible" were designated as harmful in a proceedings volume which contained passages favorable to the private sector [*303*, 55]. The bias of certain officials against the private ownership of cows was labeled as "unmitigated nonsense" [*440*, 27 August 1967]. M. Osad'ko wrote: "All attempts to encroach on the interests of the subsidiary plots and livestock holdings must be suppressed in the most determined

---

[46] This was explicitly stated in [*452*, 31 August 1968].

manner" [272, 71]. One can only assume that such attempts were still being made. In fact, it was said in the summer of 1969: "Some leading kolkhoz officials at times raise groundless demands for its administrative curtailment" [291, 79]. As for rural construction workers, one writer recommended that they be given not only apartments but also private plots and feed for their livestock in order to combat high labor turnover [452, 3 August 1968].

In his important book published in 1968, D'iachkov refuted the view of "some economists" who underestimated the private sector and attributed to it only a secondary, subsidiary role. The private sector, D'iachkov contended, was indispensable as long as the simple kolkhoznik was underemployed and while the public sector could not furnish him with an adequate variety of foodstuffs. Even with guaranteed and rising kolkhoz earnings, the private sector "only changes its social function," becoming a means "for bringing closer the real income levels of the urban and rural population. . . . The level of development of productive forces objectively demands the preservation of subsidiary farming of the kolkhozniks at the present time and during the near future" [87, 34–35]. But even D'iachkov advocated collective instead of individual gardens for kolkhozniks under some circumstances [87, 105], and did not seek a restoration of the former plots in every kolkhoz: "In those kolkhozes where the reduction of subsidiary farming was economically justified, the situation is to remain unchanged" [87, 63]. He pleaded for a differentiation of size not only by regions but also in accordance with individual socioeconomic conditions, and concluded by advocating a cautious, rather ambiguous approach [87, 94]:

If, by reason of its size, subsidiary farming hinders the development of the public sector, the undertaking of certain organizational measures in the interests of strengthening the latter is both possible and expedient. It is necessary to diminish the role of subsidiary farming of the individual kolkhozniks, to tighten control over the scale of their incomes, over the volume of work in the kolkhoz and on the private plot, [and] to grant benefits to the kolkhozniks in accordance with their labor contribution to the public sector. However, it would be politically and economically incorrect to reduce administratively the size of subsidiary plots on a large scale without any kind of justification, or to exact a high agricultural tax from them. This would make the political mood of the kolkhozniks worse and would only cause harm.

The ambiguity was even more marked in some other contributions to the debate which revealed a latent political and ideological bias against the private sector. This is exemplified in the following words taken from an important proceedings volume published in 1968:

The contradiction between the necessity for the steady development of the public sector of the kolkhozes and the existence of the personal subsidiary plots of the kolkhozniks is manifest in that subsidiary farming—economically necessary at the given time—involves the kolkhoznik in market relations in the capacity of a property owner, diverting a significant amount of the kolkhoznik's working time from the public sector. The presence of the private plot also complicates the task of overcoming the vestiges of the past in the consciousness of many kolkhozniks. Their advanced socialist consciousness as an expression of their place in the system of collective social production is often still diminished by the remaining vestiges of the private owner's psychology which is sometimes revived by the personal subsidiary farm and its concomitant mode of life.[47]

At a conference in Makhachkala in the Daghestan ASSR held on 28–30 March 1967, an oblast party secretary spoke in favor of buying livestock from private owners for fattening and of encouraging such sales by kolkhozniks and sovkhoz workers by giving them in exchange fodder and other agricultural produce. Nevertheless, an economist at the same conference, Yu. A. Babaev, said that although the practice of giving agricultural produce to private persons was widespread and could not be terminated, only amounts equal to the "scientifically based norms" of human consumption should be issued "in the future" [217, 122–123]. He thus implied no fodder or feed grain distribution. One month later, Sovetskaia Rossiia of 26 April 1967 published a sharp attack on conspicuously prosperous private sheep raisers in the same Daghestan republic. And it was this republic where the output of the public agricultural sector was reported to have declined from 1965 to 1967, while private production increased at an annual rate of some 2.5 percent [434, no. 9 (1968), 28–29].

Some authors appeared to place their hopes on the most "progressive" members of the agricultural labor force, the mechanizers with relatively high earnings who were soon expected to renounce their private plots [400, 182]. "But for the time being, this is a thing of the future, *although not a distant* [future]" [452, 11 November 1967]. [Emphasis supplied.]

There can be no doubt that no one advocated the permanent existence of the private sector, with the possible exception of L. Kalinin (cf.

[47] [180, 94]; "certain contradictions" and "divarication of psychology" in [128, 87, 88–89].

pp. 375 ff.) The relevant question is how long its temporary existence will last and how soon circumstances will change in order to permit the private sector to "wither away."

As far as kolkhozes and the kolkhozniks are concerned, the conditions for the withering away of the private sector have been defined by several Soviet writers. Of these, Aitov recorded his conditions even before the dismissal of Khrushchev, although his article was not finally approved for printing until after the events of October 1964. Aitov's conditions are essentially in accordance with the 1961 Party Program [374, III, 290] and may be taken as pertinent for both periods. What changed in 1964–1965 was not the formulation of the conditions (which was much the same as that used by two later sources) but the estimated degree of their present or imminent fulfillment. As laid down by Aitov, D'iachkov, and Ostrovskii, the conditions may be summarized as follows:[48]

1. An increase in the output of the public sector of the kolkhozes sufficient to assure the fulfillment of the state procurement plans and to satisfy completely the food requirements of the kolkhoz population.

2. An increase in the incomes of the kolkhozniks obtained from the public sector and sufficient to render unnecessary the existence of any additional private income.

3. Remuneration of kolkhoz labor in cash alone. (This would not necessarily mean that no produce would be issued to the kolkhozniks but that it would be sold and not distributed as an integral part of remuneration for labor services performed.)

4. Acceptance by the kolkhozniks of the notion that the "withering away" of the private sector is necessary and to their advantage.

5. Development of the state and cooperative retail trade and services in the villages to an extent enabling not only the satisfaction of demand for basic consumer goods and foodstuffs but also of the growing demand for more sophisticated industrial consumer goods and services. (The nature of the kolkhoz household would thus change to that of a household operating in an exchange economy on a money basis.)

At the time of writing, the third condition is near to fulfillment. The fourth can be ignored, since this is a matter of manipulating public opinion with well-known methods. It is generally acknowledged that the first

[48] N. A. Aitov, "Izmeneniia sotsial'noi prirody i klassovykh osobennostei krest'ianstva," in [354, I, 376–377]; [87, 64–65, 123–124, 178, 180]; [275, 91–92]. Essentially the same conditions were later reviewed in some detail by Shmelev [339a, 134–142].

condition is clearly far from being fulfilled; indeed, with the agricultural output goals of the Eighth Five-Year Plan not attained and with the demands of an expanding urban sector rising and becoming more refined, no fulfillment of this condition can be discerned in the foreseeable future. Equally—or even more—remote is the fulfillment of the fifth condition, but this could in part be accomplished instead by village reconstruction, by better rural roads providing access to towns, and by a decline in the numbers of the rural population and rural consumers. The attainment of the second condition devolves mainly on the question of what income will be deemed "sufficient" for the kolkhoznik and whether this should be restricted to the level of income enjoyed by the sovkhoz workers and employees. It seems symptomatic that there is generally less advocacy for the private plots of sovkhoz workers and employees than for those of the kolkhozniks. As long as the kolkhoznik's income is lower than that of the sovkhoz worker and employee, the second condition will not be considered as fulfilled, even by Soviet standards. This applies particularly to the problem of underemployment in the kolkhozes,[49] because on the average wages per man-day are about equal by now. But the time may not be far off when kolkhoz and sovkhoz incomes will be about equal, even among the lower paid categories and even when account is taken of the differing proportions of skilled workers.

It is clear that the more important conditions will only be partially fulfilled during the next few years. However, it remains to be seen whether these conditions will be strictly adhered to, or whether the extent of the underfulfillment will be interpreted away—as was done under Khrushchev. This is the old question of socioeconomic reality versus ideological zeal. Significantly, Ostrovskii elaborates on the enumeration of his conditions by stating that "such a future is near for many kolkhozes," and that although matters should not be forced on the kolkhoz population by restrictive administrative measures, neither must the Party leave things to "drift" but should "create the conditions for the withering away of private subsidiary farming" [275, 92]. But Grigorovskii and Alekseev envisage "more than one decade" for the arrival of the "withering away" stage [128, 87]. P. Rebrin appears to be no less pessimistic [306, 162–163], while D'iachkov doubts whether the first of the listed conditions concerning animal products can be fulfilled in the foreseeable future. For this reason he envisaged the maintenance of private livestock

---

[49] For a recent treatment, see [191, 36].

holdings but a decrease in the size of kolkhozniks' private plots to that of nonagricultural rural workers and employees—that is, to 0.15 hectare [*87*, 124-125]. This would mean about one-half of the present average size. Moreover, it was pointed out again that the urban population is still, to a considerable degree, dependent on the free kolkhoz markets [*211*, 73; *281, passim*]—on the private production of the kolkhozniks.

Only Kalinin's interesting views (cf. p. 375) are not far removed from an acceptance of the continued existence of the private sector—albeit greatly changed—even under full communism. But his is an exception among Soviet views. The great majority do not discuss whether the private sector will finally disappear but only when, under what conditions, and in which way. Most of them, as well as the policy makers, probably hold the view that the private sector will first cease to produce for the market and will be confined to the personal consumption requirements of the owners of plots and livestock on a gradually diminishing scale. Grigorovskii and Alexseev consider this to be a clearly defined initial stage [*128*, 96]. Yet they also warn that the "withering away" has not yet begun; moreover, although the private sector's share in total agricultural output may decline, the volume of its output may well continue to grow [*128*, 87-88].

Most Soviet authors agree that the most pertinent reason for the continued existence of the private sector is the still unsatisfactory productive performance of socialized agriculture. Thus future developments will depend, to a great extent, upon the performance of the public sector. A series of good harvest years might expedite the launching of another campaign against the private sector, especially if the latter shows no signs of withering away of its own volition. On the other hand, industrialization and urbanization may, within a few years, raise the consumer's sights so as to render inadequate a harvest which might have been deemed bountiful in, say, 1966. The methods to be applied then may be less crude than those of Khrushchev's era. It is possible that the collective gardens in urban areas and some tiny garden plots in rural districts may be exempt from any new campaign. Considered in isolation, these are less bothersome to Soviet planners if and when the larger plots and animal holdings have disappeared.

Addendum: From the Third Kolkhoz Congress
to the 24th Party Congress

As this book was being written, translated, and edited, the Third All-Union Congress of Kolkhozniks was finally convened in the fall of 1969, and the Twenty-Fourth Congress of the Communist Party of the Soviet Union followed in the spring of 1971. Because the policy toward the private sector had been rather open-ended at mid-1969, these events were clearly of great interest to all those concerned with private agricultural production.

The benevolent line of policy towards the private sector was emphatically reaffirmed as early as December 1969. More important in this respect than even the Kolkhoz Congress was the December 1969 plenary session of the Central Committee of the CPSU. The proceedings of this plenum had not been published at the time of writing (1971), but comment in the press and by Soviet leaders made it clear that the agricultural situation had been one of the main topics on the agenda. The plenum decided that the private sector should be called to the rescue to alleviate the critical shortages of meat and milk.

During the Twenty-Fourth Party Congress, more than a year later, the important thing was that the line of the December 1969 plenum was endorsed. The new Five-Year Plan approved by the congress provides for growth, albeit at a modest rate, of private agricultural production up to 1975, and for a rise in the income of the kolkhoz population, not only from the public but also from the private sector [*434*, no. 25 (1971), 14].

The Soviet press in 1970 and up to the late fall of 1971 left no doubt that the benevolent attitude toward the private sector still prevailed. A few books or booklets also appeared (not all of them available to me) which evidenced the continued, generally sympathetic interest in the subject.[50] Curiously enough, some Soviet authors consider work on the pri-

---

[50] The most important were those of V. A. Belianov [*56a*] and Shmelev [*339a*]. Both, of course, share the well-known Communist bias against private economic activities. But under present conditions they accord the private plots and livestock holdings a special and justified role. Both books abound with valuable information and show a sophisticated approach which would have been unthinkable ten years ago. Cf. the article, otherwise not quoted here, by N. A. Makarenko, "O sotsial'no-

vate plot as deterring young people from staying in agriculture, while others see the renewed relationship between the size of the private plot and participation in kolkhoz work as a means to make people, including the younger generation, return to the kolkhoz.[51]

One of the remarkable shifts of emphasis in these publications is the growing attention paid to the private agricultural activities of the non-kolkhoz population.[52] A recent booklet [55a] was devoted to the legal questions of private land use in urban areas. In fact, the output of the nonkolkhoz population as early as 1967 amounted to 44 percent of total private agricultural output,[53] and by now may well have risen to one-half.

There are two main reasons for this increasing share: 1) the kolkhoz population is continually decreasing in numbers; and 2) because of growing kolkhoznik incomes and the still inadequate performance of Soviet trade in foodstuffs, the demand for and the prices of fruit and vegetables are rising fast. Typically, privately sown areas—other than under potatoes and vegetables—decreased from 1960 to 1969, and suburban gardens increased by 4 percent, mainly from 1965 to 1968 [14a, 312–313]. The private area under fruit and vines expanded even more [8, 376 ff.; 14a, 348 ff.], especially in the Ukraine, where the expansion was by almost one-third.[54] In the western Ukraine, where private gardening is of above-average importance, one author had the following to report:

An important urban source of supply of agricultural produce are the highly developed private gardens in the towns of agricultural oblasts. According to the data of the town statistical inspectorates, roughly 30 percent of the families have plots beyond the city limits where they grow mainly potatoes and

---

ekonomicheskoi prirode lichnogo podsobnogo khoziaistva pri sotsializme," *Vestnik Moskovskogo universiteta, seriia VII: ekonomika,* no. 1 (1971), pp. 29–36. A number of other recent articles, which are not included in the bibliography, are referred to in the footnotes of this *Addendum.*

[51] For example, T. I. Zaslavskaia, ed., *Migratsiia sel'skogo naseleniia* (Moscow: 1970), p. 330, as opposed to A. M. Butenko, *Vosproizvodstvo kvalifitsirovannoi rabochei sily v sel'skom khoziaistve* (Moscow: 1970), p. 153.

[52] This was anything but common opinion a few years ago, as is illustrated by Belianov's remark [56a, 74, n. 1]: "It is not legitimate either, in our opinion, to justify assertions about the withering away of the personal subsidiary plot as a whole with reference to data on kolkhozniks' plots only, *as is being done by some* [Soviet] *authors."* (Emphasis supplied.)

[53] According to G. Ia. Kuznetsov, *Vestnik sel'skokhoziaistvennoi nauki,* no. 9 (1969), 7.

[54] I. Kravchenko [437, no. 6 (1971), 27, 29].

vegetables. According to the Khmel'nitskii city executive committee, at the present time the area of the urban population's plots, excluding villages on urban territory, within the city limits amounts to about 500 hectares. In 1969, the urban population grew about 3600 tons of potatoes and vegetables on this area.[55]

Privately-owned livestock herds also show a numerical shift in favor of nonkolkhozniks; this finally became quantifiable (the data are incorporated in Tables 12 and 20 above).[56]

The growing share of the nonagricultural population in private farming somewhat compensates for the geographical shift caused by the decrease of the rural population in most of the USSR and its increase in the south and southeast. Thus according to the 1970 census results, the rural population continued to grow during the preceding decade in all of the Transcaucasian and Central Asian republics as well as in the Moldavian SSR; the increase slowed down, it is true, by the mid-1960s, but not in the predominantly Islamic and Turkic republics of Azerbaidzhan, Turkmenia, Kirghizia, Uzbekistan, and Tadzhikistan.[57] In the four Central Asian republics, not only the size of the rural population but also the number of kolkhoz families is still increasing. The rural segment of the private sector must also be increasing in these parts of the country.

Although for agricultural policy in general, including that toward the private sector, the December 1969 plenary session of the Central Committee was the most important single event, the results of the preceding Third Kolkhoz Congress in November 1969 are also of great topical interest, because one of its purposes was the adoption of the new Model Charter for the kolkhozes. On the basis of this, each individual kolkhoz had to draft a new charter or adapt its old one. The Model Charter established new rules for private agricultural activities in the kolkhozes. The proposed regulations for private plots and livestock holdings of the

[55] N. Timchuk, "Rol' prigorodnykh raionov v snabzhenii srednikh gorodov produktami pitaniia" [437, no. 3 (1970), 79]. (The city of Khmel'nitskii, mentioned here, had 113,000 inhabitants in 1970.)

[56] Cf. the data for the Chuvash ASSR, where over the period from 1958 to 1968 the kolkhozniks' herds decreased (as did the number of kolkhoz families), and the herds of workers and employees more than doubled, as indicated in a table by V. N. Iakimov, *Problemy trudovykh resursov kolkhozov* (Moscow: 1969), p. 87.

[57] For an excellent study on the private plots in Soviet Central Asia, based on direct observation, see E. Giese, "Hoflandwirtschaften in den Kolchosen und Sovchosen Sowjet-Mittelasiens," *Geographische Zeitschrift*, vol. 59, no. 3 (October 1970), pp. 175–197.

kolkhozniks were one of the most energetically debated topics in the public discussion organized by the news media during the months preceding the Congress and following the publication of the official draft of the Model Charter.[58]

The General Secretary of the Party, Leonid Brezhnev, did not mention the private sector in his address to the Kolkhoz Congress. But D. S. Polianskii, First Deputy Prime Minister and a member of the Party's Politburo, reaffirmed his basic positive attitude toward the private sector expressed two years earlier in his article in *Kommunist* (see above, p. 331). He warned against "premature" and "artificial" restrictions of the private sector [452, 26 November 1969]. He nevertheless ignored the private sector when enumerating those aspects of the new Model Charter for which proposals for the modification of the official draft had been advanced. But his attitude should be interpreted as an expression of a defensive, rather than a negative, line on this issue, because most of the proposals for revision which were published in the course of the discussion favored a more restrictive approach toward the private sector than had been laid down in the draft charter. It is therefore important to note that the provisions of the relevant Section X of the adopted Model Charter are virtually the same as those included in the official draft version of this document. (The draft and final, adopted texts may be found in [452, 24 April and 30 November 1969].)

Article 42 of the new Charter contains the following provision:

When the dwellings of rural settlements are constructed in close proximity [*kompaktnaia zastroika*], the kolkhoz will allot to the kolkhozniks plots of a similar size situated next to their houses (living quarters). The remaining portions of the plots will be located beyond the limits of the housing area of the settlement. In such cases, the total land area allotted for use to the kolkhoznik's family (kolkhoz household) must not exceed the size of the subsidiary plot foreseen in the charter of the [individual] kolkhoz.

This provision may become—and is presumably meant to become—important at some future date. But it is not important at present (cf. pp.

---

[58] I have discussed the Kolkhoz Congress—including the preceding press discussion—and the Model Charter in greater detail in my articles: "Der Dritte Kolchos-Kongress," *Osteuropa*, no. 3 (1970), 145–151; "Das neue Musterstatut der sowjetischen Kolchose," *Osteuropa*, no. 4 (1970), 276–298; and "Le Secteur privé dans l'Agriculture soviétique de la Déposition de Khrouchtchev au Congrès des Kolkhoziens," *Cahiers du Monde russe et soviétique*, no. 1 (1970), 5–23.

300 f. and 327 f. above). Recent Soviet press reports on rural reconstruction reveal the same moderate tendency in reconstruction policy that prevailed in 1968 and 1969.[59] Some of these reports point out that reconstruction plans should not ignore the interest of the kolkhozniks in private farming (for example, *ibid.*, and [452, 3 February 1970, 25 June 1971]) and the interest of the state in the produce from this source.[60] Any rural reconstruction of the Soviet type, however, is unerringly aimed at, among other things, a long-run, indirect restriction of private agricultural activities.[61] This is especially true of the still latent idea of constructing sheds for privately owned livestock "beyond the limits of the housing zone" of the settlement [452, 28 December 1969].

According to the new Model Charter, the opportunities for private subsidiary farming in the kolkhozes depend on the size of the family as well as on active participation in the public sector of the kolkhoz. Objections were raised against possible related restrictions (for example, [434, no. 27 (1969), 19] and [452, 8 August 1969]). In particular, some Soviet jurists felt that the size of the plot should not be made dependent on such unstable factors. They pointed out that this dependence would be detrimental to the "stability of land use" and that parcels of land taken away from the inactive kolkhozniks would just be left unused [460, no. 9 (1969), 143]. Indeed, frequent changes in the plot sizes would considerably reduce the desired stimulating or deterring effect on the private sector.

The new norms for private plots and livestock holdings are, on the whole, somewhat lower than those of the old (1935) Model Charter. This is chiefly because the enlarged norms, set by the 1935 Charter for regions of extensive land use, have now been eliminated. In practice, however, most of these higher norms had already been abolished in the 1950s. As Ia. Ia. Strautmanis, professor of law at the Latvian State University, pointed out, the new norms are upper limits, and as such imperative for all kolkhozes, whereas a diminution according to family size and labor participation, or generally lower norms in an individual kolkhoz, may be decided on by the kolkhoz [460, no. 6 (1970), 60]. In addition, the new

[59] Cf. the detailed and rather objective discussion of the problems involved by V. Stern, "Puti razvitiia zhiloi zastroiki sela" [467, no. 11 (1970), 95–96, 101–102], and by E. Dorosh, "Piatnadtsat' let spustia" [445, no. 9 (1970), 49–56].

[60] The latter motive was emphasized by G. Radov [443, no. 29 (1970), 10].

[61] For a recent statement of this underlying idea, see N. Verkhovskii [445, no. 8 (1970), 166].

Charter provides for some higher norms for private livestock herds "in some regions, in consideration of national peculiarities and local conditions," including norms for horses, donkeys, camels, reindeer, and so on. Final decisions on these matters rest with the Councils of Ministers of the Union Republics.[62]

It might at first appear that the new plot size of 0.5 hectare per household is larger than the old norms which ranged from 0.25 to 0.5 hectare (except for the regionally greater norms). But this does not amount to much, because—in contrast with the provisions of the old charter—the area under yards and buildings is now counted as a part of the private plot. Thus, the actual size of the average plot in 1969 (0.31 hectare), together with the additional area under yards and buildings, was not much smaller than the new upper limit. In some regions, the average size was much greater: In the Nikolaev oblast it came to 0.6 to 1.0 hectare [452, 12 July 1969]. Those who drafted the new charter must have had such regional variations in mind when they stipulated that the old (and larger) plot sizes might be preserved, provided that they were established legally on the basis of the old charter. The plot size on irrigated land is not to exceed 0.2 hectare, but this restriction was in fact implemented some time ago.

The new norms for private livestock holdings per kolkhoz household as outlined in Chapter III (p. 30 above) are slightly lower than those of the 1935 charter, but they exceed the present actual average livestock holding per kolkhoz household by a comfortable margin and should not, therefore, be considered an additional restriction. Norms for bees, rabbits and poultry may be set locally—as has been the case before.[63]

Numerous proposals for smaller plot and livestock norms were made in the published proceedings of the discussion of the draft charter.[64] To my knowledge, no proposal for bigger norms was made, or rather, published. The only proposal favorable to the private plots was that of fixing not only an upper but also a lower limit [460, no. 9 (1969), 143].

[62] Cf. G. D'iachkov, "Podsobnoe khoziaistvo sem'i kolkhoznika (kolkhoznogo dvora)" [435, no. 11 (1970), 38].

[63] L. Zaitsev, A. Ivanov [435, no. 6 (1971), 30]; cf. B. D. Kliukin, "O nekotorykh osobennostiakh Primernogo ustava," in G. A. Aksenenok, S. V. Kuznetsov, eds., Nauchnye osnovy novogo Primernogo ustava sel'skokhoziaistvennoi arteli (Moscow: 1966), p. 59.

[64] For example, [452, 7 July and 18 October 1969]; Partiinaia zhizn', no. 13 (1969), 50–51; [434, no. 47 (1969), 14]; [435, no. 7 (1969), 39, and no. 9 (1969), 38].

Soon after the Third Kolkhoz Congress, the norms for plots and livestock holdings assumed concrete form in many parts of the country; this concretization "as a rule, did not lead to any changes in the land use by kolkhoz households as it had developed" up to 1969.[65] In "some kolkhozes" the size of the family was taken into consideration when fixing the norms, although in others it was not.[66]

The new charter does not specify clearly how family size is to determine the size of the plot. It is not clear whether this size should depend on the total number of persons in the household, on the number of able-bodied, or on the number of the able-bodied who participate in kolkhoz work.

During the discussion a proposal was made to allow for the number of minors [452, 7 June 1969], but another proposal suggested disregarding the number of elderly persons on pensions [452, 30 August 1969]. Presumably, the decisions on such details are being left to republican and lower level authorities.

Moreover, the new Model Charter does not specify which households (families) are to be considered as kolkhoz households or what should be done with the plots of those no longer considered as such. A request for guidelines on this matter was made in the course of pre-Congress discussion [452, 9 September 1969], and a proposal was made to restrict the plot to norms which apply to plots of workers and employees (0.15 hectare) when a household ceases to be a kolkhoz household [440, 4 April 1969]. But the Charter remained vague in this respect, presumably because the matter is too involved (cf. pp. 23-25 above) and because the number of mixed households is great. However, the Charter does specify that plots are not to be reduced because of failure to participate in kolkhoz work as a result of old age, military service, performance of elective office, absence for purposes of education and training, temporary work outside the kolkhoz with the consent of the kolkhoz managing board, or when minors are the only persons left in the household. This implies that the kolkhoz assembly would be expected to reduce the size of the plot in all other cases.

Because the plot is not the property of the kolkhoz household but is only alloted to it for use, there are no legal obstacles to its reduction (or, for that matter, complete withdrawal of land from the use of the household) if such actions are based on a legal decision of the kolkhoz assem-

[65] N. Vedenin (conference report) [435, no. 10 (1970), 121].
[66] Ibid.; also G. D'iachkov [435, no. 11 (1970), 38].

bly. The charter of the individual kolkhoz is considered to be of a quasi-legal (*podzakonnyi*) nature [cf. *460*, no. 11 (1969), 60]. However, privately held livestock remains the "full personal property" of the household. The Model Charter forbids the private possession of livestock beyond the stated norms, but it does not indicate what is to be done if these norms are in fact exceeded. During the pre-Congress discussion, proposals were aired for "more stringent and concrete measures" to be provided in the charter [*435*, no. 10 (1969), 45]. It was also suggested that the kolkhoz should then be entitled to buy such livestock at the state purchase price—Shmelev later proposed: at half this price [*339a*, 106]—or that the owners should be obliged to sell it to state organizations [*435*, no. 9 (1969), 38]. One participant in a conference on problems of the Model Charter proposed that livestock holdings in excess of the norms should be taxed at higher rates. Another participant wanted to give to the kolkhoz the right to "socialize" such livestock after a three months' notice [*460*, no. 9 (1969), 143]. With respect to plots, the Charter provides for withdrawal of above-norm areas together with what is planted or sown upon them. Here too, "more stringent measures" [*452*, 15 November 1969] or a higher tax rate [*452*, 4 April 1969] were requested during the discussion. The final version of the Charter did not comply with such proposals, probably because some leeway should be left to deal with local circumstances and because it was believed that the kolkhoz chairmen could deal with such problems through indirect pressure or other means.

If the kolkhoz thus exerts a restricting and controlling function with respect to the private agricultural activities of its members, it has also been called upon to assist this activity in certain ways. This has been spelled out in the new Charter (as it was in the old). Under Khrushchev, such strictures were largely disregarded, but they have been reemphasized in recent years. The new Charter is more explicit in this respect: It speaks of assistance in the cultivation of the plots, in the acquisition of livestock (chiefly by supplying young animals from kolkhoz herds), in supplying veterinary care, and in providing feed and pasture. Article 4 of the new Charter, which mentions the kolkhoznik's right to obtain transportation for personal needs (which may include transport of private produce to the market, although the Charter is conspicuously silent on this point) should also be mentioned in this context. The Charter does not say, however, to what extent such help is to be granted, and it does not place the kolkhoz management under a strict obligation to supply such services. The form and the extent of such assistance is left to the discretion of the kolkhoz management by making a reference to the standard procedures (*vnutrennii rasporiadok*) of each kolkhoz. A model of these was published ten months later [*434*, no. 36 (1970), 12–13], but it was as noncommittal on this point as the Charter. In essence, the kolkhoznik is still very much dependent on the benevolence of his *brigadir* in these matters, as was admitted by R. Kireev in *Krokodil* (no. 14, May 1971). Before the Congress convened, voices were raised asking for greater precision in these matters, especially with respect to the supply of fodder for privately owned livestock [*435*, no. 10 (1969), 45; *460*, no. 10 (1969), 65], but these were not given much prominence.

Article 44 of the new Charter deals with grants of kolkhoz land for private use by nonmembers who live on the territory of the kolkhoz. While the kolkhoznik has a firm right to a plot, plots "may" be granted to workers and employees if there is enough land available in the kolkhoz land fund destined for private plots. The relevant provision of the Land Law of 1968 (Article 27) is repeated almost verbatim in the new Charter. Both documents state that such grants are obligatory in the case of teachers, physicians, and other specialists who not only reside in a kolkhoz village but who also work there (though not necessarily for the kolkhoz itself).

In his speech at the Kolkhoz Congress, Brezhnev insisted that both the procurements of meat and the public livestock inventories must be increased in every conceivable way. Indeed, total livestock production stagnated in 1969, and meat and milk procurements declined [*14*, 317; *14a*, 291, 299]. But, although sheep and goat herds declined in both the public and the private sectors, the number of cattle in private ownership declined and that of kolkhozes and sovkhozes increased—apparently at the expense of the private sector. Only with respect to pigs did both sectors show a marked increase, more so in the public than in the private sector. At the same time, the demand for animal products was far from being satisfied at prevailing prices; incomes were rising faster than planned between 1966 and 1970, and the urban population continued to grow fast. In addition, consumption by the agricultural population increasingly drained the state resources. Data for the Ukraine show that although the private output of animal products per kolkhoz household stagnated, consumption by these families increased.[67] Less came on to the market, and more was bought from the public sector.

[67] A. Koroed, A. Babaeva, "Rol' obshchestvennogo i podsobnogo khoziaistva v biudzhete kolkhoznoi sem'i" [*437*, no. 5 (1971), 73–74].

G. Radov [*443*, 15 July 1970] said outright what until then had to be gathered from indirect evidence, namely that the disappointing numerical development of private herds since 1967 had come as a surprise to the Soviet planners and economists. After the lifting of restrictions in 1964 and 1965, a more sustained growth of the private livestock sector had been expected.

At the December 1969 plenary session of the Central Committee of the CPSU, the leadership, and especially Brezhnev, must have sounded the alarm. Breshnev himself later told an audience at Khar'kov that the plenum also discussed the situation in agriculture in detail, and that "in some regions" the demand for meat and meat products was not fully satisfied [*452*, 14 April 1970]. He made it clear that the supply of animal products constituted a major bottleneck. Not only rural but also urban inhabitants, he continued, should be encouraged to keep livestock, including poultry, in order to overcome the shortage.

Toward the end of 1970, even the chief ideologue, M. A. Suslov, spoke out in this vein, warning against the undue expansion of private agricultural activities[68] as well as against their curtailment. See also Suslov's speech on the anniversary of the October Revolution [*452*, 7 November 1970]. He admonished the representatives of the local soviets in the RSFSR [*452*, 27 November 1970]:

It is necessary to help kolkhozniks, workers, and employees buy young livestock, to help provide privately owned livestock with feed and grazing facilities, and also to help them market agricultural produce from the private plots.

In January 1970, a conference of officials dealing with family budget statistics showed concern over the inadequate statistical information about the possible contribution of the private sector to the country's food requirements.[69] Reporting on private livestock herds was to be intensified, said Starovskii at this conference. Also an all-union census of fruit plan-

---

[68] Expansion beyond the norms may come about as a consequence of the indulgence of collective and state farm managers or of local authorities. But it may also happen in spite of their vigilance where control is difficult to exercise. Thus in the Stavropol' krai, the steppe shepherds plough up stretches of unused dry land and there grow watermelons for the market. The profits thus realized are such that fines do not deter them ([*442*, 10 January 1971], as cited in [*439*, April 1971, 86]). Moreover, shepherds are in demand, and that may also influence the reluctance of the authorities to control their illegal actions.

[69] Conference report by I. Sukhoruchkina [*466*, no. 8 (1970), 79–84].

tations and vineyards, including those in private ownership, was decided on at about the same time [466, no. 6 (1970), 45–46].

The 1970 statistical report announced overfulfillment of the animal products procurement plan and increasing herds and animal production, but with total output increasing less than procurements [452, 4 February 1971]. Generally speaking, private owners had responded to the demand for meat by increasing the numbers of pigs, sheep, and calves, but not those of cows (see Table 5). Thus the private output of meat increased by 5 percent, whereas that of milk decreased by 2 percent [466, no. 6 (1971), 88–89]. The statistical report for the first six months of 1971 indicated concern about diminishing private meat sales to the state in some republics and about nonfulfillment of the overall milk production and procurement plan.[70] This must be viewed against the rather modest plan for 1971, which included an implied increase of private agricultural output of roughly 4 percent.[71] For the five-year period (1971–1975), too, an increase in the output of private animal products, although a moderate one, is implied by known data for the RSFSR.[72]

At the same time, Soviet trade is said to lag behind demand not only in meat but also in milk (Sovetskaia torgovlia, 5 June 1971). To fill the gap at least partly, purchases from private producers were greatly stepped up in 1968 and 1969. By 1967, more than half of all meat, eggs, and milk marketed by private livestock owners had been bought by the state and cooperative procurement agencies [56a, 104]. In 1969, such purchases totaled more than 2.5 billion rubles[73]—about 10 percent of all procurements and purchases. Presumably it was even more in 1970. The consumer cooperatives especially are "called on to play a considerable role in the purchases of agricultural products and raw materials," said A. P. Klimov, head of Tsentrosoiuz (central board of the consumer cooperatives) [452, 11 August 1970].

The new emphasis of policy inaugurated in 1970 emanates very clearly from one of the many indirect summaries of the proceedings of the December 1969 plenum [452, 16 January 1970]:

---

[70] [452, 24 July 1971]; cf. the comment in [434, no. 31 (1971), 18].

[71] N. Gusev [435, no. 2 (1971), 4, 8].

[72] V. Sokolov [435, no. 3 (1971), 48].

[73] [14a, 300], and the method of derivation as explained by Z. Bim, "Nekotorye voprosy razvitiia roznichnogo tovarooborota," Ekonomicheskie nauki, no. 2 (1971), p. 27.

Shortcomings in the development of agriculture and, above all, in the public livestock sector were criticized at the plenum. . . . The opportunities for increasing the supply of meat are not fully utilized in some parts of the country. Some farms do not attempt to increase their livestock herds; a decline in livestock numbers has been allowed to take place. This is an unhealthy, an incorrect tendency. . . . The raising of livestock and poultry on private plots is very important. As is well known, the meat supply of the country consists of purchases from kolkhoz and sovkhoz output, plus purchases from the subsidiary farms of kolkhozniks and of workers and employees. It would be completely incorrect to ignore the personal [private] sector as a supplementary source of output of farm products while concentrating exclusively on the future growth of public livestock production. The Party and the government removed the unfounded restrictions on livestock holdings in the personal [private] farms of the kolkhozniks and sovkhoz workers. The management of the kolkhozes and sovkhozes should assist these by supplying young animals and feed.

Two things were thus made clear for any procurement agent and for any kolkhoz chairman or sovkhoz director. He must increase herds as well as meat deliveries by relying on private resources as well, and he must also assist the private sector to facilitate its contributions. In practice, the decisions of the majority of these managers would automatically give priority to increasing herds and meat deliveries, because these will be reflected in their plan fulfillment performance. Only then would they consider ways to aid the private sector.

In subsequent press releases, more emphasis was placed on the conditions to be created for the further development of private animal husbandry. The dates of those releases indicate the influence of the December plenum rather than that of the Third Kolkhoz Congress. After January 1970, state farms and breeding stations were officially allowed (and the practice was recommended to the kolkhozes) to sell piglets and live poultry to individuals; one-fifth of profits from the sales was to be paid to the personnel of these farms in the form of bonuses [434, no. 7 (1970), 16]. On 11 February 1970, a lead article of the Central Committee's agricultural daily, Sel'skaia zhizn', admonished:

While steadily developing the output of the public sector, one should not forget about raising pigs and poultry on personal farms. The inhabitants of the villages are not only able to supply their own requirements in meat products, but they can also sell surpluses of such products to the state and on the kolkhoz markets. But some managers forget about this. In some kolkhozes the distribution of feed grains and other feed—which counts toward the labor remuneration of the kolkhozniks—was reduced, and the sale of young poultry and piglets was not organized. In fact, the procurement organizations do not purchase poultry from individuals. All this leads to a decline of the pig and poultry numbers in the subsidiary farms of sovkhoz workers and of kolkhozniks. The managers of kolkhozes and sovkhozes as well as the workers of local government agencies should correct these mistakes.

Similar assertions were made by N. Gusev, deputy chairman of the USSR Gosplan [*435*, no. 3 (1970), 4]. At its plenary session in the spring of 1970, the Ukrainian Central Committee made a statement to the same effect [*452*, 3 April 1970].

Private poultry raising was repeatedly given attention in the press.[74] Authorities in the Briansk oblast were called on to expand the breeding and procurement of geese on a large scale with the help of the private sector [*452*, 17 March 1970].

During 1970, the monthly journal of the Ministry of State Purchases of Agricultural Products printed a number of articles dealing wholly or in part with the improvement and expansion of state and cooperative purchases from private producers, and with the successes and shortcomings of such activities.[75] Among the shortcomings and difficulties mentioned were the lack of transport, the fact that the dairy industry reduced the number of procurement points, and the inadequate processing capacity of the slaughterhouses. Thus it was reported from Lithuania that the private owners must submit to great bureaucratic and other difficulties when selling animals.[76] In Pskov oblast, "an absolutely inadmissible situation has arisen with the selling of animals, especially pigs, from the private holdings": people were queuing up because the slaughterhouses could not accept all the animals [*452*, 1 August 1971]. The same difficulties were reported in fall 1971 from Dnepropetrovsk oblast [*452*, 3 October 1971].

Appeals, criticisms, and comments like those mentioned above, although not completely new, amounted to a real press campaign which may be said to have started on 27 December 1969. On that day, the leadership of Gomel' oblast was selected for sharp criticism in *Pravda* because of its failure to develop livestock production; the neglect of the private sector was mentioned as one of the causes of the unsatisfactory performance. On the same day, *Sel'skaia zhizn'* printed (and commented on) a

---

[74] For example, [*449*, 11 February 1970]; N. Rudenko [*435*, no. 7 (1970), 8].
[75] For example, [*468*, no. 8 (1970), 5–7; no. 9 (1970); no. 11 (1970); no. 1 (1971)]; cf. *Sovetskaia torgovlia*, 5 June 1971.
[76] [*442*, 16 January 1971], as cited in [*439*, April 1971, 86].

complaint from a raion in the Belgorod oblast, describing practices which kept the kolkhozniks from selling their animals directly to the state or on the free market. Such practices also imply that many private deliveries to the state are registered statistically as deliveries from the kolkhozes. It is hardly coincidental that, some time earlier, procurement and statistical agencies had again been accused of the well-known malpractice of *pripiska* (see p. 236 f. above).[77]

The fact that the extra price for young animals of more than a certain weight may be paid only to public producers offers a strong inducement for kolkhozes and sovkhozes to sell animals which are theirs "by transit"—animals which they buy from the population and, immediately or soon afterwards, resell to the state. It was deemed necessary to point out again that in such cases the extra price must not be paid.[78] For butter, a unified procurement price applying to both public and private producers was introduced as of 1 January 1971 [*435*, no. 1 (1971), 112].

In the fall of 1971, when it became evident that the potato crop and procurements would fall short of plans, it was advocated that the state procurement agencies should step up their purchases from private producers [*452*, 8 and 23 October 1971]. Such an appeal usually implies some pressure on potential sellers who otherwise might prefer to sell in the free kolkhoz market. In the case of meat it was confirmed that often—against the law—"in essence, strict plans for meat deliveries are being imposed on the population" [*468*, no. 10 (1971), 34–35]. In one raion, the state inspection for procurements ordered public agricultural enterprises to use less milk for their own needs [*468*, no. 10 (1971), 31–32], which very probably also meant a reduction of the quantities of milk sold or issued to their own workers.

Another malpractice connected with purchases from the private sector is that of exerting pressure, direct or indirect, on people to sell to the cooperative procurement network. *Sel'skaia zhizn'* reported that deliveries of butter (as a substitute for milk) were being enforced through the cooperative stores with the help of local soviets.[79] The soviet of the Central Board of the consumer cooperatives had the following to say about this at its session of 1 June 1971 [*452*, 3 June 1971]:

---

[77] [*446*, no. 12 (1969), 75], and [*457*, 1 August 1969] as cited in [*439*, January 1970, 61].

[78] V. Maslennikov, G. Kniazev, *Finansy SSSR*, no. 4 (1971), pp. 12, 16.

[79] [*452*, 11 May 1971]; for positive examples of organizing voluntary sales in Estonia and Latvia, cf. [*452*, 21 May 1971].

Severely condemned was a disgusting phenomenon, discrediting Soviet trade, such as attempts to make the selling of a certain commodity dependent upon a reciprocal sale, say, of eggs. The Central Board has [earlier] issued a special order forbidding the imposition of plans of agricultural procurements on the cooperative stores. But in various places gross infringements of this order occur.

Shortly afterwards, the Central Board reprimanded a number of officials guilty of such infringements and decided to exert close control in the future [452, 16 July 1971].

Even if the sales are truly voluntary, it is difficult to draw a line between unlawful practice of registering of private produce sold through the intermediary of the kolkhoz or sovkhoz as part of the output of the public sector and the lawful practice of procuring private output through these public farms. Among the legal forms is the "delivery by contract" (kontraktatsiia, see p. 245 above). This means that young animals become formal public property at a very early stage, but are kept in private sheds and fed with fodder from the kolkhoz or sovkhoz; the whole procedure thus becomes a payment for raising and fattening of livestock. Kontraktatsiia has been reemphasized. For the Kurgan oblast, the practice was recommended as a means of providing employment during the slack season [452, 10 January 1970]. The leaders of the Tula oblast were even reproached for waiting for "directives from above" instead of developing this method on a large scale at their own initiative. After this criticism appeared, more than two thousand calves were contracted for in that oblast within a single week [452, 22 January and 13 February 1970]. But it is doubtful whether all fodder for contracted animals comes from the public sector. Only a "small help by means of [supplying] fodder" was mentioned as necessary when purchases from sovkhoz workers were recommended [452, 22 January 1970], and the recent decrease in contracting in the Kalinin oblast was said to be caused partly by the insufficient amounts of fodder provided to the private sector for this purpose [434, no. 9 (1970), 18].

Apparently the term kontraktatsiia is not always used in a juridically strict sense. The First Party Secretary of the Briansk oblast used it when simply referring to buying young animals from private owners for fattening them in the public herds; he referred to calculations showing that in his oblast alone one hundred thousand more calves could be bought annually, and he reported that this was planned for 1970 [452, 20 January 1970]. However, he reported measures to increase the sale of piglets to kolkhozniks, workers, and employees to enable them to sell more pork to the state. At present, it seems generally true, as it had been formerly, that calves are bought from private owners and piglets are sold to them.[80]

In the unprecise meaning of the word, *kontraktatsiia* simply signifies giving fodder to the kolkhoznik or sovkhoz worker in exchange for his willingness, or his entering into an obligation, to sell to the public sector a young animal raised and fattened to a certain limit.[81] The provision of feed is the central point in such transactions, because this is vital for private animal production. It was in this very respect that the private sector has been at a disadvantage, even since the measures of 1964 and 1965. This occurred mainly in connection with the general changeover to money payments in kolkhozes since June 1966.[82] "With the changeover of the kolkhozes to money payments, in many of them the plans provided for a decrease of feed grain and roughage given to kolkhozniks as part of their wages. If, for instance, the kolkhozes of the RSFSR gave out and sold to kolkhozniks 14.1 percent of the total harvest in 1965, it was only 5.8 percent in 1968."[83] In absolute terms, this means 5.5 million tons of grain in 1965 and 3.4 million in 1968.

The price at which fodder is given (or calculated as part of the wage) also plays a role. High accounting prices enable kolkhoz leaders to boast of statistically high wages, which were the order of the day in 1966 and 1967. "A few years" before 1970, the free price—which is strongly influenced by prevailing kolkhoz prices and scarcities—for straw was 0.15 ruble per kilogram—the price of bread in the state retail stores.[84]

Following the December 1969 plenum, and right up to the summer of 1971, expansion of the feed basis for the public herds and provision of feed and fodder to private livestock owners was generally and strongly recommended.[85] Here, a conflict of ends is involved: Farm managers now are called on to utilize every small piece of meadow land, including the

[80] Cf. the examples given, and recommended for imitation, in [*452*, 9 January 1970], and by G. D'iachkov [*435*, no. 11 (1970), 41].

[81] An early example of this practice, from a Ukrainian kolkhoz in the mid-1950s, was recently described favorably by A. Berdyshev [*445*, no. 7 (1970), 201–202].

[82] In most cases, these are not pure money payments, to be sure, but the wages for kolkhoz work are now calculated in money terms instead of in work-units (*trudoden'*).

[83] V. Iakushev [*435*, no. 9 (1970), 25]; cf. [*386*, 71]; [*449*, 27 December 1969]; [*437*, no. 3 (1970), 39].

[84] A. Emel'ianov [*443*, no. 45 (1970), 11].

[85] Decree of the Central Committee and Council of Ministers, [*452*, 14 August 1970]; cf. Emel'ianov [*443*, no. 45 (1970), 11]; [*452*, 20 July 1971].

strips alongside roads, canals, and so on, for gathering hay, and to employ scythes and unskilled labor where machines cannot be put to use [*452*, 18 June 1971]. Yet it is mainly in these very places that private initiative can be used to mow hay if allowed to do so. It remains to be seen how this conflict will be solved. Shortage of labor will probably work against the widespread public gathering of hay from such places.

The emphasis on contract delivery is a sign that the regime seeks a way to utilize private initiative without expanding the private ownership of livestock. It is doubtful whether this can work. And it is even more dubious whether the private sector will again be able to increase very much its output of livestock products as it did on earlier, similar occasions in 1953 and 1954 and again in 1964 and 1965. Conditions have changed: nowadays, additional rural labor is available only in some parts of the country, or to a very limited degree in others. This is illustrated by the fact that able-bodied labor, including that of married women occupied on private plots as well as in households, is estimated by Soviet authors to have amounted to only 8 percent of all labor by 1970, whereas in 1960 it still made up 22 percent.[86] According to preliminary results of the 1970 census, the total number of people occupied in private subsidiary farming and in the household has decreased by two-thirds, as compared with the preceding census of 1959 [*339a*, 162]. In many large regions, including the area of traditional animal husbandry north of the Black Earth Belt, the agricultural labor force consists largely of old people who are now, more than ever, involved in work in the public sector, and who might be unable to find time for much additional work with their own or with contracted livestock. And after the large increase in wages for work in the public sector, further private work may no longer be as attractive as it used to be.

A policy dilemma also arises on the free kolkhoz markets. These are still supplied almost exclusively with produce from the private sector [*56a*, 107]. Even industrial enterprises, hotels, restaurants, hospitals, and so on, buy some produce on these markets—especially meat, vegetables, and fruit.[87] The Soviet statistical yearbook for 1969 showed a share of less than 9 percent in total turnover of "comparable" food products for the kolkhoz markets [*14a*, 601], but recently *Sovetskaia torgovlia* (23 January 1971) put it at "no less than 10 to 12 percent." One can only speculate

---

[86] V. G. Kostakov, P. P. Litviakov, *Balans truda* (Moscow: 1970), p. 65.
[87] A. Zaitseva, G. Moroz [*466*, no. 5 (1971), 38–39].

about why almost all information on kolkhoz markets was discontinued in the 1969 and 1970 yearbooks. Turnover increased in 1968–1970, but this was mainly—or wholly?—a consequence of an increase in prices, which were showing a sharp upward trend already by 1968 [*14*, 655; *14a*, 597]. G. Radov thinks that this came as a surprise to the planners [*443*, no. 43 (1971), 10].

The regime wants to expand this category of trade as another means of making up for the deficiencies of the public distribution network and of stimulating total agricultural production. But it abhors the "speculative" tendencies inherent in genuinely free trade, or rather the difficulty of controlling such a flow of goods.

In his speech at the Kolkhoz Congress, Polianskii came out strongly for the kolkhoz market, thus apparently opposing some preceding tendencies to restrict this sphere of economic activity. At the same time, he advocated "an important improvement in the organization of trade on the kolkhoz markets and the introduction of order there" [*452*, 26 November 1969]. The meaning of these words soon became evident when—again, after the December Party plenum—the press agitated for the improvement of the kolkhoz trade, for its quantitative expansion as well as for restrictions of the truly private elements of this trade. The signal was given in *Pravda* on 3 January 1970, and it was followed by *Sel'skaia zhizn'* a day later. Both articles made it clear that kolkhoz market trade had been declining in many places, partly because of interference by local officials, and that a reactivation was being sought.

As often happens in such cases, a good deal of information was published on the prevailing practices, revealing that measures introduced in 1964 and 1965 to help the kolkhoz market trade were, in part, not implemented. As early as 1964, funds made available for construction in the markets could not be utilized fully because of shortages of construction and other materials [*135*, 72–73]. Evidently such materials were allocated to sectors or enterprises which could claim a higher priority. Only six trucks were provided by 1970 to serve the transport needs of Moscow's kolkhoz markets, although a total of 125 special trucks were ordered. The construction of a new market hall in the same city, planned for 1968 and 1969, had not been begun by 1970, and a kolkhoz selling milk on the Moscow Central Market was criticized for engaging in this activity by the local raion newspaper [*452*, 11 March 1970]. The territory of the main kolkhoz market in Krasnodar was reduced instead of being enlarged

[*452*, 24 January 1970]. The authorities in a raion of the Belgorod oblast chose to ignore the model regulation on the kolkhoz trade which explicitly forbids making the sellers produce a document testifying to the legitimate possession of goods about to be sold on the markets [*452*, 27 December 1969]. Procurement agents fulfilled their plans by buying livestock on the markets instead of on farms.[88] "The more trouble there is with a product, the less they are inclined to procure it [themselves]" [*443*, no. 43 (1971), 10]. Some kolkhoz chairmen and sovkhoz directors forbade their kolkhozniks and sovkhoz workers to sell products on the market [*452*, 4 February 1970]. Price limits were illegitimately fixed on the markets; raion authorities forbade people to sell produce in the neighboring towns and thus forced them to sell to local procurement agencies at the lower state prices [*452*, 17 February 1970].

To be sure, such developments did not take place everywhere. From Leningrad it was reported, in the fall of 1971, that new kolkhoz markets with modern buildings and facilities were being built or planned [*452*, 3 October 1971]. But an official of the USSR Ministry of Trade complained, in *Sovetskaia torgovlia* of 23 May 1970, that the kolkhoz markets were still being neglected and that construction plans for these markets were unfulfilled almost everywhere. He deemed it necessary to make the often reiterated statement that the authorities are not allowed to set price limits for the free market.[89] Thus the overall picture still was one of numerous and varying impediments to the conduct of kolkhoz market trade in most parts of the country. And the well-known complaints about inadequate transport and other facilities for this trade were also voiced when an expansion of kolkhoz market activities was advocated.[90]

The cited sources also dealt with problems of reactivating the kolkhoz market trade. These can be grouped under five broad headings:

(1) How to improve conditions for the "honest" private producer and seller and how to combat "speculators"; this was rather a side issue and nothing new was contributed to it.

(2) How to improve the concurring procurement and purchase,

---

[88] [*457*, 1 August 1969] as cited in [*439*, January 1970, 61].

[89] Free price formation on kolkhoz markets, under the influence of supply and demand, is stipulated in Article 40 of the Fundamentals of Civil Law of 1961 [*465*, no. 50, 1961]. This article was recently referred to as still being valid [*434*, no. 1 (1971), 16].

[90] For example, G. D'iachkov [*435*, no. 11 (1970), 41]; *Sovetskaia torgovlia*, 16 June and 24 November, 1970; [*452*, 8 August 1971].

processing, transport, and distribution network of state and cooperative agencies, especially for perishable goods such as vegetables and fruit. Shortcomings and lossses in this field are a recurring subject in the Soviet press, and nothing especially new was added. But it deserves mentioning that discussion was intensified in 1970 and 1971.[91]

(3) How to induce kolkhozes and sovkhozes to take a more active part in the kolkhoz market trade.

(4) How to expand and to improve the free market activities of consumer cooperatives. In one article these were encouraged to buy products for the market not only locally, but over great distances, although such activities were said to be "not regarded favorably" by some.[92]

(5) How to improve and expand the activities of market administrations and the facilities they offer to sellers. It was advocated that the Bureaus of Sales Service (*Biuro torgovykh uslug*), recently created in many places, also be adopted elsewhere. Their Model Regulation was approved by the USSR Ministry of Trade in the early summer of 1970 [*434*, no. 23 (1970), 16]. The Bureaus collect produce of individual sellers and act as an intermediary direct seller; they seem to have been organized first in Tambov oblast, not later than 1966 [*434*, no. 25 (1970), 17]. It also seems that one of their tasks is to prevent sellers' prices from climbing over a certain level.[93] As for the rest, opinions were divided on whether the market administrations should assume the role of buyers and sellers (which they may not do legally), or whether they should continue to act merely as suppliers of technical facilities for the market trade.

The last three points leave no doubt that the Soviet leadership intends to expand the kolkhoz markets for the benefit of the public, but that it does not want them to expand as a truly free trading institution which might strengthen "private property instincts." As with livestock production, this goal is to be achieved with the aid of organizational forms which provide considerable control over the market mechanism.

[91] For example, F. Savitskii [*435*, no 1 (1971), 37-38]; E. Sorokin [*468*, no. 11 (1970), 22]; [*499*, 30 September 1970]; [*452*, 30 May, 13 August, 27 September, 1970 and 12 March, 15 June, 23 July, 1971]. The plan to create an all-union production base of fruit and vegetables in the southernmost part of Azerbaidzhan seems to have failed; cf. Radio Liberty Research, CRD 385/70, 6 November 1970.

[92] A. Karelov [*468*, no. 8 (1970), 27].

[93] This is implied in the description of their activities on the Alma-Ata market [*434*, no. 51 (1970), 16].

It remains to be seen whether, given such conditions in the kolkhoz market trade, the profit stimulus will be strong enough to induce the much needed flexibility and enlarged supplies in the distribution network. In 1966, Liniichuk had already expressed doubts about the views of those Soviet economists who expected the kolkhozes—and not the kolkhozniks —to expand their activities on the free market. He noted: "In the course of the whole history of the kolkhoz trade . . . the *kolkhoznik* appeared and appears as its central figure" [*214a*, 52]. The development of free kolkhoz trade still depends primarily on the expanding or the shrinking activities of individual sellers and not on those of state-controlled organizations. Similarly, measures designed to increase livestock production in the private sector, although clearly incompatible with short-term restrictions, reveal an apprehension about the possible uncontrolled expansion of private activities.

Not much was said about the private sector during the Twenty-Fourth Party Congress in Moscow in the spring of 1971. Brezhnev briefly mentioned what he had said before, in 1970, about the indispensability—for the time being—of the private producer and the importance of helping him with feed for his animals. Kosygin asked for an increase of private livestock holdings within the legal norms. The directives for the new Five-Year Plan (1971–1975) mentioned the kolkhoz markets—but only the "improvement of their organization"—and put these after the expanded activities of consumer cooperatives in purchases and trade. The Congress apparently considered the issue decided by the events and comments of 1969 and 1970 and had nothing new to add.

Thus, the critical supply and distribution situation has forced the regime to adopt measures that are contrary to its ideological maxims. This happened on numerous occasions in the past. It can safely be assumed that these measures will be rescinded as soon as "affluence" by Soviet standards is attained. But in the circumstances prevailing in the summer of 1971, fulfillment of this condition seemed far in the future. All the more so, because the ambivalent implementation of any "liberal" measures might severely impair their desired results.

11

Conflict and Uneasy Coexistence

Throughout this book special emphasis has been placed on the interdependence of the public and the private agricultural systems. This interdependence is most evident in deliveries to the state and to the kolkhoz market. But it transcends these boundaries. I have shown that the interdependence is actually more important, although less visible, within the confines of large socialized enterprises and that it is also found in state trade and in the provision of social services. Without such a division of labor, the Soviet state could not have existed during the four decades since collectivization, it could not have built up its industry, and it could not feed its population now.

The interdependence also affects the use of labor within the economy as a whole. Sakoff is right when he says: "The family farm is an economic unit for supplying the country with its needs, since it mobilizes labor and utilizes time resources which would otherwise be largely unused and fits in with the kolkhoz and sovkhoz system by enabling these to devote most of their production to feeding the urban population" [*315*, 11]. The application of these time and labor resources means that the soil of the private plot is cultivated in a more timely and more labor-intensive manner than are the fields of the public sector. This is also the reason why privately owned livestock is better tended and often more productive, and why farming in the private sector is profitable—under Soviet wage and price conditions—even though it has often been obliged to specialize upon that which is disadvantageous for the public sector. After all, this is also a division of labor, and it has been advocated lately as such even by some Soviet writers [for example, *170*, 69–71].

Shmelev outlined the ways in which such an involved division of labor can and should be effected, without contravening the basic principles of the Soviet argricultural system [*340*, 37]:

In farms where the social and personal interests are correctly understood, the kolkhozniks take an active part in the social farming, they cart some of the dung from their own livestock on to the kolkhoz fields. The public herds are stocked up with young animals raised in the personal farms, while an appreciable share of the output of the private plots is used to meet state procurements. On the other hand, the kolkhozes allocate draft animals for work on private plots, make available transportation for produce, provide breeding animals for servicing privately-owned livestock, allot plots for haymaking and for grazing, and so on.

A further perfection of the production relations on the countryside is possible only if the correct attitude is adopted toward the personal plot as a farm which supplements social production. [Only then] can conditions be created under which the personal farm becomes redundant both for those working on the land and for the entire society and the social output fully covers the requirements of the population for agricultural produce.

Late in 1966, Makeenko spoke out firmly on the related key issue [230, 63]:

From time to time, it is still asserted—from an inertia of thought—that work on the personal plots lowers the labor productivity of the kolkhozniks in social production. Usually such assertions are made on an a priori basis or are supported by random data which are not based on large statistical samples. Yet statistical analysis not only refutes the thesis that work on the personal plot causes a lower work performance by the kolkhozniks, but it testifies that in a number of regions the personal plot is one of the factors which raise the work performance of the kolkhozniks in the public sector—provided, of course, that the plot is not of excessive size.

Bukovskii's colorful and intimate observations of a small steppe village on the Vorona river in Tambov oblast, during the summer of 1965, demonstrate the significance of the private sector and its place in the larger Soviet context. But he also appreciates acutely the problems of such a division of labor in this ideologically determined system [68, 167–168]:

Now I saw the "division of labor." I saw that the state, above all, produced from the steppe, but that these villages by the river [produced] more from the low-lying meadows. And they were both content with one another, for the state received grain and the villages by the river did not go hungry either. . . . It was not only this dozen households in Kipets that lived well. All these villages along the river lived well, and perhaps only the social foundations here suffered more than in the state grain steppe [with villages of a different type, which Bukovskii had also visited], and yet the state was not worried here either. The people lived here, were not a bother to anyone, they fed themselves, they fed my Inzhavino with its population of ten thousand people, and they fed the inhabitants of the neighboring towns who came here to market. All summer long they fed their urban relations who came to stay, they fed towns further afield with potatoes, and supplied *makhorka* to the smokers of all that part of Russia. On the other hand, they delivered wool, meat, eggs, and butter not just for themselves but also for other near and distant consumers, and [their contribution] represented a real supplement which people should be grateful for rather than resent.

Only one thing is sad: These people withdrew from the social and turned increasingly to the personal [way of life]—already up to two-thirds. But given its steppe, the state clearly found even this [state of affairs] tolerable.

Bukovskii continued [*68, 179*]:

Ahead of us, however, there lies the social [way of life]. Only the social, with its public MTS, its public land improvement stations, its public agronomists and dredger operators, its public human beings who decide the fate of the local rivers and tributaries, of the meadows and the forests, of all the riches of this soil and water; and behind them stands an equally social interest, a kolkhoz interest and nothing else.

All three authors are concerned with the same concept of coexistence as well as with a division of labor at the farm, local, and state level. The difference is that two see economic relationships and imperatives more clearly, while the other is more conscious of the ideological and political danger. But all see a future merging of the personal (private) sector into the social (kolkhoz or sovkhoz) sector. For those who are not bound to communist ideology, two related questions emerge: can the private sector and the social sector of Soviet agriculture flourish side by side—can the concern for private interests, and the related more prosperous state of the private sector, really help the social sector and flourish in the future? And if this can happen at all, can it last and will there then finally be "a peaceful transition" to full communism for the farming population of the Soviet Union?

These questions can be meaningfully debated and answered only if one proceeds from the past and present realities of the Soviet system. If the questions are divorced from these realities, then the answers must be in the negative. On the purely theoretical plane, the following statements can hardly be disputed:

1. Plots which are at present worked privately and almost exclusively by hand would return the same or higher yields with considerably lower labor inputs (albeit with higher capital inputs) if they were farmed in an up-to-date efficient manner. The same is true for privately-owned livestock: if the animals were accommodated in large modern installations

and scientifically fed and tended, productivity per animal would increase and labor inputs per unit of product would decline.

2. The private sector requires large inputs of labor which are partly diverted from the public sector. If the Soviet farm population had no private plots and livestock holdings and were wholly dependent on earnings for work in the public agricultural sector, then a greater share of their labor would be available, especially at times of peak seasonal demand.

3. The private sector represents a potential source of disruption for a Soviet-type centralized economy and renders it partially dependent on factors which cannot be centrally controlled. The private sector exposes the defects and the chronic or temporary failures of the state sector and by contrast makes the scale and the causes of these shortcomings more visible to the population. Moreover, the private sector exploits these faults to its own advantage by using the market forces of supply and demand, and it can thereby exacerbate shortages.

4. Private output confers partial economic independence upon those active in Soviet agriculture; this makes them less amenable to both social and political controls. This is a breeding ground for the "private property" and "petty-bourgeois" tendencies of the individual, which are justifiably considered to be a real ideological-political danger by the Soviet system. Many Soviet authors continue to warn that the private plot can give birth to "unhealthy tendencies, conflicting with the principles of socialism" [230, 63].

However, the following observations are also in order, both on the grounds of principle and in the light of Soviet realities; they are listed by numbers which correspond to the above statements:

1. Given the nature and the location of the plots and the present forms of rural settlements in Soviet Russia, farming in an up-to-date and efficient manner would be possible only over a small proportion of the area concerned. "As a rule, the personal plots do not border directly on the kolkhoz fields, and this hampers the [public] utilization of that part of the personal plot fund which has been taken out of service" [340, 136]. Moreover, in most instances where the public sector is unable to operate efficiently (even with its vast areas of farmland and with its own livestock herds), where returns do not cover the costs of production nor make possible the necessary investment, its losses would be merely enlarged if it were to take over the private plots. This holds true even after the increase of state purchase prices in 1965 and in 1970. First, because of in-

creased needs for labor and material, the new prices still do not ensure genuine profitability in every region and for every sector (especially the livestock sector). Second, the state now pays unusually high purchase prices that entail enormous subsidies (the level of price supports for meat alone in 1969 was budgeted at 5.3 billion rubles [439, October 1969, 36]). Even where the farm itself would incur no losses by taking over private plots and private livestock holdings, the state would lose by virtue of the increased subsidies needed.

Furthermore, if private output were to cease, the public sector would have to take over and expand the output of precisely those products—such as animal products, potatoes, vegetables, and fruit—which are indispensable for the population but which the public sector provides at particularly high cost. Given the realities of the Soviet agricultural system, the following statement is valid for the present and for the foreseeable future: "The individual personal labor in the plots of the kolkhozniks, workers, and employees is a consequence of the inadequate development of the productive forces and an indicator of a certain imperfection of the socialist collectivization of labor" [107, 228].

2. It cannot be denied that agricultural work amounted to virtually unpaid forced labor during those decades in which the kolkhoz system and the Soviet government's price and delivery policies meant that "the personal plots and livestock holdings were, in fact, the sole incentive for participating in work in the social sector," [250, 176] because work in the kolkhoz conferred the right to a private plot.

The situation may since have changed, but the fact remains that only a small proportion of the labor presently utilized in the private sector may be drawn on for the public sector.[1] Most of the work inputs are supplied by unskilled, part-time labor, not the kind of labor which is increasingly needed by the modern, large-scale farm. Thus, the existence of the private sector permits the utilization of labor reserves which would otherwise go untapped[2]—the labor of mothers with small children, invalids, and old-age pensioners as well as the labor of able-bodied workers and employees during their free evenings, weekends, and vacations

---

[1] This is acknowledged in a book published in English for participants in the Fourteenth International Conference of Agricultural Economists held in Minsk in August of 1970; cf. V. A. Tikhonov, "Problems of Labour in Soviet Agriculture," in *Agriculture of the Soviet Union* (Moscow: 1970), 157.

[2] This was recently acknowledged by I. Glotov, in [452, 25 September 1969] and by Belianov [56a, 79].

[*88*, 44]. Many of these people can put in a few hours every day in the home, in the cow shed, or around the house, but would be unable to spend a whole day in the distant fields or the stalls of the kolkhoz or sovkhoz, either because they cannot stay away from the house for so long or because they are not physically capable of a whole day's work.[3] In terms of human nature, it is more than debatable whether, for example, a still relatively hale and hearty seventy-year-old, who enjoys working three or four hours a day in his garden, would be prepared to work for the same length of time in a distant kolkhoz field brigade. The absurdities of the wage system in kolkhozes and sovkhozes can at times make it worthwhile for able-bodied hands to put in as much time as possible on their private plots and livestock holdings.[4] But on the whole, fully able-bodied male kolkhozniks spend only up to ten percent, and often considerably less, of their total working time in private agricultural activities; with able-bodied female labor, it is true, the share amounts to about one-third of their total working time.[5] But it is doubtful whether all women could find employment in the public sector all the year round, even if they wanted to do so. Only a very few of the able-bodied kolkhozniks not working in kolkhoz production are absent because of the private plots [*118*, 22, 24]. The contention that the private sector detracts labor from the kolkhoz and sovkhoz economy was called, by a Soviet writer, "an unjustified assertion, far [removed] from reality" [*386*, 68]. And for agriculture as a whole, Belianov stated [*56a*, 51]: "The personal subsidiary farm, within the set limits and under the condition that it gets effective help [from the public sector], not only does not jeopardize the social economy, but, to the contrary, steps up the activity of the toilers and their standard of living."

There is no doubt that many mothers could be freed for agricultural work and would in fact take part in it if more kindergartens were provided on the countryside and more laborsaving devices and aids in the home were made available (running water, household appliances, a greater variety of goods in the village stores, and so on). Another inducement for voluntary participation in kolkhoz and sovkhoz work would be more

---

[3] Thus O. Pavlov, in [*440*, 11 April 1967] see also [*170*, 70]; [*140*, 9]; [*254*, 129]; [*91*, 51–52]; [*87*, 90].

[4] See, for example, [*215*, 76]. The Soviet agricultural wage system is too broad and too involved a subject to be dealt with here briefly. The reader is referred to my book *Die Bezahlung der Arbeit in der sowjetischen Landwirtschaft* (Berlin: 1972).

[5] [*275*, 129]; for greater detail, see [*339a*, 46–48].

attractive rates of pay. But such conditions are only just beginning to appear in the Soviet Union and it is debatable just how many labor-saving devices, what levels of pay, and so on, are deemed adequate. The satisfaction of wants is, after all, a relative concept. When urban living conditions and wages improve at the same time, the sights of the agricultural work force are raised correspondingly. Even with rural living standards improving at a faster rate than those in the towns (this has been the recent policy of the present administration), the vast discrepancies are still far from overcome. Until this gap is closed, other inducements are required to keep labor on the land, and the private plot is an important inducement which does not require any additional outlays by the state. Soviet sources have also clearly stated that official policy against the private sector was in part responsible for the excessive flight from the land before 1953 and again after 1960.[6] Conversely, the more tolerant policy toward the private sector immediately after 1953 has been credited, in part at least, for the growth of the agricultural labor force during the period between 1953 and 1960 [*128*, 45], and the similar tolerance displayed at present is aimed at, among other things, checking the rural exodus [*220*, 193; *452*, 25 September 1969].[7]

Another factor to be considered is that the able-bodied male members of a kolkhoz family might well be prepared to help their wives, parents, and children, in the house, cow shed and garden in their free time. But they might not always want to put in overtime in the kolkhoz or sovkhoz fields or animal sheds, even if they were well paid for it.

These men willingly put in a lot of overtime on their plots and livestock holdings, especially during the harvest season—either before, after, or during pauses in work in the socialized sector.[8] However, such overtime work would not always be of value to the public sector. The work organization of the large farm offers only limited opportunities for the use of occasional overtime hours, but there is always something to be done

---

[6] [*220*, 154–155, 193]; cf. [*258*, 116]; G. Shinakova, A. Ianov, "Trevogi Smolenshchiny" (Part II), [*443*, 26 July 1966, 2]; [*426*, 177–178]; for 1946 to 1953, see [*292*, 5] and [*153*, 56].

[7] The revival of the private sector is seen by Pavlov [*286*, 22] as the reason why the flight of labor from the kolkhozes ceased in 1964 and 1965. This is also indicated by [*279*, 27]. Makeenko, on the other hand, rightly judges this to be only partly the case. In fact, the flight from the land recommenced in 1966 and 1967; see [*414*, 287 ff.].

[8] A. M. Emel'ianov, *Metodologicheskie problemy nakopleniia i rentabel'nosti v kolkhozakh* (Moscow: 1965), 106.

on a small plot or livestock holding. It is, of course, true that if the private sector were to expand markedly—which is unlikely—this would deprive the socialized farming of a large part of its labor force, including the able-bodied [*426*, 190]. But cause and effect are often reversed: where the kolkhoz is unable to provide adequate employment for its members throughout the year, these people devote more energies to their plots and seek to extend them.[9] But none of these problems or related ones were seriously investigated until recently; they were usually dismissed by a priori assumptions [*113*, 141].

If the private sector were to disappear, the bulk of the labor applied to it would simply be lost to the economy because only a small proportion of that labor can be utilized in the socialized sector. According to the calculations of Soviet writer Sonin, out of many millions engaged to some extent in the private sector at the end of Khrushchev's administration, only one million could really be mobilized for work in the public sector [*350*, 197]. By 1968, this reserve had dwindled to about half a million.[10] And it is possible that this limited contribution would not make up for the negative psychological effects of abolishing the private sector. High yields require not only machinery, organization, capital and skills but, in the long run, also a willing workforce. "Man creates the harvest" [*68*, 136].

On the other hand, as Soviet writers have recently pointed out, the public sector could contribute a great deal by issuing feed as payment-in-kind, loaning machinery and draft animals for use on the plots and thereby saving manual labor, and so on. This would produce an incentive for the able-bodied and part-time workers to offer more of their services when the large farms are particularly in need of labor. It could also give an incentive to the retired kolkhozniks to continue their work on the kolkhoz [*443*, no. 42 (1969), 10]. A condition for this would be the continued existence of the private sector and, indeed, a qualitative if not quantitative improvement in it.

3. It is true that the private sector does represent a potential source of disruption for the Soviet command economy, but it is also a source of assistance. In the past, at present, and in the immediate future, this help is—it is now openly acknowledged—indispensable. Whether it can be dispensed with in the distant future is debatable to say the least, in

---

[9] [*161*, 23]; cf. [*51*, 59] for the Moldavian SSR, see [*116*, 70, 72].
[10] See [*87*, 119]; [*236*, 4]; [*51*, 58–59].

view of the past performance of Soviet agriculture and of the rapidly growing demands placed on this sector by a country in "the second industrial revolution." If the private sector were to disappear today or tomorrow, the deficiencies and shortcomings of the Soviet planned economy would be even more sharply exposed to both the urban and the rural population. The reaction of the population could be just as disrupting to the economy as the private agricultural sector and its free market are today.

4. Partial economic, social, and ideological-political independence within the Soviet system does not exist only in the private agricultural sector. Other ways in which the individual can evade controls have been demonstrated, even in agriculture. The most important and the most obvious of these has been the flight from the land, which went far beyond the planners' expectations; from this standpoint, the existence of the private sector has been an ameliorating rather than an aggravating factor. The "private property" and "petty bourgeois" tendencies, pilloried in the Soviet media, are not limited to the agricultural sector. The problem of partial, functional independence, even without private ownership of the "means of production," exists in the socialist society as well as elsewhere. It is hard to see how its gravity could even partially be relieved by the disappearance of the private agricultural sector.

Despite the above, it cannot be said that the existence of the private sector creates no problems for Soviet agriculture, or that harmony between its public and private sectors is natural or even attainable. Fundamentally, it is true that "in addition to the ideological, [there is] also an economic [and social] conflict situation between the collective and the private activities in agriculture."[11] But even so, it would be an oversimplification to conclude that mutually beneficial cooperation in practice is impossible at least for the present and for the foreseeable future.

For the dogmatic Communist, the word *competition* is always linked with the two opposites of victory for one side and defeat for the other. The Soviet leaders have just begun to realize that, on the whole, competition is one of the most important conditions for economic growth and rising affluence. But most Soviet authors still tend to ignore the aspect of competition in treating the problem of the private sector. They have always been aware of the dangers this sector presents to the construction

[11] Karl-Ernst Schenk, "Volkswirtschaftliche Disproportionen und Agrarpolitik," in [59, 102].

of communism, but they are now beginning to perceive its advantages. Their inner schism usually manifests itself by the expression (at the end of their remarks) of the conviction that the social sector will eventually—in cooperation with the private sector—reach such a peak of performance that the private plots will become superfluous. This conviction has become almost an incantation. It is especially noticeable in the writings of Bukovskii who, almost fifty years after the October Revolution, was quite aware of what was going on but was still reluctant to renounce his hopes for a truly Communist future [68, 160, 173]:

The people in Karai-Pushchino, Kipets, Parevka, and Iasachnyi Balyklei [names of villages in the Tambov oblast] today live in a secure way, and I merely wondered when the state would effect the change of this current, materially assured existence of the people of Karai-Pushchino and Iasachnyi Balyklei into a really broad economic development of the kolkhoz itself. For, I knew that the people as a whole and the state itself did not live from the market, they lived from the kolkhozes and the sovkhozes.

I was concerned with the same perpetual problem, the same old problem of the local villages on the steppes and the river meadows: their social and their nonsocial existence, the partial return to their past, and further—simply the life in these villages today, which changes almost from year to year but which at the same time remains unaltered in a certain respect insofar as only the share of the social and the nonsocial and its own relationship to the earth changes.

During the period between 1956 and 1964, the attempt was made to alter the relationship between the social and the nonsocial so that the private sector would contract and eventually wither away; this was carried out by a none too gentle pressure from above. As the agricultural crisis of 1963 and 1964 showed, such methods could not be used and were in fact harmful to the agricultural sector as a whole. The private sector was, it is true, reduced, but then its close interrelationship and mutual interdependence with the social sector became evident. The latter was also affected adversely, and the only way to save it was to renounce that particular agricultural policy. The conflict situation could not be thus resolved. It is only logical that a different course was subsequently tried, which might be characterized as the peaceful coexistence and cooperation of both sectors.

Yet, as is well known, peaceful coexistence does not signify any dissolution of the ideological antitheses, and, given the Soviet system and its Party leadership, only the future will show whether the new course is feasible in the long run. Whether the new course is basically feasible at all would not be irrevocably proven by a failure under present conditions, for these conditions may be subject to change in any further continuation of the Soviet system. Various reasonable compromises are conceivable within the framework of the system: these could ensure coexistence and, at the same time, a better performance from Soviet agriculture as a whole without a repudiation of the indisputable dogma of the collective use of land [cf. 265, 407].

The framework of the existing rules still offers some latitude for private agricultural production, even if the rules are strictly observed. "As long as the private plot remains within the bounds which have been set for it by society, it is not a contradiction and a disturbance to the development of the social economy but a supplement" [191, 362]. Makeenko makes it quite clear that these bounds have yet to be reached.[12]

The problem of the private sector is anything but confined to the kolkhoz sector, contrary to the apparent beliefs of many Soviet writers.[13] In a highly interesting article, Kalinin has elaborated this side of the problem. He argues against those of his colleagues who consider the private sector "merely a transient phenomenon, which will somehow disappear in the near future, as soon as the public sector develops at a high rate," and stresses that increasing numbers of the members of workers' and employees' families are working on private plots and tending private livestock [153, 53]. At present, Kalinin observes, the role of the private plots is changing rapidly, and the production of fruit and high quality vegetables is becoming more and more the distinctive feature of the private sector. Kalinin is undoubtedly right in maintaining that private agricultural production is changing qualitatively rather than quantitatively: "Under such circumstances, the main emphasis in both the marketed and the privately consumed output is laid on these [items] which are not produced by the kolkhozes and the sovkhozes. Any 'competition' between the personal and the public sectors in [the production of] the same goods is a matter of quality" [153, 54].

Expecting the private sector to supply those items, the production of which is quantitatively or qualitatively insufficient in the huge kolkhozes and sovkhozes, Kalinin wants the latter to concentrate on specific products depending on local conditions. He wants them to renounce the earlier goal of fully diversified enterprises by developing instead the more specialized and efficient branches of large scale production. Of

[12] [230, 66–67]; for an indirect allusion, see [52, 57, n. 1].
[13] See the criticism on this score in [128, 4].

course, he does not want kolkhozes and sovkhozes to give up some branches of output entirely. He apparently asks for large scale, specialized production in the most suitable natural areas and for an output large enough to supply the larger cities outside these regions. For the rest, the private sector is to fill the gap, thus relieving the distribution network of the task of supplying small towns, and especially villages, with those products. "In this connection there are no grounds to expect the fully diversified development of sovkhozes and kolkhozes, even in the distant future." This would also determine the fate of the personal plots and livestock holdings. Moreover, the private sector is "a technically necessary supplement to the process of the division of agricultural labor and the specialization of agricultural enterprises," and therefore should "enjoy the necessary support of the socialist government" [153, 57].

This was a new outlook on the future role of the private sector indeed! In essence it means that by such a division of labor, private agricultural production could not only help to feed the Soviet population but could also help to make the socialized sector a more efficient producer. Kalinin's proposed solution to the problem makes sense economically. But the implications are that the private sector would remain an indispensable part of the socialist economy and that the value of its output would increase absolutely even if not relatively, and even though its volume may decline. And what about the eventual transition to full communism? Would not the private sector continue to exist even then?

Kalinin also enumerated several reasons why small-scale production under Soviet conditions "is characterized by several specific features, enabling it to produce relatively inexpensive agricultural produce." It is located close to the consumer, therefore transportation costs are lower; it operates on more fertile soil; manual labor and individual technology enable the small producer to grow and to sell produce of a "higher and more varied quality," and to take advantage of a "monopoly position" for "products of a special kind and quality" which, for the socialized producer, are "still impossible or uneconomic" [153, 57–58].

He indicated still other advantages of the continued existence of the private plot. It "serves as a very useful school for utilizing the latest agrotechnical measures, types of fertilizers, herbicides, and insecticides, and also varieties of crops and cultures and breeds of livestock" [153, 55]. Private plots enable people to spend their spare time in a constructive way and keep them away from that kind of "activity [alcoholism, hooliganism, and so on] which has nothing in common with the conduct of the new man nor with the task of educating him" [*153*, 55]. Moreover, private farming helps to maintain the required labor force in the sovkhozes and kolkhozes [*153*, 56]. And finally, private agricultural producers are able to respond faster than the large public farms to the changing advantages of intensive labor inputs and also to the changes in demand. "Therefore, the study of the process of development of personal subsidiary agriculture under socialism is extremely important for the timely provision in national economic plans of opportunities for satisfying the rising demand for certain kinds of products, so that no shortages will arise" [*153*, 60]. Thus the private sector can act as an indicative shadow market in the centrally planned economy which is too clumsy on its own to adjust rapidly to newly changing circumstances.

The possibility of any "restoration of private ownership relations" and of "instincts [characteristic of] a small proprietor" is repudiated by Kalinin. In his opinion, private plots and livestock holdings have this effect no more and no less than any other types of personal property under socialism (that is, houses, cars, furniture, clothes, and so on), and the existing socioeconomic and political system provides enough of a safeguard against this hazard [*153*, 58, 61].

Curiously, one important precondition for the withering away of the private sector is not mentioned by Soviet authors and this is a reduction of production costs in the public sector. Although kolkhozes and sovkhozes can cover production costs only by virtue of exorbitantly high state purchase prices—and often they still produce at a loss despite low wages —the private sector profits from this high price level. The tiny plots and livestock herds can yield a profit, albeit a very small one by other standards, simply because the large kolkhozes and sovkhozes operate at an incredibly high cost and must be paid correspondingly high prices. The situation would change fundamentally if these costs could be reduced considerably. However, at the present time, with agricultural earnings rising faster than those in the rest of the economy, prospects for such a change are dim.

Thus there will be several factors influencing the decisions of the Soviet policy makers, apart from their own psychological outlook, for some time to come. One thing is certain: the option for a new campaign against the private sector is being kept open. The rural reconstruction schemes may well turn out to be the new indirect approach to such a campaign, although they at present represent blueprints rather than working plans. A full rural reconstruction program would require vast investment resources from the state budget (I estimate more than one hundred billion rubles), *in addition* to expenditures of households for similar and related purposes [*411*, 18]. There is no likelihood that resources to support the full program will be available for some time.

Another question altogether is whether, in the long run, the ideology might not after all be undermined in this fashion, and whether the absolute power of the Communist Party and its apparatus—which is inseparably bound with the ideology—might not gradually lose its authority in this area as well as in others. Up till now, the Soviet authorities have always reacted very sensitively to the merest indication of any such development, both at home and also in "fraternal" countries, as the intervention in Czechoslovakia demonstrated. But Khrushchev's policy against the private sector resulted, in our opinion, not only from ideological visions and from the strivings for power by an organized political leadership stratum, but also from a faulty appraisal of economic and social realities, an appraisal which need not be repeated. During the period from 1953 to 1956, the private sector grew even more rapidly than the socialized sector (as has been shown in Chapter VIII) and this clearly alarmed Khrushchev and his associates. At the same time, the growth of the socialized sector also aroused their hope that this would in the future no longer be dependent on the private plots. They did not realize that the upswing in one sector was insolubly bound with the advance of the other. It remains to be seen whether the Soviet leaders of tomorrow will appraise a given situation and the likely consequences of their measures more soberly than their predecessor did.

Bibliography

ALL-UNION STATISTICAL PUBLICATIONS:

[1]   *Chislennost' skota v SSSR* (Moscow: 1957).
[2]   *Dostizheniia Sovetskoi vlasti za 40 let v tsifrakh* (Moscow: 1957).
[3]   *Narodnoe khoziaistvo SSSR* (Moscow: 1956).
[4]   *Narodnoe khoziaistvo SSSR v 1956 g.* (Moscow: 1957).
[5]   *Narodnoe khoziaistvo SSSR v 1958 g.* (Moscow: 1959).
[6]   *Narodnoe khoziaistvo SSSR v 1959 g.* (Moscow: 1960).
[7]   *Narodnoe khoziaistvo SSSR v 1960 g.* (Moscow: 1961).
[8]   *Narodnoe khoziaistvo SSSR v 1961 g.* (Moscow: 1962).
[9]   *Narodnoe khoziaistvo SSSR v 1962 g.* (Moscow: 1963).
[10] *Narodnoe khoziaistvo SSSR v 1963 g.* (Moscow: 1965).
[11] *Narodnoe khoziaistvo SSSR v 1964 g.* (Moscow: 1965).
[12] *Narodnoe khoziaistvo SSSR v 1965 g.* (Moscow: 1966).
[13] *Narodnoe khoziaistvo SSSR v 1967 g.* (Moscow: 1968).
[14] *Narodnoe khoziaistvo SSSR v 1968 g.* (Moscow: 1969).
[14a] *Narodnoe khoziaistvo SSSR v 1969 g.* (Moscow: 1970).
[15] *Posevnye ploshchadi SSSR*, Volumes I & II (Moscow: 1957).
[16] *Sel'skoe khoziaistvo SSSR* (Moscow: 1960).
[17] *SSSR v tsifrakh* (Moscow: 1958).
[18] *SSSR v tsifrakh v 1966 g.* (Moscow: 1967).
[19] *Strana sovetov za 50 let* (Moscow: 1967).
[20] *Trud v SSSR* (Moscow: 1968).

REPUBLICAN AND LOCAL STATISTICAL PUBLICATIONS:

[21] *Ekonomika i kul'tura Armenii k 50-letiiu Velikogo Oktiabria* (Erevan: 1967).
[22] *Kazakhstan za 40 let* (Alma Ata: 1960).
[23] *Narodne hospodarstvo Ukrainskoi RSR: Statystychnyi shchorichnyk 1957 rik* (Kiev: 1958).
[24] *Narodne hospodarstvo Ukrainskoi RSR* (Kiev: 1957).
[25] *Narodnoe khoziaistvo Azerbaidzhanskoi SSSR v 1963 g.* (Baku: 1965).

[26] *Narodnoe khoziaistvo Kazakhskoi SSSR v 1960 i 1961 gg.* (Alma Ata: 1963).
[27] *Narodnoe khoziaistvo Kazakhstana* (Alma Ata: 1968).
[28] *Narodnoe khoziaistvo Krasnodarskogo kraia* (Krasnodar: 1965).
[29] *Narodnoe khoziaistvo Lipetskoi oblasti* (Lipetsk: 1959).
[30] *Narodnoe khoziaistvo Lipetskoi oblasti za gody Sovetskoi vlasti* (Voronezh: 1967).
[31] *Narodnoe khoziaistvo Moldavskoi SSR v 1964 g.* (Kishinev: 1965).
[32] *Narodnoe khoziaistvo RSFSR v 1958 g.* (Moscow: 1959).
[33] *Narodnoe khoziaistvo RSFSR v 1960 g.* (Moscow: 1961).
[34] *Narodnoe khoziaistvo Tadzhikskoi SSR v 1964 g.* (Dushanbe: 1965).
[35] *Narodnoe khoziaistvo Tadzhikskoi SSR v 1965 g.* (Dushanbe: 1966).
[36] *Narodnoe khoziaistvo Tatarskoi ASSR* (Kazan': 1957).
[37] *Narodnoe khoziaistvo Tatarskoi ASSR* (Kazan': 1966).
[38] *Narodnoe khoziaistvo Uzbekskoi SSR v 1965 g.* (Tashkent: 1966).
[39] *Razvitie narodnogo khoziaistvo Belorusskoi SSR za 20 let* (Minsk: 1964).
[40] *Sovetskaia Moldaviia k 50-letiiu Velikogo Oktiabria* (Kishinev: 1967).
[41] *Tadzhikistan za gody Sovetskoi vlasti* (Dushanbe: 1967).
[42] *Tatarskaia ASSR za 40 let* (Kazan': 1960).

BOOKS AND ARTICLES

[43] Abramov, F. "Vokrug da okolo." *Neva* 1 (1963).
[44] Abriutina, M. S. *Sel'skoe khoziaistvo v sisteme balansa narodnogo khoziaistva.* Moscow: 1965.
[45] Aimetdinov, A., and Petrov, V. "Trebovaniia vremeni—v ustav kolkhoza." *Ekonomika sel'skogo khoziaistva* 1 (1966).
[46] Aksenenok, G. A. "Nazrevshie problemy pravovogo regulirovaniia sel'-skokhoziaistvennogo proizvodstva." *Kommunist* 18 (1968).
[47] ———. "Obespechenie ratsional'nogo ispol'zovaniia zemli." *Sovetskoe gosudarstvo i pravo* 10 (1968).
[48] Anisimov, V. "Real'naia zarabotnaia plata i metodika ee opredeleniia." *Ekonomika Sovetskoi Ukrainy* 5 (1967).
[49] Anokhina, L. A., and Shmeleva, M. N. *Kul'tura i byt kolkhoznikov Kalininskoi oblasti.* Moscow: 1964.
[50] Arkhipov, A., and Nikiforov, L. "Posledovatel'noe osushchestvlenie printsipa material'noi zainteresovannosti." *Ekonomika selskogo khoziaistva* 12 (1966).
[51] Arutiunian, Iu. V. *Opyt sotsiologicheskogo izucheniia sela.* Moscow: 1968.
[52] ———. "Sotsial'naia struktura sel'skogo naseleniia." *Voprosy filosofii* 5 (1966).

[53] Avetisov, G. "Komu zagotavlivat' plody i ovoshchi?" *Ekonomicheskaia gazeta* 15 (1969).

[54] Auzinger, Helene. "Russischer Sprachkurs in einem Touristenlager des Kaukasus." *Osteuropa,* 5/6 (1969).

[55] Baikova, V. G.; Duchal, A. S.; and Zemtsov, A. A. *Svobodnoe vremia i vsestoronnee razvitie lichnosti.* Moscow: 1965.

[55a] Balezin, V. P. Pravo *zemlepol'zovaniia grazhdan, prozhivaiushchikh v gorodskoi mestnosti.* Moscow: 1970.

[56] Beliaevskii, I. K. *Statistika kolkhoznoi torgovli.* Moscow: 1962.

[56a] Belianov, V. A. *Lichnoe podsobnoe khoziaistvo pri sotsializme.* Moscow: 1970.

[57] Belov, V. "Sel'skie rasskazy." *Nash sovremennik* 2 (1963).

[58] Bilinsky, A. "Aktuelle Rechtsprobleme der Kolchosen." *Jahrbuch fuer Ostrecht* VIII: 1 (1967).

[59] Boettcher, E.; Lieber, H. J.; and Meissner, B.; eds. *Bilanz der Aera Chruschtschow.* Stuttgart, Berlin and Koeln: 1966.

[60] Boldyrev, V. A., ed. *Sbornik zakonodatel'nykh i vedomstvennykh aktov po sel'skomu khoziaistvu.* 3 vols. (Vol. II was not available to the author.) Moscow: 1957-1958.

[61] Bolgov, A. V.; Borodin, I.; and Karnaukhova, E. S.; eds. *Ekonomika sotsialisticheskogo sel'skogo khoziaistva.* Moscow: 1965.

[62] *Bol'shaia Sovetskaia Entsiklepediia.* 2d ed. Moscow: 1949-1958.

[63] Borisova, L. G. "Sravnitel'nyi analiz material'nogo polozheniia sel'skikh i gorodskikh uchitelei." In *Doklady Vsesoiuznomu simpoziumu po sotsiologicheskim problemam sela,* edited by T. I. Zaslavskaia. Mimeographed. Novosibirsk: 1968.

[64] Borodanov, N. M., and Cherniak, I. S. *Otvety na voprosy kolkhoznikov, rabochikh i sluzhashchikh po priusadebnomu zemlepol'zovaniiu.* Moscow: 1960.

[65] Borodin, I., ed. *Ispol'zovanie trudovykh resursov v sel'skom khoziaistve SSSR.* Moscow: 1964.

[66] Bromlei, N. Ia. "Uroven' zhizni v SSSR (1950-1965 gg.)." *Voprosy istorii* 7 (1966).

[67] Bukovskii, K. "Malye goroda." *Novyi mir* 8 (1965).

[68] ———. "Porechno-stepnye (dva nebol'shikh puteshestviia po Vorone)." *Oktiabr'* 6 (1966).

[69] ———. "Tri pis'ma iz kolkhoza." *Oktiabr'* 12 (1966).

[70] Burtin, Iu. "Tseleustremlennost' pravdy (Efim Dorosh i ego 'Derevenskii dnevnik')." *Voprosy literatury* 2 (1965).

[71] Chemekov, I. "Padenie." *Oktiabr'* 2 (1964).

[72] Cherniak, I. "Kak pravil'no primeniat' zakonodatel'stvo o priusadebnom zemplepol'zovanii? (Otvety na voprosy chitatelei)." *Sovety deputatov trudiashchikhsia* 7 (1965).

[73] Chernichenko, Iu. "Kuban'-Vologodchina." *Novyi mir* 4 (1965).

[74] ————. "Pomoshchnik-promysel." *Novyi mir* 8 (1966).

[75] ————. *Strelka kompasa*. Moscow: 1965.

[76] ————. *U nas doma*. Moscow: 1967.

[77] Cherniavskii, U. "O prognoze sprosa na neprodovol'stvennye tovary." *Planovoe khoziaistvo* 10 (1965).

[78] Chombart de Lauwe, J. *Les paysans soviétiques*. Paris: 1961.

[79] Chugunov, T. K. *Derevnia na golgofe (Letopis' kommunisticheskoi epokhi: ot 1917 do 1967 g.)*. Munich: 1968.

[80] Churakov, V. Ia., and Suvorova, L. I. *Ispol'zovanie trudovykh resursov v kolkhozakh i sovkhozakh*. Moscow: 1967.

[81] Clarke, Roger A. "Soviet Agricultural Reforms Since Khrushchev." *Soviet Studies* XX/2 (October 1968).

[82] Degras, J., and Nove, A., eds. *Soviet Planning: Essays in Honor of Naum Jasny*. Oxford: 1964.

[83] Demchinskii, Iu. "Organizatsiia torgovli na kolkhoznykh rynkakh." *Sovetskaia torgovlia* 10 (1966).

[84] Denisov, A. "Otvety na voprosy chitatelei." *Ekonomika sel'skogo khoziaistva* 7 (1968).

[85] De Pauw, John W. *Measures of Agricultural Employment in the U.S.S.R.: 1950–1966*. Washington, D.C.: October 1968.

[86] ————. "The Private Sector in Soviet Agriculture." *Slavic Review* XXVIII/1 (March 1969).

[87] D'iachkov, G. V. *Obshchestvennoe i lichnoe v kolkhozakh*. Moscow: 1968.

[88] ————. "Osobennosti vozmeshcheniia zatrat rabochei sily v kolkhoznom proizvodstve." *Ekonomicheskie nauki* 3 (1969).

[89] Dietrich, B. "Verbrauch und Lebensstandard der Sowjetbevoelkerung." *Osteuropa* 1 (1964).

[90] *Direktivy KPSS i sovetskogo pravitel'stva po khoziaistvennym voprosam. Sbornik dokumentov*. 4 vols. Moscow: 1957–1958.

[91] Dmitrashko, I. I. *Vnutrikolkhoznye ekonomicheskie otnosheniia*. Moscow: 1966.

[92] Dohrs, Fred E. "Incentives in Communist Agriculture: The Hungarian Models." *Slavic Review* XXVII/1 (March 1968).

[93] Dorokhova, G. A. "Pravovoe polozhenie dachnogo poselka." *Sovetskoe gosudarstvo i pravo* 11 (1968).

[94] Dorosh, E. "Chetyre vremeni goda (kinopovest')." *Novyi mir* 7 (1960).

[95] ————. "Dozhd' popolam s solntsem." *Novyi mir* 6 (1964).

[96] ————. "Dva dnia v raigorode." *Novyi mir* 7 (1958).

[97] ———. "Ivan Fedoseevich ukhodit na pensiiu." *Novyi mir* 1 and 2 (1969).

[98] ———. "Poezdka v Liubogostitsy." *Novyi mir* 1 (1965).

[99] ———. "Raigorod v fevrale." *Novyi mir* 10 (1962).

[100] ———. "Sukhoe leto (1960)." *Novyi mir* 7 (1961).

[101] Dumont, R. *Sovkhoz, Kolkhoz ou le problématique Communisme.* Paris: 1964.

[102] Dunaevskii, A. "Kogda k rynku otnoshenie predvziatoe." *Ekonomicheskaia gazeta* 37 (1965).

[103] Dunn, Stephen P., and Dunn, Ethel. *The Peasants of Central Russia.* New York: 1967.

[104] *Ekonomicheskie zakonomernosti pererastaniia sotsializma v kommunizm.* Moscow: 1967.

[105] *Ekonomicheskii spravochnik sel'skogo propagandista.* Moscow: 1966.

[106] Emel'ianov, A. M. "Reforma i razvitie khozraschetnykh otnoshenii v sel'skom khoziaistve." *Voprosy ekonomiki* 5 (1968).

[107] Emel'ianov, A. M., ed. *Khozraschet i stimulirovanie v sel'skom khoziaistve.* Moscow: 1968.

[108] Emel'ianov, A.; Ignatov, S.; and Romanchenko, A. "Novoe uchebnoe posobie po ekonomike sel'skogo khoziaistva." *Voprosy ekonomiki* 12 (1965).

[109] Eremina, N. M., and Marshalova, V. P. *Statistika truda.* Moscow: 1965.

[110] Erofeev, B. V. "Razvitie poniatiia gorodskikh zemel' v sovetskom zakonodatel'stve." *Sovetskoe gosudarstvo i pravo* 7 (1968).

[111] ———. *Sovetskoe zemel'noe pravo.* Moscow: 1965.

[112] Eroshkin, F. "Chitateli predlagaiut." *Vestnik statistiki* 8 (1961).

[113] Evsiukov, Iu., and Lagutin, N. "Uchenye-ekonomisty obsuzhdaiut problemy ispol'zovaniia trudovykh resursov." *Voprosy ekonomiki* 3 (1966).

[114] Ezhov, A. I. *Sistema i metodologiia pokazatelei Sovetskoi statistiki.* Moscow: 1965.

[115] Ezhov, A. I., *et al.*, eds. *Statisticheskii slovar'.* Moscow: 1965.

[116] Floria, A. M. "Problemy povysheniia zaniatosti trudovykh resursov (na primere sel'skogo khoziaistva Moldavii)." *Vestnik Moskovskogo Universiteta, seriia VII: ekonomika* 4 (1968).

[117] Gaabe, Iu. E.; Levitin, I. I.; and Pavlov, A. N. *Statistika sel'skogo khoziaistva.* Moscow: 1964.

[118] Gaevskaia, V. "Nekotorye itogi izucheniia ispol'zovaniia trudovykh resursov v kolkhozakh." *Vestnik statistiki* 8 (1969).

[119] Gaponenko, S. G. "Ekonomicheskie usloviia pod'ema sel'skogo khoziaistva." *Planovoe khoziaistvo* 5 (1965).

[120] Gaponenko, S. G.; Gritskov, M. K.; and Popova, I. K. *Osnovnye printsipy planirovaniia sel'skogo khoziaistva.* Moscow: 1965.

[121] Garipov, K. "Oplata truda mekhanizatorov na uborke urozhaia." *Ekonomika sel'skogo khoziaistva* 7 (1967).

[122] *Geografiia naseleniia i naselennykh punktov SSSR.* Leningrad: 1967.

[123] Gerasimov, E. "Puteshestvie v Spas na Peskakh." *Novyi Mir* 12 (1967).

[124] ———. "Vesna v Dubkakh." *Novyi mir* 6 (1968).

[125] Gorshkov, M. "Sochetanie obshchestvennykh i lichnykh interesov v sel'skom khoziaistve." *Ekonomika sel'skogo khoziaistva* 2 (1965).

[126] Gozulov, A. I. *Statistika sel'skogo khoziaistva.* Moscow: 1959.

[127] Gozulov, A. I.; Grankov, V. P.; and Merzhanov, G. S. *Statistika sel'-skogo khoziaistva.* Moscow: 1967.

[128] Grigorovskii, V. E., and Alekseev, M. A. *Lichnoe podsobnoe kho-ziaistvo kolkhoznikov, rabochikh i sluzhashchikh v SSSR.* Leningrad: 1968.

[129] Gsovski, V., and Grzybowski, K., eds. *Government, Law, and Courts in the Soviet Union and Eastern Europe.* Vols. I & II. New York: 1959.

[130] Gudimov, A. "Shumit kolkhoznyi rynok." *Ekonomicheskaia gazeta* 47 (1965).

[131] Gumerov, R. "Sovershenstvovanie tsen na kolkhoznuiu produktsiiu i ukreplenie khozrascheta v kolkhozakh." *Finansy SSSR* 8 (1965).

[132] Guseinov, V., and Korchagin, V. "Perepis' naseleniia i ego ekonomi-cheskaia kharakteristika." *Voprosy ekonomiki* 7 (1967).

[133] Hastrich, A. *Alltag und Recht der UdSSR im Spiegel der Sowjetpresse.* Koeln: 1967.

[134] Hazard, J. N., and Shapiro, I. *The Soviet Legal System: Post-Stalin Documentation and Historical Commentary.* New York: 1962.

[135] Holovach, A., and Ostapenko, M. "Pytannia nynishn'oho rozvytku kolhospnoyi torhivli." *Ekonomika Radians'koi Ukrainy* 9 (1965).

[136] Iakhnich, A. "Kolkhoznyi rynok v SSSR." *Ekonomicheskie nauki* 2 (1966).

[137] Ianchuk, V. Z. "Teoreticheskie predposylki sovershenstvovaniia kol-khoznogo zakonodatel'stva." *Sovetskoe gosudarstvo i pravo* 5 (1968).

[138] Iashin, A. "Vologodskaia svad'ba." *Novyi mir* 12 (1962).

[139] Ignatovskii, P. A. *Sotsial'no-ekonomicheskie izmeneniia v sovetskoi derevne.* Moscow: 1966.

[140] Ilebaev, U. *Priusadebnoe zemlepol'zovanie v Kirgiskoi SSR.* Frunze: 1965.

[141] *Ispol'zovanie trudovykh resursov v sel'skom khoziaistve Kirgizskoi SSR.* Frunze: 1968.

[*142*] *Itogi i perspektivy. Sel'skoe khoziaistvo posle martovskogo Plenuma TsK KPSS.* Moscow: 1967.

[*143*] Iurchishin, V. "Reservy povysheniia produktivnosti sadov." *Ekonomika Sovetskoi Ukrainy* 7 (1968).

[*144*] Ivanov, G. V. "Dve formy sobstvennosti." *Ekonomicheskaia gazeta* 14 (1965).

[*145*] ———. *Chlenstvo v kolkhoze.* Moscow: 1960.

[*146*] Ivanov, L. "Novye vremena—novye zaboty." *Novyi mir* 6 (1967).

[*147*] *Izmeneniia sotsial'noi struktury sovetskogo krest'ianstva: tezisy dokladov i vystuplenii na nauchnoi konferentsii "Izmenenie sotsial'noi struktury sovetskogo obshchestva."* Minsk: 1965.

[*148*] Jasny, N. "Chruschtschow und die Sowjetwirtschaft." *Osteuropa* 10 (1957).

[*149*] ———. *Essays on the Soviet Economy.* New York: 1962.

[*150*] ———. "The Failure of the Soviet Animal Industry." *Soviet Studies* XV/2 (October 1963) and XV/3 (January 1964).

[*151*] ———. *The Socialized Agriculture of the USSR. Plans and Performance.* Stanford: 1949.

[*152*] ———. *The Soviet 1959 Statistical Handbook: A Commentary.* East Lansing, Michigan: 1957.

[*153*] Kalinin, L. "O lichnom podsobnom khoziaistve pri sotsializme." *Voprosy ekonomiki* 11 (1968).

[*154*] Kalinovskii, N. P. *Raionnye razlichiia real'noi zarabotnoi platy rabochikh i sluzhashchikh.* Moscow: 1966.

[*155*] Karcz, J. F. *Appendix to Quantitative Analysis of the Collective Farm Market.* Mimeographed. Santa Barbara, California: 1963.

[*156*] ———. "Farm marketings and state procurements: definitions and interpretation." *Soviet Studies* XV/2 (October 1963).

[*157*] ———. "Quantitative Analysis of the Collective Farm Market." *The American Economic Review* LIV/4 (June 1964).

[*158*] ———, ed. *Soviet and East European Agriculture.* Berkeley and Los Angeles: 1967.

[*159*] ———. "Soviet Inspectorates for Agricultural Procurements." *California Slavic Studies* III (1964).

[*160*] Karnaukhova, E. "Eshche raz o sebestoimosti kolkhoznoi produktsii." *Kolkhozno-sovkhoznoe proizvodstvo* 1 (1964).

[*161*] ———. "Obespechit' polnuiu zaniatost' kolkhoznikov v techenie goda." *Kolkhozno-sovkhoznoe proizvodstvo* 1 (1965).

[*162*] Kassirov, L., and Morozov, V. A., eds. *Khoziaistvennyi raschet v kolkhozakh i sovkhozakh.* Moscow: 1965.

[*163*] Katal'nikov, I. F. *Statistika sovetskoi torgovli.* Moscow: 1966.

[164] Kazachkin, V. G. *Pravovoe polozhenie mekhanizatorov kolkhozov.* Moscow: 1959.

[165] Kazantsev, N. D., ed. *Kolkhoznoe pravo.* Moscow: 1962.

[166] Kazbaras, R. "Gorodskaia torgovlia i priezzhie pokupateli." *Sovetskaia torgovlia* 9 (1966).

[167] Kerblay, B. "Les avancées, les reculs et les perspectives de l'agriculture soviétique (1954–1965)." *Il Politico* XXX/3 (1965).

[168] ———. *Les marchés paysans en U.R.S.S.* Paris and The Hague: 1968.

[169] ———. "Typologie des marchés paysans en U.R.S.S." *Annuaire de l'U.R.S.S. 1965.* Paris: 1966.

[170] Khadonov, T. A. "Ispol'zovanie trudovykh resursov v lichnom podsobnom khoziaistve." *Vestnik Moskovskogo universiteta, seriia VII: ekonomika* 1 (1968).

[171] Khalevina, L. "Zemlepol'zovanie kolkhoznykh dvorov." *Sovetskaia iustitsiia* 2 (1966).

[172] Kharchev, A. G. *Brak i sem'ia v SSSR.* Moscow: 1964.

[173] Khiliuk, F. "Lichnoe podsobnoe khoziaistvo naseleniia i ego rol' v proizvodstve sel'skokhoziaistvennykh produktov." *Ekonomika Sovetskoi Ukrainy* 1 (1966).

[174] Khlebnikov, V. "Razvitie sel'skogo khoziaistva v novykh usloviiakh." *Ekonomika sel'skogo khoziaistva* 2 (1967).

[175] ———. "Sebestoimost' produktsii i rentabel'nost' proizvodstva." *Ekonomika sel'skogo khoziaistva* 3 (1969).

[176] ———. Review of *Tekhnicheskii progress v sel'skom khoziaistve* by Ia. B. Lapkes. *Vestnik statistiki* 6 (1969).

[177] Khmelev, N. "Posledovatel'no rasshiriat' khozraschet v kolkhozakh." *Vestnik statistiki* 5 (1968).

[178] Khorev, B. S. *Gorodskie poseleniia SSSR.* Moscow: 1968.

[179] Khrushchev, N. S. *Stroitel'stvo kommunizma v SSSR i razvitie sel'skogo khoziaistva.* 8 vols. Moscow: 1962–1964.

[180] *Klassy, sotsial'nye sloi i gruppy v SSSR.* Moscow: 1968.

[181] Klimov, A. "Peremeni v zhizni sela." *Ekonomicheskaia gazeta* 29 (1967).

[182] Kliukin, B. D. "Mestnye Sovety i sel'skoe khoziaistvo." *Sovetskoe gosudarstvo i pravo* 10 (1966).

[183] Knox Lovell, C. A. "The Role of Private Subsidiary Farming during the Soviet Seven-Year Plan, 1959–65." *Soviet Studies* XX/1 (July 1968).

[184] Kochin, I. N. *Preodolenie sotsial'no-ekonomicheskikh razlichii mezhdu gorodom i derevnei.* Moscow: 1964.

[185] Kolbasov, O. S. "Konferentsiia po teoreticheskim problemam budushchego Primernogo ustava sel'skokhoziaistvennoi arteli." *Sovetskoe gosudarstvo i pravo* 3 (1966).

[186] *Kolkhoz—shkola kommunizma dlia krest'ianstva.* Moscow: 1965.

[186a] *Kollektivnye material'nye interesy pri sotsializme.* Moscow: 1968.

[187] "Kollektivnyi sad." *Ekonomicheska gazeta* 30 (1968).

[188] Komiakhov, V. "Partiia i ukreplenie kolkhoznogo stroia." *Kommunist* 9 (1966).

[189] *Kommunisticheskaia Partiia Sovetskogo Soiuza v rezoliutsiiakh i resheniiakh s'ezdov, konferentsii i plenumov TsK.* 4 vols. (Moscow: 1954–1960).

[190] Koriagin, A. G. "Ukreplenie i razvitie material'no-tekhnicheskoi bazy sel'skogo khoziaistva—osnova pod'ema sel'skokhoziaistvennogo proizvodstva." *Ekonomika sel'skogo khoziaistva* 10 (1966).

[191] ———. "Vozproizvodstvo rabochei sily v derevne." *Ekonomika sel'skogo khoziaistva* 12 (1968).

[192] ———. *Vosproizvodstvo v sotsialisticheskom sel'skom khoziaistve.* Moscow: 1966.

[193] Kornienko, N. "Formy lichnoi sobstvennosti pri sotsializme." *Ekonomika Sovetskoi Ukrainy* 6 (1969).

[194] ———. "Sushchnost' lichnoi sobstvennosti pri sotsializme." *Ekonomika Sovetskoi Ukrainy* 6 (1968).

[195] Kotechenkov, A. "Razvitie obshchestvennogo proizvodstva i lichnykh podsobnykh khoziaistv." *Planovoe khoziaistvo* 1 (1966).

[196] Kotov, G. G. *Rezervy povysheniia proizvoditel'nosti truda.* Moscow: 1966.

[197] Kozyr', M. I. "Kakim dolzhen byt' novyi Primernyi ustav kolkhoza." *Sovetskaia iustitsiia* 1 (1966).

[198] ———. "Gosudarstvennoe upravlenie zemel'nym fondom v SSSR." *Sovetskoe gosudarstvo i pravo* 8 (1968).

[199] "Kratkie raz'iasneniia." *Sovety deputatov trudiashchikhsiia* 2 (1968).

[200] Krutilin, S. *Lipiagi: Iz zapisok sel'skogo uchitelia.* Moscow: 1966.

[201] Kugel, S. A. *Zakonomernosti izmeneniia sotsial'noi struktury obshchestva pri perekhode k kommunizmu.* Moscow: 1963.

[202] Kurman, M. V., and Lebedinskii, I. V. *Naselenie bol'shogo sotsialisticheskogo goroda.* Moscow: 1968.

[203] Kuzmin, M., and Strumilov, N. "Sovershenstvovat' formy godovogo otcheta kolkhozov." *Vestnik statistiki* 8 (1969).

[204] Lagutin, N. S. *Problemy sblizheniia urovnia zhizni rabochikh i kolkhoznikov.* Moscow: 1965.

[205] ———. "Uchenie V. I. Lenina o putiakh sblizheniia urovnei zhizni trudiashchikhsia goroda i derevni." *Ekonomika sel'skogo khoziaistva* 6 (1969).

[206] Laird, R. D. *Collective Farming in Russia. A Political Study of the Soviet Kolkhoz.* Lawrence, Kansas: 1958.

[207]   ———, ed. *Soviet Agricultural and Peasant Affairs*. Lawrence, Kansas: 1963.

[208]   ———, Crowley, Edward, eds. *Soviet Agriculture: The Permanent Crisis*. New York, Washington and London: 1965.

[209]   Lakshin, V. "Pisatel', chitatel', kritik." *Novyi mir* 8 (1966).

[209a]   Lapkes, Ia. B. *Tekhnicheskii progress i proizvoditel'nost' truda v sel'skom khoziaistve*. Moscow: 1968.

[210]   Laptev, I. "Osobennosti tovarnogo proizvodstva pri sotsializme i ekonomicheskoe stimulirovanie razvitiia sel'skogo khoziaistva." *Ekonomika sel'skogo khoziaistva* 5 (1967).

[210a]   Lemeshev, M., ed. *Ekonomicheskoe obosnovanie struktury sel'skokhoziaistvennogo proizvodstva*. Moscow: 1965.

[211]   Liapin, A. "Razvitie i sovershenstvovanie otnoshenii sotsialisticheskoi sobstvennosti v SSSR." *Voprosy ekonomiki* 12 (1968).

[212]   Likhonosov, Viktor. "Na ulitse shirokoi." *Novyi mir* 8 (1968).

[213]   ———. "Rodnye." *Novyi mir* 2 (1967).

[214]   Liniichuk, Ia. "Nekotorye voprosy vnutriderevenskogo tovarooborota." *Voprosy ekonomiki* 7 (1965).

[214a]   ———. *Osobyste pidsobne hospodarstvo*. Kiev: 1966.

[215]   Linkun, N. I.; Kim, S. P.; and Polina, V. I. *Oplata truda v sovkhozakh v zavisimosti ot rezul'tatov proizvodstva*. Moscow: 1965.

[216]   Lishanskii, M. "Natural'naia chast' pri garantirovannoi denezhnoi oplate truda." *Ekonomika sel'skogo khoziaistva* 12 (1964).

[217]   ———, and Zakerzhaev, D. "Dagestanskaia ekonomicheskaia konferentsiia." *Ekonomika sel'skogo khoziaistva* 7 (1967).

[218]   Lisichkin, G. "Spustia dva goda." *Novyi mir* 2 (1967).

[219]   Liskovets, B. A. *Imushchestvennye razdely i vydely v kolkhoznom dvore (Po materialam sudebnoi praktiki)*. Moscow: 1963.

[220]   Litviakov, P. P., ed. *Demograficheskie problemy zaniatosti*. Moscow: 1969.

[221]   Lobov, A. "Ne tol'ko den'gami, no i naturoi." *Kolkhozno-sovkhoznoe proizvodstvo* 1 (1965).

[222]   Logvinenko, V. K. *Kolkhoznaia sobstvennost' i voprosy ee razvitiia pri perekhode k kommunizmu*. Kiev: 1966.

[223]   ———. "Lichnaia sobstvennost' v kolkhoznom sektore narodnogo khoziaistva." *Ekonomika Sovetskoi Ukrainy* 11 (1966).

[224]   Ludat, H. ed. *Agrar-, Wirtschafts- und Sozialprobleme Mittel- und Osteuropas in Geschichte und Gegenwart*. Giessen: 1965.

[225]   Lukinov, I. I. *Tsenoobrazovanie i rentabel'nost' proizvodstva sel'skokhoziaistvennykh produktov*. Moscow: 1964.

[226]   ———. "Sel'skokhoziaistvennoe proizvodstvo i tseny." *Kommunist* 4 (1968).

[227] Lur'e, S. M. "Osobennosti pravovogo regulirovaniia kontraktatsii sel'skokhoziaistvennoi produktsii." *Sovetskoe gosudarstvo i pravo* 7 (1969).

[228] Lutsenko, A. I., and Nazarov, M. G. *Obshchaia i sel'skokhoziaistvennaia statistika.* Moscow: 1962.

[229] Makarov, A. "Doma." *Novyi mir* 8 (1966).

[230] Makeenko, M. "Ekonomicheskaia rol' lichnogo podsobnogo khoziaistva." *Voprosy ekonomiki* 10 (1966).

[231] ———. "Preodolenie sotsial'no-ekonomicheskikh razlichii mezhdu gorodom i derevnei." *Voprosy ekonomiki* 8 (1968).

[232] Malafeev, A. N. *Istoriia tsenoobrazovaniia v SSSR (1917–1963 gg.).* Moscow: 1964.

[233] Manevich, E. "Vseobshchnost' truda i problemy ratsional'nogo ispol'zovaniia rabochei sily." *Voprosy ekonomiki* 5 (1965).

[234] Maniakin, V. "Preodolet' otstavanie v razvitii sel'skogo khoziaistva." *Ekonomika sel'skogo khoziaistva* 2 (1965).

[235] Markert, Werner, ed. *Osteuropa Handbuch. Sowjetunion: Das Wirtschaftssystem.* Koeln and Graz: 1965.

[236] Markov, V. "Aktual'nye problemy ispol'zovaniia trudovykh resursov." *Planovoe khoziaistvo* 10 (1965).

[237] *Martovskii Plenum TsK KPSS o pod'eme sel'skogo khoziaistva.* Moscow: 1965.

[238] Mashenkov, V. F. *Ispol'zovanie trudovykh resursov sel'skoi mestnosti.* Moscow: 1965.

[239] Matiukha, I. Ia. *Statistika biudzhetov naseleniia.* Moscow: 1967.

[240] Matusevich, V. "Gorodskoi kooperativnyi rynok." *Ekonomicheskaia gazeta* 15 (1969).

[241] Matveev, G. K. "Voprosy lichnoi sobstvennosti v GK USSR." *Sovetskoe gosudarstvo i pravo* 6 (1965).

[242] Maurach, R. *Handbuch der Sowjetverfassung.* Munich: 1955.

[243] Mehnert, K. "Kolchose und Baumwolle in Turkestan." *Osteuropa* 2 (1956).

[244] ———. *Der Sowjetmensch.* 5th ed. Stuttgart: 1959.

[245] Meissner, B. *Das Parteiprogramm der KPdSU, 1903 bis 1961.* Koeln: 1962.

[246] Miller, Jack. *Life in Russia Today.* London and New York: 1969.

[247] Morozov, V. "O kolkhoznom rynke." *Voprosy ekonomiki* 2 (1962).

[248] ———. "O tsenakh vnutrikolkhoznogo rynka." *Voprosy ekonomiki* 8 (1963).

[249] ———. "Razvitie tovarno-denezhnykh otnoshenii na sele." *Voprosy ekonomiki* 7 (1965).

[250] ———. *Trudoden', den'gi i torgovlia na sele.* Moscow: 1965.

[251]   Mozhaev, B. "Iz zhizni Fedora Kuz'kina." *Novyi mir* 7 (1966).

[252]   Muchametshin, N. "Pochemu ubytochna torgovlia plodoovoshchami?" *Sovetskaia torgovlia* 11 (1966).

[253]   Musatov, I. M. *Sotsial'nye problemy trudovykh resursov v SSSR.* Moscow: 1967.

[254]   *Narodonaselenie i ekonomika.* Moscow: 1967.

[255]   Nazarov, R. "Nekotorye voprosy proizvodstva i zagotovok produktov zhivotnovodstva." *Kommunist* 17 (1960).

[256]   ———. "Podsobnoe khoziaistvo: ego rol' i mesto v sel'skokhoziaistvennom proizvodstve." *Kommunist* 16 (1965).

[257]   ———. "Povysit' rol' potrebitel'skoi kooperatsii v sbyte izlishkov sel' khozproduktov." *Sovetskaia torgovlia* 2 (1965).

[258]   "Nekotorye ekonomicheskie problemy kolkhoznoi derevni. Obzor pisem, zametok i statei, postupivshikh v redaktsiiu." *Kommunist* 8 (1961).

[259]   Nekrasov, A. "Stariki Kirsanovy." *Novyi mir* 9 (1962).

[260]   Nesmii, M. *Analiz khoziaistvenno-finansovoi deiatel'nosti kolkhozov.* Moscow: 1966.

[261]   Newth, J. A. "Soviet Agriculture: The Private Sector 1950–1959, Animal Husbandry." *Soviet Studies* XIII/1 (October 1961), and XIII/4 (April 1962).

[262]   Nimitz, N. *Farm Employment in the Soviet Union, 1928–1963.* Rand Memorandum RM-4623-PR. Santa Monica: 1965.

[263]   ———. *Soviet Government Grain Procurements, Dispositions, and Stocks, 1940, 1945–1963.* Rand Memorandum RM-4127-PR. Santa Monica: 1964.

[264]   Nosov, E. "Ob'ezdchik." *Novyi mir* 2 (1966).

[265]   Nove, A. "Ideology and Agriculture." *Soviet Studies* XVII/4 (April 1966).

[266]   ———. "Les paysans dans la littérature soviétique post-stalinienne." *Cahiers du Monde russe et soviétique* 5 (1964).

[267]   ———. "Rural Taxation in the USSR." *Soviet Studies* V/2 (October 1953).

[268]   "Novyi etap v razvitii kolkhoznogo zakonodatel'stva." *Sovetskaia iustitsiia* 12 (1969).

[269]   *Obshchestvennye fondy kolkhozov i raspredelenie kolkhoznykh dokhodov.* Moscow: 1961.

[270]   "Odno iz dvukh! (Delovoe pis'mo predsedateliu pravleniia Tsentrosoiuza SSSR, tovarishchu Klimovu, A. P.)." *Krokodil* 11 (1966).

[271]   Orlov, Ia. "Torgovlia v usloviiakh khoziaistvennoi reformy." *Kommunist* 7 (1968).

[272]   Osad'ko, M. "Lichnoe podsobnoe khoziaistvo kolkhoznikov i rabo-

chikh sovkhozov (konsul'tatsiia)." *Ekonomika sel'skogo khoziaistva* 5 (1967).

[273] "Osnovy zemel'nogo zakonodatel'stva Soiuza SSR i soiuznykh respublik." *Sel'skaya zhizn*, 26 July 1968.

[274] Ostapenko, N., and Golovach, A. "Voprosy metodiki rascheta ob'ema i struktury vnederevenskogo rynka." *Ekonomika Sovetskoi Ukrainy* 5 (1969).

[275] Ostrovkii, V. B. *Kolkhoznoe krest'ianstvo SSSR.* Saratov: 1967.

[276] "Otvechaem na voprosy." *Sovetskaia iustitsiia* 15 (1966).

[277] "Otvechaem na voprosy." *Sovetskaia iustitsiia* 12 (1969).

[278] Ovchinnikov, N. I. "Pravovoe regulirovanie priusadebnogo zemlepol'-zovaniia kolkhoznykh dvorov." *Sovetskoe gosudarstvo i pravo* 5 (1957).

[279] Palladina, M., and Grebennikova, L. "Garantirovannaia oplata truda v kolkhozakh." *Voprosy ekonomiki* 11 (1966).

[280] Panchenko, N., and Fedorishcheva, L. "Problemy razvitiia sotsialisticheskoi sobstvennosti." *Ekonomika Sovetskoi Ukrainy* 7 (1967).

[281] Panov, Viktor. "Moskovskii kolkhoznyi rynok." *Moskva* 3 (1969).

[282] Parigi, I. *Die Sowjetdeutschen. Zwischen Moskau und Workuta.* Guetersloh: 1965.

[283] Partigul, S. "Voprosy torgovli v tekushchei piatiletke." *Voprosy ekonomiki* 2 (1967).

[284] Paskhaver, I. *Balans trudovykh resursov kolkhozov.* Kiev: 1961.

[285] ———, and Trofimov, V. "Trudovye resursy kolkhoza." *Sel'skaia zhizn*, 7 May 1966.

[286] Pavlov, I. "O pravovom polozhenii lichnogo podsobnogo khoziaistva kolkhoznikov." *Sovetskaia iustitsiia* 6 (1966).

[287] "O printsipakh novogo Primernogo ustava kolkhoza." *Sovetskoe gosudarstvo i pravo* 2 (1966).

[288] Pavlovskii, E. N., and Konstantinov, O. A., eds. *Geografiia naseleniia v SSSR.* Moscow and Leningrad: 1964.

[289] Perekalin, S. "Za prilavkom kolkhoznogo rynka." *Zakupki sel'skokhoziaistvennykh produktov* 4 (1968).

[290] Perevedentsev, V. "Zdes' zhivet piat'desiat' millionov. Sud'by malogo goroda." *Literaturnaia gazeta* 3 (1968).

[291] Pershin, P., and Lukinov, I. "Kolkhoznoe proizvodstvo na novom etape." *Kommunist* 10 (1969).

[292] Peshekhonov, V. A. *Rol' tovarno-denezhnykh otnoshenii v planovom rukovodstve kolkhoznym proizvodstvom.* Leningrad: 1967.

[293] Petrov, V. "O primenenii norm reguliruiushchikh imushchestvennye otnosheniia v kolkhoznom dvore." *Sovetskaia iustitsiia* 4 (1967).

[294] Pikul'kin, A., and Satin, I. "Polnee ispol'zovat' trudovye resursy kolkhosov." *Ekonomika sel'skogo khoziaistva* 8 (1966).

[295] *Plenum Tsentral'nogo Komiteta Kommunisticheskoi Partii Sovetskogo Soiuza, 24–26 marta 1965 goda. Stenograficheskii otchet.* Moscow: 1965.

[296] Ploss, S. I. *Conflict and Decision-Making in Soviet Russia: A Case Study of Agricultural Policy, 1953–1963.* Princeton: 1965.

[297] Polianskii, D. "O roli soiuza rabochikh i krest'ian v pereustroistve sovremennoi derevni." *Kommunist* 15 (1967).

[298] Polina, V. "Aktual'noe v agrarnoi teorii i praktike." *Voprosy ekonomiki* 1 (1969).

[299] Poltoratskii, V. "Krasili." *Nash sovremennik* 3 (1963).

[300] "Predlozheniia, podskazannye zhizn'iu." *Ekonomicheskaia gazeta* 20 (1966).

[301] "Primernyi ustav sel'skokhoziaistvennoi arteli." *Pravda*, 18 February 1935.

[302] "Priusadebnoe zemlepol'zovanie." *Ekonomicheskaia gazeta* 18 (1968).

[303] *Problemy izmeneniia sotsial'noi struktury sovetskogo obshchestva.* Moscow: 1968.

[304] Prokhanov, A. "Intelligent v derevne." *Literaturnaia gazeta* 26 (1969).

[305] *Raionnoe zveno.* Moscow: 1966.

[306] Rebrin, P. "Glavnoe zveno." *Novyi mir* 4 (1969).

[307] ———. "Golovyrino, Golovyrino. . . ." *Nash sovremennik* 3 (1963).

[308] *Regional'nye osobennosti ekonomicheskogo razvitiia raionov strany (na primere Sibiri).* Moscow: 1966.

[309] *Resheniia Partii i pravitel'stva po khoziaistvennym voprosam.* Vols. V and VI. Moscow: 1968.

[310] Révész, L. "Das gefaehrdete Einfamilienhaus in der Sowjetunion." *Osteuropa* 4 (1964).

[311] Richter, L. "Plans to Urbanize the Countryside 1950–1962." In *Soviet Planning: Essays in Honor of Naum Jasny,* edited by Jane Degras and Alec Nove. Oxford: 1964.

[312] ———. "Some Remarks on Soviet Agricultural Statistics." *The American Statistician,* June 1961.

[313] Ruskol, A. A. "Demokratizatsiia printsipov upravleniia v kolkhozakh." *Sovetskoe gosudarstvo i pravo* 11 (1967).

[314] Ryzhikova, V. "Iz praktiki rassmotreniia sudami grazhdanskich kolkhoznykh del." *Sovetskaia iustitsiia* 4 (1966).

[315] Sakoff, A. N. "The Private Sector in Soviet Agriculture." *Monthly Bulletin of Agricultural Economics and Statistics* XI/9 (1962).

[316] Sarkisian, G. "Povyshenie zhiznennogo urovnia kolkhoznikov." *Ekonomika sel'skogo khoziaistva* 12 (1964).

[317] *Sbornik dokumentov po zemel'nomu zakonodatel'stvu SSSR i RSFSR.* Moscow: 1954.

[318] *Sbornik normativnykh aktov po kolkhoznomu pravu.* Moscow: 1965.

[319] *Sbornik postanovlenii i rasporiazhenii po trudu dlia rabotnikov sel'- skogo khoziaistva.* Moscow: 1958.

[320] *Sbornik postanovlenii Plenuma Verkhovnogo Suda SSSR, 1924–1963.* Moscow: 1964.

[321] *Sbornik reshenii po sel'skomu khoziaistvu.* Moscow: 1963.

[322] *Sbornik zakonodatel'nykh aktov po sel'skomu khoziaistvu Tadzhik- skoi SSR.* Dushanbe: 1962.

[323] *Sbornik zakonov SSSR i ukazov Presidiuma Verkhovnogo Soveta SSSR, 1938 g.–1961 g.* Moscow: 1961.

[324] Schiller, O. *Das Agrarsystem der Sowjetunion.* Tuebingen: 1960.

[325] ———. "Der neue Kurs der sowjetischen Agrarpolitik." *Osteuropa* 6 (1953).

[326] ———. "Privates Grundeigentum und private Landnutzung in den Reformplaenen fuer die sowjetische Landwirtschaft." *Osteuropa- Wirtschaft* 4 (1965).

[327] ———. "Die sowjetische Landwirtschaft nach Chruschtschow." *Osteu- ropa* 6 (1965).

[328] ———. "Stand der Landwirtschaft und agrarpolitische Massnahmen in der Sowjetunion seit 1953." *Berichte ueber Landwirtschaft* XXXV/1 (1957).

[329] Schinke, E. *Die Kostenrechnung in der sowjetischen Landwirtschaft.* Giessen: 1962.

[330] Sedugin, P., and Syrodoev, N. "Osnovy zemel'nogo zakonodatel'stva Soiuza SSR i soiuznykh respublik i zemel'nye kodeksy soiuznykh respublik." *Sovetskaia iustitsiia* 11 (1969).

[331] *Selo Viriatino v proshlom i nastoiashchem. Opyt etnograficheskogo izucheniia russkoi derevni.* Moscow: 1958.

[332] *Sel'skokhoziaistvenna entsiklopediia.* 4 vols. Moscow: 1951–1956.

[333] Semin, V. "Semero v odnom dome." *Novyi mir* 6 (1965).

[334] Serykh, A. "Na strazhe kolkhoznoi demokratii." *Sovety deputatov trudiashchikhsia* 3 (1965).

[335] Sharipov, Kh. "Obshchestvennoe i lichnoe." *Sovety deputatov trudia- shchikhsia* 1 (1965).

[336] Sheremet, K. F. *Sel'skii sovet.* Moscow: 1966.

[337] Shinn, W. T. "The Law of the Russian Peasant Household." *Slavic Review* XX/4 (December 1961).

[338] Shishkin, N. I., ed. *Trudovye resursy SSSR (Problemy raspredeleniia i ispol'zovaniia).* Moscow: 1961.

[*339*] Shmelev, G. I. "Ekonomicheskaia rol' lichnogo podsobnogo khoziaistva." *Voprosy ekonomiki* 4 (1965).

[*339a*] ——. *Lichnoe podsobnoe khoziaistvo i ego sviazi s obshchestvennym proizvodstvom*. Moscow: 1971.

[*340*] ——. *Raspredelenie i ispol'zovanie truda v kolkhozakh*. Moscow: 1964.

[*341*] Shnirlin, Iu. "O produktsii postupaiushchei gorodskomu naseleniiu iz lichnogo khoziaistva." *Sovetskaia torgovlia* 6 (1956).

[*342*] Shol'ts, S. V. *Statistika sel'skogo khoziaistva*. Moscow: 1956.

[*343*] Shul'ga, Z., and Pogorelov, N. "Lichnoe podsobnoe khoziaistvo" (book review). *Ekonomika Sovetskoi Ukrainy* 7 (1967).

[*344*] Sidorova, M. "Formirovanie i metodika rascheta fonda vosproizvodstva rabochei sily v kolkhozakh." *Voprosy ekonomiki* 5 (1967).

[*345*] Simush, P. I. "Preobrazovanie sotsial'noi prirody krest'ianstva SSSR." *Voprosy filosofii* 12 (1967).

[*346*] *Sistematicheskoe sobranie zakonov RSFSR, ukazov Presidiuma Verkhovnogo Soveta RSFSR i reshenii pravitel'stva RSFSR*. Moscow: 1967–present. (The following volumes of this multi-volume compendium were accessible to the author: I, II, III, IV, VI, VIII, IX, XI, XIII, XIV.)

[*347*] Slesarev, G. A. *Metodologiia sotsiologicheskogo issledovaniia problem narodonaseleniia SSSR*. Moscow: 1965.

[*348*] Smith, E. "Comparing Soviet Agriculture." *Soviet Studies* XVI/1 (July 1964).

[*349*] Soloukhin, V. "Kaplia rosy." *Znamia* 1 (1960).

[*350*] Sonin, M. Ia. *Aktual'nye problemy ispol'zovaniia rabochei sily v SSSR*. Moscow: 1965.

[*351*] ——. *Vosproizvodstvo rabochei sily v SSSR i balans truda*. Moscow: 1959.

[*352*] Sorokin, A. "Obshchestvennoe i lichnoe v usloviiakh sovkhoza." *Ekonomika sel'skogo khoziaistva* 3 (1965).

[*353*] Sotnikov, V. "Zemlia—istochnik bogatstva nashego obshchestva." *Ekonomika sel'skogo khoziaistva* 11 (1966).

[*354*] *Sotsiologiia v SSSR*. 2 vols. Moscow: 1965.

[*355*] *Sovetskoe zemel'noe i kolkhoznoe pravo*. Moscow: 1959.

[*356*] "Die sowjetische Landwirtschaft im Jahre 1957." *Osteuropa* 5 (1958).

[*357*] Spektor, M. "Sotsiologicheskie issledovaniia pri planirovke sel'skikh naselennykh mest." *Ekonomika sel'skogo khoziaistva* 5 (1968).

[*358*] *Spravochnik ekonomista*. Kishinev: 1967.

[*359*] *Spravochnik partiinogo rabotnika, vypusk shestoi*. Moscow: 1966.

[*360*] *Spravochnik partiinogo rabotnika, vypusk sed'moi*. Moscow: 1967.

[*361*] *Spravochnik po zakonodatel'stvu dlia kolkhoznika*. Moscow: 1961.

[362] *Spravochnik po zakonodatel'stvu dlia predsedatelia kolkhoza.* Moscow: 1962.

[363] *SSSR i soiuznye respubliki v 1967 g.* Moscow: 1968.

[364] Stadniuk, I. "Liudi ne angeli (kniga vtoraia)." *Neva* 8 (1965) and 9 (1965).

[365] Stavskii, E. "I slyshen aromat zemli. . . ." *Literaturnaia gazeta* 49 (1967).

[366] Stepanchenko, L. "Raspredelenie obshchestvennogo produkta v kolkhozakh." *Ekonomika Sovetskoi Ukrainy* 5 (1968).

[367] Strauss, Erich. *Soviet Agriculture in Perspective: A Study of Its Successes and Failures.* New York and Washington: 1969.

[368] Strelianyi, A. "Memuary tselinnika." *Novyi mir* 5 (1969). (A review of F. Morgun, *Dumy o tseline*, Moscow: 1968.)

[369] *Stroitel'stvo kommunizma i razvitie obshchestvennykh otnoshenii.* Moscow: 1966.

[370] Struev, A. "Bol'she prav—vyshe otvetstvennost'." *Sovetskaia torgovlia* 6 (1965).

[371] Strumilin, S. G., *et al.*, eds. *Ekonomicheskaia zhizn' SSSR. Khronika sobytii i faktov, 1917–1959.* Moscow: 1961.

[372] Sukharev, A. I. *Sel'skaia intelligentsiia i ee rol' v stroitel'stve kommunizma.* Moscow: 1963.

[373] Suslov, I. F. *Ekonomicheskie problemy razvitiia kolkhozov.* Moscow: 1967.

[374] *XXII S'ezd Kommunisticheskoi Partii Sovetskogo Soiuza, 17–31 oktiabria 1961 goda. Stenograficheskii otchet.* 3 vols. Moscow: 1962.

[375] *XXIII S'ezd Kommunisticheskoi Partii Sovetskogo Soiuza, 29 marta–8 aprelia 1966 goda. Stenograficheskii otchet.* 2 vols. Moscow: 1966.

[376] Syrodoev, N. "Sobliudat' zakonodatel'stvo otvetstvennosti za potravy posevov v kolkhozakh i sovkhozakh." *Sovetskaia iustitsiia* 17 (1967).

[377] Tarasov, Aleksandr. "V sem'e." *Novyi mir* 6 (1968).

[378] Terent'ev, M. L. *Kolkhozy i tovarno-denezhnye otnosheniia.* Moscow: 1966.

[379] ———. "Tovarno-denezhnye otnosheniia v period sotsializma i ikh rol' v razvitii sel'skogo khoziaistva." *Ekonomika sel'skogo khoziaistva* 1 (1968).

[380] *Territorial'nye problemy dokhodov i potrebleniia trudiashchikhsia.* Moscow: 1966.

[381] Titov, M. "Sovershenstvovat' kolkhoznoe zakonodatel'stvo na nauchnoi osnove." *Sovetskaia iustitsiia* 17 (1966).

[382] Tiukov, V. S., and Lokshin, R. A. *Sovetskaia torgovlia v period perekhoda k kommunizmu.* Moscow: 1964.

[383] Troepol'skii, G. "V kamyshakh." *Novyi mir* 4 (1963) and 10 (1963).

[384] Tromsa, F. "Istochnik kolkhoznogo bogatstva." *Ekonomika sel'skogo khoziaistva* 8 (1969).

[385] Tulupnikov, A. I., and Nikishov, M. I., eds. *Atlas sel'skogo khoziaistva.* Moscow: 1960.

[386] Turchaninov, N. "K voprosu o lichnom podsobnom khoziaistve." *Ekonomika Sovetskoi Ukrainy* 8 (1969).

[387] Udachin, S., and Sotnikov, V. "Zemel'nye resursy i ikh ispol'zovanie." *Ekonomika sel'skogo khoziaistva* 4 (1969).

[388] Urlanis, B. Ts. *Rost naseleniia v SSSR.* Moscow: 1966.

[389] U.S. Congress, Joint Economic Committee. *New Directions in the Soviet Economy.* Washington, D.C.: 1966. Part II–B, sections 3–5.

[390] Usikov, P. "Chto nuzhno znat' deputatu o razmerakh priusadebnykh uchastkov v sel'skoi mestnosti i pravilakh pol'zovaniia imi." *Sovety deputatov trudiashchikhsia* 1 (1965).

[391] *V pomoshch' izuchaiushchim ekonomiku sel'skogo khoziaistva.* Moscow: 1964.

[392] Vasil'eva, G. "Zaboty agronoma." *Kommunist* 9 (1965).

[393] Vecherskii, S. A. "Voprosy formirovaniia roznichnykh tsen na sel'sko-khoziaistvennuiu produktsiiu." *Vestnik Leningradskogo Universiteta, 5, ekonomika, filosofiia, pravo* 1 (1968).

[394] Velichko, I. "Problemy ratsional'nogo razemeshcheniia proizvoditel'-nykh sil i ispol'zovanie trudovykh resursov v ekonomicheskikh raio-nakh." *Ekonomika Sovetskoi Ukrainy* 10 (1968).

[395] Venzher, V. G. *Ispol'zovanie zakona stoimosti v kolkhoznom proizvodstve.* 2d ed. Moscow: 1965.

[396] ———. *Kolkhoznyi stroi na sovremennom etape.* Moscow: 1966.

[397] ———. "Podsobnye khoziaistva—dopolnitel'nyi istochnik proizvodstva sel'skokhoziaistvennykh produktov." *Voprosy ekonomiki* 7 (1962).

[398] ——— et al., eds. *Proizvodstvo, nakoplenie, potreblenie.* Moscow: 1965.

[399] Verkhovskii, N. "V odnom tselinnom raione." *Novyi mir* 7 (1968).

[400] Vikulov, S., and Sushinov, A. "Vokrug izby." *Oktiabr'* 5 (1966).

[401] Vinnichenko, I. *Duma o kommunizme.* Moscow: 1959.

[402] Vinogradov, I. "Po stranitsam 'Derevenskogo dnevnika' Efima Do-rosha." *Novyi mir* 7 (1965).

[403] Vinogradova, M. "Uluchshit' planirovanie zagotovok plodov i vino-grada." *Ekonomika sel'skogo khoziaistva* 10 (1968).

[404] Voloshin, N. P. *Pravo lichnoi sobstvennosti kolkhoznogo dvora.* Moscow: 1961.

[405] Vorob'ev, G. "Selo moe rodnoe (Dokumental'naia povest')." *Znamia* 12 (1963).

[406] Vovk, Iu. A. *Novoe v oplate truda kolkhoznikov.* Moscow: 1963.

[407] Vsesoiuznyi Nauchno-Issledovatel'skii Institut Sovetskogo Zakonoda-tel'stva. *Uchenye zapiski,* vypusk 12. Moscow: 1968.

[408] Wädekin, K.-E. "Betriebsleiter und Funktionaere, Die Kolchosvorsit-zenden in ihrem Verhaeltnis zu uebergeordneten Instanzen gegen Ende der Chruschtschow-Aera." *Osteuropa* 10 (1966).

[409] ———. "Die Expansion des Sovchoz-Sektors in der sowjetischen Land-wirtschaft." *Osteuropa-Wirtschaft* 1 (1968).

[410] ———. "Fuehrt der Weg zur Agrostadt?" *Sowjetstudien* 24 (1968).

[411] ———. "Housing in the USSR—The Countryside." *Problems of Communism* XVIII/3 (May–June 1969).

[412] ———. "Kolkhoz, Sovkhoz, and Private Production in Soviet Agriculture." In *Agrarian Policies and Problems in Communist and Non-Communist Countries,* edited by W. A. D. Jackson. Seattle and London: 1971.

[413] ———. "Landwirtschaftliche Bevoelkerung und Arbeitskraefte der Sowjetunion in Zahlen." *Osteuropa-Wirtschaft* 1 (1967).

[414] ———. "Manpower in Soviet Agriculture: Some Post-Khrushchev Developments and Problems." *Soviet Studies* XX/3 (January, 1969).

[415] ———. "Nicht-agrarische Beschaeftigte in sowjetischen Doerfern." *Osteuropa-Wirtschaft* 3 (1968).

[416] ———. *Privatproduzenten in der sowjetischen Landwirtschaft.* Koeln: 1967.

[417] ———. "Sowjetische Doerfer—gestern, heute, morgen." *Osteuropa* 8/9 (1968).

[418] ———. *Die sowjetischen Staatsgueter: Expansion und Wandlungen des Sovchozsektors.* Wiesbaden: 1969.

[419] ———. "Das Strassensystem in der Landwirtschaft der UdSSR." *Osteuropa-Wirtschaft* 3 (1969).

[420] ———. "Zur Frage der regionalen Besonderheiten in der sowjetischen Landwirtschaft und Agrarpolitik." *Osteuropa-Wirtschaft* 3 (1964).

[421] Whitman, J. "The Kolkhoz Market." *Soviet Studies* VII/4 (April 1956).

[422] Wronski, H. *Remunération et niveau de vie dans les Kolkhoz. Le troudoden.* Paris: 1957.

[423] "Za chto zhe sniat s raboty predsedatel' sel'ispolkoma?" *Sovety deputatov trudiashchikhsia* 7 (1965).

[424] Zaitseva, A., and Pletneva, A. "Sostoianie i blagoustroistvo kolkhoznykh rynkov po dannym edinovremennogo obsledovaniia." *Vestnik statistiki* 1 (1967).

[425] Zaslavskaia, T. I. "Ekonomicheskie usloviia vnedreniia denezhnoi oplaty truda kolkhoznikov." *Voprosy ekonomiki* 11 (1959).

[426] ———. "Nekotorye metodologicheskie problemy modelirovaniia dvi-
zheniia rabochei sily sela." In *Sotsiologicheskie issledovaniia, voprosy
metodologii i metodiki,* edited by R. V. Ryvkina. Novosibirsk: 1966.

[427] ———. *Raspredelenie po trudu v kolkhozakh.* Moscow: 1966.

[428] ———, ed. *Doklady Vsesoiuznomu simposiumu po sotsiologicheskim
problemam sela.* Mimeographed. Novosibirsk: 1968.

[429] Zaverniaeva, L. "O garantirovannoi oplate truda v kolkhozakh." *Voprosy ekonomiki* 10 (1968).

[430] Zharikov, Iu. G. "Pravo kolkhoznogo zemlepol'zovaniia." *Sovetskoe
gosudarstvo i pravo* 7 (1966).

[431] Zlomanov, L. "Po printsipu ekvivalentnosti." *Ekonomicheskaia gazeta* 6 (1965).

[432] Zybenko, R. "The Official Attitude to Kolkhoz Markets Undergoes a
Change." *Institute for the Study of the USSR, Bulletin* 11 (1965).

NEWSPAPERS AND PERIODICALS

[433] *La documentation francaise: Notes et études documentaires* (Paris,
irregular).

[434] *Ekonomicheskaia gazeta* (Moscow, weekly).

[435] *Ekonomika sel'skogo khoziaistva* (Moscow, monthly).

[436] *Ekonomika Radian'skoi Ukrainy* (Kiev, monthly).

[437] *Ekonomika Sovetskoi Ukrainy* (Kiev, monthly).

[438] *Handelsblatt* (Duesseldorf, daily).

[439] *Information Supplement to Soviet Studies* (Glasgow, quarterly).

[440] *Izvestiia* (Moscow, daily).

[441] *Kommunist* (Moscow, eighteen issues a year).

[442] *Komsomolskaia Pravda* (Moscow, daily).

[443] *Literaturnaia gazeta* (Moscow, weekly).

[444] *Neva* (Leningrad, monthly).

[445] *Novyi mir* (Moscow, monthly).

[446] *Oktiabr'* (Moscow, monthly).

[447] *Ost-Probleme* (Koeln, biweekly).

[448] *Osteuropa-Wirtschaft* (Stuttgart, monthly).

[448a] *Planovoe Khoziaistvo* (Moscow, monthly).

[449] *Pravda* (Moscow, daily).

[450] *Pravda Ukrainy* (Kiev, daily).

[451] *Problems of Communism* (Washington, bimonthly).

[452] *Sel'skaia zhizn'* (Moscow, daily).

[453] *Sel'skaia nov* (Moscow, monthly).

[454] *Sotsialisticheskaia zakonnost'* (Moscow, biweekly, continued as [456]).

[455] *Sovety deputatov trudiashchikhsia* (Moscow, monthly).

[456] *Sovetskaia iustitsiia* (Moscow, biweekly).

[457]   *Sovetskaia Kirgiziia* (Frunze, daily).

[458]   *Sovetskaia Latviia* (Riga, daily).

[459]   *Sovetskaia Rossiia* (Moscow, daily).

[460]   *Sovetskoe gosudarstvo i pravo* (Moscow, monthly).

[461]   *Sowjetstudien* (Munich, irregular).

[462]   *Trud* (Moscow, daily).

[463]   *Turkmenskaia Iskra* (Ashkhabad, daily).

[464]   *Vedomosti Verkhovnogo Soveta RSFSR* (Moscow, weekly).

[465]   *Vedomosti Verkhovnogo Soveta SSSR* (Moscow, weekly).

[466]   *Vestnik statistiki* (Moscow, monthly).

[467]   *Voprosy ekonomiki* (Moscow, monthly).

[468]   *Zakupki sel'skokhoziaistvennykh produktov* (Moscow, monthly).

Index of Geographical Names

A geographical index has been constructed because much information on private agricultural activities is available on a regional level and shows deviations from all-union totals; cf. *regional variations* and *virgin lands* in the subject index. Names of some minor places were excluded, and so was the RSFSR, which is too large to provide meaningful regional information; but regions and places within the RSFSR are included.

Subject Index